NEW STUDIES IN THE POLITICS AND CULTURE OF U.S. COMMUNISM

D1603904

NEW STUDIES IN THE POLITICS AND CULTURE OF U.S. COMMUNISM

edited by
Michael E. Brown, Randy Martin,
Frank Rosengarten, and
George Snedeker

Monthly Review Press
New York

"McCarthyism and the Decline of American Communism, 1945–1960"
      copyright © 1993 by Ellen Schrecker
"The New York Workers School, 1923–1944: Communist Education in
      American Society" copyright © 1993 by Marvin E. Gettleman
"Culture and Commitment: U.S. Communist Writers Reconsidered"
      copyright © 1993 by Alan M. Wald

Library of Congress Cataloging-in-Publication Data
Brown, Michael E., et al., editors
      New studies in the politics and culture of U.S. communism / edited by
Michael E. Brown ... [et al.].
            p.   cm.
      Includes bibliographical references.
      ISBN 0-85345-851-0 : $38.00. ISBN 0-85345-852-9 (pbk.) : $18.00
      1. Communist Party of the United States of America—History. 2.
Communism—United States—History.   I. Brown, Michael E.
JK2391.C5N49 1992
324.273'75—dc20   92-44884
                                                                               CIP

Monthly Review Press
122 West 27th Street
New York NY 10001

Manufactured in the United States of America

10 9 8 7 6 5 4 3 2 1

CONTENTS

Editors' Preface   7

Introduction: The History of the History
    of U.S. Communism   *Michael E. Brown*   15

Remaking America: Communists and Liberals
    in the Popular Front   *Mark Naison*   45

The Comintern, the Fronts, and the CPUSA
                                    John Gerassi   75

Purging the Profs: The Rapp Coudert Committee
    in New York, 1940–1942   *Stephen Leberstein*   91

McCarthyism and the Decline of American Communism,
    1945–1960   *Ellen Schrecker*   123

The Question Seldom Asked: Women and the CPUSA
                                    Rosalyn Baxandall   141

The Communist Influence on American Labor
                                    Roger Keeran   163

The Red and the Black: The Communist Party
    and African-Americans in Historical Perspective
                                    Gerald Horne   199

The Cultural World of the Communist Party:
    An Historical Overview   *Annette T. Rubinstein* 239

The New York Workers School, 1923–1944:
    Communist Education in American Society
                                    Marvin E. Gettleman   261

Culture and Commitment: U.S. Communist Writers
    Reconsidered   *Alan Wald*   281
Interview with Gil Green   *Anders Stephanson*   307

EDITORS' PREFACE

On November 9, 1989, the Research Group on Socialism and Democracy held an all-day conference at the Graduate Center of the City University of New York to mark the seventieth anniversary of the founding of the Communist Party USA (CPUSA). Ten of the eleven essays contained in this volume are revised versions of papers presented at that conference. Stephen Leberstein's essay was added later since its subject is so closely related to the other papers. Anders Stephanson's interview with Gil Green was also added because it provides unusual insights and information about the history of the CPUSA, in particular the events of the past several years. We are especially pleased to publish this interview because it was Gil Green who first proposed to us that we sponsor the 1989 conference.

From its inception in 1984, the Research Group on Socialism and Democracy has committed itself to finding a way of discussing the history of Communism that avoids simplistic labels and excessive rhetoric in favor of analysis and critique. We are particularly interested in freeing the discourse about Communism in this country of its uncritically negative biases. It was because of this point of view that we were approached by Gil Green in the early months of 1989. Green, a long-time member of the CPUSA, had read several issues of *Socialism and Democracy*, and had reached the conclusion that the journal was making an important contribution to the turn in Communist historiography exemplified by the authors in this volume; a turn that has helped to remove the barriers to understanding erected over a very long time by historians who have insisted on seeing the CPUSA as nothing but an outpost of the foreign policy and expansionist ambitions of the Soviet Union.

Many younger historians have directed their attention to the social and cultural history of the party. Less imbued than their predecessors with the enthusiasms and prejudices of the cold war, they have begun to read the documents in a new way, and above all to ask new questions. One of these questions might be phrased this way: How was it possible for a political party presumably acting as the surrogate of the foreign office of the Soviet government not only to attract a sizeable membership in the 1930s and 1940s, but also to have played an important role in a mass political movement composed of millions of people espousing a wide variety of causes and engaging in militant struggles on many fronts? In seeking the answers to this and similar questions, the writers in this volume and their colleagues elsewhere in and out of the academy have produced a body of work that deserves an attentive reading.

In response to Green's suggestion and to the efforts of the new historiography of Communism, the Research Group saw a real opportunity to deal with some of the issues it had been discussing in the pages of *Socialism and Democracy* and in a series of lectures and panel discussions at the Socialist Scholars Conference and in other settings. We felt that there was a need to situate the history of U.S. Communism in a context of struggles and conflicts that could not be adequately accounted for by referring only to Soviet policy and aims. At the same time, we were convinced that the time was ripe for some new thinking about Soviet policy. This occurred coincidentally with the advent of the Gorbachev era. The rise of a new generation of Soviet leaders committed to wide-ranging reforms of the Soviet polity and economy seemed to offer evidence in support of our belief that there was a critical public in the USSR whose needs and aspirations constituted a dynamic force in Soviet life.

On the basis of our perception of a changeable and changing Soviet Union, and operating on the assumption that the CPUSA, whatever questions remained about its relations to the Comintern and its internal political structures and processes, had fulfilled a important oppositional role in U.S. society over the past seventy years, the Research Group proceeded to plan what turned out to be a well-attended and memorable conference. About 300 people came to hear papers and to enter into lively debate concerning the significance and implications of what the various speakers had to say. We shall return to the dominant themes of these papers. At this point, there is an issue that has to be addressed, namely why, in the wake of the devastating defeats suffered by the world communist movement since 1989, especially the demise of the Soviet Union as a political entity, are we following through with a publishing venture concerned with the political and cultural history of the U.S. Communist Party?

We believe that the study of history is always fruitful, provided that the historical record is probed and interrogated with appropriate respect for the complex and contradictory nature of human activity. Such complexity is certainly to be found in the history of movements that assume the burden of advancing the cause of equity and justice. In other words, the current crisis of world Communism does not and cannot efface the significance of what has been risked and accomplished by people involved in progressive struggles that are still very much a part of our reality today. Think of the gross inequalities of class, race and gender in this country. Think of the still inadequate means at the disposal of ordinary working people to safeguard their health, and provide for themselves in times of economic distress and dislocation. Think of the still unused or underutilized human potential of the inner cities, which exist side by side with forms of economic accumulation unprecedented in their scope and magnitude. These are among the problems which the CPUSA has placed at the top of its political agenda for the past seventy years. The party's engagement in grassroots and community efforts to right the inequities of racism, poverty, and exploitation, and the strong presence it has had in the resistance of workers in the factories and fields of the U.S. heartland, are of sufficient importance to warrant the claim that its story should be better integrated into the study and teaching of U.S. history.

It is our hope that these essays will serve as a catalyst for discussions that go against the grain of the prevailing schemes of political thought. We envision discussions and debates in which it will be possible to examine all facets of the story of U.S. communism, and not just those that point to servility vis-à-vis a "foreign power." We hope that this volume will assist teachers and students to situate the history of the CPUSA in the general history of the U.S. left, which in turn requires consideration of Communism as one of many radical political projects that came into being here and elsewhere in the world as a consequence of widespread popular alienation from the capitalist system in crisis. The "elsewhere" is located on all five continents, in agrarian and industrialized areas, in town and country. One of the fascinating aspects of the Communist movement that easily gets lost today as the interlocking network of Communist governments dissolves, is that it presents to the researcher a treasure trove of resources for the study of internationalism, of coordinated and solidaristic political activity on a global scale on behalf of social groups and classes that have borne the brunt of exploitation, war and oppression. The study of the CPUSA leads inevitably to the study of other Communist parties and movements, which taken together present a far from uniform picture. On the contrary, no sooner has one begun to look seriously at the history of these parties and movements than one is struck by the extent to which they have been shaped by the contours of their national political and cultural landscapes. Fresh investigation of the CPUSA, therefore, means fresh investigation of world Communism, whose history has been marked by internationalism on the one hand, and by remarkable diversity and variety on the other.

There is a tendency for people in media-saturated societies to assume the same attitude toward the great issues of the day as the purveyors of the news. One of the outcomes of this amalgamation of media-generated opinion and public opinion is that the dominant ideology, which in the United States bears the imprint of the culture of capitalism, assumes the aspect of an ineluctable force. This book is designed to provide readers with an alternative understanding of contemporary history, one that moves beyond labels and stereotypes to substantive issues.

We think that the current crisis of world Communism does not signal the end of ideas and ideals that have animated communist movements since the days of Karl Marx. There are continuities, there are processes and struggles that link past and present, and that allow human beings in different times and places to relate to each other sympathetically, but these are not necessarily to be found in specific political formations. Thus it behooves us today to appreciate what is distinctive and original in the experience of the CPUSA, as well as in that of other Communist parties, while at the same time remaining alert to their historicity, which is to say to their ways of responding to a very particular set of problems and challenges. By adopting an approach that takes contingency into account, and that is sensitive to the less than perfect congruence between names and the realities these names designate, we place ourselves in a position to do what our late colleague Herbert Gutman did in his studies of U.S. labor history: "to see the present as a moment in time, as a part of a process and as something that has not been with us forever and is not frozen in some kind of historical ice age." Gutman worked on the assumption that "the function of the institutional arrangements that dominate everyday life ... has been to transform the conditional into the given, which means that people accept what exists as natural, as unchanging. Once we see that ... we can begin to ask critical questions about the world in which we live...." (Mimi Rosenberg, "An Unpublished Interview with Herbert Gutman on U. S. Labor History," *Socialism and Democracy* 10, Spring/Summer 1990: 54.)

We would like to highlight two points concerning the essays in this volume. The first is that while they are appreciative studies of the CPUSA they are also critical and in some instances, from various points of view, even condemnatory. Let no one think that the authors represented here have glossed over or in any way concealed what they think have been mistaken and counter-productive policies on the part of the CPUSA. Theirs is not an exercise in moral and political evasiveness. On the contrary, it seems to us that the real value of these essays lies in their ability to confront some of the hard questions posed by the history of world communism and to do so in such a way as to allow for discussion of what was actually done by the party that was creative, life-affirming, and helpful to the cause of democracy.

Secondly, it should be noted that the authors come from a range of political backgrounds, and that they bring different perspectives to their historical interpretations. Several have been long-standing members of the CPUSA. One has fought in the ranks of Trotskyist formations. Most are independent, politically unaffiliated scholars who have made important contributions to various aspects and phases of the history of communist and socialist movements. Their political presuppositions will, we think, be duly noted by readers. Yet it does not seem pretentious to assert that, whatever the particular beliefs and affiliations of the authors might be, their work springs from deep concern about their topics and is in all cases based on years of research, which in some instances is supported still further by exceptionally rich personal experiences.

As indicated earlier, the essays are in general characterized by their stress on the history of the CPUSA as part of a movement whose influence extended into many spheres and sectors of U.S. life. Mark Naison and John Gerassi, starting out from different premises, situate the CPUSA in the period of the popular front, and come to quite different conclusions about the impact of the party's commitment to alliances with non- and even anti-communist liberal, socialist, and middle-class groups. Gerassi argues that the CPUSA suffered the consequences of an involutional and ultimately self-defeating turn away from revolutionary intransigence imposed on Communist parties by the Communist International. Naison's essay gives an account of the multiple ways in which the party participated in grassroots political campaigns during the years of popular frontism. Ellen Schrecker and Stephen Leberstein analyze the attempts of local and national government to discredit the CPUSA in the early 1940s, and again, on a much more massive scale, in the 1950s. McCarthyism was an attempt to criminalize the CPUSA, and in this way helped to shape a political culture whose intolerance of organized opposition recalls the behavior of regimes recently removed from power in Eastern Europe.

Alan Wald and Annette Rubinstein review aspects of the still largely untold history of U.S. Communism's contribution to the arts. Both authors show that the vigor and depth of this contribution belies what has been generally thought of as the stultifying effects of Communist orthodoxy on the creative imagination of writers and artists. In fact, just as in the political arena narrowly defined, it was precisely their feeling of connection with a worldwide movement that gave many Communists the will to embark on projects of enduring artistic as well as social value. Marvin Gettleman looks at one of the best known but rarely studied educational institutions of the CPUSA, and argues that in its own way, the New York Workers School did a creditable job of introducing Marxist concepts into the study of U.S. culture and politics.

Rosalyn Baxandall, Roger Keeran, and Gerald Horne investigate three controversial areas in which the CPUSA has been actively engaged: the emancipation of women, the mobilization and organization of industrial workers, and the struggle for racial equality. Baxandall looks at the deficiencies in the strategy and mentality of the party with regard to "the woman question," which, she believes, was inadequately conceptualized by the Communist Party. On the other hand, her essay is by no means completely rejectionist.

Keeran attributes considerable importance to the skill and tenacity shown by Communist Party trade union organizers in their efforts to move the U.S. labor movement away from corporativism and towards class solidarity. Horne's purpose is to explain why so many blacks have readily identified themselves with the party; he illustrates some of the basic reasons for this identification through examining the remarkable political career of Benjamin Davis.

Finally, in an interview conducted by Anders Stephanson in early March 1992, Gil Green touches on some of the decisions and actions of the CPUSA that are responsible for the party's ambiguous legacy. He looks candidly at some of the reasons why the party was unable to transcend its deeply rooted and uncritical loyalty to the Soviet Union, and makes clear in the process why he felt impelled to take minority positions on such events as the Soviet interventions in Hungary in 1956 and Czechoslovakia in 1968. In addition, he offers insights into the dilemmas facing U.S. communists today, as they cope not only with widespread disaffection from Communist ideology throughout the world but also with the consequences of an ideological and political split in their own party.

We are grateful to Monthly Review Press for having given us the opportunity to make the essays in this volume available to the reading public. We take pleasure in belonging to the group of authors and editors whom MR Press has chosen to publish as part of its ongoing commitment to produce books that deal seriously with the history of oppositional political movements on the left. Susan Lowes, Director of MR Press, was among the persons who attended the 1989 conference. She was responsive to our project from the very beginning and encouraged us to transform the conference proceedings into a book.

Communist Party headquarters on Union Square, Manhattan, 1930, including *Daily Worker* office, meeting hall, cafeteria, barber shop, and bookstore; flanked on the left by offices of the *Freiheit*, the party's Yiddish-language daily. Courtesy of Robert F. Wagner Labor Archives, New York University, Charles Rivers Collection. Photo: Charles Rivers.

INTRODUCTION:
The History of the History
of U.S. Communism

Michael E. Brown

1

The 1980s were an unusual decade in the history of the historical study of North American Communism, not only because of the amount of scholarly work devoted to the topic but primarily because of the publication of a number of important books representing a distinct turn in the historiography of the field. Among the most prominent are Maurice Isserman's *Which Side Were You On? The American Communist Party During the Second World War* (1982), Roger Keeran's *The Communist Party and the Auto Workers Unions* (1980), Paul Lyons's *Philadelphia Communists, 1936–1956* (1982), Mark Naison's *Communists in Harlem During the Depression* (1983), and Ellen Schrecker's *No Ivory Tower: McCarthyism and the Universities* (1986).[1]

For the sake of convenience and brevity, and because of the significance of the generational factor, I will refer to the authors of these studies as the new historians,[2] and the earlier cohort of Theodore Draper, Daniel Bell, Joseph Starobin, and Irving Howe, among others, as the orthodox historians of North American Communism. Draper's books, *The Roots of American Communism* (1957) and *American Communism and Soviet Russia: The Formative Period* (1960), exemplify a dedicated orthodoxy of method and orientation also found in a number of later texts, most notably Harvey Klehr's *The Heyday of American Communism: The Depression Decade* (1984).

There has been some controversy over how to characterize the contribution of the new historians, and this essay addresses what is at stake in the debate.[3] On the one side, Theodore Draper considers their work to be essentially an apologist revision of

15

Communist history, which he believes to have been written more honestly and with a morally more appropriate evaluation by him and his protégés and colleagues (cf. Draper 1957; Draper 1960; Starobin 1972; Klehr 1984). Moreover, he considers its content symptomatic rather than substantive, and an expression of un-earned privilege rather than experience. Thus, he writes that:

> The new historians of American communism and the new breed of academic Marxists constitute a little-noted subdivision of the "Yuppie social stratum." (*New York Review of Books*, 9 May 1985)

On the other side, at least some of the new historians have expressed astonishment at the savagery of Draper's attack, and appear to have tried, for the purpose of encouraging dialogue, to interpret it more moderately than it was written. For example, Sean Wilentz responds to what he sees as its pathos:

> It's sad how the history of American Communism can still provoke gang warfare in the intelligentsia. In 1985, half a century after the American CP reached its peak and more than a generation after American Communism all but died, it should be possible to approach the subject with something like detachment. Not, to be sure, dispassion, which is neither attainable nor desirable when studying Stalinism; rather, the kind of distance that informs historical passions and turns them into good history. But where the CP is concerned, memories are long, and old loyalties and grudges live on like folk traditions. (Wilentz 1985)

Where Draper sees the recent scholarship as essentially promoting the Communists' point of view, or at best hopelessly naive, the new historians see themselves as relatively agnostic on the question of how and in regard to what contexts the party should be judged, attempting only to add detail and a more neutral perspective to a literature altogether too polemical, encumbered as it is with sectarianism, the attitudes of the cold war, and an overreliance on the experiences of the disaffected. The centrality of the testimony of the disaffected to orthodox methodology, in particular, is underscored by Draper's own comment that

> historians also have some reason to give thanks that so many early American Communist leaders were expelled from the party. A few of them have been consulted personally in the preparation of this work. (1957: 9)[4]

In any case, the new historians see themselves primarily as attempting to bring the history of Communism into line with *history*. To the extent that this project is interpreted from the left—that is, as part of a broadly conceived social criticism—it follows the logic of what Perry Anderson refers to as "any decent history of a communist party." Such a history

> must take seriously a Gramscian maxim, that to write a history of a political party is to write the history of the society of which it is a component from a particular monographic standpoint. In other words, no history of a communist party is finally intelligible unless it is constantly related to the national balance of forces of which the party is only one moment, and which forms the context in which it must operate. (Anderson 1981: 148)

Whether or not the new historians' evaluation of the party is too positive, or the orthodox historians' too negative, the question of judgment is, then, beside the point. If the recent studies soften or even reverse orthodox anticommunism, it is not because they avoid harsh facts, though there is no doubt that they include other facts less consistent with the "professional anticommunism" advocated by Draper (*New York Review of Books*, 15 August 1985). It is because the work of these scholars reflects the modernization of social science along precisely the lines described by Anderson.

Specifically, their research on the CPUSA refers to a North American context not well represented in earlier studies. In this regard there is no choice but to write a history that includes the activists who formed the party, those of various backgrounds and persuasions who joined it in preference to other political options, those of varying degrees of commitment who worked within and around party organizations, and the greater number of people— whether officially members or not—whose experiences of agency, moral urgency, and politics were influenced by it in the various settings in which they lived and felt the need to take action.[5] What appears to Draper as a "softening" of judgment must be seen, instead, to represent a considerably expanded empirical field and a correspondingly different sense of what is involved in writing history. What he objects to, despite what he claims to oppose, are not the opinions of the new historians, but their determination to write history rather than opinion, and to write it about an organization he believes has had no significant history beyond the very unhistorical repetition of a fixed pattern. Thus, in *The Roots of American Communism*, Draper was able to write that

> something crucially important did happen to this movement in its infancy. It was transformed from a new expression of American radicalism to the American appendage of a Russian revolutionary power. Nothing else so important ever happened to it again. (1957: 395)

Not only does such a statement beg too many questions, but it is not consistent with information gathered by many of the writers in this book, as well as, it must be added, by Draper's own research. Mark Naison's study of Communists during the Depression provides unmistakable evidence to the contrary, if evidence could even be the issue of so extravagant a claim. So does Lyons's study of the Philadelphia Communists. Nevertheless, Draper's protégé, Harvey Klehr, reiterates the point over a quarter of a century later:

> Sooner or later, Communist parties begin to repeat themselves. The rhetoric and tactics of an earlier era disappear, and party lines are far less interesting the second time around. (1984: 410)

Both Draper and Klehr write as if the party should be understood as an altogether exceptional organization. However, if this is the case, they have in no sense demonstrated it. If it is not, then their accounts of the history of the party, for all their reference to sources, are without a comprehensible conceptual foundation, therefore difficult to read as history.

Unlike their predecessors, the new historians emphasize the variations and complexities of context, a perspective C. Wright Mills once referred to, without intending to identify it with a specific discipline, as an exercise of the "sociological imagination." Above all, this implies a view of every instance of social life, of what people do together, as subject to multiple orientations and shifting conditions. This is the larger point of Anderson's remark that

> one of the besetting sins of a lot of communist party historiography is a failure to take seriously, or to weave into the picture adequately, what the non-communist sections of the national working class are feeling and doing. (1981: 148)

One would have to add: how political and non-political dimensions are articulated within populations, organizations, groups, and individuals, as part of the complexity of orientation that underlies all instances of human action.

It is the logic of this position, rather than merely the internal pressure of opinion, that impels the new historians to express a qualitatively different and less judgmental attitude toward the party and its participants and adherents. In addition to the factors mentioned by Anderson, this involves a willingness to recognize the significance of what E.P. Thompson calls "experience," and to acknowledge the ways in which settings socialize and give content, form, and direction to the collective practices that constitute experience.

One implication, incidental to this attitude but profound in regard to the debate, is that individuals who participate in social movements and movement organizations cannot be defined exclusively by their participation.[6] Rather, everyone, from leaders to rank-and-file activists to occasional participants and casual associates, must be seen as involved to varying degrees in overlapping projects and arrangements, only some of which are associated directly with the party. These, taken together as interpenetrating aspects of situation, and not in any sense separately, constitute the conditions of individual participation in the party, as in other organizations.

This means that in every instance the conduct of individuals as members must be understood in two ways: (1) as oriented toward the locally diverse conditions of participation (that is, as situated—and therefore deliberative—in regard to the rationalities of any given situation), and (2) as ambivalent toward the practical alternatives that present themselves at any given time (that is, as capable of deciding for good reasons to behave one way rather than another and then reflecting upon the decision).

This complexity defines a great deal of what is possible and reasonable for individuals in any social setting, and therefore in the party considered as a membership organization. The failure to acknowledge this allows many of the orthodox historians to depict participation in the party mechanistically and to portray participants either as functions of their membership, deceived, constitutionally compliant, or driven by relatively simple and independent motives. They are, without exception, unable to convey any clear sense of the generative processes of deliberation and reflection, and therefore of conflict and negotiation, that must have operated behind every decision at all levels, just as such processes play a constitutive role in every known social organization. Had Draper, for example, been able to recognize himself in those about whom he wrote, had he been better able to reflect on his own experience, had he been able to see the Communists as possessed of a sense of responsible agency rather than as either puppets or otherwise lacking in principle, he would have been forced to rethink his major thesis that the party was a tool of Moscow and that the activities associated with it were nothing other than the expression of this putatively irrepressible disposition.

His interpretation of many of the facts he addressed might have been quite different; for example, in his contention, not a hypothesis, that changes in party policy reflected solely the interests of the USSR.[7] He would also, no doubt, have been less blind to certain facts now considered as important as those on which he relied—the relation of the party to other organizations, the conditions under which people joined and left the party, the types of pressure placed on leadership by the attempt to coordinate local aspects of activism with more general policies, the diversity expressed in the culture of the party, the role of women and the significance of gender, forms of internal dissent, the ways in which the implementation of policies led to modifications and revisions, the complexities of structure and process within the Comintern itself, and the social, political, and economic conditions under which the party operated as a North American movement organization.

This explains to some extent why Draper is unable to tolerate, much less appreciate, the new emphasis on participation, on the fact that people choose their politics in the light of various considerations—including what those situations permit—that cannot be left out of any account of their attitudes and conduct, as well as of their organizations. This denial of process, more than any other quality, is what makes the orthodox histories implausible as history.[8] To deny that responsible deliberation played a role in the history of the party is, without even trying to make the case that the party is an absolutely exceptional social formation, tantamount to denying the significance of context and self-reflection to the development of any organization.

Bitterness on the part of the orthodox historians is certainly evident, particularly in Draper and Starobin; and the fact that it serves as an overwhelming frame of reference is perhaps, as Wilentz says, understandable. But the fact that it is so unyielding a presence in their texts in effect places them outside of social science, as exemplars of a distinctive polemical genre, an extraordinarily overtly tendentious type of satire—as if the authors most fear that their readers might not otherwise get the point.

From another perspective, to include participation (and therefore heterogeneity and process) is not merely—as Fraser M. Ottanelli claims is true of the new historians—a matter of rectifying an injustice by recognizing those whom the older historians ignored. It is rather a way of understanding the relatively organized features of social movements in terms of those aspects that bear on the connection between what organizations do and how, within charged and ambiguous contexts, they clarify their identities as organizations. In this regard, it is necessary, and not merely arbitrary, to focus simultaneously on the ways in which people respond collectively to the conditions under which they and their fellows live and the sociopolitical, cultural, and economic relations that mediate those responses.

As a result, the work of the new historians allows us to appreciate the various types of influence—latent as well as manifest—that can be attributed to the party. It also acknowledges and thereby makes available for research the democratic aspects and complexities of party life that lie beneath the surface of leadership and that have something to do with the changes in policy that have so consistently marked the party's history. On both counts, their departure from orthodox historiography allows them to reflect on the historical significance of the party to American life, something that was, for the most part, not possible for the orthodox historians.

2

These shifts in emphasis and attitude reflect yet broader changes in the human sciences, and especially in the interdisciplinary aspirations of contemporary social historians, no matter what their subject (cf., for example, Samuel 1981; Burke 1978, 1980; Jones 1971; Gutman 1976). Between the old orthodoxy and the new historiography there is an enormous difference in social and historical perspective. This is apparent in how each group of historians conceives of social movements and movement organizations, and therefore in how each addresses the issues associated with parties and the conditions under which they are formed, develop, and change (cf., for more general discussions, Newton 1989; Darnton 1985: esp. 256–63; Burke 1978; Rude 1980).

In the introduction to his recent book, *The Communist Party of the United States from the Depression to World War II* (1991), Fraser M. Ottanelli identifies two features of this reorientation. First, many of the new historians departed sharply from those studies of the CPUSA "that examined the Party's history solely from the perspective of establishing the Soviet origins of the Party's policies" (1991: 1–2). While Ottanelli does not discuss the connection directly, Draper's exclusive focus on leadership factions within the party could scarcely have supported another view but that the party was nothing more than a tool of Moscow.

Second, and perhaps the most significant change—because it was both substantive and methodological—is the discovery of the importance of the "grassroots" to the Communist movement. This emphasis on conditions of popular participation was, as we have seen, part of the rediscovery of the U.S. context and the party's role in twentieth-century U.S. history. This, and not merely ideology or opinion or naïveté, was the decisive feature of the new historians' revision of the history of U.S. Communism.

Ottanelli refers to this scholarship, as I have, as the "new history" and considers it an advance over the older literature. However, he criticizes as one-sided its emphasis on participation, which he refers to as the "grass roots." From this, he arrives at the obvious conclusion that "exclusive emphasis on the grass roots misses the interaction between local experiences and overall Party policy" (p. 3–4).[9] However, few if any of the new historical books listed in his bibliography seem to be guilty of anything even approaching such an "exclusive emphasis." Nor does Ottanelli attempt to demonstrate it by reviewing the literature and analyzing its key texts.

Given this, it would be easy to dismiss his criticism altogether. But to do so would be to ignore what it contributes, despite what it seems to say, to the clarification of his own project. Indeed, rather than identifying a problem in the new history that is corrected by his own research, Ottanelli's comment situates the latter precisely in the more complex empirical field disclosed by the newer research. Moreover, perhaps because of its scope, Ottanelli's account does less to illustrate the "interaction between local experiences and ... Party policy" than Mark Naison's more focused and detailed account of the party's work in Harlem during the Depression years. This is by no means to criticize Ottanelli's research or to qualify the importance of his book. It is merely to say that it too is part of the new turn in Communist studies and does not constitute a correction of previous mistakes. In this case, aside from noting the perspective and the empirical content of that turn, it is necessary to ask what is theoretically new about the new history, and what its own context might be.

In addition to the attempt to introduce an "American" aspect to the history of the party, there is a compelling shift of theoretical emphasis in this literature taken as a whole that reflects yet more general developments in the social sciences and humanities. Instead of identifying the history of the party exclusively with the "formal" or official aspect of its organizations—that is, with its centralist and hierarchical forms, the principal means by which leadership rationalized and documented policy decisions, and the factionalization of leadership—the new emphasis on participation invokes informal and interactive aspects of organizational life that are normally thought of as distinctively sociological.

Whatever their connection to the formal features of the party and the movement of which it was a part, the informal aspects are above all intrinsic features of the everyday experiences of people working in and associated with any organization, including the Communist Party. What follows is that the party, like all organizations, must be seen as intrinsically more changeable than it had been, as subject to internal differentiation and driven by processes neither visible nor comprehensible from a point of view that sees only fixed forms, repeated patterns, and predictable adjustments.[10]

Identifying the informal aspects of party history draws attention to the relationship between social movements and the organizations claiming to represent them, varieties of participation within and in connection to the Communist movement, the relationship between the formation of party policy and the conditions of its implementation, and the effects of numerous contexts—including political repression, the presence or absence of other political organizations, economic conditions, and the state of the labor movement—in defining the options of policy and practice at any given time. It draws further attention to the special features of the development of the Communist Party as a "movement organization" that are constituted at the practical intersection of internal tensions and external conditions. This is an understanding profoundly different from that of the party as unmitigated bureaucracy, and its development as the unmediated result of an original principle.

3

In part, this reflects a different generation's experience of the left and of anticommunism. But it also reflects changes in more general attitudes of historians to their subject matter and to their craft. During the 1970s and 1980s, graduate students in the social sciences were confronted with historical studies, like E.P. Thompson's *The Making of the English Working Class*, which, intentionally or not, treated their subject matter more sociologically and addressed their sources with greater skepticism than those of an earlier generation.[11]

To some extent, their response to those texts depended on the influence of yet far greater events, particularly those associated at first with imperialism and racism, and, somewhat later, sexism. Imperialism was signified popularly by, among other things, the invasion of Vietnam and disclosures about the CIA. Racism was dramatized nationally in the live telecast of the violent and unprovoked police response to the march on Selma, and the struggle against it was symbolized for millions by the life and death of

Martin Luther King, Jr. Sexism became visible in a number of ways. Notable among them were the growing resistance of homebound middle class women (cf. Friedan 1963), and the unwillingness of left activist women to continue compromising with "movement patriarchy"—especially, in the late 1960s, in new left organizations such as Students for a Democratic Society and the New University Conference.

These were decisive though difficult points of reference for scholars writing in the wake of the social protests of the 1960s. But what transformed that context of image and insight into a context of theory and practice were vast multifaceted mobilizations of people, extending well into the 1980s. These took forms beyond what the "paradigmatic" social sciences—in particular political science and sociology—expected after the apparent decline of "the movement" following the 1960s and the collapse of liberalism.[12]

Developing within an accelerating global instability, itself a result of capital's progressive transgressions of the older boundaries of nation and hemisphere, coming in the wake of the 1960s, these mobilizations presented scholars with an unprecedented obligation. It was no longer possible to ignore the internally contradictory universe of constantly intensifying exploitation; and it was as impossible to ignore what that intensification, according to its speed and unevenness, made increasingly volatile—enforced juxtapositions of differences in culture, forms of sociality, and interest.

Nor was it possible any longer to ignore the points of view of those who were so forcefully "differentiated," but who found themselves suddenly possessed of a politics oriented against apparently intractable systems rather than specifically identifiable opponents. These new "subjectivities" included women, so-called minorities and people of color, the geopolitically coerced populations of what had been called "third world," gays and lesbians, and increasingly impoverished workers however otherwise described.

What distinguished them was in many ways obvious: conventions of identification, geography, specific history, or their positions in regard to the interests of locally dominant others. What they shared were the general effects of intensified exploitation and violated boundaries. The latter, perhaps because of the ambivalence with which people experience both the boundaries they have taken for granted and the violations which they cannot, provided the initial theoretical and methodological challenges to critical intellectuals in the late 1970s and 1980s. The important feature of the emergent counter-hegemonic politics of the period—the refusal to vote as well as participation in social movements—was the correspondence of its sociocultural diversity with capital's homogenizing transgressions of political economic boundaries (cf., for example, Eisenstein 1988; Harvey 1989; Spivak 1987, 1988). Indeed, many intellectuals found themselves either among the newly differentiated or with no alternative but to identify in one way or another with them (cf. Grossberg, Nelson, and Treichler, 1992).

Therefore, critical scholarship could no longer evade that most difficult responsibility of criticism—to identify and articulate the perspective from which criticism is and had been not only possible but necessary. It follows from the above that the outlines of such a perspective would have to be compatible with the historically qualified and contextually limited universalism manifest in those mobilizations themselves. In other words, critical scholarship, which is to say scholarship, had and has little choice but to address the popular, the everyday, the interactive, the "grassroots," and for the study of organizations such as parties, participation.[13]

But rather than excluding hierarchy, elites, leadership factions, and policy, this perspective presents them as problematic, things to be explained and not merely taken as points of departure for explaining something else. What it does exclude is the conventional working supposition that hierarchy, as constituted, is a *necessary* condition of social rationality. Admittedly, this raises questions about what "rationality" might mean if it does not correspond to the principle of hierarchy and to comprehensive definitions of what is and is not efficient and "goal-effective." It is, nevertheless, possible to identify some of the features it must have if it is to represent a critical perspective on society.

Above all, the type of universalism and rationality represented by the "grassroots" is complicated by the heterogeneity of popular society as such. Elitist perspectives on organizations, including parties, ignore this. In doing so, they in effect treat participants either as functionaries or as comprising a relatively homogeneous population that serves as context of (or resource for) official action.

The emphasis on participation, considered as a perspective,

begins with the practices within which people act, changes in the conditions of those practices, and the multiple determinations of those conditions. In other words, it begins by emphasizing the heterogeneity intrinsic to what is meant by the "grassroots"—qualified by the greater social relations of which they are part. But applied to the history of the Communist Party, this emphasis is neither the creation of the new historians nor simply the result of opinion, loyalty, or sentiment. Apart from its logical justification, discussed earlier, it is a feature of the intellectual culture of *all* the fields in which the historians of Communism are now unavoidably implicated.

4

Writing on the history of Communism after the 1960s meant dealing with issues having to do with knowledge that affects every discipline, in particular those having to do with relations among the disciplines and the ways in which each field comes to identify its subject matter in the light of those relations.

Thus the new historiography of Communism found itself in the midst of an extraordinary academic/intellectual context of overlapping fields. Among the elements were: (1) an anthropology concerned with the connection between power and social differentiation (Willis 1977; Stephen and Dow 1990); (2) a newly critical ethnology of "resistance" and "identity" (Scott 1985); (3) an interdisciplinary feminism focused on gender and the relationship of sociality to heterogeneity (Eisenstein 1988); (4) a philosophically informed literary critique of the contradictions of text and textualization, theory and voice, and form and the labor of writing (Eagleton 1983; Spivak 1987); and (5) a new interdisciplinary sociology of the cultural dialectics of popular mobilization (cf. Brown and Goldin 1973; Hebdige 1979). Above all, it found itself enmeshed in a new humanities unable to avoid the consuming discourses of identity and otherness and driven by the increasingly obvious "deconstructive" conclusion that what "we" had once thought of as "the other" is always us (cf. Said 1978; Goffman 1963).[14]

In such a context, theoreticians—including historians—could

only acknowledge that conclusion by insisting that interpretation be as self-critical as it is critical. For historians, this meant that any account of the past must also involve questioning how it is historically possible to construct such an account. Therefore, they would have at least to consider the possibility that there is an issue of perspective in social history that points to the "grassroots."

It is this latter that provides the most general explanation for why critics of the new historians see them as unduly sympathetic to the left organizations of the past. What appears to be sympathy is in fact simply a willingness to accept responsibility for the only perspective from which a critical historiography can proceed. This, as we have seen, is not driven by a desire to apologize for the weaknesses, mistakes, and failures of any left organization, including the Communist Party. Indeed, the critical perspective allows one to see that the party historically shared many defects with all of those who have tried to participate in history rather than merely suffer it, and that the historiography of Communism can be no different from the historiography of political life in general. For the new historians, the problem of understanding supersedes the tendentious and invidious moralism of so much of the orthodox literature.

On the other hand, this intellectual culture had many opponents, and the rightist reaction after 1980 went far beyond what could have been expected even a year before. The introduction of a durable fascist element at the center of the United States polity gave extraordinary moral and political weight to interpretations of the past. It is not that representations of the past had once been free of ideology; this reaction came as an authoritarian urgency entered into the defense of a particular representation of the past as an essential part of justifying authoritarian projects in the present. The new historians of Communism, like their colleagues in other fields and disciplines, had little choice but to rethink what had been written about the political past of the nation, and therefore to engage it from a critical point of view—from the point of view of participation and the "grassroots."

Admittedly, few of the new historians have acknowledged this intellectual background, and some—perhaps most—would deny it altogether. Nevertheless, its effect is evident in their choice of perspective, their attitude toward sources, the modesty of their prose, and the ways in which they account for stasis and change in terms of the relationship between organization and participation.

5

The result is less a radical departure than a *relatively* new historical account of the party, one that operates far more cautiously on the orthodox historiography from which it seeks to depart than critics such as Draper have been willing to admit. This is evident in (1) the modesty with which the new historians address the earlier research, (2) the judiciousness with which they draw on social theory to extend the conceptual reach of their own interpretations, and (3) their refusal, nevertheless, to go beyond fairly conventional disciplinary accounts of their work.

This is, in other words, an innovative and dedicated literature. The other side of modesty and judiciousness, however, has been an unwillingness on the part of the new historians to defend as a matter of theoretical principle what they do as a matter of historiographic practice (Brown 1986/7). This may explain why they have responded to their orthodox critics, when at all, in the same terms those critics have used against them. Thus Wilentz urges detachment in research and civility in debate, and Ottanelli urges balance in choosing points of entry and perspective (Wilentz 1985; Ottanelli 1991).

But if, as I have argued, the difference cannot be reduced to something as trivial as balance or as extracurricular as civility, and if both sides of the debate—for example Draper and Wilentz—are equally self-righteous in their attribution of a lack of "detachment" to their opponents, then something important is missing from the work of the new historians. Because their work differs in fundamental respects from those of Draper, Bell, Starobin, and Klehr, and because it draws on a different intellectual setting from that of most orthodox historians, it is not unreasonable to ask for something of a theoretical and methodological defense of what is legitimately unorthodox about it. This would, in effect, clarify what constitutes their research program, thereby making it possible to evaluate and expand upon such features as their methods of gathering, evaluating, and substantiating information, the principles by which they interpret and organize material as a reflection on the conceptual validity of their fields of reference, and the ways in which their writing and analysis provide or fail to provide a "dialogical" basis for an active and critical reading.[15]

I have indicated one context in which such a program would have to be described, and conditions under which the perspective of participation has become imperative in the historiography of Communism. But only the historians themselves can clarify how the relationship between the historical (the growth of a movement) and the social (its manifestation in relatively organized form) bears on the detailed operations of their research and how their methodological innovations can be incorporated into the more general project of writing history.

The party that has been studied by the new historians is not the same sort of thing described by Draper, Starobin, and Bell; which is, perhaps, one reason why Draper so thoroughly misread their work in his reviews of 9 May 1985, 30 May 1985, and 26 January 1987. Draper's own view of the party remained constant from 1957 to 1987: "Communism is codified in its canonical literature: it is at any one time what the authoritarian Party says it is" (*The New Republic*, 26 January 1987, p. 35).

Clearly such an object—without context and lacking internal differentiation, a significantly self-critical relation of form to content, and a social base of participation—can exist only if the fields of history and social science are altogether wrong about the general attributes of human organizations, and all other knowledge in the human sciences, including history, is false. For the new historians, then, the party is in many ways a far more conventional social entity than appears in orthodox accounts: a movement organization requiring for its study a methodology consistent with that conception and providing for adequate reference to both the formal hierarchy of leadership (and leadership factions) and the extra-formal, practical, and complex realities of participation (cf. Brown 1987). Appropriately enough, the new historians are more skeptical than Draper in admitting the possibility of multiple interpretations of the same information, hence the necessity for recognizing the ambiguities of decision, policy, and practice in the history of the party.[16] They are more self-critical than their critics in refusing to separate the question of what qualifies as "source" material from that of how it came to be selected as such by historians. Finally, they are more responsive to the social dimension of their topic in their insistence that the ambiguous or unrecorded experiences of ordinary people participating in social movements are no less important for understanding political organization than the recorded activities of elites and their special situations.

6

    Nevertheless, there is an almost palpable pathos in most of the orthodox histories of the party. Many of those texts can be understood as attempts to justify their authors' disaffection with a politics to which they were once, perhaps overwhelmingly, committed. From this point of view, the persuasiveness of those studies is predicated upon a profound philosophical malaise that is more common than is usually admitted, but that is particularly pronounced in most texts written from the retrospection of personal, moral, or political conversion, even more so when the depreciation or denigration of the critical past—e.g., of conflict, struggle—is seen as virtuous, entitling one to at least a modicum of secular redemption.

    It is a malaise induced by the terms of what conversion seems to discover about a past that the converted can no longer recognize or acknowledge. In this regard the conversion text exemplifies what Hegel described as "reason" that has lost sight of its own history, which is to say its own possibility, and therefore that finds itself without the capacity to teach and, one must add, without the capacity to learn.

    What is most persuasive about those texts may be that very moral pathos, the sense they convey of a now inadmissible past, and therefore the anti-nostalgic exultation, the righteousness with which pathos is transformed into a show of strength. It may be, as Michel Foucault hinted in his critique of modernist illusions of emancipation, that dogmatism is only considered legitimate when it constitutes the rhetoric of a new beginning. The paradox is clearer when stated this way; and from this point of view, the strength of the conversion texts lies in their sheer inability to explain how their authors were once attracted to a Communism they now condemn, and therefore to account for how a reasonable and serious person who had once participated could have so thoroughly changed her or his mind. In other words, their strength, and possibly their appeal, lies in their capacity to make any participation whatsoever in the Communist movement seem incredible—and therefore make the nonparticipant seem utterly righteous.

Clearly, such a perspective can have little to say about the role of participation in the history of Communism, and is therefore all the more likely to favor a model of the party as an unyielding monolith without significant local contexts or an organizationally effective base of activity. The paradox of this perspective may be obvious, but it is nevertheless worth restating if only because of the self-defeating temptations posed by the conversion texts themselves: without the ability to conceive of what belonging to or working within the Communist Party might have meant, and how participation must have been mediated within the more comprehensive life settings of participants, as well as by the party itself, disaffection can only seem as arbitrary as the affection so many of the orthodox texts now condemn.

7

Draper makes one statement about the new historians with which I agree, though with a different interpretation from what he obviously intends:

> Instead of making sense of their own experience by confronting it directly, these post-New Left professors seem to want to make sense of it through the medium of an earlier generation. They have evidently turned back to the 1930s, 1940s, and 1950s because they are unwilling or unable to face up to their own political history (*The New Republic*, 26 January 1987, p. 29).

There seems no doubt that the new historians do wish to make connections between the politics of today and the left of an earlier period. But it is wrong to assume, as Draper does, that politics comes in packets, separate from one another, each instance or epoch without any history but its own isolated moment of self-realization.

The boldness with which Draper states this assumption is odd for someone who claims to have studied the *history* of the Communist Party, and even more so for one whose own historical account begins at a point prior to his birth—that is, with the politics of a still "earlier generation." What Draper's comment indicates, despite what it declares, is that the new historians are interested in something more than he can understand or admit to understanding. They are interested in contributing to what is now taking shape as a more honest and comprehensive social history of North America than, for example, Frances Fitzgerald found in the two centuries of school texts she studied in her book, *America Revised* (1979). But they are also interested in establishing the basis for a comprehensive, useful, and honest—which is to say self-critical—historiography of the left, something that may be less difficult to develop today than it was in the past.

On the other hand, there seems little doubt that many on the left desire, for other reasons than "professional anticommunism," to separate themselves from the history of which they are part, from the "embarrassments" of the Soviet Union, the "failures" of the parties, the "corruption" of working-class organizations, and the "excesses" of twentieth century revolutionary movements. It is especially understandable given the overwhelming political effects of capital's global projections on every national or regional society, the deformation of whatever democracy can be said to have existed, in the United States as elsewhere, in the face of massive and desocializing concentrations of wealth, and the momentary loss of international support for socialist reforms.

The tendencies to assign blame, to identify socialism with specific national experiences, to embrace total alternatives in an epoch of totalizing militarization, to think utopian thoughts about democracy in the face of the loss of whatever practical instances of democracy that once could have been identified—all of these contribute to a turning away from the history of the left, often in favor of a renewed concern with moral philosophy, certainly appealing on other grounds but predicated on that very turning away from history (cf., for example, Cohen 1982; Laclau and Mouffe 1985). This is part of the difficulty that many groups experience in reflecting on the problematic aspects of the left project, that is, those aspects that appear historically and that constitute it as a project.

The history of the party is part of the history of the left, and it is more important to understand it in all its contradictory details than to judge it, and to admit the necessity for rethinking that history as ours, rather than to insist that it was complete at its beginning, and in any case another's history; to understand that history requires a sympathetic view of the people who, as Thompson says, "made it."

This is systematically excluded in the conversion texts and in the orthodox histories in general. Critical self-recognition would require that the methodology of an author such as Draper embody a sympathy not for those "others" who participated in the movement, but indeed for himself—that is, for the possibility that anyone might have participated, or that anyone might have remained in the party despite temptations to leave or left despite temptations to stay. It requires an appreciation of the greater dimensions of participation that have to do with life itself; with the North American context of class, race, and gender; with limited options; with ambivalences and distractions; and with the always present difficulty of reconciling the radically democratic values and the possibility of a post-capitalist socialism that emerge in the midst of the active critique of capital with the unpredictable and contradictory aspects of the struggle to implement them as principles of an egalitarian society.

Notes

1. There are also, as in every social movement, memoirs and oral history. Among the names associated with this testimonial literature are Peggy Dennis, *The Autobiography of an American Communist: A Personal View of a Political Life* (1977), and Vivian Gornick, *The Romance of American Communism* (1977). While these, and others by Gil Green, Dorothy Healy, Benjamin Davis, et al., are of interest to historians, I do not consider them part of the historiography of Communism and therefore do not address their contribution in this essay. There is also a growing scholarly literature that has been surveyed elsewhere (cf. the first twelve issues of *Socialism and Democracy*). Fraser M. Ottanelli's *The Communist Party of the United States from the Depression to World War II* (1991) provides an up-to-date working bibliography.

2. Both Theodore Draper and Fraser Ottanelli use the expression "new
    historians" to refer to the recent literature on the Communist Party.
    While I use the term in part to mark the generational difference, it
    will be apparent that I consider the major difference to be between the
    new historians and a certain orthodoxy. Thus, the newness of the
    former refers to a difference in historiographical principle. However,
    I do not mean by this to identify the work of the new historians with
    what has been called "The New Historicism" in cultural and literary
    studies, though it has something in common with what Harold Veeser
    describes as its "key assumptions," which he lists as follows: (1) "that
    every expressive act is embedded in a network of material practices";
    (2) "that every act of unmasking, critique, and opposition uses the tools
    it condemns and risks falling prey to the practice it exposes"; (3) "that
    literary and non-literary 'texts' circulate inseparably"; (4) "that no
    discourse, imaginative or archival, gives access to unchanging truths
    nor expresses inalterable human nature"; (5) "finally ..., that a critical
    method and a language adequate to describe culture under capitalism
    participate in the economy they describe" (Veeser 1989: xi). While this
    program describes a set of historiographical principles consistent with
    recent discoveries in the social sciences, the new historians of Com-
    munism would add at least one other requirement, that any historical
    study at least address the source material of all other studies in its
    field and attempt to expand the common base of empirical reference.
    As will be evident from what follows, I believe that they would also
    agree that theory plays a crucial role in historical study, and that this
    role depends upon the development of theory within the social sciences
    taken as a whole (cf. Brown 1987a, 1987b).
3. Eric Hobsbawm identifies what he calls "orthodox history" with its
    emphasis on "the great actions, the great public actions," including
    especially such events and affairs as "battles, treaties, cabinets, and
    so on" (Hobsbawm 1984: 41–42). Draper's approach to the history of
    the Communist Party exemplifies this on the scale of a movement
    organization.
4. By itself there is nothing wrong with a historian consulting former
    participants. However, Draper does not provide information about
    how he made his selection of informants, whom he eliminated as
    sources, how much he relied on those he accepted, how much of his
    interpretation of the party's history reflects the perspective of those
    who had been expelled, etc. Given this, and his indifference to the
    problems posed by his statement, it is not unreasonable to approach
    his text with at least a degree of skepticism, not only regarding his
    analysis but about his selection and weighing of evidence.
5. Keeran has raised the question of how the party fit into larger

institutional contexts, specifically in regard to the automobile industry and the UAW (Keeran 1980). Naison's study of the Communists in
Harlem during the Depression places the party's agenda in the context
of the national political economy of unemployment and exploitation,
particularly in regard to the way in which relations of class and race
influenced party policy, and how the practical problems and solutions
engendered by those relations affected the activities of party workers
in the field (Naison 1983). Neither author develops an analysis adequate to the sort of history advocated by Perry Anderson, though each
provides the opening needed for such a development, and facts that
lend themselves to it. For a discussion of some of the difficulties
involved, and possible directions, cf. Brown 1987a, 1987b.

6.   This is particularly evident in Lyons's study of the Philadelphia
     Communists (1982), and it is at least implicit in Schrecker's research
     on McCarthyism (1986). The sociological literature on social move-
     ments, especially that portion influenced by "symbolic interaction-
     ism," is more systematic in its analysis of this aspect of politics (cf.
     Brown and Goldin 1973).

7.   "The Communists have held so many different and conflicting posi-
     tions that at first glance the total effect may be one of incredible
     inconsistency and confusion. They have been so inconsistent that they
     have even hopelessly confused themselves. But when the reasons for
     the changes are looked into, when the conditions that made them
     necessary are analyzed, a number of basic problems and forces ap-
     pear—a pattern emerges.

     "This pattern began to emerge at a very early stage. Once the
     Communist movement matured, it became the prisoner of its own
     development. It gradually created precedents, traditions, rituals....
     The deepest, the important secrets are hidden in the formative period"
     (1957: 4). While any study of an organization must deal with the
     internal institutionalization of its practices, the use of the primitivist
     language of ritual, tradition, etc., gives this characterization a decided
     slant. Moreover, having already decided that little need be said about
     the development of the party but its attachment to Moscow, practices
     are easily seen as automatic, mechanical, thoughtless, and first causes
     are easily identified for what seems to be little more than their
     realization in one form or another.

8.   To deny the ambiguity of situations for actors and the consequent
     ambivalence of participants, regardless of individual character traits,
     is tantamount to asserting that human action is essentially mechan-
     ical, that social life is predetermined and automatic rather than
     consisting of a complex play of forces. This is not merely an ideological
     point. To make such an assertion is to deny that there is social life

altogether, and therefore to deny the perspective from which the analysis of participation, social movements, parties, etc., stems in the first place. Therefore, the assertion itself cannot be rational. It comes, I believe, from an inability to tolerate in analysis the complexity of rational action that one cannot avoid tolerating in the world. Draper, for example, writes with a degree of impatience and intolerance toward his subjects that seems to me most easily explained by just such an inability, as if his writing is designed to allow him to vent his frustration at the intractability of that complexity. His subjects emerge, then, as puppets, monologuists, people without any history or any significant personal attachments (cf. Draper, 26 January 1987, quoted below, and 1957: 4, also quoted below). See also Starobin's description of Eugene Dennis (1972: 13–14) and compare it with Isserman's (1982: 23–24).

9. Ottanelli's criticism follows a far more judicious prologue that in my view should have led to a different conclusion: "while balancing the record, the current tendency toward emphasis on the grass roots, however, presents some dangers.... [T]he new history tends to over-shadow the fact that the Communist party was a highly centralized Leninist organization with little room for the diversity that character-ized, for instance, Populism or the Socialist party" (1991: 3). On the one hand, this should not have led Ottanelli to use the phrase "exclu-sive emphasis on the grass roots," since the above speaks only of a "tendency toward emphasis," and an "overshadowing." On the other hand, one question raised by bringing participation into the history of the CPUSA is: what is the nature of "highly centralized," "diversity," etc., and how can these expressions be used in an analysis that has been fundamentally challenged by the emergence of the problematic of "participation?" The point is that when participation is taken into account, the organization of the party needs to be reexamined as such, and the terms of that reexamination brought into line with the newly perceivable internal forces identified by an "emphasis on the grass-roots." This point is made clear in E. P. Thompson's *The Making of the English Working Class* (1963). Thompson shows that taking account of the attitudes and ideas of workers and their communities leads to necessary revisions in one's conception of the dominant structures that, before such an account, seemed to define the substance and limits of civil society. It is also clear in Dorothy Smith's critique of sociology, in which she argues that the introduction of gender in sociological analysis puts into question both the received terms of analysis and the uses to which those terms can be put once gender is taken into account (Smith 1987).

10. By this, I do not mean to say that social life is indeterminate through

and through, but that one finds stability within change rather than attributing change to the breakdown of a former stability.

11. Daniel Bell's vituperative and unsubstantiated characterization of the "American New Left" in the 1967 preface to his essay on *Marxian Socialism in the United States* was one expression of resistance to the intellectual work of those who laid some of the groundwork for the new historiography: "What is lacking in the American New Left is any precision of analysis (therefore its reliance on such vague terms as Power Structure, the Establishment, or simply 'the system') or any discussion of political philosophy. Some of this lack derives from the emphasis on 'gut feeling' and emotion (and a consequent strong anti-intellectualism); some from the inability to locate the sources of power and change in a society where three or more criteria (property, technical skill, and political mobilization) have become the bases of class and social mobility" (1967: xi). It is important to note that Bell's essay was addressed to one influence that he felt was particularly insidious, that of C. Wright Mills, and that in 1967, the same year in which his essay was published, the July issue of the *Journal of Social Issues* featured a series of articles reviewing what was known about participants in "the New Left." In every psychological measure available at the time, self-identified "new leftists" scored higher on measures of democratic tendency and lower on dogmatism and authoritarianism than conservatives and self-labelled moderates (cf., for example, Christian Bay, "Political and Apolitical Students: Facts in Search of Theory," *Journal of Social Issues* 23 [1967]: 76–91). In regard to texts that influenced social studies after the 1960s, other than by historians, Foucault's remarkable studies must be mentioned, in particular, *The Birth of the Clinic* (1973) and *The Order of Things* (1971). The later Frankfurt School's reflections on the meaning of the 1960s for "the idea of history" were an important part of the philosophical background, as was the work of the structuralists (cf. Schroyer 1973; Habermas 1971; Althusser 1970, 1971). Finally, there was a revitalization of Marxist thought generally in regard to labor, empire, urbanization, ideology, culture, and political economy that gradually worked its way into the scholarly journals of the period (Braverman 1974; Aronowitz 1973; Ollman 1971).

12. Just prior to the 1960s, social scientists were fairly confident that, at least for the universities, the forthcoming decade would continue what appeared to be (though it was not, in fact) a period of relative stability following World War II (cf. Parsons 1965). Similarly, in the early 1970s there was a sense among journalists that "the movement" had, in effect, vanished, that the period of activism had come to an end. In fact, activism throughout the 1970s continued to grow in many areas

of U.S. life. This is evidenced by the rapid development of the women's movement; the emergence of insurgencies within a number of major unions, the steelworkers' being most prominent; the expansion of the activism of "neighborhood women," continued anti-war activities, the emergence of environmentalism, and the like. By 1979, after Carter's last "State of the Union" address called for a renewed cold war, hundreds of "teach-ins" were organized at universities and colleges around the country, more than thirty in the New York region alone. The press, however, refused to cover these events—one story summarizing the considerable level of activism that was scheduled to be published in the Sunday *New York Times* was killed at the last moment, and from that point on the *Times* simply failed to cover demonstrations no matter how large, or meetings of activists no matter how prominent their spokespeople. From the standpoint of mass media, it was as if activism had vanished. In fact, it had accelerated. The mobilizations that took place in the 1970s mediated what I have called, above, the "context of discovery" in such a way that scholars could no longer avoid analyzing movement organizations— such as parties—as if they were independent of the everyday lives of people. These events provided a U.S. context for theoretical developments in North American historiography similar to what 1968 did for French critical historiography. In both cases, regardless of point of view, it was no longer possible to write as if social movements and politics were not implicit in society as such.

13. I do not mean to suggest that such a perspective is attainable, but only that the attempt to attain it is a principle guiding research. One of the most compelling findings of poststructuralist criticism is that there are radical limits to any inquiry that posits a relationship between an observing subject and another subjectivity (cf. Foucault 1970: xxiv; Spivak 1987). While this may seem to be a variant of earlier arguments about the possibility of knowing other minds, it differs fundamentally from them. Briefly, it argues that theory as we presently conceive of it transforms the subjectivities to which its attention is drawn, for reasons that are in principle outside of science, into objects of knowledge. That is to say that they are no longer practical subjects (cf. Garfinkel 1967), no longer what they were when "we" wished to study "them." Moreover, this transformation re-presents a division within the "observing subject" that contradicts the claims of that subject to "know." No doubt, this is cryptic in the context of the present essay, but it is a qualification that needs at least to be mentioned. Foucault's programmatic statement, at the end of the preface to *The Order of Things* (1970: xxiv), is one version of this insight: "The history of madness would be the history of the Other—of that which, for a given

culture, is at once interior and foreign, therefore to be excluded (so as to exorcise the interior danger) but by being shut away (in order to reduce its otherness)...."

14. I do not mean to suggest that the representative new historians of Communism cite this literature or are even directly aware of it. My point is only that there is a background to what they are doing, whether or not they deliberately take it into account. In one way or another, all of them, including those most interested in maintaining strictly disciplinary criteria, work within that intellectual culture and share the sensitivities of it.

15. Dialogical writing should be understood in contrast with the sort of preemptive text that constrains its reader and allows for little more than a passively receptive reading. The tendentiousness of tone running through Bell's and Draper's work, accompanied by a more explicitly polemicized content, illustrates one aspect of such a text. Compare Bell's pontifical characterization of the "American New Left" with Draper's more personalistic polemic against the new historians (both quoted above). The same tone adheres to much of orthodox historiography itself, as in the following passage by Draper: "Another Russian specter came to haunt the American Communist movement as it struggled to be born. To their American disciples, hurriedly catching up with decades of Russian revolutionary history, the Bolsheviks seemed to have prepared for power by spending most of their time fighting among themselves or against other factions in the Russian Socialist movement. The Bolshevik-Menshevik split of 1903 had been followed by innumerable other splits, always justified as the way to strengthen the revolutionary movement by removing foreign excrescences. If this was the school of revolution in Russia, what self-styled disciple of Lenin dared say that it could be otherwise in the United States?" (1957: 164). Needless to say, this sort of prose cannot be written today by anyone claiming to write history. But to understand the relief felt as one reads the work of the new historians, it is important is to note the preemptive tone of this passage. The rhetorical elevation of a summary authorial voice above all possibilities for rethinking the putative base of information on which the passage seems to rely, and the mix of extremely simplifying abstractions and a tone of voice that I believe must be described as snide—"American disciples hurriedly catching up ...," "foreign excrescences," "self-styled disciple"—gives the prose its unself-critical momentum. All of this is justifiable in texts that claim a primarily polemical intent, but is not when authors claim to interpret events dispassionately and to provide valid histories of them. Of course, all prose carries at least some polemical weight; but this is a case in which there is virtually no point

at which one does not find the heavy weight of Draper's attitude toward the party, and his effort to eliminate alternative points of view or questions that might show his to be only one of other possible ways of understanding the history of the party. These passages are as typical of Draper's account of the Communist Party as they are atypical of writing normally recognized as historical. The fact that, in his 1985 reviews, he upheld just this sort of writing as the standard by which the research of the new historians should be judged, suggests that tendentiousness at all levels is the historiographical principle he wishes to defend, rather than a defect he wishes to correct or a quality he wishes to moderate.

16. One type of problem particularly poignant for the history of the party has to do with the ways in which policy deliberations among leadership groups are transformed when final statements of policy are received by deliberating groups of participants engaged in day-to-day activities within communities, and by others who might be considered audiences (occasionally called "constituencies") of such statements and activities. What is for one group a conclusion is for the other the beginning of deliberation, not merely of implementation. The failure to have conceptualized party organization in appropriate organizational terms may account for the orthodox view of the party as a monolith, without context or the expected properties of political formations. Few organizations have solved the problem of democratizing decision, and for good reasons, though for reasons that must always be challenged if the organization is to endure. This would involve exposing the processes, including debates, that underlie any instance of policy-making, and encouraging participants to reengage those debates in the course of organizationally salient action itself. The party seems only rarely to have provided exceptions to this typical organizational dilemma, and one might argue that any movement-based organization that hopes to grow will have to find one way or another to promote the circulation of its deliberative practices within the contexts of its political practices, though the difficulties of this will and must always encourage resistance to it. The failure of the party to have done so on an appropriate scale, however, does not imply the model invoked by Draper in his *New Republic* article. Rather, given what we know about organizations, it suggests the unavoidable presence of change-inducing tensions among various practices, therefore tendencies of each practice to interfere with the others. This is clear in Gerald Horne's essay in this volume on the relationship between the party and the Davis campaign, in Naison (1983), and in Lyons (1982).

Bibliography

Abraham, D. *The Collapse of the Weimar Republic: Political Economy and Crisis*. Princeton, NJ: Princeton University Press, 1981 (rev. ed., New York: Holmes and Meier, 1986)

Althusser, L. *For Marx*. New York: Vintage, 1970.

Althusser, L. *Lenin and Philosophy*. New York: Monthly Review Press, 1971.

Anderson, P. "Communist Party History," in Samuel, R. (ed.), *People's History and Socialist Theory*. New York: Routledge & Kegan Paul, 1981: 145–156.

Aronowitz, S. *False Promises*. New York: McGraw-Hill, 1973

Bay, C. "Political and Apolitical Students: Facts in Search of Theory," *Journal of Social Issues* 23, July 1967: 76–91.

Bell, D. *Marxian Socialism in the United States*. Princeton, NJ: Princeton University Press, 1967 (originally published in 1952).

Braverman, H. *Labor and Monopoly Capital*. New York: Monthly Review Press, 1975.

Brown, M. and A. Goldin. *Collective Behavior*. Goodyear, 1973.

Brown, M. *The Production of Society: A Marxian Foundation for Social Theory*. Lanham, MD: Rowman & Littlefield, 1986.

Brown, M. "Issues in the Historiography of Communism, Part One. *Socialism and Democracy* 4, 1987a: 7–38.

Brown, M. "Issues in the Historiography of Communism: Part Two: Some Principles of Critical Analysis." *Socialism and Democracy* 5, 1987b: 1–34.

Brown, M. "History and History's Problem," *Social Text* 16, 1986/7: 136–61.

Burke, P. *Popular Culture in Early Modern Europe*. New York: New York University Press, 1978.

Burke, P. *Sociology and History*. Concord, MA: Allen & Unwin, 1980.

Cohen, J. *Class and Civil Society: The Limits of Marxian Critical Theory*. Amherst: University of Massachusetts Press, 1982

Darnton, R. *The Great Cat Massacre and Other Episodes in French Cultural History*. New York: Vintage, 1985.

Dennis, P. *The Autobiography of an American Communist: A Personal View of a Political Life, 1925–1975*. Berkeley, CA: Creative Arts, 1977.

Draper, T. *The Roots of American Communism*. New York: Viking, 1957.

Draper, T. *American Communism and Soviet Russia: The Formative Period*. New York: Viking Press, 1960.

Draper, T. "The Myth of the Communist Professors: The Class Struggle," *The New Republic*, 26 January 1987: 29–36.

Draper, T. "The Popular Front Revisited," *The New York Review of Books,* 30 May 1985.

Draper, T. "American Communism Revisited," *The New York Review of Books*, 9 May 1985.

Eagleton, T. *Literary Theory*. Minneapolis: University of Minnesota Press, 1983.

Eisenstein, Z. *The Female Body and the Law*. Berkeley: University of California Press, 1988.

Foner, E. *History of the Labor Movement in the United States*. 5 vols. New York: International Publishers, 1972.

Foucault, M. *The Order of Things*. New York: Random House, 1971.

Foucault, M. *The Birth of the Clinic*. New York: Vintage, 1973.

Fitzgerald, F. *America Revised: History Schoolbooks in the Twentieth Century*. Boston: Little, Brown and Co., 1979.

Garfinkel, H. *Studies in Ethnomethodology*. New York: Prentice-Hall, 1967.

Goffman, E. *Stigma*, New York: Prentice-Hall, 1963.

Gornick, V. *The Romance of American Communism*. New York: Basic Books, 1977.

Grossberg, L. C. Nelson, P. Treichler (eds.), *Cultural Studies*. Routledge, 1992.

Gutman, H. *Work, Culture, and Society in Industrializing America*. Knopf, 1976.

Habermas, J. *Knowledge and Human Interest*. Boston: Beacon Press, 1971.

Harvey, D. *The Condition of Postmodernity*. Cambridge, MA: Blackwell, 1989.

Hebdige, D. *Subculture: The Meaning of Style*. New York: Routledge, 1979.

Hobsbawm, E. MARHO interview, in MARHO (eds.), *Visions of History*. New York: Pantheon, 1984: 27–46.

Howe, I. and L. Coser. *The American Communist Party: A Critical History*. Boston: Beacon Press, 1957.

Isserman, M. *Which Side Were You On? The American Communist Party During the Second World War*. Middletown, CT: Wesleyan University Press, 1982.

Jameson, F. *The Political Unconscious*. Ithaca, NY: Cornell University Press, 1981.

Jones, G.S. *Outcast London*. New York: Oxford University Press, 1971.

Keeran, R. *The Communist Party and the Auto Workers Unions*. Indianapolis: Indiana University Press, 1980.

Klehr, H. *Communist Cadre: The Social Background of the American Communist Party Elite*. Stanford, CA: Hoover Institution Press, 1978.

Klehr, H. *The Heyday of American Communism: The Depression Decade*. New York: Basic Books, 1984.

Laclau, E. and C. Mouffe, *Hegemony and Socialist Strategy* (transl. by W. Moore and P. Cammack). New York: Verso, 1985.

44   NEW STUDIES IN U.S. COMMUNISM

Liebman, A. *Jews and the Left*. New York: Wiley & Sons, 1979.

Lyons, P. *Philadelphia Communists, 1936–1956*. Philadelphia, PA: Temple University Press, 1982.

Naison, M. *Communists in Harlem During the Depression*. Champaign: University of Illinois Press, 1983.

Newton, J. "History as Usual? Feminism and the 'New Historicism,'" in Veeser, H. (ed.) *The New Historicism*. New York: Routledge, 1989: 152–167.

Ollman, B. *Alienation: Marx's Conception of Man in Capitalist Society*. New York: Cambridge University Press, 1971.

Ottanelli, F. *The Communist Party of the United States from the Depression to World War II*. New Brunswick, NJ: Rutgers University Press, 1991.

Rude, G. *Ideology and Popular Protest*. New York: Pantheon, 1989.

Said, E. *Orientalism*. New York: Random House, 1985.

Samuel, R. *People's History and Socialist Theory*. New York: New York: Routledge & Kegan Paul, 1981.

Schroyer, T. *The Critique of Domination*. Boston: Beacon Press, 1973.

Schrecker, E. *No Ivory Tower: McCarthyism and the Universities*. Oxford University Press. 1986.

Scott, J. *Weapons of the Weak: Everyday Forms of Peasant Resistance*. New Haven: Yale University Press, 1985.

Smith, D. *The Everyday World as Problematic: A Feminist Sociology*. Boston: Northeastern University Press, 1987.

Spivak, G.C. *In Other Worlds: Essays in Cultural Politics*. New York: Methuen, 1987.

Spivak, G.C. "Can the Subaltern Speak?" in Nelson, C., and L. Grossberg (eds.), *Marxism and the Interpretation of Culture*. Champaign: University of Illinois, 1988: 271–313.

Starobin, J. *American Communism in Crisis, 1943–1957*. Cambridge, MA: Harvard University Press, 1972.

Stephen, L. and J. Dow (eds.). *Class, Politics, and Popular Religion in Mexico and Central America*. Washington DC: American Anthropological Association, 1990.

Thompson, E.P. *The Making of the English Working Class*. New York: Knopf, 1963.

Veeser, H. (ed.). *The New Historicism*. New York: Routledge Chapman and Hill, 1989.

Wagner, R. *The Invention of Culture*. Chicago: University of Chicago Press, 1981.

Willis, P. *Learning to Labour*. Aldershot: Saxon House, 1977.

Wilentz, S. "Red Herrings Revisited: Theodore Draper Blows His Cool," *Voice Literary Supplement*, June 1985.

REMAKING AMERICA: Communists and Liberals in the Popular Front

Mark Naison

From the summer of 1935 through the fall of 1939, the Communist Party USA became an influential actor in a popular upheaval that transformed U.S. life. Given a green light by the Communist International (Comintern) to reconcile itself to U.S. liberalism, the CPUSA participated in an industrial union drive of unprecedented breadth and effectiveness and contributed to a process of political and cultural change that gave immigrant workers and blacks an enhanced sense of citizenship. Dispensing with revolutionary rhetoric, the party leadership wrapped itself in the mantle of militant populism, devoting its energies to building trade unions, mobilizing support for New Deal legislation and trying to awaken popular vigilance to the dangers of fascism. In doing so, it not only sparked a large growth in party membership (from 26,000 in 1934 to 85,000 in 1939), but engendered a spirit of cooperation between liberals and radicals that facilitated the empowerment of North America's least privileged citizens and placed ethnocentrism on the defensive in U.S. political and intellectual life.[1]

The announcement of the popular front policy, in the summer of 1935, set in motion change in party life that gave it greater flexibility to adapt to popular attitudes and pursue opportunities for political influence. Seeking support from an American working class in revolt against corporate tyranny, Communists found their leadership skills valued by people whose major political language was U.S. republicanism and who responded to symbols of equal opportunity and fair play. Seeking anti-fascist alliances in the mainstream of U.S. politics, Communists found themselves courted by union leaders and politicians anxious to facilitate New Deal reforms. For people who had been outsiders, and who in some cases had experienced jail and exile, this was heady stuff—but it invariably involved the condition that Communists keep a low profile and push "utopian" goals to the background. Yet on most levels of the party, this transmutation of political identity aroused more enthusiasm than resentment. With apparent Comintern approval, party general secretary Earl Browder took extraordinary steps to ease the party's path to political influence, loosening the demands of party membership, disavowing armed revolution as a goal and affirming the continuity of Communism with the great reform traditions of the U.S. past. Only on one issue—support for the foreign and domestic policies of the Soviet Union—did party leaders define a political identity markedly different from liberals and New Dealers.[2]

However, the CPUSA's effort to shed its "foreign" image betrayed glaring inconsistencies. At the very moment that Browder described the party as a "consistent fighter for democracy," he was still making trips to Moscow to get Comintern approval of major policy initiatives. Moreover, party leaders still functioned as though their real constituency, the one that could make or break them as leaders, was in the Soviet Union. Without the slightest embarrassment, they translated the Soviet obsession with internal opposition into a U.S. setting, demanding the excommunication of "Trotskyites" from the labor movement and the left while elevating praise of Stalin to cult-like proportions. Browder's exhortations to the party membership to stamp out factionalism "with a red hot iron" and eradicate Trotskyite "poison" raised questions about the sincerity of his pledge to party allies to "use ... democratic methods as the sole method of resolving disputes between us." To some intellectuals, the popular front became the moment when Communism revealed its profound moral corruption.[3]

Nevertheless, it would be a mistake to see the popular front merely as a facade for Communist manipulation of liberal constituencies. Because of the dangerously charged international atmosphere, some U.S. liberals were willing to ignore many warts and blemishes to assure Communist participation in anti-fascist activities. Sometimes, they took the most hardheaded approach to securing Communist aid, insisting that Communists sacrifice their power, and even their identity, as the price of political cooperation. Secondly, Communists could not help but be influenced by the varying moods of optimism and foreboding that swept through the constituencies among whom they organized. The party's reputation as a center of practical activism drew hundreds of thousands of people into its orbit. Among Jews and blacks, Eastern European immigrants and displaced farmers, the popular front ethos evolved from a formula for liberal-radical cooperation into an ambitious effort to reformulate U.S. nationality. As the party hastened to embrace "progressive" elements in the U.S. political tradition, it attracted a diverse array of cultural figures, from folk and jazz musicians to non- conformist ministers and sportswriters. In their hands, the popular front developed a unique U.S. chemistry, a vision of a nation repudiating ethnic prejudice and class privilege and employing the strength and resilience of its common people to prevent a fascist triumph. If changes in Comintern policy and party rhetoric helped create such a world view, the energies it unleashed far transcended their control.

The popular front marked the emergence of Earl Browder as an enthusiastic partisan of the party's Americanization and the first U.S. Communist to become a media figure. Prior to the Seventh World Congress of the Comintern, where the popular front policy received full articulation, Browder had been a cautious, inconsistent leader, privately encouraging initiatives that would expand the party's influence while engaging in strident denunciations of the Roosevelt administration and trade union and socialist leaders. Placed in power by the Comintern, he never overstepped his mandate for innovation, fearful that a resentful William Z. Foster would move rapidly to unseat him if he lost Comintern support. But the Seventh Congress proved a godsend to Western party leaders like Browder, removing some of the tight supervision they labored under (to defuse accusations of Soviet interference in the affairs of democratic nations) while encouraging them to discard their image as colorless bureaucrats and become "patriotic" leaders with broad national constituencies. After years in the shadows, Browder discovered long-suppressed ambitions to become a public figure. No longer would he censure innovative political strategies "sprouting at the grassroots"; he would lead by example, showing how a Communist could become respectable in the highest councils of the nation.

The Communist election campaign of 1936 provided a perfect stage for Browder to unveil his aspirations to national leadership.

Nominated as the party's presidential candidate, Browder coined the slogan "Communism is Twentieth Century Americanism" and sought to identify himself as the heir of Jefferson, Lincoln and John Brown. Dropping references to the New Deal as "fascist," Browder described the main danger in the campaign as the election of a Republican candidate backed by the Liberty League, the Hearst newspapers, and other centers of anti-labor and anti-Soviet sentiment. For Browder, the logic of the popular front not only meant dropping references to a "Soviet America," but deemphasizing agitation for socialism: "the direct issue of the 1936 election," he declared, "is not socialism or capitalism, but rather democracy or fascism." While broadcasting these views over national radio, Browder ordered a reorganization of the party at the local level to make it less conspiratorial in appearance and more capable of competing within the electoral process. Party street units, averaging ten to fifteen members in size and meeting in apartments and private homes, consolidated into party branches of fifty to 100 members that met in storefronts and meeting halls. The *Daily Worker* underwent an equally dramatic change, unveiling a daily sports page, expanded cultural coverage, and a Sunday magazine that featured portraits of popular sports figures, musicians, labor leaders and historical personalities. Mike Gold, with typical pungency, summarized the new party credo: "When you run the news of a strike alongside the news of a baseball game, you are making American workers feel at home.... Let's loosen up. Let's begin to prove that one can be a human being as well as a Communist. It isn't a little special sect of bookworms and soapboxers."[4]

The formation of the Committee for Industrial Organization, marked by Communist participation at all levels, helped give substance to Browder's rhetoric and the party's new strategy. In the fall of 1935, leaders of the three largest AFL unions, the United Mine Workers Union, the Amalgamated Clothing Workers Union, and the International Ladies Garment Workers Union, decided to place their "prestige and resources" behind the creation of industrial unions in unorganized U.S. industries—steel, auto, rubber, maritime, and electric. Encouraged by rank-and-file organizing efforts, spontaneous strikes, and the passage of New Deal legislation which facilitated unionization (the Wagner Labor Relations Act), they hired organizers, publicists, and lawyers to aid incipient

unions and created a Steel Workers Organizing Committee to take
on North America's largest open-shop industry. Astonishingly, the
CIO's director, John L. Lewis, solicited Communist involvement in
this daring endeavor. Not only did Lewis and his associates meet
privately with top party leaders to secure their support (Browder,
Clarence Hathaway, and Wyndham Mortimer all met with CIO
officials in the winter of 1935–1936), but he hired Communist
sympathizers as CIO general counsel and director of publicity and
placed almost sixty Communist organizers on the Steel Workers
Organizing Committee payroll. This unanticipated political alliance, initiated by a leader who had brutally purged Communists
from his own union, provided Browder with a striking example of
the opportunities that awaited Communists as they pursued the
people's front. Rejecting warnings of Communist perfidy, Lewis
gambled that he needed Communist shock troops to win battles for
union recognition and that he could maintain the upper hand if
their interests ever diverged from his.[5] As their part of the bargain,
Communists in the CIO kept a low profile and sometimes tolerated
humiliating constraints on their power and attacks on their political philosophy. In the Steel Workers Organizing Committee, Communists accepted, without protests, a structure that gave
dictatorial powers to SWOC head Philip Murray, assuring that
Communists could be eased out when the hard work of organizing
was done. In the automobile industry, where Communists had won
influence through persistent advocacy of industrial unionism, their
major spokesman, Wyndham Mortimer, declined to run for the
presidency of the new United Auto Workers Union while their cadre
agreed to the passage of a resolution denouncing "Fascism, Nazism,
and Communism." To protest their position and avoid embarrass-
ing Lewis, Communists in the CIO, with rare exceptions, denied
their party affiliation and threw themselves into the task of building unions with single-minded devotion. Throughout industrial
America, the party placed its ethnic associations, legal defense
groups and black community networks at the disposal of the CIO,
but abjured revolutionary rhetoric as that might offend conservative workers. Indeed, Communists in labor conducted special party
functions—recruiting, caucusing, and propaganda—so circum-
spectly that some workers couldn't tell where the party ended and
the union began (Irish transport workers in New York, Josh Free-

man points out, called their left-wing leadership's philosophy "Communionism"). This approach, Harvey Levenstein argues, meshed perfectly with the needs of CIO officials: "They could avoid defending the right of Communists to dominate unions by claiming ignorance of the extent of Communist power in the CIO while enjoying the benefits of having superb Communist organizers and talented Communists on the CIO staff."[6]

In their electoral activity, Communists displayed a similar determination to remain within the mainstream of working class sentiment and accommodate powerful allies willing to give them a "piece of the action." After the Seventh Comintern Congress, Browder's main electoral goal had been the creation of a "working-class-led farmer-labor party" fielding its own ticket in the 1936 elections. To advance this objective, Communists began joining third party movements they had previously assailed (in October 1935, Browder held a secret "peace" conclave with Minnesota Farmer-Labor Governor Floyd Olson) and began pressing for independent labor political action on a state and local level. Despite past indiscretions, Communists received a suprisingly warm welcome from strategically placed politicians who cultivated labor support. In Minnesota, Harvey Klehr points out, Governor Olson "welcomed the Communist Party as a legitimate partner in Minnesota politics" and incorporated them into his electoral machine by putting key party members on the state payroll. In Washington, Communists drew the executive director of the Commonwealth Federation, Howard Costikyan, into the party's inner circle, enabling them to become "the single most powerful force in the organization." Using similar inside dealing, Communists built a base in the Wisconsin Progressive Farmer Labor Federation and local labor parties in Michigan, Ohio, Massachussets, and Connecticut. But Communist participation did not mean Communist control. Faced with a grassroots New Deal groundswell among industrial workers and a CIO decision to support Roosevelt's candidacy, Communists decided to confine agitation for a farmer-labor party strictly to state and local elections. With Comintern approval, they decided to use Browder's independent candidacy largely to warn of the dangers of a Republican victory, thereby becoming the first party in U.S. history to use a presidential campaign largely to assure the victory of one of its opponents![7]

Browder's bizarre campaign strategy, while it did little to affect the outcome of the election, helped Communists expand their influence in state and local politics. By 1937, party trade unionists and neighborhood activists had become securely ensconced in New York's American Labor Party, while securing similar bases within the Minnesota Farmer-Labor Party, Washington's Commonwealth Federation, and Wisconsin's Progressive Farmer Labor Federation. Ironically, all four of these organizations had clauses barring Communists from membership, but in the atmosphere of the popular front, Communists blended into the scenery so effectively that there was little incentive to expel them. Presenting their organization as a disciplined secret fraternity willing to fight for liberal goals (a kind of left-wing version of the Masons!), Communists drew elected officials, administrators of state agencies and ambitious politicians into their inner circle. Possessed of the power to make careers as well as fight for social reforms, the party, Peggy Dennis recalled, attracted a new breed of recruit: "experienced activists, mainly from other organizations" who had little exposure to Marxism. Fearful of jeopardizing their liberal cover or driving them away with excessive demands, the party approached their political education on a hit-or-miss basis, undermining the core of common beliefs that united the party and bluring the lines that separated members from sympathizers and fellow travelers.[8]

The drive for industrial unionism, stirred to a fever pitch by Roosevelt's reelection, also served to erode some of the insularity that had previously characterized the party. Throughout industrial America, workers interpreted the New Deal victory as confirmation of their right to organize; the number of strikes rose from 3,720 in 1936 to 4,740 in 1937, more than half over the demand for union recognition. The CIO registered particularly dramatic victories, some of them sparked by spontaneous worker protest. In Schenechtady, New York, Ronald Schatz observes, "immigrant workers who went to the polls for the first time in their lives discovered overnight that there were thousands ... in their factory who shared their convictions"; two months later, they selected the United Electrical Workers Union as their bargaining agent with General Electric, stunning previously pessimistic union organizers. In the Midwest, a proliferation of spontaneous sit-down strikes during the early months of 1937 idled over 100,000 workers, forcing

General Motors to begin negotiations for a national contract with the UAW. During the same period, steel workers rallied with such enthusiasm to the CIO that U.S. Steel chose to recognize the SWOC as a bargaining agent rather than face a crippling strike. Strikes with significant left involvement occurred in rubber, meatpacking, lumber, East Coast maritime, and New York transit.[9]

Told by the party leadership that building the CIO represented their highest priority, Communists became enmeshed in the spirit of this popular upheaval. Struggles for union recognition not only challenged employer domination at the workplace, particularly the authority of foremen and supervisors, they spilled over into politics and civic affairs where immigrants and blacks sought representation in local governments long dominated by Protestant elites or established Catholic ethnics. In Detroit, in the Mesabi range, and the Bronx, Communist ethnic workers clubs rallied to the CIO, giving union organizers meeting places and social networks safe from vigilantes and company spies, while Americanized party organizers provided publicity, legal assistance and contact with sympathetic public officials. "The spiritual and moral awakening" these efforts engendered fired the imagination of a generation of party activists and gave them an unmatched sense of practical accomplishment. CIO organizing drives in the mining, lumbering, steel, automobile and textile industry, one Finnish-American Communist recalled, "...brought to fruition the dreams of the older generation of radical Finns, many of whom rallied their clubs, associations, and cooperatives to support the second generation Finnish radicals who helped to spearhead the drive.... As a consequence of unionization, immigrant workers, Finns among them, who had largely been voiceless and powerless in company dominated towns throughout industrial America finally gained actual meaningful citizenship."[10]

The atmosphere of communal warfare that characterized CIO organizing surfaced with particular clarity in the Flint sit-down strikes of 1937. UAW Vice President Wyndham Mortimer, assigned to organize Flint, found a workforce pervaded by spies and informers and a local government totally dominated by General Motors. Fearful of company retaliation, Mortimer based his first union support groups entirely upon Communist Party units and Macedonian, Finnish, Russian, Czech and Slovakian workers clubs attached to the IWO. Thereafter, Mortimer and his successor, Bob Travis, gradually won the confidence of other workers by printing exposés of General Motors espionage based on information supplied by a Communist investigator for the La Follette Civil Liberties Committee. When spontaneous sit-down strikes erupted on the basis of local grievances, Travis and Mortimer used party networks to spread the movement and their role as UAW representatives to bring national support to the strikers. What followed was an epic struggle in which Communists, operating only as "good union men," blended their efforts in a total mobilization of the Flint working class and the CIO top leadership. "Here was a classic labor-capital confrontation," Bert Cochran writes, "encompassing scores of corporation executives intent on beating back the union challenge, property minded judges issuing sweeping injunctions, sheriffs and police with drawn guns, vigilante workers trying to organize a back to work movement, heroic wives, excited labor agitators.... And Communists were in the center of it all. Mortimer was one of the negotiators, the only UAW officer presiding in the decisive stage of negotiation, Travis was the Flint director, Kraus was running the union newspaper and publicity." Significantly, none of these strategically placed individuals used their positions to build the party or publicly propagate a socialist outlook; when the strike ended, the UAW had become a force in community affairs, but the Communist Party in Flint remained small and isolated. "So politically covert were the Communists," Roger Keeran writes, "that Roy Reuther, who worked closely with Travis, believed that the sit-down leader simply acted as a 'good trade union guy' who had no politics until later."[11] The victory over General Motors persuaded Browder to focus even more Communist energies on building the CIO. After April 1937, when the CIO became an independent labor federation, several Communist-led unions bolted the CIO, among them the Transport Workers Union, the National Maritime Union, the Fur and Leather Workers Union, the Maritime Federation of the Pacific, the International Wood Workers Union and a section of the International Association of Machinists (which joined up with the UE). By the CIO's 1938 convention, Harvey Klehr writes, "no less than 40 percent of the international unions were either led by Communists and their close allies or significantly influenced by them." The largest of these were the United Automobile Workers

Union, where Communists constituted the strongest force in a divided and contentious leadership, and the United Electrical, Radio and Machine Workers of America, where party members used their positions as secretary-treasurer and director of organization to hire much of the union's staff.[12]

However, the terms of Communist success in the CIO dramatized party concessions to pragmatism in the name of the popular front. With the exception of Ben Gold of the Fur and Leather Workers Union, not one Communist CIO official made his convictions publicly known and participated openly in the affairs of the party. Although party union heads met privately with the party's political elite, they were treated with great deference, given access to party resources while being allowed considerable freedom to shape day-to-day union policy. Moreover, in campaigns for union recognition and survival, CIO Communists rarely risked dividing their constituency by projecting heterodox views. They did try to incorporate party perspectives into union newspapers, particularly those on race and foreign policy, but rarely in a manner that might offend conservative members. This new version of Communism, a private faith attuned to practical union realities, seemed to exercise a disproportionate attraction for those with leadership ambitions. "In union after union," Harvey Klehr writes, "party influence was concentrated among the leadership and paid bureaucracy." Rank-and-file workers, who were not easily decieved, viewed Communists as effective spokesmen for their interests, to be evaluated strictly on their ability to deliver the goods. "Smart boys," an NMU member told Fortune. "They're going where we want them to right now —democratic unions with a firm tie-up to shore workers. The Coms, they say, are fighters, they've got ideas on strategy and they keep their noses clean on money."[13]

If labor organizing represented the key focal point of the popular front, mobilization against fascist aggression represented the second. Anti-fascism gave U.S. Communists an enlarged constituency among intellectuals and ethnic minorities. The party's advocacy in behalf of China and Ethiopia, each invaded by a fascist nation, its continuous agitation against Hitler's Germany, and above all its campaign to support the embattled Spanish Republic represented one of the most ambitious mobilizations around international issues ever attempted by an organization of the U.S. left. The enthusiasm stirred by these protests belies accusations of cynicism often directed at U.S. Communists. Though the Comintern may have employed anti-fascist appeals largely for Soviet *raisons d'état*, neither the rank-and-file party membership, or the much larger network of party sympathizers and allies, approached this activity in a spirit of mechanical obedience. It did not take much persuasion to make a Jewish printer or a Croatian steelworker hate Hitler, or a black school teacher denounce Mussolini, or an Austrian refugee actor raise funds for victims of the Dolfuss regime. Such individuals, the bones and sinews of the Communist movement, approached the anti-fascist cause with the feeling that their own lives were at stake. Moreover, the proliferation of U.S. apologists for fascism (led by Father Charles Coughlin, who possessed the largest radio audience in the world), the growth of the Black Legion, the Ku Klux Klan and the German-American Bund, and the persistence of racial and religious discrimination throughout U.S. society provided a powerful incentive for radicals, liberals and exponents of minority rights to unite their forces. "While the hydra-headed monster of fascism is threatening our rather weak democratic institutions in America," A. Philip Randolph was quoted as telling one popular front gathering, "it is imperative that the mass voice of Negroes and all their allies be spoken."[14]

In arousing vigilance against fascism, Communists sought a constituency that extended far beyond the organized left. During the summer of 1935, party activists, working through the American League Against War and Fascism, spearheaded a campaign to boycott the 1936 Olympics that included congressmen, AFL leaders, the head of the Amateur Athletic Union and Protestant, Catholic and Jewish clergymen. Although the campaign failed to prevent the U.S. team from competing (the head of the American Olympic Committee, Avery Brundage, was a Nazi sympathizer), it helped publicize Hitler's suppression of German Jewry and his aggressive intentions toward neighboring countries. During the same period, Communists helped organize an interracial protest movement against Italian agression in Ethiopia that incorporated representatives of the black clergy, the NAACP and black nationalist organizations. The high point of this movement, a 25,000-person march through Harlem organized by the American League Against War and Fascism, featured a contingent of 200 Italian-

American radicals chanting anti-Mussolini slogans, helping to defuse a potentially explosive confrontation between neighboring black and Italian communities. In Southern California, a recent convert to the party, Donald Ogden Stuart, joined with Dorothy Parker, Fritz Lang, Frederick March and Oscar Hammerstein to organize the Hollywood Anti-Nazi League, a movement to raise funds for victims of Hitler's terror and press the Roosevelt administration to impose sanctions on the Nazi regime. At its high point, the League had over 4,000 members, sponsored its own newspaper and radio show, and organized an "endless series of meetings, demonstrations, speeches, banquets, parties and panels focusing on every conceivable fascist menace to the peace and freedom of the world."[15]

The party's campaign in behalf of the republican government in Spain, however, dwarfed all these efforts in breadth and political significance. The revolt of the Spanish army against a freely elected, popular government, undertaken with German and Italian support, provided a textbook case of the conflict between democracy and fascism which Communists constantly spoke of. Astonishingly, not one Western government would provide military aid to the Spanish Republic; the United States, Britain and France all kept out of the conflict while Mussolini sent troops and Hitler used the war to test his most advanced military technology. The Soviet Union's decision to send arms to the Spanish Republic and the Comintern's sponsorship of an international brigade to fight on the republican side inspired a groundswell of good will among U.S. liberals. Spanish aid committees quickly formed throughout the country, incorporating trade unions, religious bodies, ethnic associations, and artists' and writers' groups as well as the party. But the most dramatic manifestation of U.S. support was the formation of the Abraham Lincoln Brigade, a contingent of more than 3,000 young Americans who volunteered to fight with the republican armies. Although people of many political backgrounds participated in the brigade, rank-and-file Communists, drawn from unions and neighborhood organizations, composed more than 60 percent of the recruits. Their experience dramatized the spirit of heroism and sacrifice which U.S. Communism could inspire in its best moments. Half of the brigade died in battle; half of those who returned had serious wounds. Their "matter of fact common sense and tragic humor," Joseph Starobin writes, "deeply moved journalists who covered the war; poorly trained and poorly armed, they stoically gave their lives against a militarily superior enemy because they believed that fascism had to be stopped on the battlefields of Spain."[16]

While constituting a "red badge of courage and honor for American Communists," the Spanish conflict offered a glimpse of the seamier side of the Comintern and the U.S. party. The Soviets brought political commissars and secret police along with their military advisors and launched a campaign of assassination, intrigue, and outright military assault against Spanish Trotskyists, syndicalists, and independent socialists who dared criticize their tactics and goals. Although Lincoln Brigaders did not, with rare exceptions, participate in this grisly episode, U.S. party leaders shamelessly praised the Soviets for their vigilance, urging Americans to "emulate the Soviet Union in doing battle with Trotskyism, in driving it out of the ranks of the working class." For anti-fascists unfortunate enough to doubt Stalin's omniscience, such arguments added a distasteful element to Spanish relief efforts. But weighing Soviet abuses against the ostrich-like behavior of democratic governments, many liberals chose to refrain from public criticism of the republican side. From Hollywood to Harlem, "Spain became the great unifying symbol of the popular front," the subject of frenetic fundraising, of efforts to prod Roosevelt out of his posture of neutrality, and of solemn memorials for Americans who died in battle. If Soviet realpolitik raised questions about the long-term compatibility of Communism and liberalism, it did little to undermine the sense of urgency of loyalist supporters. The tough Jewish street kids who decided to give Hitler a taste of his own medicine, the black sailors and steelworkers who saw a blow against Franco and Mussolini as a blow against the Klan, the mid-American journalists appalled by Falangist bombing raids on unarmed villages embodied a powerful democratic impulse in U.S. anti-fascism, something even the worst Stalinist intrigues could not fully corrupt.[17]

Aware of the force of popular passions that fueled antifascism, the party leadership began to find virtues in manifestations of ethnic awareness and pride that had a "progressive" political content. During the popular front era, party leaders encouraged the

International Workers Order, once regarded as a grudging concession to atavistic ethnic sentiments, to launch a massive recruiting
drive among immigrant workers sympathetic to the party. Claiming 150,000 members in 1939, less than 10 percent of whom were
Communists, the IWO emerged as a force among several Eastern
and Southern European nationalities who played a key role in the
industrial union movement (among them Jews, Hungarians,
Czechs, Italians, Slovakians, Finns and Serbo-Croatians). Regarded as assets to the labor movement and reservoirs of anti-fascist sentiment, ethnic fraternal groups received a mandate to
transform their theatres and newspapers, language schools and
summer camps into exponents of ethnic pride and a "progressive
Americanism." In the process the IWO and the party set forth a
vision of America as a land of minorities, each making a special
contribution to the democratic national culture. "Our national
journal, the *Fraternal Outlook*," an IWO official told Paul Buhle,

> had as many as sixteen different language supplements.... Among
> the children, particularly, we developed the idea that America was
> a multicultural society.... There was a dual aim: number one, to
> acquaint them with the specific progressive national traditions in
> their own nationalities.... Second, we tried at the same time to unite
> all groups, to show that there were certain things bringing us
> together.[18]

The new ethnic policies had a special impact on party work in
the Jewish community. "From 1936 on," Arthur Liebman writes,
"the Communist Party ... made a concerted effort to reach Jews
using Jewish problems." At a time when physical assaults against
Jews were a common feature of big-city life (whether practiced by
Coughlinites or schoolyard gangs) and when Jews met with discrimination in most universities and places of employment, Communists attracted attention by using their press, their trade unions
contacts, and civil rights organizations to excoriate anti-Jewish
practices. Equally important, party leaders began to encourage
expressions of Jewish pride and solidarity within the party subculture. For the first time since bolshevization, Jewish Communists
found themselves free to celebrate Jewish holidays, speak respect-
fully of Zionism, and celebrate the Jewish contribution to U.S. life.
In a movement where assimilationist pressures had driven many

Jews to take gentile party names (e.g., Sol Auerbach = James Allen), the imperative to restore Jews to "their full stature in history" came as a welcome relief. Not only did Communists recover some of their credibility among Yiddish- speaking Jewish workers (the Jewish section of the IWO grew to 38,000 in 1938), but they began to expand their influence among U.S.-born educated Jews. By 1939, when party membership rose above 80,000, Jews composed over 40 percent of that total and second generation Jewish Communists had begun to play major roles in the party as union organizers, middle level functionaries, and writers for The *Daily Worker* and other party publications.[19]

As Jews gravitated to popular front causes, Jewish left-wing cultural activities expanded even more rapidly than the party. The summer camps, bungalow colonies, "shules," (children's schools) and neighborhood workers clubs of the Yiddish-speaking generation found their counterpart in slightly more upscale institutions catering to college-educated Jewish leftists. Thousands of Jewish school teachers, social workers, lawyers, and technicians, facing discrimination at the workplace, joined militant unions in their professions, agitated against nazism and Spanish fascism, and carried their political passions into their leisure time activities. Their hiking clubs and theatre parties, lecture series and sports clubs, benefit concerts and dances, infused with a pop front version of progressive politics, attracted large numbers of Jewish liberals who looked to Communists both as workhorses of the antifascist cause and purveyors of a good time. Within this subculture, the myth of Soviet philo-Semitism gave Communists a special panache. Pointing proudly to the 1936 Soviet constitution which outlawed anti-Semitism, the establishment of Birobidjan as a Jewish national region and "guardian of the Yiddish socialist national culture," and the prominent role of Jews in the Soviet government (including its foreign minister, Maxim Litvinov), Jewish Communists argued that their movement represented the only real protector of Jews in a dangerous world. Although most Jews remained skeptical, the argument had enough force to gain Communists entry into the mainstream of the Jewish community, working side by side with rabbis, Zionist leaders, and "old guard" socialist unionists with whom they had once bitterly clashed.[20]

However, it was in the sphere of race relations that popular front

During the 1930s, the National Negro Congress was arguably the most successful of popular front coalitions in the United States.

Communism may have had its greatest long-term impact. Defining support for racial equality as the hallmark of anti-fascism, Communists solicited liberal and labor support for campaigns against discrimination in employment, organized protests against lynching and the poll tax, called for the teaching of black history and the non-discriminatory treatment of black artists and athletes, and spawned numerous organizations that encouraged social interaction between blacks and whites.

More than ever, interracialism became the trademark of the Communist left. It meant a Workers Alliance office in Birmingham, Alabama which refused to maintain separate toilets for black and white members; a cooperative housing project in the Bronx that welcomed interracial couples; a nightclub in Greenwich Village that featured black and white entertainers and seated patrons without regard to race; summer camps and resorts which solicited black patronage; picket lines at ball parks demanding the integration of major league baseball; interracial marches through Harlem celebrating Joe Louis's victories; pagaents celebrating black history and concerts extolling the black contribution to U.S. popular music. [21]

Courtesy of Robert F. Wagner Labor Archives, New York University, Charles Rivers Collection. Photo: Charles Rivers.

This passionate interracialism, coupled with a willingess to cooperate with traditional black organizations, helped make the party a force in the life of a generation of black labor leaders, intellectuals, and community activists. In Harlem, Rev. Adam Clayton Powell, Jr., solicited Communist support in a campaign to open jobs for blacks in public utilities, department stores, and government agencies, building a power base that would elevate him to the New York city council and the U.S. Congress. In Washington, a black economist named John P. Davis obtained party support for the creation of a federation of black organizations that would employ mass protest techniques to fight for legal equality and encourage black participation in organized labor. Davis's brainchild, the National Negro Congress, became an important aid to industrial unions in their efforts to enroll black workers. In Birmingham, black Communists, operating from within the Steelworkers Union, the church, and the NAACP, helped organize a "Right to Vote Club" that challenged the disenfranchisement of blacks and poor whites. By blending their efforts with other leaders and fighting in the name of fair play and democratic rights, Communists won a new measure of acceptance in African-American life.

"Communist Party headquarters," a *Saturday Evening Post* writer observed in 1938,

> is a place where every Negro with a grievance can be sure of prompt action. If he has been fired, the Communists can be counted on to picket his employer. If he has been evicted, the Communists will guard his furniture and take his case to court. If his gas has been cut off, the Communists will take his complaint, but not his unpaid bill to the nearest office.... There is never a labor parade, nor a mass meeting of any significance in the colored community in which Communists do not get their banner in the front row and their speakers on the platform.[22]

Communist influence among black creative artists, if anything, exceeded its influence among political activists. Perhaps the three most respected black cultural figures of the late 1930's, poet Langston Hughes, novelist Richard Wright, and actor-singer Paul Robeson, maintained close ties with the party. The personal odysseys that took them to the left were very different, but all found the popular front party to be supportive of their artistic endeavors. Here, they benefited from a substantial liberalization of party cultural policies. Anxious to create a more "American" persona for their movement, party cultural critics, themselves often new recruits, began to argue that Communists should sponsor and promote black artistic activity because it possessed an inherently democratic content. By 1937, for example, party publications began to print laudatory articles about swing and hot jazz, using arguments unprecedented in the annals of "socialist realism." "Swing is as American as baseball and hot dogs," wrote one Young Communist League critic. "A good hot band can claim as many raucous rooters as the Dodgers. There is a good deal of audience participation in swing, a kind of give and take and mutual inspiration for the musician and the crowd, a rough democratic air invading the sacred halls of music."[23]

With puritanism giving way to populism in party circles, a new generation of black and white intellectuals began to use the party to elaborate a multicultural image of U.S. history and culture in which the black contribution would be recognized and accepted. The popular front evoked an interest in hearing black musicians, whether jazz players, folk singers or opera stars; in attending plays about black life; in reading novels and poetry by black authors, in rooting for black athletes. Although old time sectarians assailed this indiscriminate enthusiasm, American-born pop-fronters responded in a spirit of genuine curiosity, feeling that an understanding of black culture helped give them a better understanding of their own identity as Americans. That a party whose top leadership was largely indifferent to cultural matters, and whose theoretical documents were written in "Marxist-Leninese" could spawn grassroots cultural movements of such vitality represents something of a paradox. But the popular front represented a special moment in party history, when the leadership, anxious to shed its foreign image, allowed popular enthusiasm for music, sports and the arts to invade the party milieu. For the first and possibly the last time in its history, the party allowed fellow travelers, as well as cadre, to shape its cultural stance. In 1936, for example, the *Daily Worker* actually polled its reader to see if they wanted a regular sports page. When they voted in favor six to one, the paper hired a young sports enthusiast named Lester Rodney, who wasn't a party member, to handle the task and gave him one-eighth of the paper. Rodney, largely on his own initiative, shaped one of the distinctive crusades of the popular front left—a campaign to integrate major league baseball.[24]

In the field of music, pop-fronters made an even greater contribution to U.S. cultural history. During the late 1930s, John Hammond, a left-leaning record producer who believed that jazz "was the most important cultural exhibit that America has given to the world," enlisted writers from the *New Masses* and The *Daily Worker* in his crusade to win recognition for black musicians. In 1938, Hammond secured *New Masses* financial backing—with no political strings attached—for a series of Carnegie Hall concerts designed "to bring together ... before a musically sophisticated audience Negro music from its raw beginnings to the latest jazz." Excited by the success of this venture, Hammond then threw his energies into an interracial night club in the Village founded by party members and fellow travelers—Cafe Society. The performers at opening night, including Teddy Wilson, Billie Holiday, and the comedian Jack Gilford, symbolized the fusion of jazz, interracialism and left politics that would make Cafe Society a seminal part of New York's jazz scene for ten years. Guided by Hammond's uncanny eye for talent, the club became a place where "known and unknown performers could be heard, where jazz and blues and gospel were blended, ... where Negro patrons were as welcome as whites."[25]

The party subculture also served as a catalyst for what one historian called the "All-American Left-Wing Folk Song Revival Movement." Urban intellectuals in the party, like their counterparts in the New Deal, felt moved by the resilience of America's common people in the face of the Depression and responded emotionally to the music people sang in churches, union halls, and homes when they needed their spirits lifted. No person symbolized this chemistry more than an itinerant balladeer and radio personality named Woody Guthrie, who offered his services to California farm workers organizing under party auspices. Invited to perform at a San Franciso rally for Tom Mooney, Guthrie transfixed an audience of urban radicals with haunting ballads of Depression life, infused with humor, contempt for privilege and a visceral patriotism. In a gesture typical of the popular front, California Communists made him the musical symbol of their movement, inviting him to union meetings and fund raising parties throughout the state and giving him a column in the West Coast Communist daily. Coincidently, New York Communists adopted a black Texas blues singer named Huddie Ledbetter whom folklorist Alan Lomax had rescued from a Texas jail, making him a fixture at parties and meetings. His inventive guitar playing and mournful songs, about hard living, love and the evils of Jim Crow, impressed a twenty-one year old journalist-musician named Pete Seeger who literally placed himself at Ledbetter's feet to absorb his skill and wisdom. The interaction of these three musicians, David Dunaway writes, would change U.S. musical history. "No political commissar declared folk songs in vogue.... It was as spontaneous as musicians sitting down to sing, among them a trouble-tough Louisiana black, a New England boy, bouncy as a kid in sneakers, and soon a wandering Okie." Guthrie, Ledbetter and Seeger, employing rhythms and harmonies harking back to 16th Century England and Africa, but writing of contemporary themes, created music that both sentimentalized and affirmed the populist aspirations of U.S. radicals, enabling them to feel part of the country they were trying to change. For Seeger, the youngster of the group, the popular front ethos would serve as the spiritual reference point for forty years of musical activism; "folksongs, radicalism, and patriotism blended in his mind."[26]

The party's love affair with popular culture, ironically, did not advance its standing with the literary intelligentsia. The popular front's romanticization of the "common man," its quest for influence in Hollywood and Tin Pan Alley, and its hunger to identify "progressive" elements in folk culture and U.S. traditions, offended intellectuals whose artistic preferences were more avant-garde and who wished to maintain a critical distance from the policies of the New Deal and the cultural tastes of U.S. workers.

But the achilles heel of popular front Communism, the phenomenon which most damaged its standing among the intellecuals, was the Moscow Trials. When the Soviet government, in late 1936, put hundreds of founding leaders of the Soviet Revolution on trial for treason, sentencing them and thousands of others to death, it highlighted the brutality of Soviet society in a manner that had special poignancy for those who viewed ideas as living forces. Other murderous trends in Soviet life—famines, collectivization, deportations to gulag—had occurred in out of the way regions, among individuals who had few links to the West, but the purge trials took place before an invited audience of the world press and involved individuals (e.g., Bukharin, Zinoviev, and Kamenev) who had been leaders of Soviet society and heads of the Comintern. The "confessions" of those accused did little to reassure observers of the trials; at best, they revealed a society traumatized by divisions among its founding generation. For those who chose to look deeper, a more devastating picture emerged; Soviet Communism had evolved into something truly evil, a society in which paranoia, thought control, and murder had become institutionalized.

Because of the Soviet Union's role in resisting fascist military incursions in Spain and the CPUSA's centrality in campaigns to democratize U.S. life, many liberals chose not to make the trials the basis of a final and decisive break. But a number of prominent writers and academics, weary of pressures to adapt literary and social theory to the latest Comintern line, decided to take a stand in defense of the victims of the trials, even if it meant being excommunicated from popular front coalitions. A literary magazine that had grown out of the New York John Reed Clubs, *Partisan*

Review, became a rallying point for left intellectuals who wished to maintain their integrity in the face of Communist pressures for conformity and silence. It not only denounced the trials as a sham, but argued for the autonomy of art from political direction. Other important intellectuals rallied to the defense of Leon Trotsky, the one important Bolshevik who had escaped Stalin's net, and launched a campaign to prove his innocence. The party's venomous attack on former sympathizers like John Dewey, Sidney Hook, and James Farrell, who participated in an independent investigation of charges against Trotsky, revealed the brutal, authoritarian side of popular front Communism. Sympathizers of Trotsky, Browder solemnly averred, were "slime," "scum," "assassins," and "wreckers," heirs of "Benedict Arnold and Aaron Burr," who deserved the same fate as their Soviet counterparts.[27]

By the beginning of 1939, Communists confronted a significant left opposition in academic and literary circles. Rooted in Trotskyist organizations and the board of *Partisan Review*, the anti-Stalinist left disseminated a devastating critique of the undemocratic features of Soviet life and of the hypocrisy of the CPUSA's endorsement of liberal reform. The image of Communism as a movement at war with the humanistic impulses that had given rise to it had begun to enter the discourse of U.S. intellectuals, even though many hesitated to make the trials the occasion of an open break. But serious doubts had been raised about the party's claim to leadership of the U.S. left, arguments that would surface with renewed force when Soviet diplomacy underwent its next radical reversal.

Rising opposition to the party in intellectual circles coincided with a larger conservative trend in U.S. life, directed against the New Deal and the CIO as well as the party. The unionization of millions of workers and the proliferation of New Deal agencies that regulated industries and gave jobs to the unemployed frightened local elites, particularly in parts of the country where paternalistic labor relations had once prevailed. The spectre of urban intellectuals reshaping the United States created a powerful backlash against New Deal reform, uniting white supremacists, Protestant fundamentalists and Catholic conservatives with large farmers and corporate spokesmen. When a severe recession struck in 1938, eroding popular hopes of recovery, grassroots anti-radicalism moved into the hall of Congress. In the spring of 1938, the House of Representatives formed an Un-American Activities Committee, headed by Martin Dies of Texas, which immediately launched investigations of Communist penetration of CIO unions and New Deal agencies. Parades of witnesses accused leaders of the Federal Theatre Project and key unions of Communist sympathies, arguing with some justice that it was impossible to distinguish between Communists and liberals on key social issues. Republicans used the Communist issue to great effect in fall 1938 elections, capturing eighty seats in the House, eight in the Senate, and eleven governerships previously held by Democrats.[28]

The CP leadership responded to conservative attacks by further efforts to disguise its identity and tailor its program to the needs of liberal allies. During 1938, Earl Browder, with Comintern approval, redefined the popular front to conform in essence with the New Deal wing of the Democratic Party and announced that Communists would postpone agitating for socialism in the interests of the "unity of progressive forces." Communists applauded Roosevelt's cautious initiatives against fascist aggression, lobbied to protect New Deal legisltion from conservative attacks, and virtually suspended independent electoral efforts in favor of campaigns for progressive candiates in the two major parties. Moreover, the party took extraordinary steps to avoid compromising cadre who had achieved positions of power, or government and trade union leaders with whom it had secret understandings. In 1938, the party eliminated shop units and shop papers—the major manifestations of an independent party presence in the trade union movement. From now on, Communists in the trade union movement would not meet separately as a group; rather top trade union officials close to the party would communicate privately with party leaders, leaving the rank and file to discover party positions through neighborhood branches, the party press, or actions of union leaders.[29]

The party's new posture represented a startling admission of political vulnerability. Browder virtually conceded that Communists could achieve power in the United States only by pretending to be somebody else and by deferring to the interests of liberal allies. In the Steel Workers Organizing Committee, party leaders failed to protest when Philip Murray began systematically purging Communists from the union staff in 1938, fearful that opposition might jeopardize their relations with John L. Lewis. In the United Auto Workers Union, party leaders went to the 1939 convention to persuade their own members to vote against candidates of the Progressive Caucus who had the votes to win control of the union, arguing in favor of moderates favored by Sidney Hillman and John L. Lewis. In several CIO unions, Communists voted for resolutions that equated nazism and Communism, rather than expose their identities to conservatives who wished to purge them from the movement.[30]

As boundaries between Communists and liberals blurred, popular front Communism, in the words of Bert Cochran, assumed "something of the character of a religious encampment." On its top levels, the party still functioned as an orthodox Marxist-Leninist organization. The Politburo, in consultation with the Comintern, defined the party line on key international and domestic issues and disseminated that line to heads of party publications and leaders of the district and state organizations. Its paid staff of 4,000 to 5,000 people functioned under tight discipline and defended party orthodoxy, particularly on matters relating to the Soviet Union. But the party rank and file, moving in and out of the party at a rapid rate, functioned with a great deal of autonomy. The popular front party attracted many upwardly mobile, ambitious people—trade union officials, government employees, teachers, social workers, lawyers and journalists. By allowing such "influentials" to disavow their party membership, the top party leadership inevitably relinquished control. Communication became irregular, meetings unsystematic, directives confined to "critical" issues. An atmosphere of pragmatism pervaded the movement, reflected by the huge number of individuals who chose to be sympathizers or fellow travelers rather than disciplined party members. "To this category," Joseph Starobin observed, "a political movement was a vehicle, an instrument to be repaired when it functioned badly or abandoned when it had been wrecked."[31]

The atmosphere of popular front Communism infuriated both orthodox Communists and the party's numerous enemies. Almost no prominent Communist academics, union leaders, and government officials would admit party membership; if pressed, they would say they were progressives! Because of the informality of popular front Communism, it was difficult to prove them wrong. How do you demonstrate that an influential state legislator is a Communist? He possesses no party membership card. He attends no party meetings. His meetings with top party leaders are secret and hard to document.

What all pop-fronters shared was a set of principles and affinities: unwavering support for the Soviet Union, domestically and internationally; unity of progressive forces, even at the expense of socialist principles; support for racial equality; vigilance against domestic fascism; suspicion of all groups on the left that did not defer to the Communist Party; identification of the CIO and the New Deal as major vehicles of social change. Hundreds of thousands of individuals espoused this ethos, some as a result of organizational discipline, more through personal choice or communal identification.

With the wisdom of hindsight, it is easy to see grave inconsistencies in this world view. But in the dangerous, tension-filled atmosphere of the late 1930s, it had considerable appeal to strategically located constituencies. The Depression had given new vitality to ethnocentric impulses, threatening vulnerable peoples and nations with extermination, while simultaneously creating opportunities for sweeping political change. Groups who had historically been marginal in the United States—blacks, Jews, Eastern Europeans—saw an opportunity to make a major breakthrough in their social and political status, but also feared a backlash against their progress that might imitate the fascist movements wreaking havoc in Europe. To activists from these groups, popular frontism was a strategy that used the power of the Soviet Union to keep fascism at bay while encouraging pragmatic adaptations to achieve domestic reforms. The most important causes of the popular front left— the defense of the Spanish Republic, the battle for industrial unionism, campaigns for citizenship rights for blacks, resistance to Nazism and domestic anti-Semitism—all dramatized the heroism of Communists in defense of liberal goals. Because of this, many people who doubted that Communism had a future in the United States concluded they needed Communists to bring liberal visions to fruition.

But making the affirmation of American dreams dependent on Soviet power involved grave risks. Some popular front causes had indigenous political roots. The movement for black equality, the organization of industrial unions, even the vision of a multi-ethnic United States proud of its varied cultural heritage, represented long repressed impulses flowering within a left milieu, not Soviet dictats being implemented on U.S. soil. But the insistance on linking these democratic currents to a brutal Stalinist dictatorship and a political party as highhanded in its decision making as Ford or General Motors, exposed the popular front left to charges of hypocrisy and political cynicism. A temporary expedient for committed Marxist-Leninists, the popular front served most of its adherents as a Faustian bargain, a well-intentioned but dangerous gamble that Communism would accommodate itself to U.S. values and U.S. political reality. A strategy that unleashed powerful forces in behalf of worker and minority rights, it rested on the most fragile and vulnerable political foundations.

Notes

1. For the figures on party membership, see Harvey Klehr, *The Heyday of American Communism: The Depression Decade* (New York: Basic Books, 1984), pp. 240, 307.

2. See Joseph Starobin, *American Communism in Crisis, 1943–1957* (Cambridge: Harvard University Press, 1972), pp. 29, 39, and Al Richmond, *A Long View from the Left* (Boston: Houghton Mifflin, 1973), p. 254.

3. See Earl Browder, *The People's Front* (New York: International Publishers, 1938), pp. 54, 145–49, 167–72, 266–69. On Browder's trips to Moscow during the popular front, see Klehr, *Heyday of American Communism*, pp. 189–90, 207, and Philip Jaffe, *The Rise and Fall of American Communism* (New York: Horizon Press, 1975), pp. 39–40. On intellectuals' disillusionment with the popular front, see Alan H. Wald, *The New York Intellectuals: The Rise and Decline of the Anti-Stalinist Left from the 1930s to the 1980s* (Chapel Hill: University of North Carolina Press, 1987), pp. 128–63.

4. On the 1936 presidential election campaign, see Klehr, *Heyday*, pp. 192–96, and George Charney, *A Long Journey* (New York: Quadrangle, 1968), pp. 60, 64–97. On organizational changes in the party during the popular front, see Robert Jay Alperin, "Organization in the Communist Party, USA, 1931–1938," Ph.D. diss., Northwestern University, 1959, pp. 45, 74–75; and F. Brown, "New Forms of Party Organization Help Us Win the Masses," *Party Organizer* 10 (July–Au-

gust 1936): 11. For the Mike Gold quote, see the *Daily Worker*, 31 August 1935.

5. See Bert Cochran, *Labor and Communism: The Conflict That Shaped American Unions* (Princeton: Princeton University Press, 1977), pp. 95–102; Klehr, *Heyday*, p. 228; and Harvey A. Levenstein, *Communism, Anticommunism and the CIO* (Westport: Greenwood Press, 1981), pp. 47–50.

6. See Roger Keeran, *The Communist Party and the Auto Workers Unions* (Bloomington: Indiana University Press, 1980), pp. 144–47. On the clandestine character of Communist leadership in the Transport Workers Union, see Joshua B. Freeman, *In Transit: The Transport Workers Union in New York City, 1933–1936* (New York: Oxford University Press, 1989), pp. 69–72, and Levenstein, *Communism, Anticommunism*, p. 46.

7. See Klehr, *Heyday*, pp. 252–80, and Kenneth Waltzer, "The Party and the Polling Place: American Communism and An American Labor Party in the 1930s," *Radical History Review* 23 (December 1980): 109–11.

8. See Peggy Dennis, *The Autobiography of an American Communist: A Personal View of a Political Life* (Westport: Lawrence Hill and Co., 1977), p. 98, and Starobin, *American Communism in Crisis*, pp. 38–40.

9. See Richard A. Cloward and Frances Piven, *Poor People's Movements* (New York: Pantheon, 1977), p. 133, and Ronald W. Schatz, *The Electrical Workers: A History of Labor at General Electric and Westinghouse, 1923–1960* (Urbana: University of Illinois Press, 1983), p. 72.

10. On the impact of the CIO on worker self-esteem, see Schatz, *The Electrical Workers*, p. 117, and Carl Ross, *The Finn Factor in American Labor, Culture and Society* (New York Mill, MN: Parta Printers, 1977), p. 173.

11. See Cochran, *Labor and Communism*, pp. 118–21, and Keeran, *Communist Party and Auto Workers*, pp. 148–85.

12. See Klehr, *Heyday*, p. 238, and Levenstein, *Communism, Anti-Communism, and the CIO*, pp. 55–71.

13. See Klehr, *Heyday*, p. 240, and Freeman, *In Transit*, pp. 128–34, 157–61. On the subordination of Communist identities in union organizing, see Levenstein, pp. 40–46; for the quote about Communists in the NMU, see p. 56.

14. On right-wing movements in the United States during the Depression era, see Geoffrey S. Smith, *To Save a Nation: American Countersubversives, the New Deal, and the Coming of World War II* (New York: Basic Books, 1973). For the Randolph quote, see the *Daily Worker*, 13 January 1936.

15. On the Olympic boycott movement, see Mark Naison, "Lefties and Righties: The Communist Party and Sports During the Great Depres-

sion," *Radical America* 13, no. 4 (July-August 1979): 53–54. On inter-
racial protests against the invasion of Ethiopia, see Mark Naison,
Communists in Harlem During the Depression (Urbana: University of
Illinois Press, 1983), pp. 155–58. On the Hollywood Anti-Nazi League,
see Larry Ceplair and Steven Englund, *The Inquisition in Hollywood*
(Garden City: Anchor Press, 1980), pp. 104–12.

16. See Starobin, *American Communism in Crisis*, p. 29.

17. On the role of Stalin's secret police in Spain, see Fernando Claudín,
The Communist Movement: From Comintern to Cominform (New
York: Monthly Review Press, 1975), pp. 240–42. For Browder's justification of anti-Trotskyist purges in the Spanish Republic, see Browder, *The People's Front*, p. 310. On grassroots activism in defense of
the Spanish Republic, see Ceplair and Englund, *Inquisition in Hollywood*, pp. 112–19, and Naison, *Communists in Harlem During the
Depression*, pp. 196–97.

18. On the IWO, see Starobin, p. 25, and Klehr, pp. 382–85. The IWO
leader's quote is from Paul Buhle, "Jews and American Communism:
The Cultural Question," *Radical History Review* 23 (December 1980): 24.

19. On physical assaults against Jews by Coughlinites, see Ronald H.
Bayor, *Neighbors in Conflict: The Irish, Germans, Jews, and Italians
of New York City, 1929–1941* (Baltimore: Johns Hopkins University
Press, 1978), pp. 97–103. On the encouragement of "Jewish consciousness" in the popular front CP, see Arthur Leibman, *Jews and the Left*
(New York: John Wiley and Sons, 1978), pp. 350–51, 427; Buhle, "Jews
and American Communism," pp. 22–26; and Nathan Glazer, *The
Social Basis of American Communism* (New York: Harcourt, Brace
and World, 1961), pp. 160–61.

20. On the Jewish subculture in the American Communist movement, see
Leibman, *Jews and the Left*, pp. 307–22, 359–70, and David Leviatin,
Followers of the Trail: Jewish Working Class Radicals in America
(New Haven: Yale University Press, 1969).

21. On interracialism in the Communist movement, see Naison, *Commu-
nists in Harlem*, pp. 136–37, 193–219; Junius Irving Scales and
Richard Nickson, *Cause at Heart: A Former Communist Remembers*
(Athens: University of Georgia Press, 1987), pp. 76–83; "The Utopia
We Knew: The Coops," *Cultural Correspondance* 6–7 (Spring 1978):
95–97; and Robin D.G. Kelley, *Hammer and Hoe: Alabama Commu-
nists During the Great Depression* (Chapel Hill: University of North
Carolina Press, 1990), pp. 155–58.

22. On Powell's alliance with the CP, see Naison, *Communists in Harlem*,
pp. 267–69; on the National Negro Congress, see Naison, pp. 177–84;
on the Birmingham Right to Vote Club, see Kelley, *Hammer and Hoe*,
pp. 181–84; the final quote is from Stanley High, "Black Omens,"
Saturday Evening Post, 4 June 1938, p. 38.

23. See James Dugan, "Stop Before You Jitter," *Young Communist Review* 4 (July 1939): 2, 22.
24. See "Sports for the Worker: An Interview with Lester Rodney," *In These Times*, 12–18 October 1977.
25. See Naison, *Communists in Harlem*, pp. 211–13; John Hammond with Irving Townshend, *On Record, An Autobiography* (New York: Penguin Books, 1977), pp. 199–210; and Martin Bauml Duberman, *Paul Robeson* (New York: Alfred A. Knopf, 1988), p. 284.
26. See Robbie Lieberman, *"My Song is My Weapon": People's Songs, American Communism, and the Politics of Culture* (Champaign: University of Illinois Press, 1989), pp. 32–49; Joe Klein, *Woody Guthrie: A Life* (New York: Alfred A. Knopf, 1980), pp. 119–29; Richmond, *A Long View From the Left*, pp. 278–79; and David King Dunaway, *How Can I Keep From Singing: Pete Seeger* (New York: McGraw Hill, 1981), pp. 62–63.
27. On the disillusionment of left-wing intellectuals with Communism, see Klehr, *Heyday*, pp. 356–64 and Wald, *The New York Intellectuals*, pp. 128–63; for Browder's comments on Trotskyists and the Moscow Trials, see *The People's Front*, pp. 211–16, 297–310.
28. See Walter Goodman, *The Committee: The Extraordinary Career of the House Committee on Un-American Activities* (New York: Farrar, Straux and Giroux, 1968), pp. 24–58.
29. See Cochran, *Labor and Communism*, pp. 135–39; Starobin, *American Communism in Crisis*, p. 39; and Levenstein, *Communism, Anti-Communism, and the CIO*, pp. 78–79.
30. See Cochran, pp. 140–43; Levenstein, *Communism, Anti-Communism, and the CIO*, pp. 80–85; and Keeran, *The Communist Party and the Auto Workers Unions*, pp. 199–204.
31. See Starobin, *American Communism in Crisis*, p. 21.

THE COMINTERN, THE FRONTS, AND THE CPUSA

John Gerassi

In every country in the world, socialist and communist parties have claimed to represent the working class. Sometimes they have struggled together to better that class's lot. When the alliances were made from above, by their leaders, they were called united fronts. When, on the contrary, the union of forces was the result of street action, of rank-and-file agitation, the cry was popular front. In both cases the demand for "unity of popular forces" came primarily from communists, most often on orders received from the Soviet leadership and transmitted by the international agencies of the Communist Party of the Soviet Union. For years, the most active of such organizations was the Comintern. It did its job very effectively—and helped undermine the strength of most communist parties, including the CPUSA.

The Comintern was originally launched by Lenin as a democratic assembly of representatives from all communist parties. Its primary purpose was to find ways to bring about world revolution. But by 1928 it was totally controlled by Stalin and, hence, was no longer democratic. And since Stalin believed that fascism was the consequence of monopoly capitalism, the Comintern made very little distinction between such liberal capitalist democracies as Britain and fascist capitalist dictatorships as Italy.

But after Hitler's rise to power in 1933, the threat from Nazi Germany convinced Stalin, and therefore the Comintern, to develop a policy which could successfully stop the spread of fascism. That policy was based on the theory of the united front. In 1934, the Comintern ordered all communist parties, which were regarded as national "sections" of the Comintern, to make tactical alliances with socialist, social democratic, even liberal democratic parties under a common anti-fascist banner.

It was a tough order to follow—for both parts of the proposed alliance. Most communist leaders, after suffering decades of repres-

75

sion by their now-would-be allies, were reluctant to abandon their conviction that their task was to organize for the revolutionary seizure of power. Also, they pointed to the history of socialist and social democratic party "betrayals" of the working class and its organized movement as proof that an alliance with socialists and social democrats could easily lead to their own demise.

The first such betrayal, of course, was in Germany, where Lenin and his followers were certain that a Bolshevik-style revolution would succeed as soon as World War I ended German imperial rule. But by then the German Social Democratic Party (SPD) was much too integrated into the bourgeois structure to risk losing its sinecures and hopes for electoral victory. Indeed, it had refused to take such risks even before the war: its 1 million members, solid control of major unions, coffers so full it could subsidize scores of vacation resorts for its members, and 34.4 percent of the vote in 1912—all this success within the existing order led to a certain complacency, and it finally became just another bourgeois national chauvinist party. On August 4, 1914, it ordered its parliamentary delegates to vote for war credits—thus virtually guaranteeing the outbreak of World War I, a strictly imperialist war fought over colonies and access to resources. Then, after the war, as it lost legitimacy among the very workers it was supposed to represent, the SPD called upon the old imperial army to maintain it in power and ordered the murder of Rosa Luxemburg and Karl Liebknecht, the two former SPD leaders who had opposed the war. The thugs who were sent by the SPD to carry out the murders were the *Freikorps,* which later became the nucleus of the S.S.[1]

But the defeat of the worker's movement in Germany by socialists was only one such example of their betrayal during the postwar years. Socialists also crushed Bolshevik revolutions in Austria and Hungary, and helped bourgeois regimes hunt down, jail and often kill hundreds of communists throughout Europe. As a result, most communist organizers preferred to call social democrats "social fascists" and would have nothing to do with them. And likewise, for their part, most socialists and social democrats, convinced that communists who offered alliances for electoral or trade union struggles were in fact only waiting to "seize the time," as Lenin had advocated, were reluctant to trust them in any joint action or program.

Stalin, however, was both a realist and an opportunist. Because

Russia had been invaded by the troops of no less than eleven capitalist countries after World War I, he had concluded that no capitalist leader would rest until communism, and the only state which claimed to be working toward its establishment, were destroyed. Any means capable of hampering that capitalist drive was therefore justified; and one such means might well be the creation of an apparatus inside capitalist countries whose task would be to divide the capitalist forces. Such an apparatus could include legal electoral parties, unions, civic organizations, guilds, professional clubs, etc., as well as guerilla units and terrorist bands if necessary. In general what it meant was the policy of defending the Soviet Union as the bastion of socialism, what came to be known as the doctrine of socialism in one country. One of its consequences, of course, was a revival of Russian nationalism and the transformation of the Comintern from a genuine international organization into an agency for the propagation and execution of Russian (i.e., Stalin's) directives.

Stalin's objective was to neutralize those right-wing forces in capitalist countries bent on crushing the Soviet state. Thus he decided, as soon as he had successfully defeated Trotsky and his internationalist allies, to order some key alliances between communist and bourgeois forces, especially if those forces were themselves in opposition to a dominant capitalist imperialist country. The first such key alliance was in China where communists were ordered to work with the Kuomintang, the national bourgeois party of Sun Yatsen and his son-in-law, General Chiang Kaishek.

Despite his antipathy for Sun, whom he considered nothing more than a liberal patriarch, Mao Zedong was one of those communists who followed orders well. He worked with Sun until the latter died in 1925, and then with Chiang, though he considered him a glorified and corrupt warlord. He even continued to obey party orders after Chiang purged a thousand communists from the Kuomintang and subsequently had them murdered in 1926. (In the second great purge in 1927, in which as many as 50,000 communists and sympathizers were arrested, tortured and killed as Chiang tried to consolidate his power over all China, Mao managed to escape into high grass barely two hundred yards from the wall where he was to be shot.)[2]

To Stalin, the alliance between red and national forces in China was a success: though most of the reds were destroyed, Chiang's Kuomintang did make life more difficult for British, French and Japanese imperialist forces, and eventually brought about a Japanese invasion of China, not of the USSR. But for most communist party leaders of the world, that alliance was an unmitigated disaster: thousands of comrades dead and years of struggle and gains reversed. Thus when the Comintern, under Stalin's orders, called for the creation of united fronts against fascism in 1934, most party leaders hesitated. After so many defeats, they were more committed than ever to the revolutionary seizure of power.

For the CPUSA, that commitment manifested itself in various ways, but primarily in its continuing public analysis of the Socialist Party, the Democratic Party, indeed of all liberal elements in the U.S. as pro-capitalist and hence ultimately as pro-fascist.[3] An editorial in the *Communist*, the CPUSA's ideological journal, stressed the fact, in 1934, that fascism could only be eliminated totally "when the working class under the leadership of its Party forcibly overthrows capitalism and establishes the dictatorship of the proletariat." Only then can it proceed with "the planned, economic, political, and cultural reconstruction of society."[4]

Still, the view from the top was neither uniform nor clear. On March 18, 1933, for example, the executive committee of the CPUSA had insisted, in the *Daily Worker*, that all communist parties were expected to "approach the central committees of the Social Democratic parties... with proposals regarding joint actions against fascism and against the capitalist offensive." But in July 1934, top CPUSA ideologist and leader V.J. Jerome condemned Socialist chief Norman Thomas for supporting FDR's National Reconstruction Act. "The promises of Roosevelt are now bared to all as so much demagogy designed to conceal the class character of the New Deal. The government subsidies to bankers, railroad magnates and insurance companies...." Yet, Jerome went on, this "Loyal Norman Thomas [and] the silk-gloved gentry in the party," rally to Roosevelt because they believe that his capitalists, as Thomas himself wrote in the *New York Herald Tribune* (September 10, 1933), will "advance toward a truly Socialist society."[5]

Concluded Jerome: "Present-day 'Left' social-democracy on the contrary, is the extension of Centrism to the stage of 'Left' social-fascism. It arises, not to attack, but to protect and salvage social-

Daily Worker political cartoonist Fred Ellis adopted the "fighting worker" image to symbolize party policy. Left: Depression-era militance. Right: Mid-1940s support for the war effort and Roosevelt administration. From *A Selection of Drawings from the Worker* (New York: The Worker, 1960).

democracy as the main social support of the bourgeoisie. It stands in the way of the unification of social-democratic and Communist workers. It leads against Socialism, against Communism."[6] Added Alexander Bittelman, another of the CP's first-rank ideologists: "More than ever, it is becoming clear [in August 1934] that the Roosevelt New Deal, hailed by the Socialist Party as a 'step to socialism' and by the A.F. of L. bureaucracy as a 'genuine partnership of labor and capital,' is a weapon for a more rapid fascization [sic] of the rule of the U.S. bourgeoisie and for imperialistic war preparations."[7]

Despite genuine efforts by New Dealers and social democrats to fight the disastrous effects of the Depression on working people, the majority of the CPUSA big guns refused to temper their denunciations of the non-Communist leftists. During the election campaign of 1934, for example, Earl Browder, the party's general secretary, attacked such radical-liberals as LaGuardia, LaFollette, even Upton Sinclair for helping the "ruling apparatus" by "restraining the mass upsurge ... in those places where the problem is the hottest for the moment." Browder cited the *New York Herald Tribune*:

Prior to the primary yesterday, Mr. Roosevelt, it is known, received communications from prominent California Democrats which took Mr. Sinclair's nomination for granted and urged that the national administration be prepared to get behind him. The tenor of this advice was that Mr. Sinclair should be surrounded with practical New Dealers who could keep him from going too far or too fast. It was pointed out that he was bringing into the Democratic Party a great many thousands of votes which otherwise would go to more radical candidates outside of both major parties.... According to this analysis ... Mr. Sinclair is a powerful deterrent to the breaking away of large blocks of votes, especially among the unemployed, into the arms of Communism.[8]

Thus, as late as August 1934—and in the case of Browder, October 1934—the leaders of the CPUSA, viewing their party as a vehicle for the revolutionary seizure of power in the name of the proletariat, considered any united front headed, even only symbolically, by a liberal or social democrat as a step toward fascism. Yet on September 6, 1934, the CPUSA did make an offer to Norman Thomas and the Socialist Party (SP) to join in a "united front" on the following political, trade union and legal struggles:

1. For decisive wage increases and a shorter working week; for driving company unions out of the industries; for an energetic strike movement to win these demands; for a decisive fight against the policies of the A.F. of L. bureaucracy and for building a revolutionary trade-union leadership.

2. For the immediate enactment of the Worker's Unemployment and Social Insurance Bill (H.R. 7598); for a struggle of immediate relief; for building a strong, unified Unemployment Council movement.

3. For the immediate enactment of the Farmers' Emergency Relief Bill.

4. For the immediate enactment of the Bill for Negro Rights and to Suppress Lynching; for the liberation of the Scottsboro boys.

5. For the united struggle against war and fascism; to stop shipments of munitions; to defend the Soviet Union; for the freedom of Thälmann and all anti-fascist prisoners in Germany.

6. For united action in localities, factories, and trade unions, on every question affecting the toiling masses.[9]

The offer was of course rejected by the Socialist Party. In response to this rejection, Jerome shouted: "'Left-Wing' Thomas, the militant crusader, is still Reverend Thomas, the peacemaker with capitalism."[10] But North America was not in a pre-revolutionary state and the main issue was not fascism—yet—but jobs. Or, as Browder said, "The biggest political struggle now going on in the United States is the fight for unemployment insurance."[11] The A.F. of L. was officially against it but the locals were for it. John L. Lewis was against it because it would free union members from their dependency on the union's slush funds. But after the miners, the molders, the textile, smelter and hosiery workers, the newspaper guild and various local SP chapters supported it, Norman Thomas jumped on the bandwagon—and a compromise between the CP and the SP was worked out.

And the CP changed. It lost its revolutionary zeal. Most analysts claim that to survive it had no other choice. Pointing out that in Germany the CP was totally destroyed by its refusal to compromise with other anti-Nazi forces, mainstream as well as leftist historians insist that, as the New Deal gained adherents in all working-class organizations, for the CP to maintain its revolutionary rhetoric and activity would have been suicidal. It is the argument of this paper that the reverse is true.

First, it is important to note that Hitler crushed all anti-Nazi forces, not just the CP. Indeed, a united front of left-wingers in Germany would not have fared better than any of its components. Hitler and his party were extremely popular. The reason was the unjust punishment inflicted upon Germany by the greedy victorious allies, making each German pay—through reparations, occupations, the loss of the Ruhr and the Saar—for having lost a war which benefitted only the rich. Under such conditions the appeal of nationalism always strikes the louder key than international solidarity of workers.

Second, while it is quite possible that the CPUSA would have dwindled drastically had it maintained its uncompromising revolutionary line, once liberal democracy had been exposed as a system whereby the rich got richer and the poor poorer, the CP's tough line would certainly have been to its credit. As it turned out, that exposure never came, or at least few North Americans saw it as an endemic part of the system, but the only chance the CP did have of surviving the popularity of the New Deal was to have continued to denounce it.

Third, had the CP stuck to its revolutionary line, it would not have totally caved in during the postwar witch hunts. Instead of trying to hide under liberal beds, it would have fought openly. For example, by letting the Rosenbergs proudly proclaim their belief in communism, while denying any spying, they might have saved their lives, and brought credit to their party.

And fourth, even if decimated by wartime patriotism and during the McCarthy period, the party would have been resurrected during the civil rights movement and taken the lead of the anti-war left during the Vietnam War. Today, it would be in a position to make itself heard as the United States pursues its imperialist ambitions in the third world.

In any case, the CPUSA did commit virtual suicide by joining with social democrats in a class collaborationist united front. It worked hard for the New Deal, even furnishing some of Roosevelt's top "braintrusters." No wonder that during World War II Earl Browder felt he had no choice but to call for the dissolution of the CPUSA, to be replaced by a movement inside the Democratic Party.[12]

The Communist Party did regain much of its militancy during the Spanish Civil War, but the volunteers it sent to fight and (so many) to die in Spain went, they claimed, to stop fascism, not to help "establish the dictatorship of the proletariat ... [and] the planned, economic, political, and cultural reconstruction of society," as the CPUSA's ideological organ had insisted in 1934 was every Communist's purpose.[13] Browder was chastised by French Communist senator and party leader Jacques Duclos after the war, and was expelled from the party. But the CPUSA remained on the defensive ever since. Understandably, therefore, the United States never experienced a mass movement for a popular front, and the kind of alliance which did exist in the U.S. between socialists and communists was organized from the top. It had neither political weight nor vast support. It faded as quickly as did its two components.

In France and Spain, however, the failure of united fronts led to the creation of popular fronts. The French alliance came about despite the leaders of both the socialist and communist parties. So much did they despise each other that they even refused to allow their rank-and-filers to march together. But when both groups faced each other in one anti-fascist demonstration in 1936, those rank-and-filers rushed into each others' arms shouting "unity, unity" and their contrary leaders were booed into oblivion. The demonstrators then chose as their common standard-bearer Socialist Leon Blum and he carried the front to electoral victory a few weeks later. Like the German SPD, however, the French Socialists were reluctant to buck bourgeois legalisms; they obeyed the dictates of the reactionary British government in closing the French border during the Spanish Civil War and in refusing to aid the legitimate Republican government in Spain, thus contributing to Franco's victory.[14] That betrayal of a natural ally—another of the great outrages perpetrated by socialists—eventually guaranteed the unleashing of World War II, which Hitler might not have initiated with a popular anti-fascist government on the other side of the Pyrenees. The French Communist Party (PCF), allied to Blum and holding cabinet posts in his government, could offer only verbal protests and minor illegal support for the Republic (including a network to filter the International Brigade troops into Spain). It did not dare denounce the front by taking a principled position and thus lost much of its prestige.

It regained this prestige during its magnificent resistance struggle during German occupation and became France's leading party after the war. But instead of using that prestige to establish principled policies and to struggle toward the revolutionary seizure of power—which the events of 1968 proved was not as far-fetched as all historians and political analysts pretended—the PCF resorted again to united-frontism. Obeying Moscow's orders in 1945, it gave up its arms as de Gaulle demanded. It even refused to come to power in 1946 when de Gaulle resigned and offered First Vice President Maurice Thorez, head of the PCF, the provisional presidential mantle. Stalin's argument was that such a move by any Western European CP—and the Italian CP was in a similar situation—would lead to U.S. intervention, civil war and the crushing defeat of the CPs. Stalin restricted CP takeovers to those countries with borders touching the USSR, in case of invasion or internal chaos.

Stalin's argument may have been correct. The United States

might indeed have intervened. But as Jean-Paul Sartre said, "when a so-called revolutionary party with five million armed members or followers refuses to seize power, it can no longer claim to be revolutionary. By 1947, every Frenchman knew that the CP had become a traditional party in a bourgeois state, reformist perhaps, revolutionary certainly not."[15] Indeed, from that time to the present, the PCF (as well as the Communist Party of Italy, PCI) played bourgeois politics and promoted alliances with the Socialists. It joined the tripartite government of Guy Mollet in 1952, and voted to give him special powers to wage war on Algeria's FLN, thus alienating not only third world revolutionaries but also the substantial number of Algerian workers in France. And it joined François Mitterand's "common-front" government in 1980, only to suffer the consequences of Mitterand's anti-labor, anti-CP policies. (It was Mitterand, as Mollet's Minister of Justice, who had bellowed in a 1954 speech "l'Algérie sera toujours française," from which the right derived the chant "Al-gé-rie fran-çaise," accompanied by car honks: ta-ta-ta taa-taaa). These alliances (read: collaborations) gradually destroyed the PCF (as well as the CPs throughout Europe; in Italy, the PCI committed suicide, and in 1990 was derisively called "the thing.") Parties everywhere lost their revolutionary fervor, focusing on gaining, or rather holding on to, adherents, voters not fighters.

In her book *The Romance of American Communism*, Vivian Gornick described what it was like to be a rank-and-filer in a party that only pretended to maintain revolutionary visions:

> For thousands of Communists, being a Communist meant years of selling the *Daily Worker*, running off mimeographed leaflets, speaking on street corners, canvassing from door-to-door for local and national votes, organizing neighborhood groups for tenants' rights or welfare rights or unemployment benefits, raising money for the Party or for legal defenses or bail bonds or union struggles. Only that and nothing more. They never set foot inside Communist Party headquarters, they never laid eyes on a Central Committee member, they were never present at a major Party meeting or convention. Yet all this grinding ordinariness was fed and nourished, offset and borne by a continually resuscitated vision of the Marxist ideal: the bonds of comradeship and "revolution around the corner."[16]

But no matter how hard, discipline and motivation rarely failed:

the rank-and-filer believed in the vision and would have gone to any length to help make it come alive. As Sarah Gordon told Vivian Gornick:

> My God! How I hated selling the *Worker!*.... And then canvassing! Another horror. A lady would shut the door in my face before I'd gotten three words out—and if she was a socialist she'd *slam* the door—and I'd stand there sick. I'd tell myself a thousand times: It's not *your* face she's shutting out—God, I felt annihilated. But I did it, I did it. I did it because if I didn't do it, I couldn't face my comrades the next day. And we all did it for the same reason: we were accountable to each other. It was each other we'd be betraying if we didn't push down the gagging and go do it. You know, people never understand that. They say to us, "The Communist Party held a whip over you." They don't understand. The whip was inside each of us, we held it over ourselves, not over each other.

Added Gornick: "Sarah, during her years in the Party, would have done anything that was demanded of her—up to and including going to jail."[17] But the party made no revolutionary demands on Sarah, or on the others, during those united front days. Only selling the *Worker* and canvassing.

The CPUSA was probably the only large and effective progressive party in the United States then. It created workers' councils—democratically. Of the 350 members of the council in Flint, Michigan, for example, only eleven were Communists and, though they had launched the council, they insisted that everyone had equal vote and did not seek leadership status. The CP organized unemployment councils, bread kitchens, and immigrant camps. As John Steinbeck's novel *In Dubious Battle* accurately illustrates, it was CP organizers who defended the Mexican "wetbacks," got them shelter, food, and, when possible, jobs. These organizers were beaten, jailed, framed and often shot. Their dream was to fight back with all their personal and collective might. But the orders were to stick to labor issues, and they followed orders. As Gornick wrote:

> Throughout the Thirties and Forties, wherever major struggles were taking place between American labor and American capital, it was almost a given that CP organizers were involved. In the fields of California, in the auto plants of Flint, in the steel mills of Pittsburgh, in the mines of West Virginia, in the electoral plants of Schenectady:

they were there. They fought for the eight-hour day, the minimum wage, worker's compensation, health and welfare insurance. And for one glorious moment—during the brief life of the CIO—they brought genuine worker politics to the American labor movement. What happened to many of their organizers, in fact, was that while they were unable to convert the nation's workers to socialism, they themselves became gifted American trade unionists.[18]

When the Spanish Civil War began, these trade unionists unhesitatingly showed that they were revolutionary combatants as well. The key is not that so many U.S. Communists joined the international brigades, but that so many wanted to go. And not just Communist Party members. According to the Spanish embassy in Washington, in August 1936 alone, no less than 300,000 Americans asked how to join.[19] The embassy's response: See your organization, a veiled but clear reference to the SP or CP. But since the network to Spain was set up by the Comintern, it was the CPUSA which decided. Hamstrung by very limited funds, it obviously screened out all those it deemed "questionable" for health, economic or political reasons. The passion to bring about a better world was there, as it had always been. A revolutionary passion. The passion that made so many struggle so hard in the party for so long. The passion to join the party in the first place. The passion of a George Charney who wrote:

> I had come of age in the era of the Great Depression in which I could witness the general poverty and experience the personal galling sense of estrangement from society. I had a keen interest in life, and yet I was adrift with an evermore insistent yearning to become part of something, some group, some movement with a purpose.... Living through the Great Depression, our generation had been exposed to all the negative features of our social order—the stark contrast between wealth and poverty, the terrible waste of resources, the bewildering paradox of want in the face of plenty, the ineffectiveness of government.... I was persuaded that fascism was basically a symptom of the decay of capitalism, and that it would be absurd to expect effective resistance from protagonists of a system that spawned it. In times of crisis they would choose fascism as a bulwark against social revolution. The communists were the first victims of Hitler because they were his most stalwart and consistent opponents and represented not only the special interest of a class, but of all humanity: Growing up in the twenties without contact with the

Negro community, I had been affected by the prejudice prevailing in our own. Scottsboro was a transforming experience. It dramatically illustrated the evil institution of Jim Crow that was not only embedded in our social structure but in the hearts of the white majority of which I was a part. I could not view it objectively as a social problem. It became a personal problem as well, which forced me to purge myself of the moral guilt of years of indifference and insensitivity and hence complicity with this immoral condition.... Thus, the economic crisis, fascism, and the upsurge around Scottsboro all combined to propel me into the party.[20]

That was the passion that made a Communist. "What I remember most deeply about the Communists," when she was sixteen, wrote Gornick, "is their passion."[21] But the united fronts, the compromises, the opportunism was bound to destroy that passion. In 1946, when I was helping Don West, the poet, build an interracial camp in North Georgia, I was witness to a lynching. I was fifteen then and very angry. I passionately wanted to do something about it, perhaps join the Young Communist League. Nat Ross, the CP's chief in the South (and West's brother-in-law) talked me out of it. "You have to understand, to reason, to think logically. Only logic can make you a good Communist." How I remembered those words when Ross squealed on his fellow Communists before the House Un-American Activities Committee a few years later!

The passion disappeared, the logic stayed. The CP analyses may have been correct after all. When the New Deal was over, the rich still controlled the wealth, the laws, the courts, the police, the newspapers, the colleges. FDR was a hero, but the system of waste, inequality, concern for profits over human need was intact. And everywhere so-called socialists helped fortify that system: from France where Mitterand ordered the riot police to crush New Caledonia's pro-independence dissenters and offered subsidies to corporations setting up factories paying low wages in the "de-communized" Eastern bloc, to Peru where President Alan Garcia gave free reign to his army to massacre dissatisfied peasants, blaming it on the revolutionary Sendero Luminoso, who are currently being attacked by joint Peruvian-U.S. military might under "war on drugs" cover. No united front could ever stop these outrages. No popular front could put an end to U.S. exploitation of the third world, where five million people die every year just from the lack of the potable water used by U.S. multinationals to process their goods. Fronts demand too many compromises to be able to stop uncompromising imperialists.

In the early 1930s, the CPUSA came to the conclusion that the best hope for blacks in the United States was to exercise their rights to self-determination and establish their own nation in the eleven states where they made up a majority of the people.[22] Had that ever happened the United States would have been substantially weakened and hence could not have maintained its imperial bullyism to the extent practiced today. Of course it probably would never have occurred, but it was united frontism which stopped the CPUSA from working for that policy, since the socialists and other liberal lefts, supporting an electoral process which refuses proportional representation and genuine democracy, opposed it. Logic prevailed. And it continued to do so.

The conclusion seems to me inevitable: united/popular frontism, motivated originally by legitimate concern for the survival of the Russian Revolution, ultimately destroyed the revolutionary fervor and hence the *raison d'être* of the world's communist parties. As those parties lost ground, they became less and less principled, and felt obliged to tighten dogma more and more, giving up their democratic foundation and eventually becoming the authoritarian opportunistic parties that have been so easily crushed in the bourgeois electoral process in which they mistakenly staked most of their fates.

Notes

1. See *Failure of a Revolution: Germany 1918–1919* (Chicago: Banner Press, 1986), a brilliant history and analysis by Sebastian Haftner, a Social Democrat. See also Alfred Döblin's fabulous historical novels, *A People Betrayed* and *Karl and Rosa* (both New York: Fromm International, 1983).
2. For a vivid fictional but credible description of China's "night of the long knives," see André Malraux's classic novel, *Man's Fate*.
3. As far-fetched as that may sound today, it is nevertheless relevant to point out that the U.S. Socialist Party initially supported the United States in Vietnam and was in fact responsible for discovering "Democrat" Diem. The French Socialist Party waged war in Algeria, and the

leaderships of all European socialist parties supported the U.S. colonial war in the Arabian Gulf.

4. See "Editorial," *The Communist: A Magazine of the Theory and Practice of Marxism-Leninism* 13, no. 7 (July 1934): 615.
5. V.J. Jerome, "The Socialist Party Convention: A Communist Estimate," *The Communist* 13, no. 7 (July 1934): 618.
6. Ibid.: 638.
7. See Alexander Bittelman, "For a Bolshevik Anti-War Struggle," in *The Communist* 13, no. 8 (August 1934): 758.
8. See Earl Browder, "The Struggle for the United Front," in *The Communist* 13, no. 10 (October 1934): 937–38.
9. See Jerome, "The Socialist Party Convention," pp. 634–35.
10. Ibid., p. 635.
11. See Browder, "The Struggle for the United Front," p. 959.
12. Similarly, in the early 1970s, the U.S. Socialist Party fractured over the question of working in the regular Democratic Party. One faction formed Social Democrats USA, oriented toward the labor leaders and hawks in the Democrats' right wing. Another, the Democratic Socialist Organizing Committee (DSOC), supported liberal welfare staters and doves. DSOC later merged into the Democratic Socialists of America. Today, except among a few leftist intellectuals and academicians, it has lost the prestige and influence it may once have had.
13. See the statements of sixty-five survivors in my edited oral history, *The Premature Antifascists* (New York: Praeger, 1986).
14. Julio Alvarez del Vayo, Republican Spain's last foreign minister, a close personal friend, often told me that when he appealed, once even begged, for help, Blum literally cried as he claimed that he could not anger the British government.
15. Interview in Paris in 1972. See my *Jean-Paul Sartre: Hated Conscience of His Century*, Volume I (Chicago: University of Chicago Press, 1989), and Volume II, scheduled for publication in 1993.
16. See Vivian Gornick, *The Romance of American Communism* (New York: Basic Books, Harper Colophon Books, 1977), pp. 109–10.
17. Ibid., p. 110
18. Ibid., p. 146.
19. See Academy of Sciences of the USSR, *International Solidarity with the Spanish Republic, 1936–1939* (Moscow: Progress Publishers, 1974), p. 365. For each country represented in this volume, an article was written by an International Brigade volunteer of that country (e.g., Max Stern on Austrian volunteers, Nan Green on the British, Roger Michaut on the French, Michael O'Riordan on the Irish, Arthur H. Landis on the Abraham Lincoln Brigade, etc.). The "Afterword," which cites the statistics herewith noted, was put together by the Soviet editorial board and verified by the international editorial board

which included representatives of Britain, France, Germany, Italy, Poland, Czechoslovakia, USSR and Yugoslavia, and by Dolores Ibárruri of Spain. I cite these facts because some of the Lincoln vets have wanted to deny that so many North Americans wanted to volunteer, as if that belittled their own sacrifice, which of course it does not.

20. See George Charney, *A Long Journey* (Chicago: Quadrangle Books, 1968), pp. 24–27.

21. See Gornick, *Romance of American Communism*, p. 13.

22. The "self-determination" line was revived briefly after the war. See *The Communist Position on the Negro Question* (New York: New Century Publishers, 1947). Articles therein are all by the top CP leaders of 1946, including William Z. Foster, Benjamin J. Davis, Alexander Bittelman, etc. The introduction is by Nat Ross.

PURGING THE PROFS:
The Rapp Coudert Committee in New York, 1940–1942

Stephen Leberstein

Since the turn of the century U.S. academics have often been the targets of reactionary attacks. Defenders of the status quo did not attack them because college instructors were prominent as social activists and labor organizers, roles they only occasionally played. Instead, such academics as Richard Ely at Wisconsin in the 1890s, Scott Nearing at Toledo after World War I, and many others in the period around World War II, became targets because their work was seen as lending legitimacy to movements for social justice. As Merle Curti pointed out in *Roots of American Loyalty*, academics who supported progressive movements and causes were frequently branded "disloyal."[1]

In New York as elsewhere in the nation college teachers were attacked in the early decades of the century for their alleged or real radicalism. An example of such attacks was the Lusk Committee of the New York State legislature, which raided the offices of the Workers Party in 1919, at the same time that U.S. Attorney General A. Mitchell Palmer was launching a national "red scare." Pressure to find Communists in the schools increased during the 1930s. In 1930 the New York State legislature authorized the Hamilton Fish Committee to conduct an "investigation of Communist propaganda," which found surprisingly little evidence of Communist activity in the colleges when it issued its final report in 1931.

During the 1930s the evident risks of political engagement must have led some teachers to see the value of caution as more compelling than that of their First Amendment rights as citizens, a caution, not surprisingly, more easily indulged when their own academic freedom was protected by tenure. But the haven afforded by tenure was restricted to a relatively small part of the college teaching profession through the 1930s, and the rewards of teaching were meager enough during the Depression so that caution was a luxury unavailable to most. Repeated campaigns to enforce teachers' loyalty to the status quo foundered on these facts of life. As the decade advanced, college teachers became more politically active, whether on their own behalf in attempts to unionize, or on behalf of Spanish Loyalists, Soviet-American friendship or other trade unionists. This increasing political activity brought renewed attempts at repression.

From the time of its creation in 1938, the House Un-American Activities Committee under Martin Dies had been actively unearthing Communist influence everywhere, including the public colleges of New York City, and the Hearst press had started to headline news of the threat that Dies had discovered. In 1939 U.S. Attorney General Frank Murphy began investigating Communist Party leaders for alleged passport violations, probed the *Daily Worker*, and oversaw FBI arrests in Detroit and Milwaukee for illegal recruitment of volunteers for the Abraham Lincoln Brigade. Campaigns to repress political dissent in colleges grew more intense after the signing of the Nazi-Soviet Non-Aggression Pact in August 1939. Another national red scare emerged in 1940, a presidential election year. In June 1940 Congress passed the Alien Registration (Smith) Act, authorizing deportation of aliens belonging to revolutionary organizations. The Smith Act also established the first peacetime federal sedition law since 1798, making conspiracy to advocate the overthrow of the government a crime. Under this law, it was not necessary to prove that an individual had advocated any such act, but only that the accused belonged to an organization that favored such advocacy.[2] State legislatures set up "little Dies Committees" in California, Oklahoma, Texas, and New York. By 1940, twenty-one states across the country had loyalty oaths for teachers, and the era of the legislative committee was dawning.[3]

Origins of the Rapp Coudert Committee

New York's own "little Dies Committee," the Rapp Coudert Committee, emerged from a wave of anti-intellectual hysteria directed at City College of New York (CCNY), the oldest and largest of the city's four public colleges. In 1940, the City College philosophy department tried to hire Bertrand Russell, who was looking for an U.S. position after his pacifism had made him unwelcome in his native Britain. Russell was pilloried in the right-wing press for his supposed advocacy of "godlessness" and "free love." The *Tablet*, the newspaper of the Brooklyn diocese of the Catholic Church, branded him the "leading anti-Christian" in its March 2, 1940, issue.[4] Although the appointment fell through when Mayor LaGuardia deleted Russell's line from the city budget, State Senator John J. Dunnigan of New York City used the incident as an example of the "ungodly and un-American" ways of those in control of New York schools in order to press the state legislature to start an investigation.

Minutes after the legislature adopted an anti-Russell resolution, The *New York Times* reported, Senator Dunnigan introduced another resolution calling for a "sweeping investigation." Dunnigan explained why the investigation was needed:

> Many complaints have been made by citizens that various prominent educators who have rendered loyal and capable services to the City of New York have been compelled to retire, solely for the reason that their philosophy has not been in accord with the Godless, materialistic theories of those now governing the New York school system, and that other teachers had been denied reappointment despite the fact that their scholastic accomplishments have measured up to the highest standards.[5]

The same month saw news of an investigation of school textbooks by Dies's Un-American Activities Committee, and of an effort by the Bronx borough president to have the New York City Board of Estimate investigate subversion in the public schools and colleges. In a move typical of the political atmosphere at the time, State Senator Frederic Coudert, also of New York City, co-sponsored a bill to allow religious teachers to work in the public schools. After some maneuvering in Albany, both houses of the state legislature quickly approved the investigation Dunnigan had called for.

Approved by a joint resolution of the state legislature in 1940, the Rapp Coudert Committee (named after its co-chairmen, Assemblyman Herbert Rapp of upstate Genesee County and Senator Coudert) was formally established "to investigate the procedures and methods of allocating state moneys for public school purposes and subversive activities." It carried out investigations of the public schools and colleges of New York City mainly in 1941 and 1942, and issued a report on educational administration and finance toward the end of World War II. The committee's attacks on teachers and staff in the city's four public colleges (Brooklyn, City, Hunter, and Queens) was its major effort, one that played as front page news during much of 1941. It was at City College, the oldest, largest and most famous of the four, where most of the investigation took place.

Virtually the only investigation the committee carried out, however, was the work of a New York City subcommittee (hereafter called the committee) chaired by Senator Coudert. The committee counsel, Paul Windels, a former New York City corporation counsel under Mayor LaGuardia, took charge of the committee's investigations and hearings. The committee spent most of its energies looking into the issue of "Communist subversion" in the city's public schools and colleges.

When the committee made its report to the legislature, it stated that its aim had been to explore the "Communist problem" that it saw as endemic in the schools and colleges for the previous twenty years. A further aim, according to the report, was to make the educational institutions themselves responsible for vigilance against the alleged menace.[6] Expanding on the nature of this problem, the report attributed the spread of Communism among the teaching staff to the attitude of "that amorphous section of the public referred to under the collective heading 'liberals' and 'intellectuals,'" which evidently regarded Communism as a legitimate form of political dissent.[7] The committee's specific aim was to destroy this liberal tolerance of political dissent, and particularly to make Communist Party membership and activity unacceptable to the public, to the faculty and to the colleges' governing board.

In its initial 1942 report to the legislature, the committee had nothing to say on issues of school finance or administration, or even on allegations of fascist activity at a time when the nation was at war with the Axis powers. The nature and timing of this official report, concerned exclusively with purging political dissidents, testifies to the committee's aims. Not until 1944 did a subsequent report to the legislature discuss issues of educational reform. And in the initial 1942 report the question of fascists or Nazis in the schools and colleges was dismissed in a brief paragraph. In 1943, however, the FBI did arrest a member of the City College history department on charges that he was a paid Japanese agent.[8]

What is most significant about the committee's 1942 report is that none of the teachers suspended from their posts and charged as a result of the investigation was ever accused of any breach of law or ethics in their teaching or scholarship. Their sole "crime" in the eyes of the Rapp Coudert Committee was their alleged membership in the Communist Party; they were accused of conduct unbecoming a member of the staff only for their unwillingness to testify about their party membership. No one was ever charged with a specific instance of misusing his or her office as an instructor. Later research, none of it friendly to those who were dismissed, found the committee's victims to have been generally outstanding as teachers and scholars. The political intent of the committee and the impartiality of its findings must also be judged against this evidence.

What was new about the Rapp Coudert Committee was its isolation of the Communist Party as the target of its attack, its aim of developing a cadre of informers, its sophistication in organizing and mounting its attack, and its ability to see that its suspects lost their jobs even though the committee itself did not have the power to fire them. In all these respects, the investigation marked a turning point away from the virulent and energetic but blundering attacks of the past decades, like the Lusk raids, toward the more systematic repression of the McCarthy era.

As the investigation got underway in 1940, it did so in an atmosphere of increasingly shrill right-wing attacks on public education. One of the chief critics of City College during this period was the Taxpayers Union of New York City, whose president, Joseph Goldsmith, called for the closing of the college and a reduction of $10 million in the budget of the remaining colleges, after publication of the testimony of the committee's first informer. "A majority of the students [at CCNY] are Communists," Goldsmith declared, "and we are in favor of closing down the college until the situation is cleaned up."[9] The crusade carried out by the Rapp Coudert Committee gave critics of public spending a rationale for their choice of targets and spurred on their attacks against the public colleges. And the dual themes—of profligate public spending and of Communist "subversion"—reinforced one another in the course of the investigation.

Some might argue that the Rapp Coudert Committee was established for the honest purpose of looking into school finance and administration, and that its interest in "subversion" resulted from a political compromise forced upon the legislature by reactionary groups and individuals. Many political and public figures, however, saw the committee's activities as an attack on public education, trade unionism, and civil liberties. These included such groups as the American Committee for Democracy and Intellectual Freedom, the New York Teachers Union, and a wide range of civic, labor, and religious groups at the local and, later, at the national level.

Typical of the problems that vexed the investigators was a rally that took place on April 7, 1940, just a week after the legislature voted to authorize the investigation. Sponsored by the American Committee for Democracy and Intellectual Freedom, a civil libertarian group headed by Franz Boas, the noted anthropologist, the rally was called to protest what was seen as an attack on public education. The rally's sponsors included Ordway Tead, Harry J. Carmen, and Joseph Schlossberg, chairman and members, respectively, of the Board of Higher Education, the governing board for the city's public colleges. Among its other sponsors was Stanley Isaacs, the Manhattan borough president, and one of its featured speakers was Newbold Morris, president of the City Council.[10] Meanwhile, the diatribe against subversion in the schools continued: at a breakfast of the Holy Name Society of the Fire Department in early May, for example, former District Attorney William F.X. Geoghan warned against "godless subversives" in the schools.[11]

Paul Windels, the committee counsel, claimed that the investigation had not been set up to conduct a witch-hunt, and that it was only through the exertion of both public and private pressure that he was forced to pursue the matter of subversion. In his recollections for the Columbia University Oral History Project, Windels attributed the investigation's nature to the "public impatience and anxiety" over disorder at the colleges, including such breaches of the peace as strikes, which some saw as orchestrated by Communists.[12] Windels further claimed that the aim of the investigation had not yet been decided when Senator Coudert approached him with an offer to head it in the summer of 1940 at the Republican National Convention, where both were delegates. The staff, he claimed, would have preferred to start in on the constructive part of the job, looking at such issues as school finance and curriculum, had it not been for "the pressure of public opinion on the committee."[13] Coudert's choice of Windels, an expensive and highly political lawyer, appears to have been calculated to impart an aura of respectability and legitimacy to the committee. If Coudert had been truly interested in examining such conventional legislative concerns as finance and administration, why then did he hire Windels?

When Lawrence Chamberlain, then dean of Columbia College, studied the Rapp Coudert Committee some years later, he repeated the claim that Coudert's aim had been to look into educational reform.[14] This information probably came from Windels himself. Chamberlain attributed his source to "high ranking, responsible members of the committee's staff," who, he claimed, were persuaded that it was urgent to investigate subversion by "persons actively interested in the New York school system," and who in turn convinced Coudert. Chamberlain concluded that the decision to ferret out subversives "was dictated by the presentation of such compelling evidence that [the committee] could not ignore it."[15] While Chamberlain cautiously defended the committee's work, he did not report either the evidence or its source that led Coudert to set aside his purported original interests. It is far more logical to conclude, as the Teachers Union did at the time, that Coudert was engaged in a witch-hunt to discredit teacher unionism and to justify reduced spending on public education, than that circumstances forced him to investigate Communists in the schools. On one hand, it is ironic that it was Coudert who headed the investigation in New York City, for he had been one of the sponsors of the 1938 bill creating a tenure system for faculty members of the public colleges, a law that had been the object of the "democratization plan" put forward by the Teachers Union and some of the very individuals who would soon be dismissed as a result of the committee's investigation. On the other hand, can it be mere coincidence that those dismissed from the colleges in 1941 and 1942 included all those activists who had been earlier targets of City College's reactionary president, Frederick Robinson, who had tried unsuccessfully to have them fired in 1936?

The Role of the Colleges and of the Board of Higher Education

In its effort to rid public college faculties of suspected Communists, one of the greatest obstacles that the Rapp Coudert Committee faced was administrative indifference to political dissent. Board of Higher Education officials were reluctant to concern themselves with the political affairs of their employees, a mark of the very tolerance that the committee complained about in its report. And of course it was not illegal to belong to the Communist Party, a major impediment to having the accused fired. When the investigation began, Ordway Tead, the chairman of the board, joined prominent civil libertarians in a public protest against what he saw as an attack on public education. Windels later recalled that the Rapp Coudert investigation was initially "deprecated" by the educational authorities, who "looked upon the committee's activities as what was then termed by so-called liberals, a witch-hunt."[16] In its report to the legislature, the committee did, indeed, criticize the board for its laxity in the face of allegations of subversion in the colleges.[17] The committee pointedly singled out one board member, S.J. Woolf, for daring to criticize the investigation publicly. As a member of Philip Foner's trial committee (when the board tried him on charges that he had not cooperated with the Rapp Coudert Committee), Woolf lashed out at the informers who had testified about Foner's political associations. In his eyes, the informers' testimony was damning evidence of their own unfitness as college teachers.[18] In the committee's eyes, however, Woolf's public criticism of the investigation made *him* unfit to hold public office. By the time the committee had drafted its report to the legislature in 1942, Woolf was the sole member to raise a question about the investigation, and even he played his prescribed role in the public trial of accused teachers. Tead had long since become silent.

Two men utterly hostile to the activists accused by the Rapp

Coudert Committee took office as presidents of Brooklyn College and City College in 1939 and 1940, respectively. Their presence made the committee more effective in rooting out suspected radicals at the two colleges. The reactionary if somewhat ridiculous president of City College, Frederick Robinson, was forced to retire in 1938, and Nelson Mead of the history department was named acting president. Mead defended the college against the committee's attacks by denying that it was a center of Communist activity, by citing its accomplishments, and by urging the committee to devote its energies "to investigating the means of our continuing our service to the community." Mead's attitude toward the investigation was what the committee wanted to destroy. In a public statement at the beginning of the investigation, Mead admitted that there might be "a few" Communists at City College, but asserted that their presence was common in urban colleges, and simply stated that "Not a single instance has ever been brought to my attention of Communist indoctrination in the classroom."[19] Mead resigned and returned to teaching history at the end of 1940.

In his place, Harry Wright of the mathematics department was named acting president. Wright's attitude differed sharply from Mead's. At a special college assembly in early March 1941, Wright spoke up in defense of the committee's work, not by denying the presence of a Communist "problem" at City College, but by pledging his cooperation in rooting it out. While he denied that the committee was attacking academic freedom, Wright acknowledged that such freedom is a "relative thing," which "does not mean unrestricted license for a man to say or do anything he pleases at any time." Understating his case, Wright concluded by admitting that "We would be ridiculous if we thought such a thing."[20] The new president amply lived up to his pledge of cooperation, taking the initiative, for example, to turn over to Windels the names of faculty members who might be persuaded to inform against their colleagues.[21] Wright held the view that Communists had long been troublemakers at City College, and that the best remedy was to be rid of them, as he explained his position to officials of the American Committee for Democracy and Intellectual Freedom.[22] It was clear that the new City College president was ready to play his part in the investigation, which in any case he apparently saw as a useful way to settle old scores.

In July 1939, Harry Gideonse took charge of Brooklyn College and quickly took on the faculty radicals. Once the Rapp Coudert Committee began its investigation, Gideonse defended his college by trying to anticipate the charges it was likely to make, and to act before they were made public. An example of the Gideonse strategy emerged at a meeting of the Board of Higher Education, when a board member read what he said were notes made during a lecture on art history at Brooklyn College that demonstrated the subversive views of the instructor.[23] Gideonse rose to defend this instructor from his inquisitor on the grounds that the Rapp Coudert Committee had given the suspect its absolution as an appropriately repentant ex-Communist. The token of his repentance was his willingness to name names.

Mechanisms of Repression

In its 1942 report the Rapp Coudert Committee claimed to have "exposed" sixty-nine instructors as Communists, and to have gathered evidence implicating another 434 members of the faculty and staff.[24] While the city's Board of Education and Board of Higher Education dismissed many teachers and staff members after trials before conduct committees, and many more resigned under charges, only a single individual was ever charged with a crime and tried in a court of law.[25] While there were not yet any laws banning Communist Party membership, the Rapp Coudert Committee argued that the mere fact of membership in the party rendered a teacher or staff member unfit to work in the public schools and colleges. Party membership was assumed to demand a discipline that, in itself, was improper for a teacher, whose conduct thereby became "fraudulent" and "deceptive." The logic behind this assumption was that the Communist Party was by definition a "subversive," conspiratorial organization, whose members were ipso facto guilty of subversion. By this logic, akin to that of the Smith Act, it was therefore unnecessary to prove any particular deed or subversive act, but merely the fact of membership in the party. But in the absence of a law making party membership illegal, the committee's challenge was to find a way to force public employers to fire the individuals it could prove were members of the not yet illegal party.

In the system the Rapp Coudert Committee set in motion, the burden of proof came to rest on the accused who denied membership in the party, or who refused to testify when such testimony would oblige them to name names. Yet the committee proclaimed that its investigation showed "no inconsistency between the concept of freedom of political belief and the conclusion that Communists cannot be permitted to hold employment in the public schools."[26] But legislative committees themselves did not have the power to fire workers. The task of the Rapp Coudert Committee was to force a reluctant Board of Higher Education to dismiss the alleged Communists. Its chief accomplishment was to invent a means to achieve its repressive end. For months the board floundered, passing a convoluted set of resolutions in an attempt to keep its employees from belonging to a legal organization. Ultimately, the issue on which the dismissals hinged was the willingness of college employees to admit their membership in the Communist Party in their testimony before the committee.

In recruiting informers, developing a list of suspects, and then prosecuting them in the press, the committee and its staff were highly sophisticated. For those caught in its investigation, the Rapp Coudert Committee's tactics effectively reversed the concept of the presumption of innocence. Once accused, the teachers bore the burden of disproving the committee's charges. But because membership in the Communist Party was not a crime, the committee developed the tactic of trying the accused in the press in an effort to sway public opinion against its victims. Windels congratulated himself on revealing the names only of those who had been named by two corroborating witnesses and who had also refused to testify at the committee's private hearings, often a one-man interrogation that seemed like a "star-chamber proceeding" to those called to appear. The accused were not allowed legal counsel, the right to cross-examine witnesses, or even transcripts of the proceedings. The committee's techniques worked outside the law; with a single exception, no indictments were sought from a grand jury. And with that one exception, no trials were held in a court of law. Only in the minds of the investigators were the norms of due process observed.

As the committee's work gained momentum and wider press coverage, the Board of Higher Education surrendered its independence and increasingly accommodated itself to the aims of the investigation. In November 1940, the board resolved to cooperate fully in the investigation.[27] When the press reported that some teachers had refused to testify before the committee, the board called a special meeting at which it decided to ask the committee to forward the names of those of its employees who had challenged the committee's authority.[28] The board also sought the advice of the city's corporation counsel concerning its power to discipline recalcitrant staff members. The corporation counsel, W.C. Chanler, ruled that teachers who refused to testify before the committee were guilty of insubordination in light of the board's policy commanding them to do so.[29] Chanler further argued that a teacher's dismissal on such charges would be upheld in the courts if it were challenged. The board's final action at that meeting was the creation of a conduct committee of three to cooperate with the Rapp Coudert Committee by bringing disciplinary charges against those of its employees who had run afoul of the committee.[30]

Overcoming its earlier reluctance to concern itself with the political sympathies of its employees, the Board of Higher Education eventually prohibited Communist Party membership in the spring of 1941: the fact of membership alone would now lead to dismissal. However, none of the dismissals of teachers and staff at the colleges resulted from trial on that charge. Instead, the suspected staff and teachers were charged with refusing to testify before a legislative committee concerning their membership in the party, or more commonly with perjury in denying their membership. The charges were all based on the testimony of at least two and occasionally three cooperating witnesses. (In the case of those accused at City College, there were never more than three friendly witnesses: Martin Canning, Oscar Zeichner and Annette Sherman Gottsegen.) None of the charges involved misconduct as a teacher, and indeed the trial records offer ample evidence that the accused were generally dedicated, effective teachers and serious scholars. With the complicity of board and college officials, the committee was then able to have fired the faculty and staff members who it believed were Communists on the grounds of conduct unbecoming a member of the staff—that is, either non-cooperation with a legislative committee or perjury. Prohibiting teachers from belonging to the party meant that the suspects could be dismissed either for admitting their membership or for denying it if two cooperating witnesses were available to prove perjury. Faced with the committee's deus ex machina, the accused were at a loss for determining how to resist.

In devising these tactics, the committee had helped to pioneer a new mechanism for repressing political dissent. The committee's repressive machinery gave the accused few choices in defending themselves. They could cooperate in the investigation, which most found unacceptable on ethical and political grounds; they could deny the accusation and risk dismissal for perjury on the basis of conflicting testimony from those few witnesses who cooperated; or they could publicly admit membership in the party and face certain dismissal. Those who would have willingly admitted their own party membership under oath found this an unacceptable course since they would have then been compelled to name others or face a contempt citation. The trap had been set, and those it caught had no honorable way of escaping.

In the early months of 1941, the Board of Higher Education took a series of steps to put more pressure on the students, staff and faculty of the four public colleges, compelling them to cooperate with the Rapp Coudert Committee. In January 1941, for example, the board read into its minutes the legal arguments by which it felt its employees were obliged to testify before the one-man subcommittee of the Rapp Coudert Committee that was carrying out the investigation in New York City.[31] The board also warned its employees that it would take disciplinary action against anyone who refused to testify before this particular subcommittee, the private proceeding widely denounced as a "star-chamber hearing."

In February, the board adopted a new measure in its bylaws allowing the board itself, rather than the colleges under its jurisdiction, to try employees for disobeying its bylaws or resolutions.[32] Finally in March 1941, the board made it a policy "not to retain as members of the collegiate staffs members of any Communist, Fascist or Nazi group or society, or to retain any individual who, or member of any group which, advocates, advises, teaches or practices subversive doctrines or activities."[33] At this same meeting it was noted that Morris Schappes, English tutor at City College, had been suspended two days earlier pending trial on charges brought by the three-member board committee, and that the charges against him would be amended to include the violation, ex post facto, of the new policy just voted.[34]

At its meeting in April 1941, a month later, the board tried to clarify its definition of banned political activities in a resolution concerning the Rapp Coudert investigation. The board stated that it would have "sufficient cause" for dismissal if any employee is proved to have "counselled subversion, or to have belonged to a group advocating subversive doctrines, or to have engaged in activities disruptive of the educational system, or to have accepted the discipline of any group which requires its members to act in the interests of a foreign national group, or to follow any predetermined policy of course or conduct...."[35] This last resolution set the stage for the trial and dismissal of those singled out by the Rapp Coudert Committee, although it was so broad in its scope that it would also have allowed the board to catch Catholics, Masons and others in its net, if by some twist of fate they had displaced Communists as the enemy. It made membership in the Communist Party synonymous with misconduct and thereby circumvented the need to prove—or for that matter, even charge—the suspects with actually committing a crime. The first suspensions of faculty and staff were reported in mid-March 1941, just before this resolution clarified the crimes of the accused, and the first trials by the board were scheduled for early June. The first employee dismissed was the City College registrar, John Kenneth Ackley, on June 30, 1941. From then until the end of 1942, at least thirty-one members of the City College faculty and staff were suspended on charges brought against them by the specially constituted conduct committee of the Board of Higher Education.

With the exception of a single individual, David Goldway, who worked in Townsend Harris High School, the preparatory school for City College then under the jurisdiction of the Board of Higher Education, none of the accused relied on their constitutional privileges to defend themselves. Of course, the proceedings were not criminal trials in a court, but rather legislative hearings followed by administrative trials before a conduct committee. The Fifth Amendment protection against self-incrimination was not used except for criminal cases at that time, and the First Amendment protection of the freedom of speech and association did little to help David Goldway, who was suspended and later dismissed by the

Board of Higher Education after he invoked the First Amendment to justify his refusal to testify before the Rapp Coudert Committee after having waived its offer of immunity. His case and those of several other Townsend Harris employees were decided on the basis of Section 903 of the City Charter, a section since deleted, which made it a misdemeanor for any city employee to refuse full cooperation with any legislative investigation. Years later, David Riesman suggested that the accused might have held higher moral ground had they based their defense against the Rapp Coudert investigation on constitutional principles, but by then the Goldway case must have faded from his memory.[36] Whether such a strategy would have helped the accused to retrieve a measure of public sympathy and political tolerance is far from clear.

What is clear is the intimate cooperation that took place among officials of the Rapp Coudert Committee, the public colleges and the Board of Higher Education. While the initiative for what can only be described as a purge came from the committee, officials at the colleges and at the board, though perhaps reluctantly at first, nevertheless quickly rose to the challenge in carrying out the aims of the Rapp Coudert Committee. By the end of 1942, nineteen individuals had been dismissed from City College alone, another seven had resigned under charges, and other cases were still pending at year's end.

One additional incident in 1946 serves to show how contrived the investigation had been. Francis J. Thompson, a public speaking instructor at City College, was tried and found guilty of misconduct by the board conduct committee in 1942, but the disposition of his case was delayed because he had enlisted in the armed forces. Upon his discharge from the service in 1946, Thompson was promptly dismissed by the board, but he appealed the decision to the state education commissioner. Thompson was ordered reinstated with back pay after the commissioner found, first, that membership in the Communist Party was not grounds for dismissal under state law, and second, that there was no evidence to prove his membership in any case.[37] Apparently, none of the other victims of the committee appealed through this channel, one that led to an unequivocal decision that might have been rendered in any of the other cases as well. We can only wonder why no one thought to file such an appeal five years earlier.

It was not until the early 1950s that Lawrence Chamberlain published a serious study of the Rapp Coudert Committee as part of a larger series on American loyalty. Hardly sympathetic to the accused activists, Chamberlain knew both Coudert and Windels well enough to enjoy their confidence and to be given access to Coudert's private papers. Since he was no partisan of those who lost their jobs as a result of the investigation, Chamberlain's conclusion about their professional performance cannot be viewed as biased in their favor:

> No one can read through the verbatim [trial] testimony... without being impressed with the generally superior character of the group here under scrutiny. There seems no doubt from evidence presented elsewhere that some of the group were Communists, but the impressive and inescapable fact is that the *only evidence presented by either side* points to: (1) outstanding scholarship, (2) superior teaching, (3) absence of indoctrination in the classroom.[38]

Whatever else they might have been, the victims of the Rapp Coudert Committee were dedicated teachers, serious scholars and hardworking staff members at City College and the other public colleges of New York City.

The Accused

What were the circumstances particular to the situation in New York City in 1940 that allowed the Rapp Coudert investigation to unfold in the way that it did? Several issues need to be considered: first, the role of the Communist Party, its relative strength in this period, and the motives and actions of its members and sympathizers among those accused by the committee; second, the effect of international and national events on the party at the local level; and third, the situation in the Teachers Union.

In considering the circumstances that gave rise to the Rapp Coudert Committee, it is important to remember that City College and the other public colleges in the 1930s were not ivied campuses, isolated from the tensions of the Depression. Along with the growth of the student body at the public colleges during the 1930s came a groundswell of organized political activity, reflecting national and international issues. The rise of fascism in Europe was particularly troubling to a largely immigrant, Jewish student body and to the younger faculty and staff. During the decade of the 1930s, the day-session student population of the four public colleges grew by two and one-half times. At City College, in the freshman class of 1938, for example, only 17 percent of the students' fathers and 22 percent of their mothers were born in the U.S. Most of their parents came from Russia, Poland, and the former Austro-Hungarian Empire. In one estimate, 80 percent of the total student enrollment was Jewish or "of Jewish background."[39] And it was also found that 52 percent of all faculty members at City College who had earned their bachelor's degrees after 1930, did so at City College.[40] At City, many Jewish immigrants who graduated from the college were hired, at low ranks and meager salaries, to teach other immigrant youth. Contrary to the oft-heard charge that it was the left-wing teachers who improperly influenced their students, it is far more likely that it was the militant students who brought their teachers into politics.[41] By the early 1930s, both the League for Industrial Democracy, successor to the Intercollegiate Socialist Society, and the Young Communist League were active on campuses like City, and their activities often took the form of a Social Problems Club.

During the period of the greatest student activism, the president of City College was Frederick B. Robinson (1928–1938), a conservative, short-tempered man who often acted as though it were his personal responsibility to civilize the "unwashed" masses and train them for useful jobs. At City, the 1930s were marked by continual warfare between Robinson and student activists. In 1931, Robinson banned the Social Problems Club from the campus. In 1932, he fired Oakley Johnson, an English instructor who was advisor to the Liberal Club, was active in the Communist Party, and who had organized an expedition to Harlan County, Kentucky in support of striking coal miners. His dismissal led to student protests, including a mock trial of Robinson in which Joseph Starobin, then a student at City College, acted as prosecutor.[42] Nearly thirty students were suspended for their role in the protests.

Two incidents characterize the political tone at City College in this decade. The first was a student demonstration against the college ROTC unit at its review at the end of May 1933 in Lewisohn Stadium, located in the center of the campus. When student demonstrators blocked the way of Robinson and his military entourage, the president flailed at them with his umbrella and in the ensuing scuffle the students disarmed him. He had to be rescued by the police. The following year Robinson invited an official delegation of Italian students to a required convocation in the college's Great Hall. The college student council opposed the invitation and urged Robinson and other college officials to cancel it. But Robinson insisted that the president of the student council greet the Italian delegation, and Edwin Alexander obliged him by bringing "anti-fascist greetings from the student body of City College." A brawl followed, after which Robinson told the press that student leaders at the college were worse than "gutter-snipes." Another group of twenty students was dismissed.

In the early 1930s, the faculty and staff of the college organized an Instructional Staff Association (ISA) and then an Anti-Fascist Association. The former was an attempt to address some of the concerns of the younger, junior faculty over their abysmally low salaries and poor conditions of employment. However, it proved ineffective, and a "caucus" of activist teachers began joining the New York Teachers Union instead (Local 5 of the American Federation of Teachers, which later formed a separate New York College Teachers Union, Local 537). The concerns that led the younger teachers to join one organization also led them to take part in others. In their eyes, these organizations and the issues they addressed were important because they were the children of immigrant workers and Jews, and because of the material conditions of their lives. Morris Schappes, the most prominent of the Rapp Coudert victims and an English tutor at City College for thirteen years, remembers that, in the year of his marriage in 1930, he and his wife had a combined income of a little more than $2,000, a sum sufficient for what his friends called "bed and bookcase."[43]

These teachers did not become activists because they were members of the Communist Party. If they joined the party during the 1930s, as most did, it was because the party represented the only political organization that fought militantly for the issues that mattered most to them. Schappes, for example, remembers that his political coming of age happened in the early 1930s, after he began teaching at City College but before he joined the party. Even Bella Dodd, the legislative director of the Teachers Union in the 1930s and 1940s who later turned against her former comrades, remembers that she became a Communist in part out of admiration for "the selfless dedication of many who belonged to the party," and in part for their support of the Instructors Association and "the way they fought for the forgotten man of the city."[44] Except to justify her own choice, it is unlikely that Dodd would heap unwarranted praise on her former associates.

In his testimony before the Rapp Coudert Committee, Bernard Grebanier, who taught English at Brooklyn College and who was one of the first informers, gave his reasons for having joined the party in 1935. First, it seemed to him the most effective force for combatting fascism. And then, he continued, the party in the mid-1930s was "out-democrating the Democratic Party" and often sounded patriotic.[45] Although Grebanier's testimony is self-serving, it is consistent with that of the accused.

As another ex-teacher remembered years later in his unpublished memoirs, he turned to radicalism because he had been brought up as such a patriotic American. When the experience of the Depression years did not match the expectations of textbook Americanism, Sidney Eisenberger, like many others, sought understanding and aid where he could find it. But Eisenberger did not transform himself from what he called an "ipsy pipsy Yankee Doodle boy" into a Communist Party member overnight.[46] By 1933, "angry that my country seemed to have no use for me," he joined the Instructional Staff Association, but soon followed the Communist "caucus" from the ISA to the Teachers Union, where, "For the first time, a militant, rapidly-growing organization came into being and effectively promoted the economic interests of college teachers." In Eisenberger's eyes, as in the eyes of many others, the party fought for what mattered to them, their immediate economic interests as well as their broader interest in social justice. "I was impressed with their militancy, their courage, their tenacity, their incorruptibility, and their good sense," Eisenberger remembered. "I had been looking for ways to resist what society was doing to me and I had finally found allies whom I could trust." It was neither Comintern dictates nor Marxist ideology that prompted people like him to follow the party but rather the party's leadership on pressing issues.

Sometimes these issues were simple and mundane. For Eisenberger and others in the science departments at City College, this meant a campaign against corruption, as in the "Kem-Kit" affair. Students in chemistry courses at City College were required to purchase a "Kem-Kit," containing supplies needed for their lab work. But some members of the chemistry department had a financial interest in the company selling the kits, which cost substantially more than the price of their contents. A campaign to expose this practice led the Board of Higher Education to ban it, after which students bought their supplies at cost directly from the college. Similar campaigns focused on contracts for the purchase of coal for the college heating plant. Corrupt practices were reformed; the students, junior staff and the city benefitted, and the campaigners undoubtedly earned the undying enmity of those who had lost a source of lucrative income.

Far more significant as a local issue was the absence of blacks on the faculty and of black studies in the curriculum. Again, it was the politically active teachers and staff who took up this issue and carried it forward with the same conviction and energy that they did with other causes. Pressure by this group led City College to hire Max Yergan in 1936 to teach the first course on Negro history and culture that it had ever offered. Schappes remembers accompanying Yergan with some others on the day of his first class to the faculty dining room, which happens to command a view of Central Harlem, only to be refused service.[47] Apparently, no black person had ever come into the dining room before, but persistence led to desegregation, at least in this one case.

Yergan had worked in South Africa for years, and on his return to the United States became head of the National Negro Congress. Black students at City College, at least those who belonged to the Frederick Douglass Society, knew him and also pressed for his hiring. Yergan's role as a teacher at City brought him considerable personal prestige and the "greatest prominence in Harlem."[48] In a public statement issued at the time of his dismissal in 1941, Yergan explained that the purpose of his course was

to disclose the culture of the Negro people and its place in world culture; to study those forces which account for the present status of the Negro population of America; to expose and correct the misrepresentation of the past of the Negro people; and to discuss how Negroes may continue their contributions to cultural progress and the strengthening of democracy in America.[49]

Contribution to a collection of graphics in support of City College teachers. **Art:** Sylvia Wald. From *Winter Soldiers: The Story of a Conspiracy Against the Schools* (New York: Committee for Defense of Public Education, 1941). Courtesy of Annette T. Rubinstein.

When Yergan was named before the Rapp Coudert Committee, he was removed from his position without benefit of charge or trial. As a non-tenured lecturer, he was not entitled even to rudimentary due process, and the official explanations for his dismissal ranged from his chairman's claim that special lectureships were rotated "in order that the students may get the benefit of different personalities," to the president's assertion that he did not meet the college's standards of scholarship. His dismissal thus deprived City College of its first and, at the time, only black instructor, and its only course on black history.

The college president did give Yergan the chance to "come clean," the same chance he offered all the other accused teachers who were not protected by tenure. Morton Gottschall, then dean of the college, admitted that this offer put the burden of proof upon the accused.[50] Yergan declined. A massive protest followed Yergan's dismissal, one that the president termed "a Communist storm." Those who protested included labor, civil rights and civil liberties groups, as well as churches, both black and white, and academics. In naming Yergan, the committee was seen as using its anti-communist crusade to attack the limited gains that blacks had made in academic life.

Others active on behalf of black students and in the campaign to bring Yergan to City College were also dismissed for their efforts. Lewis Balamuth, a physics instructor, had served as faculty advisor to the Frederick Douglass Society during the 1930s. In a statement at a public hearing of the Rapp Coudert Committee in March 1941, Balamuth took pride in the fact that his work with the Douglass Society had been "a natural development ... to involve me with broader movements in the Negro community, especially those related to educational opportunities."[51]

Many former members of the society wrote in Balamuth's support. Clinton Oliver, an ex-president of the society, cited Balamuth as "a man respected and admired by every Negro student and graduate of the college who knew him as a liberal whose principles of democracy led him at all times to insist upon equal rights and opportunities for all students."[52] Another former member of the society noted that those named by the committee included all those faculty members to whom black students "looked as being sympathetically cognizant of just those problems toward the solution of which the Douglass Society was founded."[53] Balamuth too was fired.

In his statement to the committee, Balamuth commented sardonically that some prominent Americans would find in his efforts on behalf of black students proof of his "Communistic interests."[54] Those named by the committee shared in common with Balamuth an interest in racial equality; they were anti-fascists and supported the Loyalists in the Spanish Civil War; they were militant trade unionists, and they spoke out against corruption. To take a stand and act on these issues, during most of the 1930s in New York City, meant gaining support from the larger community outside the college, especially in times of crisis. When President Robinson fired thirteen teachers he regarded as troublemakers in 1936, organized labor took up their cause and fought for their reinstatement, making that demand a prominent part of the annual May Day march. The teachers were all rehired that June. Membership in the party did not isolate the teachers from their supporters; if anything, it added to their stature.

From the time the committee started its investigation, Windels focused on the Teachers Union and its college local as the means by which the Communist Party sought to control the public colleges. In fact, he began the investigation by subpoenaing the union's membership list. Never wavering in its support of those who were called before the committee, the union organized a Committee to Defend Public Education in order to arouse public sympathy for the accused, and it sent its lawyer, William J. Mulligan, to represent the accused at their hearings. At the private hearings where each one of the accused was first given the chance to cooperate, the right to legal counsel was denied. In the public hearings which began in December 1940, Mulligan tried to present Coudert with a motion to allow for the cross-examination of witnesses. When Coudert refused to hear the motion and Mulligan persisted, the senator had the police forcibly remove Mulligan from the hearing room.[55]

Charles Hendley, president of the Teachers Union, was summoned to the public hearing, where he appeared after Henry Linville, the former union president. Linville, now a friendly witness, had resigned his office in 1935 in frustration at the growing influence of the Rank and File Caucus organized by younger activist members, and since then had pressed the American Federation of Teachers to revoke Local 5's charter. Hendley, however, treated as an unfriendly witness, was grilled on Communist influence in the union, and Windels pressed him to admit that the union was a tool of the party. Difficult though it was to defend himself against Windels's attack, Hendley never admitted that he was a member of the party (he probably was not) and he never named names. Instead, he reiterated the principle that the political beliefs of members were none of the union's business.[56]

The New York Teachers Union was important to the accused teachers, all of whom were active in it. It was the instrument of their attempt to improve their wages and to gain some minimal democratic rights on the job. Their efforts helped the union to win tenure rights and some democratic reforms from the Board of Higher Education in 1938. After those reforms the union gained in its ability to defend the teachers; the possibility that the politically active teachers might survive further attacks depended on the continued strength of the union.

The connection between political activism and the union at the public colleges was a strong one. Clara Zitron, in her history of the New York City Teachers Union, suggests that reactionaries intent on throttling public education aimed to destroy the union in order to stifle dissent and trim budgets. As evidence she cites the statement of John F. Kavanagh at the December 4, 1940, conference of the Taxpayers' Federation:

> The solution of the problem of reducing the cost of education ... has been the subject of a number of investigations by the Board of Regents, state legislative inquiries and of research by newspapers.... The only known benefit from these studies has been to acquaint the civic-minded citizen with the faults of the public education administration. *But corrective measures have been frustrated by the Teachers Union.*[57]

Membership in the Teachers Union had grown greatly during the 1930s. The younger teachers joining the union brought with them their political concerns and a zeal for organizing. Their Rank and File Caucus succeeded in ousting Henry Linville and Abraham Lefkowitz from leadership in 1935, and replacing them with a coalition slate headed by Charles A. Hendley. Linville and Lefkowitz, Socialist Party members who had helped found the union in 1916, bitterly opposed the efforts of the caucus to make the union more militant. So adamant were they in their opposition to the caucus that they tried to expel a group of six teachers active in it on charges of disrupting the union in 1932 and 1933. The six, including Isador Begun, an official of the Communist Party in New York state, were tried by a committee headed by John Dewey and found guilty, but were not suspended from the union for want of a necessary two-thirds vote of the delegates. After Linville and Lefkowitz lost power in the local, they began pressing the AFT to revoke the local's charter on the grounds that it had been taken over by the Communist Party. They finally succeeded at the AFT convention in the summer of 1940, when the charters of the New York, Philadelphia, and several other left-wing locals were revoked. Both Zitron and Dodd agree that Linville and Lefkowitz were responsible for this act of revenge, which undermined the union and made it vulnerable to the committee.[58]

These events would have been harmful enough to the teachers and their union had it not been for the signing of the Nazi-Soviet Non-Aggression Pact in August 1939 and the national red scare which soon followed. Any organization to which party members belonged became vulnerable to attack in the period between the signing of the pact and U.S. entry into the war. In the minds of the committee investigators, the Communist Party and the Teachers Union were the same. Their identification of the union with the party was part of a simmering reactionary campaign against teachers' unions and public education, one that could now see possible victory thanks to changed circumstances.

The investigators were particularly eager to track down the teachers who contributed to the Communist Party "shop" papers at Brooklyn College and City College.[59] Because they wrote anonymously for the papers, these teachers were branded by the committee as guilty of "conspirative fraud." The investigators believed that these same people had captured control of the Teachers Union. The committee saw the union as no more than a front for the party at the colleges, as the "legal apparatus" created for Communist teachers who could not disclose their membership in the "illegal apparatus" of the party.[60] Yet the party remained a legal political organization and its supposed illegality was never defined. The investigators might be thought disingenuous for believing that members of the Communist Party working at the public colleges in the 1930s and early 1940s hid their identities solely for conspiratorial reasons. While there might have been other reasons for a party member to conceal that fact, it is undeniable that fear of administrative reprisals, including firing, was very real indeed.[61] The investigators believed that the party had intended to "capture" City College by first capturing the Teachers Union, then by extending the union's influence throughout the college, and finally by imposing its "democratization plan" on the Board of Higher Education.[62]

Isolated and probably unaware of the peril they faced, the activist teachers at City College sought in vain for a way to defend themselves. The defense strategy they did adopt may have hastened their demise. The sudden announcement of the Nazi-Soviet Pact in late August 1939 and the deepening isolation of the party in the following year probably left the activists at City uncertain of how to react, unsure even how dramatically their political context was changing. Their fortunes were no longer what they had been in 1936, when dismissal of the thirteen City College activists led to labor demonstrations and widespread and ultimately successful demands for their reinstatement. Now the times were different, but in later years many of the committee's victims acknowledged that they were unaware of this sea-change at the time it occurred.

Their strategy, as Morris Schappes recounted it, was based on an insight attributed to Morris Raphael Cohen, the well-known philosopher who had left City College to teach at Harvard. Cohen is reported to have said: "Why should you tell the police the truth? They wouldn't know what to do with it." And Schappes and the others were convinced that, just as the police would not recognize the truth when they saw it, so too the public would not think the worse of them for concocting a story that would save them from betraying their comrades to the committee. They decided that Schappes alone would admit he had been a member of the party until he resigned in 1939 to devote more time to scholarship. He also testified at the committee hearing that during the years of his membership he knew only four other people at City College who were also members of the party, and that three of them went off to fight in the Spanish Civil War, never to return, and the fourth resigned. This allowed him to testify and still avoid naming names. Since the accused could not refuse to testify and still hope to hold on to their jobs (the Board of Higher Education had voted to fire those who did not cooperate), and no one had yet used the Fifth Amendment defense in such cases, Schappes' testimony looked, from their point of view, like the way to escape the impossible dilemma of betrayal on the one hand or certain firing on the other. But not only was Schappes probably the most prominent of all the party members at City College in the 1930s, he was also the only teacher who was known as a contributor to the party "shop paper," the *Teacher-Worker*. His testimony, acknowledging party membership but refusing to name anyone beside the three fallen comrades and the one who resigned, rang false and outraged the committee.

In the spring of 1941, the Manhattan district attorney and future governor, Thomas Dewey, sought to have a grand jury indict Schappes for perjury in lying to the Rapp Coudert Committee. Schappes was a potential target because of his visibility, but the indictment probably became inevitable when he testified that there had been only five party members at City College, and that he alone remained.

Convicted of perjury in 1942, Schappes served thirteen and one half months in state penitentiaries. David Riesman, who had been an assistant district attorney in Dewey's office, wrote Schappes to congratulate him when the City University Board of Trustees (the successor to the Board of Higher Education) apologized to the Rapp Coudert victims in 1981. Riesman claimed an "inconsequential part" in his prosecution, one that "gave me great ambivalence at the time, and many moments of remorse since then."[63] He acknowledged that the Fifth Amendment was not an appropriate defense at the time, but suggested that a First Amendment defense would have allowed the accused to talk "freely about one's own past" although "running the risk of a contempt citation by refusing to name accomplices...." Whether a First Amendment defense was plausible for those called before the committee cannot be known; those who refused to name "accomplices," as Riesman put it, would probably have lost their jobs anyway. That Riesman was troubled by his part in the affair is clear from his comments on it in an earlier article, where he lamented the absence of "resignation [as] part of the American official culture," probably by way of regretting that he himself had not resigned to protest Schappes' persecution.[64] Schappes was the only Rapp Coudert victim ever charged with committing a crime.

Conclusion

Two conclusions are readily apparent and nearly self-evident from the record. The first is that the Rapp Coudert Committee succeeded brilliantly in its goal of purging the public colleges, and indeed the public school system as well, of those it suspected of belonging to the Communist Party or of working with the party in trade union and related activities. It did this by enlisting the cooperation of public education officials, who quickly succumbed to the pressure the committee exerted on them. It was the board members and the college presidents who actually constructed the means of purging the accused professors and staff, a purge that the committee sought but did not have the power to carry out on its own. At the time, little help was available to those who were, in essence, tried, convicted and punished by the Rapp Coudert Committee, often in the press, and always without benefit of due process or the opportunity even to testify fully in their own behalf. The first successful legal challenge to such means of repression did not come for nearly twenty years.[65]

The second conclusion follows directly from the first: the Rapp Coudert Committee succeeded in making the board and the colleges themselves responsible for prohibiting certain kinds of political dissidence. After some initial hesitation, the board acted swiftly to carry out its part in trying, on charges of conduct unbecoming a member of the staff, and dismissing those people the Rapp Coudert Committee brought to its attention. The presidents of Brooklyn College and of City College also fully supported the committee's goal of purging their campuses of political activists. Some time was needed for these officials to figure out how to do the committee's bidding, but the record shows clearly how hard they worked at this task.

Finally, it was the faculty and staff of the colleges that the Rapp Coudert Committee wanted to imbue with vigilance in policing their own institutions. To some extent, the committee saw success even as it worked in the early 1940s: it reported six cooperative witnesses on the basis of whose testimony the charges against the others were brought. Ultimately, to what extent the committee succeeded in changing the climate of tolerance for political dissent within the faculty of the public colleges, and among intellectuals in general, remains to be measured and judged. Yet, to replace that tolerance with a vigilant orthodoxy was the broad purpose of the committee's work. It is clear, even from this brief account, that the committee's activities had what could be termed a "chilling effect" on the employees of the public colleges. In this measure, the Rapp Coudert Committee did achieve its broad goal, at least for a time.

By World War II, the influence of the Communist Party and of the causes it was allied with in the 1930s was broken in the public colleges of New York. Teachers suspected of being Communists were fired and subsequently banned from teaching in public institutions. Those named by informers but not fired by 1942 were subsequently investigated by the McCarran Committee on Internal Security of the U.S. Senate, which took on one of Windels' investigators, Robert Morris, and presumably his unfinished business as well.[66] Those who lost their jobs continued to contribute to U.S. democracy in whatever ways were available to them. But New York's public colleges were free of them, and later generations of teachers and students could see from their example the risks of unorthodox political activity.

In October 1981, more than forty years after the Rapp Coudert Committee opened its investigation, the victims of its purge won vindication. After a year-long campaign, the City University Board of Trustees adopted a resolution apologizing to the victims for the injustice inflicted on them, although it offered no promise of any compensation. Instead, it expressed "its profound regret at the injustice done to former colleagues on the faculty and staff of the university who were dismissed or forced to resign because of their alleged political associations and beliefs and their unwillingness to testify publicly about them." The board also pledged "diligently to safeguard the constitutional rights of freedom of expression, freedom of association and open intellectual inquiry" in the university. For the several score teachers and staff members who lost their jobs in the early 1940s, this resolution offered little consolation, but for those working in the public colleges at other threatening moments in U.S. history, it does offer some hope for an outcome better than the one their elders faced forty years earlier.

Notes

The author wishes to acknowledge the help of Barbara Caress, who shared in the early research for this study and who participated actively in the 1981 campaign to win a Board of Trustees apology to the victims of the Rapp Coudert Committee. Also, Marvin Gettleman generously shared his vast archival material on the Rapp Coudert affair and lent his encouragement to this project. Morris Schappes provided his own records and recollections of the era and inspiration to pursue the truth.

1. See Merle Curti, *Roots of American Loyalty* (New York: Columbia University Press, 1946), p. ix. See also Robert Iverson, *The Communists and the Schools* (New York: Harcourt Brace, 1959), p. 13; David Caute, *The Great Fear: The Anti-Communist Purge Under Truman and Eisenhower* (New York: Simon and Schuster, 1978), p. 403; and Ellen Schrecker, *No Ivory Tower: McCarthyism and the Universities* (New York: Oxford University Press, 1986), passim.
2. See Maurice Isserman, *Which Side Were You On? The American Communist Party During the Second World War* (Middletown, CT: Wesleyan University Press, 1982), pp. 67–69.
3. See Caute, *The Great Fear*, p. 404.
4. Cited in Clara Zitron, *The New York City Teachers Union, 1916–1964* (New York: Humanities Press, 1968), p. 191.
5. See *New York Times*, 26 March 1940.
6. See *Report of the Sub-committee Relative to the Public Educational System of the City of New York*, New York State Legislative Documents, 165th Session, X(1942), no. 48: 22.
7. Ibid., p. 23.
8. See transcript of interview with Morris Schappes by Lawrence Chamberlain, 12 August 1949, p. 2 (in possession of the author).
9. Cited in Lawrence Chamberlain, *Loyalty and Legislative Action* (Ithaca, NY: Cornell University Press, 1951), p. 162.
10. See *New York Times*, 7 April 1940.
11. See *New York Times*, 6 May 1940.
12. See Paul Windels, Columbia University Oral History Collection, vol. II, p. 145.
13. Ibid., p. 147.
14. See Chamberlain, *Loyalty and Legislative Action*, p. 79.
15. Ibid., p. 80.
16. See Windels, Columbia University Oral History Collection, vol. II, p. 162.
17. See *Report of the Subcommittee, passim*.
18. Ibid., pp. 339–40.

19. See typewritten mss., signed Nelson Mead, n.d. (late fall 1940), in CCNY Archives.
20. See "Remarks of Dr. Harry N. Wright, at a Special Assembly, March 12, 1941," mimeoed mss., in CCNY Archives.
21. See Wright to Windels, 14 July 1941, in CCNY Archives.
22. See Robert T. Lynd to Wright, 12 June 1941, and Wright to Lynd, 25 June 1941, in CCNY Archives.
23. See Minutes, New York City Board of Higher Education, 21 April 1941, pp. 292 ff.
24. *Report of the Subcommittee*, p. 12.
25. Morris U. Schappes, a tutor in the English Department at City College, was indicted, tried, and convicted of perjury in 1941 as a result of his testimony before the Rapp Coudert Committee.
26. *Report of the Subcommittee*, p. 10.
27. See Minutes, Board of Higher Education, calendar no. 79, 18 November 1940, p. 773.
28. See Minutes, Board of Higher Education, 6 December 1940, p. 790.
29. See Minutes, Board of Higher Education, 16 December 1940, pp. 791–93.
30. Ibid., p. 795.
31. See Minutes, Board of Higher Education, 20 January 1941, p. 77.
32. See Minutes, Board of Higher Education, 17 February 1941, p. 189.
33. See Minutes, Board of Higher Education, 17 March 1941, p. 244.
34. Ibid.
35. See Minutes, Board of Higher Education, 21 April 1941, pp. 270–71.
36. See David Riesman, "The U-2 Affair: Aftermath and After Thoughts," *Commonweal* (8 June 1962), p. 273.
37. See Chamberlain, *Loyalty and Legislative Action*, pp. 178–79.
38. Ibid., p. 125 (emphasis in original).
39. See *Report of the New York City Subcommittee*, New York State Legislative Document, No. 60 (1944): 401, 413.
40. Ibid., pp. 556-57.
41. See Iverson, *Communists and the Schools*, chap. 6, *passim*.
42. Ibid., pp. 128–29.
43. See interview with Morris Schappes, 18 September 1981.
44. See Bella V. Dodd, *School of Darkness* (New York: P.J. Kennedy and Sons, 1954), pp. 72–73.
45. See transcript, Rapp Coudert Committee Public Hearing, 2 December 1940, vol. I, pp. 23–24, 35, in Board of Higher Education Archives.
46. See Sidney Eisenberger, "Communism on Campus: Recollections of a Former Communist Teacher at CCNY" (unpublished mss., 1981), chap. 7, p. 6.
47. See Schappes interview, 18 September 1981.
48. See Mark Naison, *Communists in Harlem During the Depression* (Urbana: University of Illinois Press, 1983), p. 293.

49. See "Statement by Dr. Max Yergan on his non-reappointment as Lecturer in Negro History at the College of the City of New York," 16 May 1941, p. 2, mimeographed mss. in CCNY Archives.
50. See "Interview between Dr. Lloyd Motz and Professors Wright, Gottschall and Sonkin concerning the reappointment of Dr. Motz to the Evening Session," September 1941, typewritten mss. in CCNY Archives.
51. See Lewis Balamuth, "Statement at Rapp Coudert Public Hearing," 24 March 1941, mimeographed mss. in CCNY Archives.
52. See Oliver letter, n.d., in CCNY Archives.
53. See letter, dated 9 March 1941, signed by six former officers of the Douglass Society, in CCNY Archives.
54. See Balamuth, "Statement," pp. 5–6.
55. See transcript, Rapp Coudert Committee Public Hearing, 2 December 1940, Vol. I, pp. 5–7.
56. Ibid., pp. 132–33.
57. Cited in Zitron, *The New York City Teachers Union*, pp. 192–93. Emphasis is Zitron's.
58. Ibid.; Dodd, *School of Darkness*, pp. 127–28.
59. See Marvin Gettleman, "Communists in Higher Education; CCNY and Brooklyn College on the Eve of the Rapp Coudert Investigation, 1935–1939," unpublished paper presented at April 1977 meeting of the Organization of American Historians, *passim.*, for discussion of the party "shop" papers.
60. See *Report of the Subcommittee*, p. 246.
61. Almost all of those charged with party membership were in the lower ranks, ineligible for tenure until the reforms of 1938.
62. See *Report of the Subcommittee*, p. 291.
63. See Riesman to Schappes, 5 January 1982, copy in possession of the author.
64. See Riesman, "The U-2 Affair," p. 273, 275.
65. See Chamberlain, *Loyalty and Legislative Action*, especially pp. 110–25.
66. See Caute, *The Great Fear*, pp. 105–06, 439.

McCARTHYISM AND THE DECLINE OF AMERICAN COMMUNISM, 1945–1960

Ellen Schrecker

The U.S. Communist Party (CP) has been around for seventy years. Since the late 1950s its impact on U.S. society has been marginal. Such was not always the case. During the 1930s and early 1940s the party was at the center of a dynamic social, cultural, and political movement that challenged the status quo and served as the primary conduit for a socialist critique of U.S. society. Its position as the institutional core of that broader movement of political activists and organizations enabled the CP to dominate the U.S. left and exert its authority far beyond the reach of its own membership. When that movement disappeared, the party's influence waned as well. Thus, if we are to understand the decline of U.S. Communism, we must look at the *movement* as well as the *party*. Once we do that and we examine U.S. Communism as part of the broader communist movement, we must reassess the reasons for its decline. This is because even the best of the earlier scholarship on the issue is dominated by the top-down approach that characterizes most CP historiography. These studies focus on party policy and on the response of the party leadership to the crises of the early Cold War era in the late 1940s and 1950s. While the party's leaders and policies can hardly be ignored, a top-down approach excludes much of what is essential about U.S. Communism and its day-to-day activities. Such an approach argues that most of the party's problems were self-inflicted, the product of the leadership's obedience to the dictates of Moscow and its unimaginative response to the political repression of the McCarthy era.[1] Even those scholars who recognize the importance of outside forces nevertheless focus on the party's leadership and claim that many of the CP's errors resulted from misguided attempts to fend off the onslaught it faced, if not—as in the well-documented story of the FBI's COINTELPRO program of direct disruption—actual governmental initiatives.[2] However, once we get beyond the leadership of

U.S. Communism and look at the movement from the bottom up, external factors seem increasingly more important to its decline.

This essay will explore the actual process through which those external forces—of which the state was by far the most important— contributed to the collapse of U.S. Communism. Much of that process can be identified with the anticommunist crusade of the late 1940s and 1950s that, for want of a better word, we call McCarthyism. There was nothing random about the McCarthyist onslaught against the CP. It targeted the party, of course, but it also attacked the movement, imposing sanctions on the entire constellation of organizations and individuals that lay within the CP's orbit. Of particular importance were the so-called "front groups" or "mass organizations" that all good communists were expected to join.[3] These were the groups through which the party was able to amplify its influence and reach far beyond its own membership. And these were the groups whose demise, directly attributable to McCarthyism, was so lethal to the party.[4]

Historians have only recently begun to study these organizations.[5] Accordingly, it may well be that the relatively lopsided interpretation of the decline of U.S. Communism stems from the lack of available studies of its front groups. Certainly, during the heyday of U.S. Communism, the importance of these organizations to the party was widely recognized. There were hundreds of them, ranging from summer camps and choral societies to trade unions and legal defense groups. They created a separate culture, a separate world, really, that reinforced and strengthened their members' political commitments.[6] In addition to their specific work promoting such causes as racial equality, anti-fascism, and labor organizing, these groups brought in new members and provided full-time jobs for party activists. Thus, for example, of the 766 delegates to the New York State Communist Party convention in 1938, 106 were full-time CP functionaries, 208 were labor union officials, and 253 held positions in the front groups.[7]

The relationship between the party and its adjunct organizations was close. Many, if not most, of the leaders of these groups belonged to the party, but many others did not. These Communists with a small "c" were crucial to the movement, if not to the party. In his memoir, *Loyalties*, Carl Bernstein offers us a detailed portrait of this type of communist. His parents had become involved with the left during the 1930s: his father as a union organizer, his mother as a supporter of the Spanish Republic. They joined the party in 1942 and resigned in 1947; but they did not desert the movement. They functioned as full-time activists—in labor unions, civil rights groups, and the Committee to Defend the Rosenbergs—until the demise in the mid-1950s of virtually all the organizations through which they expressed themselves politically.[8]

The broader movement that the Bernsteins, and thousands of small "c" communists like them, embraced did not survive the destruction of its constituent organizations; nor did the Communist Party survive in a politically significant way the disappearance of that broader movement. Their specialized functions did protect the adjunct organizations and labor unions from some of the CP's misguided directives.[9] But, as the political repression of the McCarthy period intensified, nothing could protect these organizations and their members from the ravages of the official campaign against U.S. Communism. Here, I must stress the word "official." The McCarthyist assault of the late 1940s and early 1950s owed its effectiveness to the federal government, which committed all the resources of the modern state to the eradication of U.S. Communism. Private groups and individuals were involved as well, but their activities were if not the direct result of a governmental initiative (as with the firing of witnesses who refused to cooperate with a Congressional investigation) at least legitimized by official support. The anticommunist furor defies a simple explanation.[10] At the time, most observers identified McCarthyism with the bizarre demagoguery of the senator for whom it was named and, accordingly, viewed it as a kind of aberrant right-wing populism.[11] By the early 1970s, however, scholars had revised that interpretation and had come to see McCarthyism as an elite phenomenon, the product of a complex interaction between the Truman administration's need to enlist public support for its foreign policy and the Republican Party's search for a popular domestic issue.[12]

The advent of the Cold War was crucial. There has always been a strain of hostility to socialism and communism in U.S. political culture, but, until the struggle with the Soviet Union pushed anticommunism to the top of the national agenda, it had usually been a peripheral issue whose main proponents tended to congregate on the extreme right of the U.S. polity.[13] By the late 1940s, however, these anticommunists suddenly found that the rest of the nation shared their concerns. As a result, in large part because they had been fighting the CP for years, and had like FBI director J. Edgar Hoover become, as it were, "experts" in the field, these groups and individuals were in a position to impose their own methods and ideology on the rest of the nation.[14] The widespread political repression that ensued was the result.

Although extreme manifestations of McCarthyism such as the removal of *Robin Hood* from the shelves of school libraries in Indiana clearly reflected the ideological fixations of the far right, Americans of all persuasions joined the crusade. Political opportunists like Joe McCarthy and Richard Nixon were eager converts. Still, most of the bureaucrats, politicians, journalists, and private employers who investigated and then punished supposed subversives were moderate, decent, often liberal individuals who viewed Communism as a threat to the nation's security and took part in the political repression of the McCarthy period out of essentially patriotic motives. Even at the time, some of these people, President Truman among them, feared that the red scare was getting out of hand.[15] Yet, because they refused to protect the civil liberties of U.S. Communists, these liberals created an opening for the violations of individual rights that they were ultimately to deplore. They seemed almost helpless when professional anticommunists like Hoover expanded the definition of Communism to embrace a wide spectrum of left-wing and liberal groups and activities.[16]

The combination of right-wing direction and mainstream collusion was deadly to the Communist movement. The federal government's activities were central here—both in fostering the anticommunist consensus that legitimized the repression, and in administering it as well. There seem to have been two separate components in the official campaign against Communism. One sought to decapitate the Communist movement by harassing and prosecuting party leaders and full-time cadres, the other to discourage people from joining the movement by punishing its rank-and-file members. Every branch of the government was involved. While the FBI was preeminent, other participants included the State, Treasury, and Justice departments, the White House, the Immigration and Naturalization Service (INS), the Civil Service Commission, the Internal Revenue Service, the Subversive Activities

Control Board (SACB), the National Labor Relations Board (NLRB), the Post Office, and, of course, Congress and its investigating committees. The federal judiciary collaborated indirectly by failing to place any substantive constitutional limits on what the rest of the government was doing.

Local governments and private institutions were also involved, especially in those aspects of the anticommunist drive that were directed against rank-and-file radicals. As employers of supposedly "subversive" individuals, corporations, universities, school boards, and labor unions administered the economic sanctions that were perhaps the most important weapons in the McCarthyist arsenal. They took action against those of their employees who had been publicly associated with Communism or had been labelled as politically undesirable by official bodies like the FBI or the House Un-American Activities Committee (HUAC). From Harvard to Hollywood, private employers fired, blacklisted, or otherwise punished the men and women who had been involved with the Communist movement in the 1930s and 1940s.[17]

The multi-pronged nature of the onslaught ensured its success. The cumulative effect of thousands of separate attacks on individuals and organizations ultimately destroyed the political base of U.S. Communism. None of this is news. Historians have documented many of the various phases of this assault on the Communist movement. What they have yet to do is integrate their findings and show how the apparently disparate actions directed against the movement's leaders and its rank and file were interrelated.[18]

The first part of that assault, the campaign against the party's top leaders and most active cadres, involved direct governmental harassment, often in the form of criminal prosecutions. The government relied on legal proceedings for several reasons. In the first place, the tools of criminal justice were already at hand. Precedents existed, statutes were on the books, and the various bureaucracies had already developed techniques for dealing with political dissenters through the criminal justice system. Moreover, the sanctions that federal prosecutions involved—prison sentences and deportations in particular—were effective means of stifling the activities of individual leaders.[19]

Even more important was the role that criminal prosecutions played in publicizing Washington's view of the Communist danger.

Political trials, as Otto Kirchheimer notes, are invaluable for "dramatizing the struggle with the foe and rallying public support."[20] The major Communist cases of the late 1940s and early 1950s helped the government promote its campaign against the party. The first Smith Act prosecution of Eugene Dennis and the other top leaders of the Communist Party was crucial. Limited though it was by the language of the statute, with its emphasis on "teaching and advocating" revolution, the prosecution was nonetheless able to use the trial to create and disseminate a politically useful image of the party as a dangerous conspiracy under the direct control of Moscow. This interpretation, crucially reinforced by the Supreme Court's 1951 decision to sustain the Communist leaders' conviction, deprived the CP of all legitimacy in the eyes of most U.S. citizens and made it considerably easier to enlist private sector support for the imposition of sanctions against individuals identified with this now officially designated "subversive" organization. Successful though it was, the use of legal sanctions to marginalize U.S. Communism was not without problems. The government wanted to use criminal proceedings to dramatize its case against the party and its affiliated organizations, but the structure of the U.S. legal system required prosecuting specific individuals for specific offenses.[21] Nonetheless, whenever they could, officials at both the state and federal levels did try to administer sanctions directly against the party, the front groups, and the left-wing unions. But few tools were available; and some of them, such as the 1950 Internal Security Act's requirement that the party and its front groups register with the Subversive Activities Control Board, raised serious constitutional issues and involved prolonged litigation. As a result, the government usually prosecuted individuals, even though the circumstances of these prosecutions made it clear that the CP and the rest of the movement were the real targets. Top party officials and leaders of the left-led unions and adjunct organizations often faced as many as three or four separate proceedings. Smith Act indictments were the most important, but a high-level party leader or union official could also be prosecuted for perjury, contempt of Congress, failure to register as an individual with the Subversive Activities Control Board (SACB), and, if he or she was foreign born, threatened with deportation or denaturalization as well. Thanks to the work of Michael

The "second string" of CP leaders indicted under the Smith Act, approximate date June 1951. Seated, left to right: party legal aide Marion Bachrach, whose indictment was later dropped due to ill health; Harlem party leader Claudia Jones, a West Indian who was deported to England; former Unemployed Councils leader Israel Amter; Elizabeth Gurley Flynn, a legendary figure from the heyday of the Industrial Workers of the World; Betty Gannett, CP organization secretary. Standing, left to right: party theoretician Alexander Bittelman; founding member William W. Weinstone; Bronx party leader Israel Begun; Arnold Johnson, a party administrator; V.J. Jerome, editor of the party theoretical journal *Political Affairs*; Simon Gerson, formerly legislative assistant to Manhattan borough president Stanley Isaacs; Painters Union leader Louis Weinstock; maritime labor leader Al Lannon; CP Negro Commission chair Pettis Perry; Alexander Trachtenberg, founder of International Publishers; Manhattan organizer George Blake Charney. Photo courtesy of the Reference Center for Marxist Studies.

Belknap and Peter Steinberg, the impact of the Smith Act cases on the Communist Party has been well-documented. The other prosecutions have received less attention. David Caute, Stanley Kutler, and Carl Beck have studied some of them, though there is as yet no systematic examination of the SACB proceedings or the INS's deportation campaign. In any event, none of the relevant literature has assessed the impact of federal prosecutions on the communist movement as a whole.[22] Party leaders and key activists were also prosecuted by state and local authorities. Pennsylvania's attempt to convict Steve Nelson for sedition was the most well-known of these actions. Nelson, who also faced contempt of Congress, Smith Act, and deportation proceedings, won his case in the Supreme

Court, but not until after he had spent considerable time in jail.[23] Clearly designed to harass party leaders, some of these prosecutions involved the selective enforcement of trivial regulations. Ohio party leader Frank Hashmall, for example, went to prison for falsifying his address when he applied for a driver's license.[24] Again, we know very little about these state proceedings; with the one exception of the fine work of Don Carleton on Texas, the literature on the state and local red scares is either dated or inadequate.[25]

Left-wing unions, their leaders, and rank-and-file activists were special targets. These unions were, after all, the most important institutions to have been influenced by the CP. The literature on Communists in the labor movement is growing, with some useful work by Steven Rosswurm, Josh Freeman, Harvey Levenstein, Bruce Nelson, Bert Cochran, Roger Keeran, and others. But most of these scholars emphasize the internal purges within the labor movement and acknowledge the federal government's activities only in passing.[26] Thus, for example, there are only sporadic references to the impact of the many congressional investigations into the labor movement and the contempt citations that often accompanied them, this even though many of the key prosecutions involved such top officials of the Communist-led unions as Julius Emspak and James Matles of the Union of Electrical, Radio, and Machine Workers (UE) and Abram Flaxner of the United Federal Workers (UFW). Similarly, although the INS's decades-long struggle to deport the Longshoremen's leader, Harry Bridges, is well-known, its attempt to deport dozens of lesser known union officials or their spouses is not.[27] Equally unstudied is the federal prosecution of union officials for falsifying the non-communist affidavits required by the Taft-Hartley Act. Here, NLRB records and the pattern of these prosecutions, especially the 1956 conspiracy indictment of fourteen Mine, Mill, and Smelter Workers Union leaders, make it quite clear that the government was trying to punish unions, not individuals.[28]

The leaders of the front organizations also faced criminal prosecutions and deportation proceedings. Because the scholarship on these groups is still rather scant, the standard accounts of the McCarthy era often ignore the significance of the officially sponsored attacks on these people. They treat their cases as individual prosecutions, rather than as part of an attack on the organizations that they led. Again, as with the party's top leaders, many of these important cadres found themselves facing several different prosecutions at once. Rose Chernin, the Los Angeles director of the party-linked immigration defense organization, the American Committee for Protection of Foreign Born (ACPFB), had to contend with denaturalization proceedings as well as a Smith Act indictment.[29]

At the same time as the Communist movement's leading cadres were fighting their own individual cases, they also had to fend off attacks on their organizations. First, there was the attorney general's list to contend with, then the requirement to register with the SACB. After the passage of the Communist Control Act of 1954 extended the reach of the SACB to labor unions, the Eisenhower administration ordered UE and Mine-Mill to register. The labor left faced other sanctions as well. The government's security regulations barred left-wing unions like UE from representing workers in sensitive defense industries. The National Labor Relations Board tried to use the anticommunist provisions of the Taft-Hartley Act to decertify the left-led unions. There were financial sanctions as well, directed against both the party and the adjunct organizations. The IRS was active here, so too were New York State authorities. The insurance commissioner simply forced the International Workers Order (IWO) out of business; and the attorney general tried to deprive the ACPFB of its status as a charity.[30]

The individuals and organizations involved fought their cases with all the legal weapons at their command—and often won. Thus, for example, although as many as 15,000 people may have been affected by the INS's anticommunist proceedings, only 253 aliens were officially deported as political subversives between 1946 and 1966.[31] Similarly, only 28 of the 145 party leaders indicted under the Smith Act actually served prison sentences after their convictions, though many of them were, it is true, incarcerated at one time or another during the course of their trials or appeals.[32] Lengthy litigation and the Supreme Court's increasing willingness to offer procedural, if not substantive, protections to the targets of anticommunist prosecutions enabled most of these people to avoid prison, deportation, or having to register with the SACB. Though the Supreme Court initially sanctioned most of the federal government's anticommunist project, by the late 1950s and early

1960s it had begun to reverse itself and void many of these people's convictions and deportations. Nonetheless, despite the widespread assumption that the judicial dismantling of the structure of political repression proved that McCarthyism had done little damage after all, these legal victories did not save U.S. Communism.[33]

The fight itself undermined the Communist movement. The cost in money, manpower, and morale was exorbitant. The struggle to fend off the government's onslaught turned the party and its adjunct organizations into self-defense groups, preoccupied with fundraising and legal strategies. The CP abandoned its other political activities and, in the words of Joseph Starobin, "became at least a case in civil liberties, at best an object of sympathy, but no longer a power."[34]

The party survived. Most of the other groups disappeared completely. Only three of the adjunct organizations outlasted the SACB's attempts to register them. For the others, the financially and personally draining struggle for institutional survival which occurred at a time when the red scare made it impossible for them to carry out their missions except on the margins of U.S. society was simply overwhelming. The Civil Rights Congress, the party's main vehicle for fighting legal repression and racial inequality, was typical. Hounded by the Justice Department, SACB, IRS, and the New York State Legislature, Banking Department, and attorney general, the organization was forced to devote most of its resources to its own defense. By the time the board of directors voted to dissolve the organization in 1956, it had essentially stopped functioning.[35] Most of the left-wing unions went under as well. With their leaders often fully engaged in staying out of jail and their locals fending off raids from other unions, the once vibrant Communist-led labor organizations became increasingly preoccupied with their own defense. Only the Longshoremen survived intact. Those unions which could arranged friendly mergers, while most of the others simply disappeared or, like the UE, dwindled into insignificance.[36]

As they fought to stay in the United States or out of jail, the men and women who were concerned with maintaining the viability of the Communist movement paid little attention to the task of recruiting. At a time when the most eager "recruits" were often FBI informers, enrolling new members was not a high priority. This failure to recruit was damaging. While the party's most important cadres remained active for decades, at the rank-and- file level political activity tended to be more sporadic. The work of Vivian Gornick and Paul Lyons, among others, shows how people joined the party or involved themselves in its adjunct organizations for a few years and then became inactive when the patterns of their lives changed and the needs of their careers and families took precedence over the often demanding requirements of political work. Ideological disillusionment was important, too; but until the McCarthy period, much of the turnover that characterized U.S. Communism is attributable to ordinary burn-out.[37]

Once McCarthyism brought recruitment to a halt, there was no way to replace the men and women who had dropped out of the movement. The formerly dynamic world of U.S. Communism turned inward. Existing organizations lost members and, except for groups dedicated to legal defense and civil liberties, no new ones appeared. Thus, for example, the Korean war, despite its controversial nature, spawned no significant peace movement. The U.S. left was both too beleaguered and too stigmatized to attract new members. At the same time, the party was becoming increasingly sectarian, which increased its isolation.

Even so, it is hard to avoid the conclusion that the federal government's attack on the Communist movement accounts for much of its failure to recruit. The ideological offensive that was such an important element in the official drive against the party and its affiliated organizations succeeded. By the 1950s, Communism was so thoroughly discredited that any ideas, organizations, or individuals associated with it were unacceptable to most North Americans. Once marginalized in this way, the Communist movement became ineffective and, thus, could no longer attract the kind of political sympathizers who had previously been willing to collaborate with, if not join, the party and its affiliated organizations. More importantly, however, working with the Communist movement had become too dangerous.

Here, we encounter the second half of the McCarthy-era onslaught against U.S. Communism: the attack on its rank-and-file members and former members. This is the aspect of the red scare that received the most attention at the time. Certainly, it had the widest reach. Unlike the federal government's more direct attack on the party and its constituent organizations, the sanctions employed were economic, not criminal. First, the supposed Communists were identified, usually by an official agency like the FBI or a congressional investigating committee. Then, they were punished, usually by the loss of their jobs. The willingness of private employers—from GM and MGM to New York University and the *New York Times*—to collaborate with this process and fire their politically undesirable employees indicates the effectiveness of the government's campaign to stigmatize the Communist movement and make its elimination a matter of national security.

The imposition of political tests for employment affected millions of Americans; Ralph Brown estimated that as many as 13.5 million Americans, perhaps one-fifth of the entire workforce, were involved. The actual number of victims, of course, was much less, probably only in the tens of thousands.[38] The most common targets were Communists, former Communists, or people who had once belonged to or worked with the organizations that formed the Communist movement. They were not, in that sense, innocent victims. Nor were they dispersed randomly through the U.S. population, but were rather concentrated in those sectors of society where the Communist movement had been most influential—organized labor, education, the communications industries, and the legal and helping professions. Scholars have been examining this aspect of McCarthyism for years and the literature on such subjects as the Hollywood blacklists, academic purges, and federal loyalty-security program is both sophisticated and extensive.[39]

We know only too well the human costs of this aspect of McCarthyism, the professional and psychological toll that unemployment and blacklisting exacted. But less attention has been given to the political costs of these economic sanctions. Nevertheless, once we place the politically motivated dismissals of the McCarthy era in the broader context of the overall attack on U.S. Communism, their specific function becomes clear. The economic sanctions that were directed against the people who had participated in the adjunct organizations or their activities made it impossible for those organizations to retain their ordinary members or recruit new ones. The cost of involvement with any aspect of the Communist movement was too high for all but the most dedicated activists. As a result, with both its leadership and its base under attack, the Communist movement that had once been such a vibrant force in U.S. life disappeared.

Although the CP survived, without that broader movement to spread its influence beyond the confines of its own membership, it became marginal and ineffective. Governmental repression, by destroying all the institutional connections between the party and the rest of U.S. society, had succeeded in isolating the CP. Isolation, of course, only enhanced the party's penchant for sectarian in-fighting. As a result, when Khrushchev's revelations about Stalin's crimes at the twentieth Soviet party congress in 1956 precipitated an internal struggle, many of the protagonists recognized the futility of an all-out battle to regain control of a ghost organization and left the party instead.[40] Had there been something more worthwhile to fight for, had a major Communist movement still existed, perhaps these people would not have deserted the battlefield. In that case, the history of U.S. Communism, and perhaps of U.S. politics itself, might well have been different. We'll never know.

Notes

1. Perhaps the most convincing, certainly the most informed, of the self-destruction interpretations is that of Joseph Starobin, the former foreign editor of the *Daily Worker*. In *American Communism in Crisis* (Cambridge, MA: Harvard University Press, 1972), Starobin amplifies the earlier mainstream interpretation, best exemplified by David Shannon's near contemporaneous *The Decline of American Communism* (New York: Harcourt, Brace and Co., 1959) that views the party's disintegration as the product of such mistakes as its support for the third party presidential campaign of Henry Wallace in 1948, its decision to send large numbers of cadres underground, and its unfortunate political purges and "white chauvinism" campaign. More recently, Maurice Isserman's *If I Had a Hammer* (New York: Basic Books, 1987) reinforces this interpretation by emphasizing the "shock of 1956" and the way in which the revelations about Stalin's crimes made by Nikita Khrushchev at the Twentieth Soviet Communist Party Congress in 1956 forced the more independent and idealistic cadres to criticize and then ultimately leave the party.

    Another version of the self-destruction scenario is offered by scholars who are primarily concerned about the disappearance of a militant working-class movement. These people insist that the CP's reformist behavior before and during World War II prevented it from challenging U.S. capitalism and building the militant working-class constituency that could have offered it the mass support it needed to defend itself during the cold war. See John Gerassi, "The Comintern, the Fronts, and the CPUSA," *supra*; James R. Prickett, "New Perspectives on American Communism and the Labor Movement," Frank Emspak, "The Breakup of the CIO," and Ronald Filippelli, "UE: An Uncertain Legacy," all in Maurice Zeitlin and Howard Kimeldorf, eds., *Political Power and Social Theory*, vol. 4 (Greenwich, CT: JAI Press, 1984).

2. For information on COINTELPRO, see Athan Theoharis, *Spying on Americans* (Philadelphia: Temple University Press, 1978), pp. 133–40, and Frank J. Donner, *The Age of Surveillance* (New York: Random House, 1980), pp. 177–95. The studies that stress the external reasons for the party's demise are Michal Belknap, *Cold War Political Justice: The Smith Act, the Communist Party, and American Civil Liberties* (Westport, CT: Greenwood Press, 1977) and Peter Steinberg, *The Great "Red Menace": United States Prosecution of American Communists, 1947–1952* (Westport, CT: Greenwood Press, 1984).

3. It is difficult to find an appropriate term for these organizations. "Mass" only few of them were; and "front" was a derogatory term, though not always an imprecise one. The groups were Communist-dominated, but that is not all they were. This essay reflects that underlying reality by referring to these organizations by several different terms.

4. Mark Naison, "Remaking America: Communists and Liberals in the Popular Front," *supra*, is a good summary of this interpretation by the most sophisticated historian of U.S. Communism.

5. One reason why the literature is so sparse is because the writers assigned to deal with the "front organizations" and the labor movement in the Fund for the Republic's series on Communism in American Life never completed their assignments. The most comprehensive account of these groups is by Harvey Klehr, *Heyday of American Communism* (New York: Basic Books, 1984), but it only deals with the 1930s. Roger Keeran is working on a study of the International Workers Order. See also Gerald Horne, *Communist Front? The Civil Rights Congress* (Rutherford, NJ: Fairleigh Dickinson University Press, 1987). There is somewhat more information about the Communist-influenced labor movement, a few studies of specific unions, Harvey A. Levenstein's useful survey, *Communism, Anticommunism, and the CIO* (Westport, CT: Greenwood Press, 1981) and Steven Rosswurm, ed., *The CIO's Left-led Unions* (New Brunswick, NJ: Rutgers University Press, 1992).

6. Robbie Lieberman, *"My Song Is My Weapon": People's Songs, American Communism and the Politics of Culture, 1930–1950* (Champaign: University of Illinois Press, 1989), pp. xiv, 14–19.

7. Nathan Glazer, *The Social Basis of American Communism* (New York: Harcourt, Brace & World, 1961), p. 219.

8. Carl Bernstein, *Loyalties* (New York: Simon and Schuster, 1989).

9. One of the most notorious instances in which party dictates caused serious problems for cadres in its auxiliary organizations was its insistence on having them endorse Henry Wallace's third party presidential campaign in 1948. That demand led directly to the defection of one of the CP's most important labor union leaders, Mike Quill of the Transit Workers Union. See Joshua Freeman, *In Transit* (New York: Oxford University Press, 1989).

10. Again, terminology creates problems. Despite my own sense that the term "McCarthyism" is historically specific and refers quite clearly to the anticommunist furor of the 1940s and 1950s, I have been criticized for using it. For a more extended discussion of this problem, see Ellen W. Schrecker, "Archival Sources for the Study of McCarthyism," *Journal of American History* 75, no. 1 (June 1988): 197.

11. The most influential proponents of the populist interpretation of McCarthyism were Richard Hofstadter and his fellow contributors to the collection of essays, edited by Daniel Bell, *The New American Right* (New York: Criterion, 1955).

12. Michael Paul Rogin demolished the populist interpretation in *McCarthy and the Intellectuals* (Cambridge, MA: MIT Press, 1967). For a few of the many studies that present McCarthyism as an ordinary political phenomenon, see Robert Griffith, *The Politics of Fear* (Lexington, KY: The University Press of Kentucky, 1970); Athan Theoharis, *Seeds of Repression* (Chicago: Quadrangle, 1971); and Richard Freeland, *The Truman Doctrine and the Origins of McCarthyism* (New York: Schocken, 1971).

13. For an intriguing discussion of the countersubversive ideology, see Michael Rogin, *Ronald Reagan: The Movie* (Berkeley: University of California Press, 1987). A useful survey of the long history of U.S. anticommunism is M.J. Heale, *American Anticommunism: Combating the Enemy Within, 1830–1970* (Baltimore: The Johns Hopkins University Press, 1990).

14. The best discussions of J. Edgar Hoover and his role in the McCarthy era can be found in Athan Theoharis and John Stuart Cox, *The Boss: J. Edgar Hoover and the Great American Inquisition* (Philadelphia: Temple University Press, 1988); Athan Theoharis, ed., *Beyond the Hiss Case* (Philadelphia: Temple University Press, 1982); Kenneth O'Reilly, *Hoover and the Un-Americans* (Philadelphia: Temple Univer-

sity Press, 1983); and Richard Gid Powers, *Secrecy and Power: The Life of J. Edgar Hoover* (New York: Free Press, 1987).

15. Truman's disenchantment with the loyalty-security program he officially inaugurated is documented in Alan Harper, *The Politics of Loyalty* (Westport, CT: Greenwood Press, 1969). The most important recantation to date is that of Father Charles Owen Rice, a Catholic priest who masterminded many of the most effective attacks on the left-wing labor movement.

16. The best study of the collapse of the liberal community is Mary S. McAuliffe, *Crisis on the Left: Cold War Politics and American Liberals* (Amherst: University of Massachusetts Press, 1978).

17. For an extended discussion of the way in which private employers, in this case academic institutions, collaborated with the federal government during the McCarthy era, see Ellen W. Schrecker, *No Ivory Tower: McCarthyism and the Universities* (New York: Oxford, 1986).

18. Richard Fried's *Nightmare in Red* (New York: Oxford, 1990) is a brave attempt to put McCarthyism in perspective, though it, like David Caute's encyclopedic *The Great Fear* (New York: Simon and Schuster, 1978) is more descriptive than analytical.

19. Fruitful discussions of the political use of criminal proceedings can be found in Otto Kirchheimer, *Political Justice: The Use of Legal Procedure for Political Ends* (Princeton: Princeton University Press, 1961) and Robert Justin Goldstein, *Political Repression in Modern America: From 1870 to the Present* (Cambridge, MA: Schenkman, 1978).

20. Kirchheimer, *Political Justice*, p. 17.

21. The Justice Department attorneys who drafted the original Smith Act indictment in the Dennis case were quite aware of the problems that prosecuting individuals involved. In fact, they did not decide which party leaders to indict until the very last minute. George Kniep, memo, nd., in John F.X. McGohey Papers, Box 1, Harry S. Truman Library, Independence, MO.

22. Caute, *The Great Fear*; Stanley I. Kutler, *The American Inquisition* (New York: Hill and Wang, 1982) and Carl Beck, *Contempt of Congress* (New Orleans: Hauser Press, 1959). My own research has yielded some preliminary information on the SACB and INS proceedings. See Ellen W. Schrecker, "Introduction" to *Records of the Subversive Activities Control Board, 1950–1972*, microfilm (Frederick, MD: University Publications of America, 1989) and "'No Golden Door': McCarthyism and the Foreign Born," unpublished paper presented to the Organization of American Historians, Reno, Nevada, 1988.

23. Steve Nelson, James R. Barrett, and Rob Ruck, *Steve Nelson, American Radical* (Pittsburgh: University of Pittsburgh Press, 1981).

24. For information on the Hashmall case, see Motion to Reduce Bail,

United States v. Frank Hashmall, etc., U.S. District Court for the
Northern District of Ohio, Eastern Division, May 1955; Thelma C.
Furry to Hyman Schlesinger, 21 May 1954, in Hyman Schlesinger
papers, Series VI, Archives of Industrial Society, University of Pittsburgh, Pittsburgh, PA.

25. Don Carleton, *Red Scare! Right-Wing Hysteria, Fifties Fanaticism,
and Their Legacy in Texas* (Austin: Texas Monthly Press, 1985).
Walter Gellhorn, ed., *The States and Subversion* (Ithaca: Cornell
University Press, 1952) is excellent, but incomplete.

26. The most recent work on these unions is Steven Rosswurm, ed., *The
CIO's Left-Led Unions* (New Brunswick: Rutgers University Press,
1992). It includes an essay by the author on the federal government's
campaign against the labor left. See also Levenstein's *Communism,
Anticommunism, and the CIO*, cited *supra*; Bert Cochran, *Labor and
Communism* (Princeton: Princeton University Press, 1977); Roger
Keeran, *The Communist Party and the Auto Workers Unions* (Bloo-
mington: Indiana University Press, 1980); Freeman, *In Transit*; Bruce
Nelson, *Workers on the Waterfront* (Urbana: University of Illinois
Press, 1989); and the essays in Zeitlin and Kimeldorf, *Political Power
and Social Theory*, cited *supra*.

27. For a good discussion of the Bridges case, see Kutler, *The American
Inquisition*, pp. 118–51.

28. Ellen W. Schrecker, "McCarthyism and the Labor Movement: The
Role of the State," in Rosswurm, ed., *The CIO's Left-Led Unions*.

29. Caute, *The Great Fear*, pp. 226, 244, 367–68.

30. Caute, *The Great Fear*, lists many of these prosecutions. See also
Schrecker, "Introduction," and "'No Golden Door.'"

31. Immigration and Naturalization Service, *Annual Report*, 1956–1966.

32. Belknap, *Cold War Political Justice*, pp. 152 ff; Caute, *The Great Fear*,
p. 208.

33. The most useful compilation of the various McCarthy era legal decisions is Thomas Emerson, David Haber, and Norman Dorsen, *Political
and Civil Rights in the United States*, 3rd ed. (Boston: Little, Brown,
1967). For a fully developed presentation of the triumph-of-the-law
thesis, see Kutler, *American Inquisition*.

34. Starobin, *American Communism in Crisis*, p. 191.

35. Horne, *Communist Front?*, pp. 48–50.

36. The standard literature on the left-wing labor unions describes their
decline. See also David Brody, *The Butcher Workmen* (Cambridge:
Harvard University Press, 1964), pp. 260–61, for the story of the end
of the Fur and Leather Workers Union, and Robert S. Keitel, "The
Merger of the International Union of Mine, Mill and Smelter Workers

into the United Steelworkers of America," *Labor History* 15 (1974): 36–43, for the demise of Mine-Mill.

37. In addition to Vivian Gornick, *The Romance of American Communism* (New York: Basic Books, 1977) and Paul Lyons, *Philadelphia Communists, 1936–1956* (Philadelphia: Temple University Press, 1982), see Schrecker, *No Ivory Tower*, pp. 24–62.

38. The most useful survey of the reach of the political tests for employment is Ralph Brown, *Loyalty and Security* (New Haven: Yale University Press, 1958), pp. 166–82. Caute, *The Great Fear*, contains the most extensive listing of the victims.

39. On the entertainment industry, see Victor S. Navasky, *Naming Names* (New York: Viking, 1980) and Larry Ceplair and Steven Englund, *The Inquisition in Hollywood* (New York: Doubleday, 1979). On academe, besides Schrecker, *No Ivory Tower*, see Vern Countryman, *Un-American Activities in the State of Washington* (Ithaca: Cornell University Press, 1951) and the recent case studies by David Holmes, *Stalking the Academic Communist* (Hanover, NH: University Press of New England, 1989) and Charles H. McCormick, *This Nest of Vipers* (Urbana: University of Illinois Press, 1989). On the federal loyalty-security program, besides Brown, *Loyalty and Security*, see Bernstein, *Loyalties* and Eleanor Bontecou, *The Federal Loyalty-Security Program* (Ithaca: Cornell University Press, 1953).

40. The best account of the 1956 struggles is in Isserman, *If I Had a Hammer*, pp. 9–34.

THE QUESTION SELDOM ASKED:
Women and the CPUSA

Rosalyn Baxandall

For many working-class and immigrant women in North America, the Communist Party opened up new horizons, providing opportunities for activism in both their jobs and communities. The rich party cultural and social life educated women in the political and international arena.

Women fed and clothed sit-down strikers in the auto, steel and rubber industries, raised money by going door to door, put up posters, and threw parties for a democratic Spain, Russian war relief, and the communist insurgents in China. Members traveled, both within North America and abroad, learned to speak publicly, argue forcefully, and write articles and leaflets. No matter how disillusioned female party members I interviewed are with communist doctrine, they still acknowledge that the Communist Party of the United States enriched their lives and opened up their hearts and minds. The splits that ripped the upper echelons apart often didn't affect the rank and file directly.

The party was by no means a feminist organization, but women within it were no doubt freer and had more opportunities for activism than did those in other parties and organizations. Communists wrote books about women, like Yuri Suhl's book about Ernestine Rose, a Jewish socialist equal rights agitator; Howard Fast's short story "Rachel and Her Daughters," about an indentured servant; and Philip Foner's volumes on labor history, which included women, albeit as tokens—but at the time, even this was an advance. The Communist Party of the United States of America (CPUSA) bolstered and provided an alternative to the nuclear family, supported family members of those in jail or underground (most often only the leadership), and created a supplementary space and counterforce to U.S. nationalism and consumer culture. During the McCarthy years, the party kept the embers of female militancy alive and nourished the feminists of the 1960s and 1970s, many of whom, like myself, were red diaper babies, daughters of party members, who had read communist history books and participated in Communist picnics, hootenannies and camps.

Theory

In comparison to their focus and advanced thinking on class and race, the CPUSA and CPs internationally have shown little interest in "the woman question." For communists, and the other socialist and working-class parties of the nineteenth and early twentieth century, feminism was associated with the bourgeoisie, and therefore was not a primary contradiction or arena for militant, mass mobilization. As the majority of women did not work for wages outside the home until the 1970s, women workers were not key to their organizational drives. However, in spite of the Communists' lack of advanced feminist ideology and special practice, women were inspired to activism in the CPUSA. Aside from the anarchists, who were few in number and small in political significance, more females joined the CP than any other socialist party, and especially in the 1930s and 1940s engaged in workers' and community struggles.

The CP was narrow in its ideas about women, never straying from Marx's early classics or transforming their ideas to suit women's changing position in society. Neither the writings and biographies of dissident communist feminists like Alexandra Kollontai, Angelica Balabanoff and even Eleanor Marx, of feminists like Mary Wollstonecraft, Harriet Mill, Elizabeth Cady Stanton, and Susan B. Anthony, of all the recent radical feminist writers like Simone de Beauvoir, nor the books and pamphlets prepared by Redstockings and the Boston Women's Health Collective, were ever translated or available in communist countries or sold in party bookstores in the United States. The dissident nineteenth century tradition of the early feminists directly inspired the radical and new left feminists in the 1960s and 1970s in North America and Europe. For this generation, Communist Party ideologues and ideology seemed autocratic, dull, and irrelevant, in comparison to the multilayered ideas of the council communists, existentialists, and critical theorists, who made room for perceptions about culture, sexuality, and grassroots democratic participation.

In the CP, ideological guidance on the woman question came and still comes from Marxism's nineteenth century classics, although many CPUSA members and even some leaders had never read them, or had only read short excerpts of Engels's *The Origin of the Family, Private Property and the State*, some passages in Marx's *Communist Manifesto, The Holy Family*, and *The German Ideology*, Lenin's *Women and Society* and Bebel's *Woman and Socialism*. (The last title was more widely quoted and read than Engels in the United States.)[1] These classics did offer women a theorization from the standpoint of the family of "the social relations of reproduction" and a historical and materialist approach to the family. Engels saw the family as a changing and changeable institution, rather than as something sacred and static. Thus, Marxism could rescue women and their cause from the defeatist ring of patriarchal discourse and open women's oppression to human and political intervention. Women as part of the proletariat could become subjects as well as objects of emancipation; they could change the world as well as themselves.

In contradiction to institutions which were capable of being altered, the specific feminist project was subsumed in the universal and fixed. The basic tenets of classic Marxism assumed that (1) the sexual struggle predated capitalism and therefore didn't exist in capitalist or socialist society except as an anachronism; (2) the natural division of labor based on the ability of women to bear children is universal; (3) sexuality is relevant only from the point of view of procreation, not pleasure; and (4) the emancipation of women will occur when they join the proletarian struggle in the workplace. These key assumptions have not shifted or even been seriously challenged, in spite of North American and European feminists in the 1970s calling them into question, and despite the transformation of women's lives by monopoly capitalism and the struggle for liberation. A new feminist-Marxist synthesis, drawing on the Marxist classics and the lived experience (albeit bureaucratic and backward) of socialism, along with radical feminism and the dissident and utopian Marxist currents, might occur now that women in Eastern Europe are making contact and reading the works of Western socialists and feminists.

1919–1935

The history of the CP internationally shaped its approach to women in North America. The CPUSA has never been a dissident or important party numerically or theoretically. No internationally noteworthy leaders or innovative ideas ever emerged from the CPUSA. Intense factional disputes during the 1920s left the CPUSA, then in its infancy, extremely dependent on the Comintern for ideological and organizational guidance. For most of the 1920s the CPUSA was consumed from top to bottom by a struggle of highly organized factions, ending only when Stalin himself removed Jay Lovestone, who wanted a more mass-oriented party, as general secretary in 1929. Historian Van Gosse notes: "The hermetic character of this struggle had accentuated what Simon Gerson, a young field organizer in 1930 and later a longtime party leader, damned as an inability to carry out 'mass work,'" an inability rooted in an immigrant-centered "sectarianism" toward the English-speaking population of workers.[2] The shifting requirements of the Soviet Union dictated permutations in the party's strategy, and these in turn affected the Communist Party's approach of benign neglect toward women.

In North America, 1920 marked a decline for activist feminism.[3] Bourgeois feminists and Socialist Party feminists lost their previous militancy and ability to motivate diverse sectors of women. Suffrage, which had been a dynamic issue since the 1840s, became narrowly relegated to the individualist aspirations of professional women and their splintered groups. The pioneer generation of women's rights and abolitionist activists had died, and their daughters were more focused on single issues and didn't participate in a broad social movement for freedom, justice and equality for working women and African-Americans. The Palmer raids, the jailing and harassing of radicals, left many socialist veterans weary and without a movement. Radicalism was no longer chic, in fact it had become downright dangerous; as a result, many of the bohemian, classy set abandoned politics for art. It is in this context of political repression and the decline of militant, multifaceted feminism that the CPUSA was launched and their ideas on women articulated.

Some active Socialist Party feminists joined the CP in the 1920s and shed their Socialist as well as feminist past. Even such a leading figure as Ella Reeve Bloor—called Mother Bloor, an appellation used for most party women, since motherliness denoted a woman's special strength—complained in her autobiography "that there has been some hesitancy in giving women full, equal responsibility with men."[4]

Juliet Stuart Poyntz, who was much better educated than most party leaders in the United States, having graduated from Barnard and the London School of Economics and earned a living teaching a course at Columbia University in history, set up an education department for the International Ladies Garment Workers Union and became a foremost Communist trade union leader during the 1920s. She disappeared in New York City's Central Park in the 1930s, and many well-known liberals, academics, and trade union leaders suspected that the Comintern killed her because she had contemplated leaving the CPUSA and knew too much about the party's machinations. John Dewey organized a committee of scholars to investigate her death, but nothing came of it. Theodore Draper believed that only Poyntz was "ever considered a threat to the male monopoly in the top leadership."[5]

When Rose Pastor Stokes, a leading birth control and suffrage advocate who gained fame for being a poor Jewish working girl who married into the ruling class, joined the CP, she militantly affirmed her indifference to purely feminist matters and denied that there was even a special women's problem.[6] It is ironic that with these views, Stokes was appointed the first national secretary of the CP Women's Commission in 1922, which was an organization in form only, without any program that was ever put into practice.

The Soviets were more conscious of women's importance during this period than was the CPUSA. *The Communist*, weekly journal of the party in the United States (founded in 1921) mentioned women or the family in its first years only when reprinting a foreign article.[7] CP women in North America were either unaware of their foremothers' militant history or chose to ignore it. They dated the founding of International Women's Day to 1913, when the Bolshevik women first instituted celebrations, rather than recalling its U.S. origin, commemorating a New York City working women's suffrage march held in 1859.[8] International Women's Day took on the coloration of a supremely proletarian holiday; its feminist origin was buried. A 1922 edition of the *Worker* featured a special section devoted to the woman worker and "The Mothers of the Proletariat." The CPUSA even renamed the holiday "International Women's Labor Day," as if to communize it.[9]

The largest group of women who made the transition from the Socialist to the Communist Party were immigrants, who organized along ethnic lines and spoke and wrote in foreign languages, and in those ways were less under the control of the party leadership. Among the Finnish, the largest national group in the party in the 1920s, women appeared to have their most prominent profile. There was even a Finnish-language women's paper, *Toveritar*, that predated and had a larger circulation than the CPUSA's English-language *Working Woman*.[10] Thousands of Jewish, Finnish, and Slavic women served the new Communist movement as they had the old Socialist one, in strike support activities and in an ever widening, sustaining web of fraternal institutions. During the 1930s, when real opportunities presented themselves, these women would make major contributions to labor and community activities.

U.S. Communists, weakened by and preoccupied with feuds, made few attempts to organize women during the 1920s; they tried to follow the Russian mandate rather than building on the U.S. or immigrant activist feminist traditions. The Comintern held an International Women's Conference in Moscow in 1920 and 1921, and urged all Communist Parties to set up women's departments. The CPUSA complied in 1922 and set up a Women's Bureau, and supported several local women's organizations. The largest was the United Council of Working Class Wives. Most of these groups were underfunded and short-lived. Typical of these activities was Women Friends of Soviet Russia, which (as described in the 1922 International Women's Day edition of the *Worker*) planned to organize "women's sewing circles, women's collecting relief circles, nursing mother's relief circles," etc.[11]

The Theses of the Communist Women's Movement, a document of the Comintern, advocated a dual approach to women's oppression: the full incorporation of women in public life at work and in politics, and the reorganization of the private sphere through the socialization of household tasks. In North America, the second point was gradually abandoned in favor of a single focus on industrial struggles. Within this productivist perspective the special interests of women were subordinated to the perceived interests of

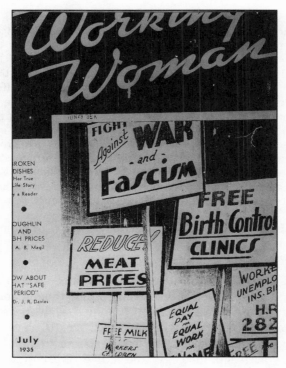

Cover of the CP's publication *Working Woman* demands equality, July 1935. Courtesy of Tamiment Institute Library, New York University.

the working class. In the party's iconographic pantheon a worker signified a brawny male in overalls, sweating in the mines, on the docks or in huge industrial auto, rubber and steel plants, with a rock-like jaw and heavy brow. Not included in this panoply were the millions of exploited laundry workers, domestics, or stenographers, and certainly not housewives. Nor did it include Southern textile workers, even though they were engaged in mass industrial strikes in the late 1920s.[12] In terms of the domestic sphere, women's right to motherhood was stressed, rather than choice or a combination of possibilities. The party's attitude toward women in the 1920s is well summed up by Vera Buch Weisbord, a working class activist in the 1926 Passaic, New Jersey textile strike and wife of Albert Weisbord, the leader of the Passaic strike:

... the situation of women in the Party and of wives in particular was an ignominious one. Few were just housewives minding children. Many who held no posts contributed a devoted activity. If they were married they were considered to be the direct echoes of their husbands in any question of opinion. ... We could only be resentful to find such bourgeois attitudes in our ranks. No matter what the women's contribution, it was taken for granted. I remember a meeting of Party activists in New York at that time in which some special questions were being discussed. In the hall outside the closed door stood about a dozen women, some among us holding important posts in the needle trades, all activists having no interest outside the Party. We had been excluded as women, for no other reason. As one man went in, before the door closed we heard him say, "There's a bunch of wives outside."
When the leaders, under pressure from the C.I. [Communist International], set up a department of "Women's Work," they felt that everything was taken care of.[13]

On the other hand, most women who have spoken or written about their party experiences readily admit that in spite of male chauvinism, the CPUSA empowered women. Women were exposed to international politics, had opportunities to travel to attend conferences and meetings, and were exposed to political debate, community activism, ideology, and a diverse group of people and projects. Tillie Olsen, a prominent writer, said, "the CP took me out of a life of drudgery and into a life of action."[14] For other women the party represented upward mobility and an introduction to a world of rich cultural activities and opportunities. It was an international organization and provided new horizons for women usually confined by family and community.

The 1930s and 1940s

With the Depression, the CPUSA grew in size and prestige. The party had predicted the disaster and had the program to meet it. Even its policy on women shifted and this change didn't come from Moscow at first; it came from the practice and everyday organizing of the rank and file.
When the Depression first turned the world upside down, the CP

continued to insist, by omission, that the domestic world and the personal tragedies of the crash, the lost homes and jobs—that is, the elements of survival—didn't count; it was only the industrial workers marching in protest that were worth organizing around. But at some time from 1930 to 1931, a subtle shift took place in rhetoric, organizing, and daily life. For the first time in the history of the CPUSA, the members were in contact with masses of working people. The struggle, no longer restricted to the shop floor, spread to the ghettos and farms. Communists mobilized to deal with mortgage foreclosures, suicides, disease, evictions, lack of food, and lack of clothes for children to wear to school. This emphasis on the broad social and economic problems of workers meant that women and the home front could no longer be ignored. According to Van Gosse, Communist neighborhood women pioneered "a new practice of constant contact around community issues: canvassing and home visits, attending and recruiting for every meeting, cultivating all possible allies, taking on the meanest tasks, embedding themselves in the minutiae of working class life instead of 'going to the workers' with a revolutionary message from afar."[15]

In the South, the CPUSA organized the unemployed as early as 1931. In Birmingham, Alabama, they held a series of demonstrations in the spring and summer of 1931 against the Red Cross, whose efforts to meet the crisis were inadequate and autocratic. A Birmingham black worker wrote to the *Daily Worker*, "The Red Cross boss stands with a pistol over us while we work, like we are prisoners working out a term."[16] The Red Cross sometimes required applicants to sell personal belongings considered superfluous like radios, watches, clothes or new furniture. They also had demeaning practices like searching trunks for hidden items. The party's unemployed councils held demonstrations against the Red Cross, who had stopped giving cash benefits and only provided food, fuel, and medication, and called for a boycott of the Community Chest, free utilities for all unemployed and underemployed workers, free lunch for school children, and the right to vote irrespective of race. Robin D.G. Kelley notes that this campaign against the Red Cross "was crucial to a formation of a local cadre, serving especially to increase the number of black female members, who often proved more militant than their male comrades."[17]

The CP also organized neighborhood relief committees to present their demands to the Birmingham Welfare Board and to deal with members' specific grievances on an individual basis. As Kelley recounted:

> These committees also fought evictions and foreclosures, and unlike militants in New York and Chicago, they tried to avoid confrontations with authorities by adopting evasive tactics, ranging from flooding landlords with postcards and letters to simple reasoning. Representatives of the unemployed councils often dissuaded landlords from evicting their tenants by describing the potential devastation that could occur once an abandoned house became a free for all for firewood. When a family's electricity was shut off for non-payment, activists from the unemployed council frequently used heavy-gauge wire as "jumpers" to appropriate electricity from public outlets and other homes.[18]

Women were often in the leadership of these integrated black and white neighborhood committees.

During this economic downturn, which hit the South first, black female domestics were either laid off, cut back, or got reduced wages, often as low as $1.50 or $2.00 a week. Twenty-seven percent of the Birmingham black community was receiving welfare.[19] Of course male chauvinism prevailed as usual. As Esther Cooper Jackson, a black CP organizer, observed, "The men deliberately kept [their wives] from advancing."[20] The Depression was doubly difficult as many husbands left due to stress or to enhance the chances of getting relief and therefore the bulk of the burden of providing for their families fell on the shoulders of women and especially black women. Meredith Tax described the practical results:

> In 1935, the Seventh World [Comintern] Congress formally announced a shift in policy—which had already taken place in practice in the rank and file of the CPUSA—called the Popular Front. This new line attracted recruits who were native-born and middle class. Anti-fascism rather than revolution was stressed and the party agitated around peace, consumer and neighborhood interests; more women joined and became active especially at the neighborhood and local levels. Women's Councils conducted bread strikes and meat boycotts and were successful in lowering the price of bread and meat in hundreds of shops, in Detroit and in several sections of New York City. Large numbers of middle and working class women joined

Unemployment Councils, which organized rent strikes and prevented evictions. Some participated in campaigns of the League of
Women Shoppers, which used the buying power of middle class
women to force department stores to deal fairly with their female
employees.[21]

In the party, especially in the late 1930s and 1940s, many women
found an arena for political action and a rich social life, one that
was freer than the dominant culture. Ambitious, rebellious women
with energy and ideas had more room in the party at this time than
they had in the professions or other political parties. CP cultural
life was exciting and fulfilling, with picnics, dances, discussion
groups, theatrical events, and several magazines. Women had more
sexual freedom than they had in the mainstream and some of the
bohemianism of the 1910–1917 period lingered in the ranks, if not
in the ruling party circles. Although the party was a refuge from
dull bourgeois life, the U.S. totems of family, monogamy, and
heterosexuality were never officially questioned. This is perhaps
due to party functionaries equating bohemians with the bourgeois
and their politics of artistic and sexual freedom with frivolity. There
were, however, significant numbers of lesbian women in the party.
But members pretended they weren't gay, as homosexuality was
equated with the decadence of capitalism.[22]

It has to be noted that due to the Depression and later the war
many women were called on to support their families. The party
praised women workers during the war for doing their part in the
fight against fascism, but never thought of them as permanent
workers. This was the prevailing attitude as well. Women could do
anything and everything, be lumberjacks, stevedores, welders, drill
press and overhead crane operators; but when the war ended, they
were to return home to their families and give up their well-paid,
rewarding jobs to returning veterans.

During the popular front period in the 1930s and early 1940s,
the party provided a stimulating, almost countercultural, environment. However, this was the exception, rather than the rule,
because on the whole, and more and more so after 1956, it was as
culturally and socially conservative and conformist as mainstream
America. The preferred music was folk, rather than avant-garde or
rock. Freud was rejected, as psychiatrists couldn't be trusted (and
some of them did give incriminating testimony), and in any case

A publicity photo: knitting to support the loyalist side in the Spanish Civil War, from the *Daily Worker,* 1936. Reproduced from *Isms,* 2nd ed. (Indianapolis: American Legion, 1937).

psychology could be explained by economics. Women's economic dependence was assumed and all marital problems were seen in terms of poverty. As Earl Browder explains in *The People's Front*:

> Permanent and healthy family life is best built upon the secure possession by all people of the material basis for the family; that is, adequate housing, plenty of food and clothing, and an assured income.... Abolish poverty and the problem of divorce will largely disappear.[23]

Men defined women, in the party as in society. In the labor movement, in the 1930s and 1940s, women were organized into ladies' auxiliaries, which made coffee, organized day care and built morale by staging rallies. Occasionally women took action, as did the CIO-affiliated Woodworkers Ladies' Auxiliary in Portland, who rode on fuel trucks with baseball bats to protect their husbands from AFL opponents.[24] In Alabama the auxiliaries sometimes rivaled union locals in membership, as well as in the stridency with which they advocated labor organization. One worker there recalled, "that whenever union members failed to recruit a recalcitrant worker, the women would send a committee to talk with the worker's wife or the worker and they would always win their point."[25] Female direct confrontation, however, tended to occur when it was too dangerous for men to act on their own behalf, banking on the fact that the police were sexist too. The film *Salt of the Earth* depicts an example of women taking the lead when men weren't able, although here, women's picketing catapults them into taking action on their own behalf, on the home front as well. Action in one area inspired action in others.

Especially in literature, working-class women were often romanticized and seen as instinctively more radical and wholesome. A good example of this is the figure of the mother in Mike Gold's *Jews Without Money*.[26] The implication was that men are the intellectual and theoretical leaders, while women, who are nearer to nature, are the sustainers of life and militant struggle. This is somewhat of a contradiction: if women were so instinctive, why wasn't their input more valued? Some of this imagery resonates with Stalinism. After the war there was a shortage of women in Russia, and so women's maternal qualities were elevated. Awards were even given for bearing over five offspring. In mainstream U.S. culture fecundity and domesticity were elevated as well, as the returning troops took back the jobs that Rosie the Riveter once held.

Women were viewed in the party as mothers of sons and creatures of sentiment, not carriers of reason. During the Nazi-Soviet Pact when the CP was taking a pacifist stance, Elizabeth Gurley Flynn, one of the few token women in the top leadership, wrote a pamphlet called "I Didn't Raise My Son for Wall Street." Party leader William Z. Foster wrote an editorial on election eve, in 1940, in which he stated that "Communist women candidates express what the vast majority of the women of America want—peace, safety in their homes and for their loved ones.... Let us give our closest attention to the problems of the women tied down by their household tasks and care for their children—provide squads of automobiles that will carry them to the polls and help in caring for their children."[27] This special consideration was especially necessary around election time. Communist men were a vanguard, but the women were ordinary run-of-the-mill Americans, except when they worked for the party. There were contradictions, as women were expected to be ordinary hausfraus and weak, and yet wonder women—but not capable of leadership.

The CPUSA was noted for outworking the other left parties and was respected for it. An indication of the CP's hard work, growth, and women's activity in the late 1930s and 1940s was the journal *Working Woman*. In the 1920s this was a little mimeoed sheet with a hammer and sickle on the masthead. In 1933, it became a magazine designed to reach a larger audience. The paid circulation grew from 2,000 to 7,000, and organizers began to sell it at factory gates. In 1936 it became *Woman Today*, a slicker journal that played down its party connections.[28] This new version contained love stories, beauty hints, and homemaking advice. All that distinguished it from other women's journals was its articles on trade unions. One could hardly call the journals, in any phase, feminist or for the liberation of women.

Women's activism did, however, sometimes lead to feminist consciousness and the realization that party leaders and even husbands were oppressors. On July 5, 1936, the women's page in the *Sunday Worker Magazine*, which usually featured recipes and advice to mothers, presented a "Dear Mr. Husband" contest in which women wrote letters "telling him in what ways he treats you as an inferior, why he does it, and in what ways he is harming himself by doing so." Anne Rivington, a columnist, describes on the same page a conversation at a women's committee meeting at a party convention, where women discussed their husband troubles. An unnamed Detroit leader complained that she and her comrades were allowed to keep house and go to meetings, but when they "forge ahead and become speakers and leaders, that's when their husbands clamped down. They don't want us to surpass them."

The overriding assumption in the party was that problems were basically caused by the capitalist system, while in the Soviet Union women had achieved freedom. The lesson was that U.S. women would wait for socialism to achieve full equality. Women's oppression was not important in itself, and women's lives could not be improved by taking female complaints seriously. Women were advised in the party press that, rather than fight with their husbands about housework, they should accommodate at home and build a good society where equal rights would be possible.[29] Elizabeth Gurley Flynn sums this up succinctly: "Happier homes are possible when families work together to speed socialism," meaning when men are in the driver's seat and women are compromising.[30] No alternatives to the nuclear family, such as cooperatives or sharing child care and housework, were explored. In fact, after the 1960s, the CP was even more conservative culturally than most people in North America under thirty years of age. The sexual revolution, hippy culture, and rock and roll were seen as capitalist consumerism and trivial.

The CP attacked the Equal Rights Amendment, an important feminist platform of the time, as anti-working class; but then the ERA was not supported by many other left and liberal groups at the time either. Mary Anderson, of the Women's Bureau and Department of Labor, and Mary Van Kleek, a social worker, drew up a Women's Charter to reunite feuding women's groups. The charter called for equal opportunity for women in employment, education, and politics, as well as economic security, including maternal insurance. Few women's groups supported the charter idea, but the party opened its pages to defend the charter and sponsored a conference in support of it in 1937.[31] It was not until 1976, after almost a decade of organized women's agitation under the banner of women's liberation, and the formation of the Coalition of Labor Union Women in 1974, that the CPUSA and the AFL-CIO opportunistically changed their minds and supported the ERA. The United Auto Workers, for example, supported the ERA in 1970. Until the late 1970s, the CPUSA decided that only middle- and upper-class professionals would benefit from equal job opportunity. On the other hand, working class women would suffer, by being forced to lift heavy loads, work in unpleasant environments, and work overtime. It didn't occur to them that some working class women would want these opportunities and that they were support- ing their families as single wage-earners.

Female membership in the party grew during the 1930s and World War II years. In 1930, 10 percent of the membership was female. By 1943 women were 50 percent of the membership. How- ever, women still remained a distinct minority in the leadership of the CPUSA. With men at war, women had more space in commu- nity and popular front organizations, but not in the party hierarchy. In fact, CP women were told that they should ignore their own needs and assist the war effort, imitating their Soviet sisters who were sacrificing their lives. During the war, women were encour- aged to join the work force and fight for day care. However, after the soldiers returned the party encouraged women to step aside and return to their rightful place in the home. The party, unlike many liberal organizations, didn't protest when day care centers were closed or women lost their jobs. After the war, Elizabeth Gurley Flynn, who was usually uncritical of party policy, claimed that even the National Association of Manufacturers took women more seriously than the CPUSA, and she noticed more male chau- vinism in the party than ever.[32]

The case of Mary Inman shows the unwillingness of the CPUSA to debate the woman question openly and freely in the period before and just after the war. In 1935 Inman, an active CP member, wrote *In Women's Defense*, a book about housework as productive labor. The party refused to publish it; the excuse they gave was that Inman didn't use a Marxist anthropological interpretation of use value. However, the *People's World,* the party's more open West Coast daily newspaper, serialized the pamphlet. Because Inman felt that housewives were workers, she organized a Committee for the Advancement of Women and put out a newsletter as well as a program for a new kind of housewives' labor union. The party understood that blacks were a special group and had to organize as such; but women, on the other hand, could not organize separately around their unique oppression. To do so was heretical.

An attack on Inman followed. Avram Landy, who was the national education director of the CPUSA, wrote *Marxism and the Woman Question*, which reasserted the CP's position that the housewife is not part of social production and therefore that women and men face the same problems of class. Landy concluded that women should organize with men in trade unions to fight issues of capitalism rather than gender. Housework, Landy claimed, was no longer a burden or issue because of technology. "Motherhood is nature, the material prerequisite of society," and had nothing to do with woman's role in capitalist production, because it took place outside of industry, he asserted. For Landy the family was an institution of "sex and blood," divorced from the production process and had no social importance.[33] It didn't occur to Landy that many women wanted to enter the paid work force, but were excluded by sexism, undeveloped skills and lack of child care.

Others in the party, including Gurley Flynn (who had originally liked Inman's ideas), Bloor, and Ruth McKenney, a novelist and editor of *New Masses*, launched an attack on Inman in the party press. Many readers, however, were sympathetic to Inman's position and wrote letters supporting her ideas on housework. Inman taught at a Marxist school and on the last day of her class a party representative, Eva Afran, came to her class and told the students that her views were not Marxist.[34] In the end, despite Inman's appeals, she was purged from the party. Organizing or discussing women's special oppression proved too threatening for the party to handle. Women would have to wait until 1956 to debate the issues of female liberation.

1956–Present

During the brief period of reevaluation and openness after the Khrushchev revelations, women began again to speak out about male chauvinism in the party, about their lack of support with children and housework from CP husbands and lovers, and about formerly taboo subjects like homosexuality and psychoanalysis.

The *Daily Worker's* letter columns contained a rich patchwork of these debate fragments.

However, on the whole the 1950s were dismal "scoundrel times," especially for the stalwarts who remained within the CPUSA fold. Many women were called upon to make enormous emotional and economic sacrifices, as men lost their jobs, and were tried and often jailed. When the Smith Act wives organized speaking tours and a defense committee, instead of gratitude, the wives' activism and publicity generated resentment by party officials, many of whom were jealous because their wives were better and more dynamic speakers than they.[35]

During this period very few younger women joined the party, and at least half of those who had joined in the later 1930s and 1940s left or became inactive. It wasn't until the 1960s, with the resurgence of campus, black and factory militancy, that a new crop of activists joined the CP ranks. However, many of those who joined left quickly, as it was hard to put up with the aging, bureaucratic, culturally and politically stagnant, conservative leadership.[36]

Activists like Bettina Aptheker, one of the leaders of the Berkeley Free Speech Movement, dropped out of the party on feminist grounds. Angela Davis introduced many women to issues of sex and race, as her writing was popular and exciting; but it was not feminist. In fact Davis attacked the early first and second wave feminists (who had begun as abolitionists and civil rights workers) for ignoring race and class. Her most important political and intellectual work had been done before she joined the CPUSA. As a CP spokesperson, she had the unfortunate task of defending the Soviet Union in an uncritical way. The party also paraded her and used her as a pin-up, auctioning full-faced posters of her at fundraising functions.

The CPUSA, unlike the Socialist Workers Party (SWP) and International Socialists, was slow to realize the importance of the women's liberation movement in the late 1960s and early 1970s. The SWP infiltrated the women's liberation movement, ran feminist candidates, and actively backed abortion and gay rights. Basically the CPUSA dismissed the second wave of feminism as it had the first, as bourgeois. However, when it became clear that women's rights, affirmative action, day care, etc., had become mainstream mass issues, they tagged along behind and created Women for

Racial and Economic Equality (WREE), organized initially as a local group in 1974, and then as a national organization in 1977. WREE holds conferences and takes positions; it has not engaged in grassroots organizing, and tends to attract functionaries rather than activists.

However, even though the CPUSA gave women's emancipation a low priority, the party played an important role in keeping the flame of women's political activism burning from the 1920s through the 1950s. A number of women's liberation activists of the late 1960s, including myself, were "red diaper babies" who grew up with such terms as "male chauvinism" and the "woman question" and heard frequent gossip about which party families were backward about women. "The woman question" was itself a radical nineteenth century term, and only the CP maintained its use. The party never saw sexism as a deep structural economic problem or as a political obstacle inherent in U.S. society, as it did racism. But even though the CP perceived of women merely as an interest group and the reconciliation of sexism and male chauvinism as a personal problem to be solved individually within the family, usually by women's willingness to compromise, they were still—until 1968—more advanced on women's issues than most mainstream organizations, and thus their legacy proved important.

What about the future? At present, it appears as if "the party is over"—at least in the United States. Communists are no longer seen as dangerous, as they were in the 1920s and 1950s; they are now merely insignificant, and have withered away as a political force. In 1992, most of the party's most vital and visible members have left, or more accurately were locked out by the Gus Hall leadership for daring to imply that the CPUSA needed a glasnost and perestroika, a major overhaul. These include Angela Davis, historian Herbert Aptheker, and the Depression era leader of the unemployed Louis Weinstock. If anything finally rises from the remains of the party, Communist women will have to transform their role and agenda if they hope to play a significant political part in North America. Opportunities abound; the time is ripe for a new feminist communist agenda.

Notes

1. From my interviews with female CPUSA members, and the interviews of CPUSA members in the Tamiment collection, Bobst Library at New York University; and Mari Jo Buhle, *Women and American Socialism 1870–1920* (Champaign: University of Illinois Press, 1981).

2. Van Gosse, "'To Organize in Every Neighborhood, in Every Home': The Gender Politics of American Communists Between the Wars," *Radical History Review* 50 (1991): 125.

3. Nancy Cott, in *The Grounding of Modern Feminism*, disputes this point, but I disagree. See my review of Cott's book in *National Women's Association Journal* 1, no. 1 (1988).

4. Ella Reeve Bloor, *We Are Many* (New York: International Publishers, 1940), p. 308.

5. Theodore Draper, *The Roots of American Communism* (New York: Viking, 1960), p. 1.

6. Mari Jo Buhle, *Women and American Socialism*, p. 321.

7. Van Gosse, "Gender Politics of American Communists," p. 120.

8. Mary Jo Buhle, *Women and American Socialism*, p. 322.

9. Van Gosse, "Gender Politics," p. 123.

10. Ibid., p. 138, fn. 23.

11. Ibid.

12. See Elizabeth Waters, "In the Shadow of the Comintern: The Communist Women's Movement, 1920–43," in Sonia Kruks, Rayna Rapp, and Marilyn B. Young, eds., *Promissory Notes: Women in the Transition to Socialism* (New York: Monthly Review Press, 1989), p. 40; and Van Gosse, "Gender Politics," p. 118.

13. Vera Buch Weisbord, *A Radical Life* (Bloomington: Indiana University Press, 1977), p. 144.

14. Presentation by Tillie Olsen, Modern Language Association panel, December 1988.

15. Van Gosse, "Gender Politics," p. 110–41; and Mark Naison, *Communists in Harlem During the Depression* (Urbana: University of Illinois Press, 1983).

16. See Robin D.G. Kelley, *Hammer and Hoe: Alabama Communists During the Great Depression* (Chapel Hill: University of North Carolina Press, 1990), p. 20.

17. Ibid., p. 33.

18. Ibid., p. 21.

19. Ibid., pp. 32–33.

20. Ibid., pp. 136, 277.

21. See Kim Chernin, *In My Mothers's House: A Daughter's Story* (New Haven: Ticknor and Fields, 1983); and Meredith Tax, "Women's Coun-

cils in the 1930s," paper presented at the Berkshire Conference of Women Historians, June 1984.

22. Information based on personal interviews with Peggy Dennis and Dorothy Healey in July 1985. In fact the tough guy, Atlas-like steel worker was the masculine ideal. "Manly" was synonymous with proletarian, so obviously women were considered the weaker, unproductive sex. On this question see also Elsa Dixler, "The Woman Question, Women and the American Communist Party, 1929–1941," Ph.D. diss., Yale University, 1974, pp. 44–46.

23. See Earl Browder, *The People's Front* (New York: International Publishers, 1938), p. 201.

24. See Mary Heaton Vorse, *Labor's New Millions* (New York: Modern Age, 1938), pp. 205, 217, 234.

25. Kelley, *Hammer and Hoe*, p. 69.

26. See also Meridel Le Sueur in the *New Masses*, 18 February 1941.

27. Van Gosse, "Gender Politics," p. 134.

28. See *Working Woman*, 17 January 1936; and *Woman Today*, March 1936.

29. See Van Gosse, "Gender Politics," p. 140, fn. 39; and *Sunday Worker Magazine*, 4 October 1936, 5 July 1936, 16 August 1936, 23 August 1936, 30 August 1936, 2 February 1938, 27 February 1938, 6 March 1938, 1 June 1938, and 17 July 1938.

30. See *Sunday Worker Magazine*, 19 December 1937.

31. See *Sunday Worker Magazine*, March 1936, February 1937, 10 January 1937; and *Political Affairs* 53 (May 1974).

32. See Rosalyn Baxandall, *Words on Fire* (New Brunswick, NJ: Rutgers University Press, 1987), p. 50.

33. See Avram Landy, *Marxism and the Woman Question* (New York: Workers Library, 1943), pp. 18, 33.

34. Most of my knowledge about Inman comes from Sherna Gluck, who interviewed Inman extensively. I tried to interview Inman myself, but she was too mistrustful. See *Words on Fire*, pp. 223–26; and an undergraduate paper by Heike Stuckert, "Inman Versus Landy: The Communist Party USA and the Woman Question 1936–1949," (March 1989).

35. See *FBI Reports*, San Francisco, 2 May 1949; 27 June 1949; 23 June 1949. See also Deborah Gerson, "Smith Act Defense Committee," paper presented at the Berkshire Conference for Women Historians, 19 June 1987.

36. Views expressed in conversations in August 1989 with many CP youth members, who would like to remain anonymous.

THE COMMUNIST INFLUENCE ON AMERICAN LABOR

Roger Keeran

A central concern of historians who have written on the Communist Party and labor has been the extent and quality of Communist influence on labor unions. In this essay I will survey the high points of this history and propose a new way of looking at the .party's influence on U.S. labor.

Ten years ago in the introduction to my book, *The Communist Party and The Auto Workers Unions*, I suggested that three generalizations had a prominent place in most historical writing about the Communist Party and labor: that the Communists were not legitimate trade unionists, that they had no significant influence on labor, and that they were not good Communists. My own research led to sharply different conclusions about Communists in the auto industry: that they were legitimate, even exemplary trade unionists, that they played an important, even crucial role in the development of the union, and that they were as good Communists as they could have been under the circumstances.[1]

Since that time, some historians, like Harvey Klehr, have continued to question the Communists' legitimacy as trade unionists by stressing their subservience to Moscow.[2] Others, like August Meier and Elliott Rudwick, have continued to question the extent of Communist influence on such issues as black equality, relative to the influence of others such as black advancement groups and the federal government.[3] Still others, like Malcolm Sylvers, have continued to question the party's commitment to a consistent radicalism by focusing on its moderation during the period of the Popular Front.[4] Since the question of Communist legitimacy hinges on assumptions about whether or not one can be both a revolutionary or a supporter of revolutions abroad and a legitimate trade unionist, and since the question of what constitutes a good Communist (or radical) hinges on a value judgment, it is doubtful that any amount of evidence will ever resolve these questions to the satisfaction of everyone.

The question of Communist influence, however, is of a different order, since the determination of the extent and kind of Communist influence is less value-laden and more clearly tied to evidence. Here, the preponderance of evidence produced by the last decade of scholarship decisively supports the conclusion that the Communist Party was an important and distinctive influence on the labor movement and that Communist influence was decidedly beneficial to unions and workers. In addition, research has added to our appreciation of the variety of that influence, as well as shed more light on the reasons for its increase in the 1930s and decrease in the late 1940s.

Before examining this evidence more closely, several preliminary observations can be made about the party's role in the history of labor. In the seventy-year history of the Communist Party, its influence on and within the trade union movement was largely confined to the two decades between 1929 and 1949. Even during the Communists' twenty-year heyday, their influence was more limited than that of their European counterparts. The U.S. Communists never had the kind of sway over U.S. labor that the French party had over the largest French labor federation, the CGT, where over half of the leaders were either party members or close to the party. Nor did U.S. Communists enjoy the status of the parties of Great Britain, Italy, Portugal, and the Scandinavian countries where they competed openly for power and often shared the leadership of the trade unions with Socialists and others.[5] U.S. Communists, noted Len DeCaux, a Communist ally and editor of the *CIO News*, never achieved full citizenship in U.S. unions.[6] Only on rare occasions were they able to operate openly in leadership positions as party members. Still, operate they did, and their influence was all the more remarkable for occurring in such a hostile environment.

It is also necessary to consider what is meant by Communist influence. In 1938 journalist Edward Levinson said, "Communist influence in the CIO is a figment of imagination."[7] Thirty years later, historian Irving Bernstein echoed this conclusion, when he said that Communist penetration of the labor movement had been "clouded by myth, exaggeration, and nonsense.... In the late thirties the issue was not very important."

Such conclusions depended, however, upon a very narrow conception of influence. Bernstein argued that the Communist influence was unimportant in the late 1930s because the Communists "worked with non-Communists for trade-union objectives" and because "the Communist Party never became a mass movement and failed almost totally to convert U.S. workers."[8] To assess Communist influence by the degree to which Communists swayed workers to act or think in ways that went beyond trade unionism, that is to join the party, vote Communist, or support a socialist revolution, is to overlook the work Communists performed and the influence they had in the day to day activities of trade unions and in class struggle. The way in which influence is defined can determine whether or not it is seen as important. That the party never generated a mass movement for socialism does not imply that it did not contribute to the shaping of other movements and organizations. Moreover, to assess Communist influence by gross indices rather than accounts of activities is to treat the party and its role in altogether different terms than those used to assess the influence of other groups and organizations. More instructive in terms of appreciating the activities of Communists is to realize that much Communist influence occurred in a practical way in regard to issues close at hand.

Moreover, influence itself is not a unitary thing but occurs in different ways and to different degrees. There are three sorts of influence relevant to evaluating the party's role. First, did Communist activities contribute to the underlying motivational context of government, business or labor policies, even when Communists did not determine the actual content of the policies? Second, to what degree and in what ways were the Communists instrumental in determining the content of labor policies? Third, what role did the Communists play in implementing policies whose content they may or may not have determined? In what follows, I will refer to these three aspects of influence as policy impetus, policy making, and policy implementation.

Communist influence in the labor movement can be traced at least to the early 1920s. Like other Communist parties, the U.S. party was the child of a marriage between "a national left and the

October Revolution."[9] Many former Wobblies (Industrial Workers of the World members) and left-wing Socialists, including the black labor socialists of the African Blood Brotherhood, either helped form the Communist Party or joined the party in the early 1920s. With the decline of the Wobblies, the Communists were, according to historian Paul Buhle, "able to assume the mantle of leadership in the struggle for industrial unionism and the organization of the unorganized."[10] The center of the party's early labor agitation was the Trade Union Education League (TUEL) headed by William Z. Foster, the leader of the massive but ill-fated 1919 steel strike. The obstacles the TUEL faced were enormous. Foster lamented that "American labor is still asleep, drugged into insensibility by bourgeois propaganda.... And the worst of it is that it is making no effort toward ... awakening."[11] Still, TUEL militants were active in the Chicago Federation of Labor, and among railroad, mine, and garment unions. Until a disastrous strike in 1926, the Communists actually controlled the International Ladies Garment Workers Union (ILGWU) in New York and were able to assemble 40,000 cloak and dress makers at a rally in Yankee Stadium.

Though the TUEL's agitation and education produced little real change in the labor movement, they were nonetheless notable for their size and vision. In 1922 the TUEL had nuclei in forty-eight cities and circulated 11,000 copies of its newspaper, *Labor Herald*, and 250,000 copies of its pamphlet, *Amalgamation*. The TUEL movement for amalgamation of trades into industry-wide organizations won the support of fourteen international unions and seventeen state federations. Moreover, at a time when the number of international unions barring blacks was actually increasing, Foster and the TUEL campaigned "to open all unions to the Negro workers."[12]

In 1928, the Communists began organizing independent industrial unions. Though Theodore Draper[13] emphasized the decisions of the Sixth Congress of the Communist International as the cause of this new line, national conditions played an equally important role. Only after Communists were expelled by unions in mining and textiles did they set up the National Miners Unions (NMU) and the National Textile Workers Union (NTWU).[14] Later, the Communists transformed the TUEL into the Trade Union Unity League (TUUL), an independent federation of industrial unions, and helped organize industrial unions of more than local scope in a dozen other industries: the needle trades, auto, steel and metal, marine transport, cannery and agricultural, food, shoe and leather, tobacco, lumber, furniture, packinghouse, and machine tool and foundry. They also helped organize fourteen local industrial unions in other industries such as dry goods and pharmacies in New York. After the Depression created a whole new set of problems around unemployment, evictions, and relief, conditions that made union organizing difficult, the Communists created scores of local Unemployed Councils.[15] In each case, the Communist initiatives, while consistent with the line of the Sixth Congress, responded to national and local conditions. This was particularly evident in the case of strikes by textile workers and miners.

During the years 1929 to 1931, TUUL unions led massive strikes of textile workers in the Loray Mills in Gastonia, North Carolina, and miners in Ohio, Pennsylvania, West Virginia, and Harlan County, Kentucky. These strikes followed a similar pattern: the workers spontaneously walked out to protest wage cuts and speedup, and turned to Communist leaders when the existing leadership sought to curb their resistance. The strikes were broken by employer-sponsored violence and repression. This included the murders of Harry Sims, a miner, and Ella May Wiggins, a textile worker. It also included persecution, such as the conviction on trumped-up murder charges of Fred Beal, a Communist who was one of the textile strike leaders.[16]

Before 1930, Communist influence outside the organizations the party directly controlled was largely agitational and educational. After 1930, Communist activities began to exert influence as policy impetus. The Communists began to influence specific policies of AFL unions, employers, and federal and local governments. In conjunction with the spontaneous outbursts of workers, the Communists were instrumental in forcing debate on the plight of unorganized industrial workers and the unemployed. Since few if any of the Communist-led unions obtained signed collective bargaining agreements, none succeeded in organizing the majority of their industries, and none established themselves on a permanent basis, it is easy to underestimate their influence on these debates. Yet, the Communist-led unions played key roles in the organizing and major strikes that occurred in this period, often influencing the direction of government and employer policies toward measures of material benefit to workers.

The most easily overlooked of all of these was the Communist organization of farm workers. In 1930, under fascist-like conditions, marked by the murder of a number of organizers, African-American Communists in Alabama formed the Croppers' and Farm Workers' Union (later the Share Croppers' Union). By 1933, this union had 2,000 members in seventy-three locals, and had formed eighty women's auxiliaries and twenty youth groups. The union fought against evictions and for relief, and led a strike in Lee and Tallapoosa counties that, according to Robin Kelley, won "substantial victories" in raising the prices landlords had to pay for cotton.[17] Similarly, in California the Communist Agricultural Workers Industrial League (AWIL) and the Cannery and Agricultural Workers Industrial Union (CAWIU) led scores of strikes and protests involving thousands of lettuce, cherry, pea, cotton and other workers between 1930 and 1934. By 1933, these actions not only forced the federal government to intervene but also gave many farm employers no choice but to change their wage policies or face further resistance. Cletus Daniel concludes that, of 37 agricultural strikes involving 47,575 workers in 1933, the CAWIU led 24 of them involving 79 percent of striking workers. Only four CAWIU strikes ended in total defeat, while the others won higher wages for 32,800 workers.[18]

The Marine Workers Industrial Union (MWIU), one of the strongest unions of the TUUL federation, led struggles that also led to changes in federal and employer policies in the maritime industries. Daniel Nelson writes that an MWIU protest in Baltimore, against the inept administration of unemployment relief by the Seaman's YMCA, resulted in a federal agency turning over the administration of relief to a rank-and-file committee of workers. Another MWIU struggle resulted in the creation of a worker-controlled hiring hall that for a time was used by every shipping company in Baltimore except Standard Oil.[19] In 1936 and 1937, the MWIU organized protests against the Copeland Bill, then before Congress, that would have required seamen to carry their discharge books. The union claimed that the bill's main effect would have been the facilitation of blacklisting. According to Herbert Tank, "by mass pressure on the government the maritime workers

forced the House Merchant Marine Committee to recommend to
Congress that the Fink Book Law be optional rather than compul-
sory."[20]

The most important series of strikes in the auto industry before
the formation of the CIO occurred in 1933. They illustrate, in two
ways, how Communists were able to provide the impetus for modifications of policy. In November 1932, the Auto Workers Union
(AWU) began organizing and agitating against anticipated wage
cuts in Detroit auto body shops. When these cuts finally came in
January 1933, the AWU led a series of walkouts which culminated
in a strike of 6,000 Briggs and 4,000 Motor Products workers.

Since the membership of the union was small (no more than 800)
and the element of spontaneity was large, these strikes could not
be attributed wholly to the decisions of Communists. Yet, the
Communists had a great deal to do with setting the conditions
under which the workers responded to the wage cuts by developing
their own demands and staging a walkout. In this regard, Joyce
Peterson writes:

> That many auto workers did what the Communists wanted them to
> do, choosing to join a strike wave that was rapidly gaining momen-
> tum after three years of declining conditions of work does not of
> course make them Communists, but neither does the small number
> of the Communists mean their influence was unimportant.... The
> most important Communist influence lay ... in their long history of
> keeping the Auto Workers Union alive and with it giving repeated
> legitimation to the idea that auto workers had rights and that unions
> existed to secure and protect those rights.[21]

The strikes themselves provided further impetus for changing
management policies in the industry. Thus, short strikes early in
the month led to the rescinding of wage cuts at Briggs, Motor
Products, Hayes, and Hudson. These successes encouraged the
organization of larger strikes later in the month against Briggs and
Motor Products with more ambitious demands. While these ended
in failure,

> the epidemic of auto strikes ... resulted in an improvement in the
> conditions in other factories that did not strike. The series of strikes
> brought the orgy of wage cutting by the auto barons to an instant
> and complete stop.[22]

In the early 1930s, the organizing and strikes by TUUL unions provided some of the background conditions for industrial unionism. Many TUUL unions became the nuclei for the new industrial unions of the CIO. Moreover, the struggles of the TUUL unions and other Communist activity among the unemployed provided background conditions for legislative reform, in particular the National Labor Relations Act. Michael Goldfield has argued that the National Labor Relations Act of 1935 was the result of the impact on government officials of the labor movement's growth and activity and "the increasing strength and influence of radical organizations, particularly the Communist Party."[23] Though the labor agitation and radical organizations embraced more than Communists, from the point of view of businessmen, AFL officials, and politicians, the Communists were the most prominent and disturbing element. The radical activity to which Goldfield referred began with the Communist-initiated Hunger March on March 6, 1930, that brought over a million people into the streets of major cities, including New York, Detroit, Chicago, Pittsburgh, Milwaukee, Philadelphia, and Cleveland. In the following years, unemployed protests occurred regularly and occasionally led to deadly confrontations and stunningly well-attended funeral marches for victims of police violence. All told, fifteen workers were killed in Communist-led unemployment demonstrations. In 1931, in Chicago, 60,000 people marched behind Communist banners in commemoration of three activists killed during a struggle to prevent an eviction of a family in a black neighborhood. The following year in Detroit, 25,000 marched for the four victims of the "Ford Massacre." Communists and other radicals were also active in farmers' protests against evictions and low prices, in movements of students and intellectuals, and in nationwide protests on behalf of the black Communist Angelo Herndon and the Scottsboro Boys.[24] All of this radical activity contributed to growing sentiment for labor law reform.

More directly related to the passage of the NLRA was insurgency at the workplace. Many strikes led by Communists or other radicals in the early 1930s assumed an insurrectionary aspect as workers and unemployed fought police and strikebreakers in the streets. Eighty-eight workers died in strike-related violence from 1934 to 1936.[25] In 1934, the number of strikes increased as the membership of trade unions increased by twenty percent. In that year, general strikes under radical leadership occurred among marine and dock workers in San Francisco, teamsters in Minneapolis, and auto workers in Toledo. "After the 1934 San Francisco general strike," Goldfield notes, "the longshore and maritime industries along the whole West Coast remained aflame with militancy, largely under communist leadership."[26]

The threat of the labor upsurge expanding and the fear of radicalism deepening provided the major conditions contributing to the passage of the Wagner Act in 1935. Goldfield notes that the belief that "government regulation was necessary to constrain, limit, and control the increasingly militant labor movement," was "a central feature of the preamble and section 1 of the bill" and ran "like a bright yellow thread through the hearings and floor debates of both Houses."[27] On March 28, 1935, Francis J. Dillon, an AFL organizer in auto, told a congressional committee:

> It is significant to here record the fact that Communists and communistic theories are more prevalent and substantially stronger among employees within the auto industry now than one year ago, constituting an actual menace to the future of the industry and a challenge to our form of government.[28]

Dillon blamed this on the failure of business to fulfill the promise of section 7(a) of the National Industrial Recovery Act that granted workers the right to organize. Consequently, though the Communists hardly determined the content of the Wagner Act, and even testified against it, their actions contributed mightily to the passage of the New Deal's most significant piece of labor legislation.

In assessing the Communist Party's Third Period (1929 to 1934), some historians have lampooned such sectarian excesses as the slogan "Toward a Soviet America" and the characterization of opponents on the left as "social fascists."[29] Others believed the CP at that time expressed a more consistent radicalism than during the following period of the Popular Front.[30] No one could deny, however, that the Third Period unleashed a period of political creativity. In a span of four or five years, the Communists created an élan that rivaled the pre-war Wobblies and the 1960s' civil rights movement, and sparked a dizzying flurry of activity—creating organizations, mobilizing demonstrations, conducting protest meetings, leading strikes, publishing shop papers, and issuing broadsides. The number and variety of these efforts dwarfed those of any previous period of political agitation. By 1935, the party had over 600 shop nuclei and published some 300 newspapers. By then, the party had increased its membership to 30,000 and "nearly a quarter of the ... membership (as well as many others, several hundred thousand at the least, who felt close to the party) were concentrated in heavy industry."[31] This political creativity was central to the Communists' growing influence.

Of course, such creativity was a product of a certain historical conjuncture—the worldwide crisis of capitalism, the paralysis of traditional political and labor leadership, and the progress of Soviet socialism. By 1934, the political landscape was radically different from the beginning of the Third Period and the onset of the Depression. In Germany, the new Nazi government was already systematically suppressing the Communist Party, the labor movement, and democratic liberties. At home, the most liberal and pro-labor Congress in the history of the country was elected in 1934. President Roosevelt and the New Deal provided a political climate more favorable to workers than at any time in the past. In the labor movement, other forces besides the Communists attempted to organize the unorganized into industrial unions. Among the leaders were John L. Lewis of the mine workers and Sidney Hillman of the garment workers. Socialists, Trotskyists, and non-political militants were also active in these efforts. Even before the Seventh Congress of the Communist International officially reoriented its policies in 1935, U.S. Communists began building alliances with progressive non-Communist movements and organizations in what would become known as the Popular Front.

During the period of the Popular (or Democratic) Front, roughly from 1934 to 1938, stunning changes occurred in the labor movement. Beginning as an AFL committee in 1935, a new labor federation, the Congress of Industrial Organizations (CIO), was formed, including the United Mine Workers Union, the United Automobile Workers, the United Electrical Workers, the National Maritime Union, the International Longshoremen and Warehousemen Union, and the United Rubber Workers. Mass organizing by both CIO and AFL unions increased the number of union members from 2.6 million in 1934 to 7.3 million in 1938. Strikes and the threat of strike led to collective bargaining agreements for the first time in

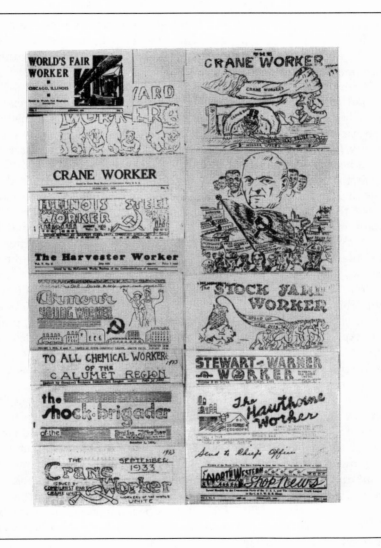

Communist shop papers, usually mimeographed, circulated by party "factory nuclei" at work sites in the early 1930s. Drawing (center, right) depicts Tom Mooney and the "Scottsboro Boys." Reproduced from Harold D. Lasswell and Dorothy Blumenstock, *World Revolutionary Propaganda* (1939; Westport CT: Greenwood Press, 1970).

mass production industries. Through Industrial Union Councils, Labor's Nonpartisan League, the American Labor Party in New York, and the Minnesota Farmer Labor Party, the CIO unions became an active political force.

Unlike the Third Period, when the Communists formed unions, called strikes and protests, led demonstrations, and exercised a clearly discernible influence on the most active sections of the labor movement, in the Popular Front period they were simply one of many forces pushing the labor movement in the same direction. Just because Communist influence during this period was difficult to factor out did not mean, however, that it was not significant. On the contrary, Communist influence was even more significant after 1934 than it had been before. Whereas in the Third Period the Communists provided impetus for the development of policies, including those designed and implemented by others, during the Popular Front they assumed positions from which they could more directly devise and implement policies.

The most striking consequence of the party's activities during the Third Period was that it gave thousands of Communists and their close supporters the organizing and leadership skills, practical experience, self-confidence, and rank-and-file support that enabled them to attain staff and leadership positions in the new CIO industrial unions and organizing committees as well as in several AFL unions.

The formation of the United Electrical Workers resulted from the amalgamation of three distinct groups (all of which favored an industrial union over merger with an AFL craft union, and two of which were closely linked with the party): a federal labor union organized within the AFL and headed by James Carey, an independent union of radio and allied trades headed by Julius Emspak, who was close to the party, and a union headed by James Matles that was formerly part of the TUUL. Carey became president of the new CIO-affiliated union, Emspak secretary-treasurer, and Matles the director of organization.[32]

The connection between the Communists' Marine Workers Industrial Union (MWIU) and the CIO unions in the maritime industry was complicated. The MWIU had the largest following of any TUUL union on the East Coast. It had won some notable struggles and was the parent of the National Maritime Union (NMU) that, as Daniel Nelson writes, proudly proclaimed itself the "legitimate heir of the MWIU." NMU president Joe Curran allied himself with Communists, including Al Lannon and Tommy Ray, originally with the MWIU, and Jack Lawrence, Blackie Myers, and Ferdinand Smith. On the West Coast, Communists organized the MWIU for longshoremen, but they also worked with Harry Bridges to strengthen the AFL's International Longshoremen's Union in ways that would enable it to contest the company-oriented Longshoremen's Association of San Francisco and the Bay District (the corrupt "Blue Book union"). In 1932, party district organizer Sam Darcy, the Communist Harry Hynes, and Bridges began publishing the influential *Marine Worker*. They provided the leadership of the great 1934 strike, and eventually formed the International Longshoremen's and Warehousemen's Union (ILWU) with Bridges as president.[33] In the electrical and maritime industries, Communists and their close allies achieved positions of leadership by serving as the founders of CIO unions.

The Transport Workers Union (TWU) offered yet another example of how Communists and their allies came into positions of direct influence. As Joshua Freeman shows, the TWU formed as a result of a coalition of two earlier efforts at unionization among New York transit workers in the early 1930s. One was led by Communists, while the other was led by former members of the Irish Republican Army (IRA), some of whom eventually became Communists.

Communists began organizing workers in the New York transit industry in 1932. Because the party feared that the transit workers, who were mainly Irish Catholic, would reject a union openly associated with the party, the early efforts were undertaken independently of the TUUL. At the same time, in 1932, the party established an Irish social and cultural organization, the Irish Workers Club, headed by Austin Hogan. The group associated with the IRA, led by IRT conductor Gerald O'Reilly and IRT ticket agent Mike Quill, decided to throw in their lot with the Communist union after failing to find support in the AFL. The Communists and the Irish Republicans united their organizations as the TWU in April, 1934. Quill became president and remained a close supporter of the party until the late 1940s; Hogan became president of the New York local and O'Reilly joined the party and became a member of the TWU staff.[34]

A. F. OF L. TRADE UNIONISTS

Read This Message From the Communists
It Will Help You Win Better Conditions

TO THE MEMBERSHIP OF THE A. F. OF L.

FELLOW WORKERS:

Your delegates to the San Francisco Labor Council June 22nd, adopted a resolution denouncing the Communist participation in the Waterfront strike, and calling for a drive against all members who have Communistic leanings. This resolution was introduced by the members of the Seamen's Unions, with Scharrenberg as the leading spirit. It had the full support of the old reactionary clique of the Labor Council.

Do you realize that this means the denying your membership the right to their own political beliefs? Why should you turn your union into an agent for the Republican, Democratic or any other capitalist party and deny your members the free right to support any political party they want? You should be especially interested in favor of their supporting a working-class party — the Communist Party. The Central Labor Council endorsed Rossi for Mayor—the same Rossi who sent the cops to shoot the waterfront strikers down. Naturally, they are against the Communists. For the same reasons they are against the strike. But you shouldn't be. You should not split your ranks. The Communists are the source, and have been the best mobilizer, of support for the strike.

What motives were behind this action? Was it that the bureaucrats were interested in strengthening the unions? Were they acting as friends of the longshoremen? What is their record as "friends?"

Scharrenberg fought to charter the "Blue Book" Company unions instead of the I. L. A.

O'Connell signed a decision of the Regional Labor Board endorsing the "Blue Book" as a bona fide union.

Casey has been the chief obstacle standing in the way of a strike vote of the Teamsters.

Vandeleur ruled out of order the motion of the I. L. A. delegates for discussion of a general strike vote in support of the longshoremen

These facts speak for themselves. Their only interest is to use the A. F. of L. membership as a weapon to feather their own nests by gaining political favors for themselves from capitalist politicians.

The action of such fakers must not go unchallenged. The rank and file of each union must immediately repudiate it. Introduce a resolution into your local, demanding the right of members to their own political opinions. You must fight against making your union a tool of the Republican and Democratic parties. These same capitalist parties have been responsible for every vicious attack against striking workers. Instruct your delegates to the Labor Council to rescind their action. Fight for rank and file control of your unions. Remove the fakers who try to split your ranks.

Don't be Drawn Into Police Activity Against Your Fellow Workers who are Communists!

The Communists Party is Your Party—it Fights for Workers in All Industries—it Fights for a Workers and Farmers Government!

VOTE COMMUNIST!   **JOIN THE COMMUNIST PARTY!**

COMMUNIST PARTY, U. S. A.
   37 Grove Street,
   San Francisco, California.
I Want to Become a Member of the Communist Party.

Name ....

Address ....

City ....

San Francisco leaflet, summer 1935. In the wake of the 1934 West Coast waterfront strike, the CP rallies support in response to an attack on party members by local AFL leaders. Reproduced from *Isms*, 2nd ed. (Indianapolis: American Legion, 1937).

In many other CIO affiliates, the Communists' role in founding unions or reviving moribund unions led them to positions of leadership. For example, Local 1199, the Retail Drug Employees Union, began as a TUUL union.[35] Communist leadership in the International Woodworkers of America,[36] and the International Union of Mine, Mill and Smelter Workers,[37] reflected a radical tradition that reached back to the Wobblies. In the fur industry, Communists Ben Gold and Irving Potash left a TUUL union to revive an old AFL union which they later brought into the CIO. Communist Donald Henderson gathered together the remnants of unionizing efforts among agricultural and cannery workers and, with John L. Lewis's blessing, created in 1937 the United Canning, Agricultural, Packing and Allied Workers. By virtue of having established the Farm Equipment Organizing Committee in 1938 and leading a strike against International Harvester, Communists assumed leading positions in the United Farm Equipment Workers Union, which was finally chartered by the CIO in 1942. The Communists led a breakaway from the AFL union in the retail and wholesale industry to form the CIO union, the United Retail and Wholesale Employees of America. In each of these cases, the pattern of movement was from activism to leadership.

Similarly, Communists helped combine several AFL federal labor unions into a small CIO union of office workers, the United Office and Professional Workers of America. With the help of Harry Bridges, they organized and led two other small CIO maritime unions on the West Coast, the Marine Cooks and Stewards and the Allied Fishermen's Union. Among telegraphers in the New York area, Communists organized the American Communications Association. Its first president, Mervyn Rathbone, was, Harvey Levenstein writes, "widely regarded as a party member or fellow traveler." Its second, Joseph Selly, had, according to Levenstein, "been active in the TUUL."[38]

The most glamorous unions, in which the Communists assumed responsibility for policy, were the three Hollywood talent guilds—the Screen Writers Guild, the Screen Actors Guild, and the Screen Directors Guild. Writer Victor Navasky pointed out that the first two questions the House Un-American Activities Committee (HUAC) asked the Hollywood Ten in 1947 were, "Are you now or have you ever been a member of the Communist Party?" and "Are you now or have you ever been a member of the guild?"[39] Though Communists were never more than a minority in the actors and directors guilds, the writers guild was another story. Lester Cole recalled that none of the ten writers who started the Screen Writers Guild in 1933 were party members at the time, though many, like himself, joined later. By the time the guild won an NLRB election in 1938, party members among its leadership included the guild's president, John Howard Lawson, Cole, Dalton Trumbo, and Ring Lardner Jr., and they effectively controlled the guild's executive board.[40]

Even in a few AFL unions, the Communists' role in forming new organizations or reviving dormant ones led to their assuming positions of leadership. Most notable among these was the Hotel and Restaurant Workers Union (AFL), where Communist influence in the industry dated back to the Food Workers Industrial Union (TUUL). The TUUL Food Workers' leader, Jay Rubin, became prominent in the AFL union in the 1930s.[41]

Though Communists were able to attain positions of leadership in many of the new CIO unions and organizing committees, and in a few AFL unions, the question remains as to whether there was anything distinctive about their contributions to the formation or implementation of union policies. During the Popular Front, broad agreement existed between Communists and others in the CIO on central policy goals and strategies, including aggressive organizing of the unorganized, establishing inclusive industrial unions regardless of workers' skills, race, or political beliefs, using mass strikes as a tactic of last resort, and mobilizing workers to elect New Deal Democrats. Though not distinctively communist, these objectives were nonetheless to the left of the traditional AFL leadership. In such cases as auto and steel, the Communists made distinctive contributions in the formation and implementation of policies designed to meet these objectives.

The United Automobile Workers Union resulted from the merger of a number of AFL federal labor unions and several independent unions, including a faction of the Mechanics Educational Association of America led by Communist John Anderson. The struggle for an industrial charter within the AFL was spearheaded by a rank-and-file movement led by Wyndham Mortimer, formerly the head of a TUUL auto union in Cleveland, and Bob Travis, a Communist from Toledo Chevrolet. Mortimer became first vice president of the UAW, Travis the director of organizing in Flint, and Anderson president of Local 155.[42] A most notable example of the distinctiveness of the Communist influence on policy implementation occurred during the General Motors sit-down strike of 1936–1937, which was a turning point in the history of the UAW and the CIO, and according to Sidney Fine, "the most significant American labor conflict in the twentieth century."[43] At the UAW convention in 1936, Communists pushed the UAW to target General Motors for organization and prepare for a strike in 1937. Wyndham Mortimer and, later, Bob Travis headed the union drive in Flint, Michigan, which was the heart of GM's empire.[44] To reach auto workers in a company town filled with spies and run by officials who were openly hostile to the union, Mortimer and Travis had assets others lacked, namely contacts with local Communists, former AWU members, and left-wing fraternal orders, such as those affiliated with the International Workers Order (IWO).

Formed by Communists in 1930 as a mutual aid society to provide low-cost life insurance for workers, the IWO had by the mid-1930s fourteen nationality sections and over 62,000 members concentrated in New York and midwestern industrial cities and towns. In Flint, Travis recalled, "I had the IWO. I'd get [the] IWO, they were the best people, too. You'd just bet if you had IWO members that I'd trust those, but you had to be very careful about the rest. You're talking about the time when ... of the thirteen guys on the [local executive] board, eleven of them were stool pigeons.... You could depend on them [IWO members]—maybe a couple of hundred, but they were scattered all through [the plants]." To handle distribution of the union newspaper, Mortimer recruited Charles Killinger, a local Communist. To build the organization in the Fisher Body 1 plant, Travis relied on a group of former AWU members headed by Bud Simons. In short, Communists were prominent among those who laid the groundwork and prepared for the momentous sit-down strike of 1936–1937.[45] Their influence would prove significant in defining the strike strategy and sustaining the effort to achieve an industry-wide agreement.

Though many groups and individuals contributed to the victory of the sit-down strike, the Communists deserve much of the credit for the bold tactics. According to several sources, Communists were primarily responsible for the adoption of the sit-down as a tactic. In any case, Bud Simons was most responsible for the efficiency and discipline with which strikers in the key Fisher Body 1 plant conducted the struggle. Moreover, CIO counsel Lee Pressman and UAW counsel Maurice Sugar, two lawyers closely associated with the party, were able to resist the impulse of another UAW lawyer to capitulate to a court injunction early in the strike. Travis in particular was a tower of strength, resisting the vacillations of CIO representatives Adolph Germer and John Brophy, supporting the seizure of Chevrolet 4 midway during the strike, and holding out for an agreement that covered all seventeen struck plants.[46]

In the packinghouse and steel industries, union recruitment occurred through organizing committees appointed and financed by the CIO. When the CIO eventually transformed the organizing committees into the Packinghouse Workers Union and the United Steel Workers (USW), this top-down control successfully denied Communists the positions of leadership that they enjoyed in unions whose origins were more in the grassroots. Still, the Communist role in the TUUL unions in both industries led to Communists exercising considerable influence in the Packinghouse Workers Organizing Committee and the Steel Workers Organizing Committee (SWOC).[47]

In August 1932, Communists formed the Steel and Metal Workers Industrial Union (SMWIU), which eventually claimed a membership of between 10,000 and 15,000. Meanwhile, inspired by a 1933 strike of coal miners in the mines owned by steel companies, thousands of steel workers joined the AFL's moribund Amalgamated Iron and Steel Association, where they formed a rank and file movement under the leadership of Clarence Irwin, a worker at Youngstown Steel. The rank and file movement aimed to achieve union recognition through a nationwide steel strike in 1934 and 1935. Had the SMWIU and the rank and file movement coalesced, unionization might have occurred as in the auto or electrical industries. Instead, a new union was aborted by the anticommunism of outside advisors of the rank and file movement and by the rigidity of the Communists in steel. The rank and file movement fell under the influence of four social democratic advisors—Clint Golden, Herbert Blankenhorn, Harvey O'Conner, and Stephen Raushenbush. They opposed Irwin's attempt to cooperate with the

Communists and favored relying on government intervention to obtain union recognition rather than a strike. In 1934 the Communists unwittingly played into the hands of Golden and the others by opposing any strike in which the SMWIU role was not primary. After the party line changed in 1935 and the Communists abandoned the SMWIU for the Amalgamated, the party again missed a chance to unite with the rank and file by refusing to leave the Amalgamated after it expelled thousands of members of the rank and file movement who were determined to strike.[48] Any possibility of organizing a steel union from below was finally preempted in June 1936, by John L. Lewis's establishment of SWOC, headed by United Mine Workers vice president Philip Murray.

Nevertheless, the Communists' previous experiences in the industry led to their securing of positions in which they were able to help implement Murray's organizing strategy. Murray had a two-fold strategy—a campaign to sign up steel workers and a campaign to secure endorsements for the union drive by African-Americans and other national groups in the steel communities. Murray hired outside organizers to conduct the recruitment campaign. William Z. Foster recalled that sixty of SWOC's first two hundred organizers were party members,[49] and John Williamson, the party's district organizer in Ohio, recalled that "our entire party and Young Communist League staffs in the steel area were incorporated into the staff of the committee."[50] The International Workers Order, with a large membership among the nationality groups in steel, also played a direct role in recruitment. David Greene, an IWO officer in Pennsylvania, recalled, "When the CIO drive started amongst the steel workers ... the CIO organizer couldn't get into many towns, but we had lodges there, with members there who were miners and who were steel workers. And they went around to ... the steel workers in their town and organized them for the CIO ... so that we played quite a role that added directly, and of course, indirectly." Similarly, John Schmies, the IWO leader in Chicago, reported that the order was active in Chicago, Indiana Harbor, Gary, and Hammond, and that "all of our members who are steel workers joined the union [and] many of them are now active in the leading committees."[51]

To implement the second part of his strategy, building community support, Murray appointed Bill Gebert, the Communist district organizer in Pittsburgh and former organizer of the National Miners Union (TUUL). Gebert relied heavily on the IWO and on a well-respected African-American Communist in Pittsburgh, Ben Careathers, in organizing a series of local and regional conferences in 1936 and 1937. Among participating groups were African-American, Croatian, Slovakian, Slovenian, Lithuanian, Ukrainian, Greek, Hungarian, Czech, and Russian fraternal organizations representing hundreds of thousands of workers. All supported the union drive.[52] Many factors doubtlessly contributed to the decision of Myron Taylor and U.S. Steel to recognize SWOC in March 1937. Not the least of these was the success of the organizing drive, which by that time had generated widespread community support, had recruited 125,000 steel workers, and had caused the collapse of the company unions.[53] The Communists had played a major role in implementing the strategy of this drive.

When John L. Lewis was asked about the prominence of reds in the steel drive, he replied, "Who gets the bird, the hunter or the dog?" Lewis thus indicated his intention to limit the ultimate role of Communists. Since SWOC functioned under an appointed leadership for six years without elections or conventions, the Communists never had a chance to translate their influence as organizers into positions as elected union leaders. Moreover, they found themselves increasingly marginalized by Murray. Bert Cochran notes, "In the case of steel organizers, Communists were simply removed from the payroll, district by district, once the union established itself in the industry."[54]

Besides organizing, Communists also distinguished themselves in implementing union policy regarding political action. In the unions where they had leadership, and in city and state industrial union councils, Communists became major players in the CIO's orientation to local and national politics. The Communist contribution was greatest where labor moved toward politics independent of the Democratic Party, as in the case of the American Labor Party (ALP) in New York.

The ALP was formed in New York in 1936 by leaders of the needle trades unions. It had the backing of unions representing 400,000 members, and in the years from 1936 to 1946 it carried between 5 percent and 50 percent of every election district in New York City. The ALP was the base for the most consistently pro-labor

candidate elected to national office, Congressman Vito
Marcantonio. State chairman of the ALP until 1953, Marcantonio
represented East Harlem in Congress between 1938 and 1950. The
ALP and Marcantonio relied on the energetic campaign efforts of
Communists and the unions under their leadership. Gerald Meyer
points out that "through its control of the neighborhood clubs and
via the affiliation of Communist-led unions, the party rapidly
became a major force within the ALP. By 1948 [party leader
Eugene] Dennis privately noted that virtually every ALP club
leader throughout the city was a party member."[55]

If a distinctive Communist influence can be identified in certain
aspects of organizing unions and in their political action, was it also
evident in the development of other union policies? The policy area
most central to the functioning of trade unions was collective
bargaining. Did it make any difference to collective bargaining
outcomes whether or not a union was led by Communists? The
prevailing view among historians is that the political beliefs of
union leaders had little effect on collective bargaining. Jack
Barbash concludes that "there is no progressive or conservative
method of conducting a strike or negotiating an agreement."[56]
Harvey Levenstein says that neither the politics of Communists
nor anticommunists "played any major role at the bargaining
table."[57] Martin Halpern found that the Thomas-Addes-Communist
group and the Reuther group differed on politics, race, and international affairs, but that "shop floor issues and labor-management
philosophy played only a minor part in the battle for control of the
UAW."[58] Even Earl Browder asserted, after leaving the party, that
"in the matter of *wage policy* there has developed no sustained and
principled difference between the *practice* of the various big, strong
unions of the CIO, whether their leadership has been Left, Center or
Right."[59]

A few historians have claimed that politics did affect collective
bargaining. On one side, Richard Boyer and Herbert Morais have
suggested that Communist-led unions were "the pace-setters for
the whole trade union movement by reason of wage scales and
conditions won."[60] On the other side, Walter Galenson has asserted
that the unions led by non-Communists "never sacrificed their
economic interests at the behest of an alien power," but Communist-dominated unions did.[61] Some historians have suggested that

Communists' political commitment to defeating fascism contributed to the slighting of workers' economic interests during World
War II. Since wage restraint and the no-strike pledge were the
official policies of both the CIO and AFL, the Communists' turn
away from militancy during the war did not constitute a distinctive
feature of Communist policy.[62] In any case, the claims that there
were neither positive nor negative effects have until recently been
supported by evidence of actual bargaining outcomes.

Recently, Judith Stepan-Norris and Maurice Zeitlin examined
the effects of politics on collective bargaining in industrial unions
that were led by Communists, those led by anticommunists, and
those where leadership shifted between Communists and anticommunists. Their examination of a sample of contracts won by
industrial unions between 1937 and 1955 led to the conclusion that
contracts "won by the locals of Communist-led unions were consistently more likely to be pro-labor ... than those won by locals
affiliated with international unions in the shifting and anticommunist camps." More specifically, the contracts of Communist-
led unions, in contrast to the others, were more likely to be short
(one year), to limit management prerogatives, to permit strikes
during the term of the contract, to require a union representative
at the first step of a grievance procedure, and to have a grievance
procedure with few steps and specific time limits. Historians may
have differed widely on whether the politics of union leaders
affected collective bargaining, but in the only systematic study of
the question Stepan-Norris and Zeitlin show that Communist leadership made a difference in bargaining outcomes, and this difference benefitted the shop floor interests of workers.[63]

In two other areas, besides collective bargaining, Communists
made a difference in union policies—union democracy and the
treatment of African-Americans. Social democrats and cold war-
riors have commonly charged the Communists with being undemocratic. This conclusion, however, is based on inferences drawn
from the Communist support of Stalin's dictatorship and from the
consultation on union affairs by Communist union leaders with
party officials. It is not based on an analysis of the actual practices
of Communists and Communist-led unions.[64]

In the most elaborate study of those practices to date, Jerry
Lembcke compares the constitutions and conventions of five Com-

munist-led and five non-Communist-led CIO unions according to
two standards of democracy: a "liberal, pluralist" standard that
measures the amount of rank-and-file control and an "associa-
tional" standard that measures internal unity and minority representation. Lembcke finds that the Communist-led unions were
more likely than the non-Communist to provide for the direct
election and direct recall of officers by the members and for limitations on the appointment power of officers. Moreover, since the
"disqualification of members for political reasons was by far the
most serious means by which democracy in CIO unions was circum-
scribed," it was noteworthy that constitutional clauses forbidding
discrimination on the basis of political affiliation were "a virtual
hallmark of Communist unionism," whereas "many non-communist unions specifically excluded Communists from eligibility for
office and even membership." Lembcke concludes, contrary to conventional wisdom, that the evidence shows that Communists were
"vastly more democratic, by pluralist standards, than their opponents." Lembcke also finds that the Communist unions scored
better on indices of unity and minority representation. He concludes that "Communists advocated organizational forms that
maximized the unity of the largest numbers of workers in an
industry or geographic region."[65] Using different criteria, Bruce
Nelson and James Prickett come to similar conclusions. Nelson
finds that Communist leadership of the ILWU was compatible
"with a vibrant local democracy and a good deal of rank-and-file
independence."[66] In his examination of the treatment of dissidents
in ILGWU, UAW, NMU, and UE, Prickett finds that Communist
union leaders practiced tolerance toward their opponents, while
non-Communist leaders tended to suppress opposition and favor
expulsion of opponents. Prickett concludes that "Communist union
leaders ... were considerably more democratic than their anti-Communist counterparts.... There is no evidence that the Communist-
led unions were undemocratic in any way."[67]

The most consistently distinctive feature of Communist behavior
in unions was their opposition to racial discrimination. Though
critics have sometimes alleged that the Communist support for
racial equality was unprincipled, that is expedient, ritualistic, and
inconsistent, particularly during World War II,[68] the evidence is
overwhelming that those allegations are, in general, false. Even

before 1928, when the party adopted its controversial line calling for the self-determination of blacks in the South, the Communists had rejected the traditional color-blind approach of socialists and argued that combatting racism required special attention and a special strategy. This distinguished their efforts in the trade unions from those of Socialists and many other non-communists.

During the Third Period, Communists gave special attention in their shop papers and union demands to the need to overcome racial discrimination. Frank Marquart, a Socialist auto worker, credited Communist shop papers in the early 1930s "for making me conscious of the fact that Negroes have special problems as a minority group, apart from the general conditions of wage earners."[69] Such agitation, however, did not endear the Communists to all white workers. During the Briggs strike of 1933, the Communist Phil Raymond had to resign as leader of the strike committee after his call for "the solidarity of the workers both white and black" provoked opposition.[70] Because Unemployed Councils and TUUL unions recruited and promoted African-Americans and provided them with organizing and leadership experience, many ended up with positions in the new CIO unions. August Meier and Elliott Rudwick note that it was "not accidental" that three of the first six UAW black organizers had previous experience with the TUUL-organized Auto Workers Union.[71] Similar personal histories occurred in the South. Robin Kelley points out that the Birmingham Communists Hosea Hudson, Henry O. Mayfield, Ebb Cox, and Andy Brown "started out as local leaders of the unemployed and went on to become CIO organizers in Birmingham's mines, mills, and factories."[72] Similarly, Michael Honey observes that both the black leaders and white business agents of the CIO's strongest industrial union in Memphis, Local 19 of the United Cannery, Agricultural, and Packinghouse Workers, "either belonged to or worked closely with the Memphis Communist Party," and some had previously been active in the Southern Tenant Farmers Union.[73]

During the Popular Front, the CP "played a significant, and possibly determinative role" in the creation of the National Negro Congress (NNC), an organization of fraternal, civic and church organizations. Supported by such prominent leaders as Ralph Bunche and A. Philip Randolph, financed in part by the CIO, and led by John P. Davis, a close associate of the CP, the Congress served as a public supporter of CIO organizing drives in Detroit and elsewhere and as a counterweight to the early anti-CIO sentiments of the National Urban League and the NAACP.[74]

Communists consistently advocated racial equality, raised workers' consciousness about discrimination, supported the advancement of blacks to union leadership positions, fought against job discrimination, and helped to implement CIO organizing policies in the black community. Moreover, many African-Americans who rose to union leadership positions were Communists or ex-Communists. The undeniable evidence of the distinctive attention that Communists gave to the race issue undercuts the idea that the Communists' racial policies were unprincipled.

Some historians, while not denying the generally progressive role Communists played on race issues, have, however, raised more subtle issues. August Meier and Elliott Rudwick, for example, suggest that no important differences existed on racial issues in the UAW between Communists and their opponents, like Walter Reuther. They say, "the Communists within the union were usually very similar to other factional groupings in the way they acted on racial matters." All the UAW leaders, according to Meier and Rudwick, believed in interracial trade unionism, and all looked forward to the end of job discrimination, but all were also constrained in their behavior by the deep-seated prejudices of the rank and file.

Though it was true that UAW leaders shared similar progressive views on racial issues, differences did exist. At the 1943 UAW convention, for example, Communists and Secretary-Treasurer George Addes supported the creation of a black seat on the executive board, which Walter Reuther, the leader of the opposing faction, opposed as reverse discrimination. Moreover, Martin Halpern argues that the Thomas-Addes-Communist faction had a more consistent record on racial issues than the Reuther faction and was viewed more favorably by African-Americans in the union. During World War II, Thomas had vigorously opposed the "hate strikes" against black upgrading, had supported housing for blacks, and proposed a program for dealing with the causes of the Detroit race riot of 1943. Addes had advocated the hiring of blacks on the staffs of regional directors. Reuther's faction, however, contained a regional director "who (as Halpern noted) had come under harsh criticism for his anti-black bias," and the Reuther group had defeated the hiring policy advocated by Addes.[75]

Donald Critchlow argues that Communist practice sometimes failed to conform to their rhetoric. He says that while the unions led by Communists and their allies consistently opposed racial discrimination, their opposition differed in strength, depending on the size of the minority membership. The National Maritime Union (NMU), which was 10 percent black and 25 percent Spanish-speaking during World War II, diligently fought to integrate ships and the union. Blacks were well represented as convention delegates, and the union elected Ferdinand Smith, a black West Indian, as secretary-treasurer. Similarly, because of a sizeable black membership in the Marine Cooks and Stewards Union and the Longshoremen's Union, Bruce Nelson writes that Communists and their allies "played a vital role in pushing the unions ... toward a break with white supremacist ideology and practice."

A different situation developed in the electrical industry, according to Critchlow. There African-Americans constituted only 5 percent of the workers in 1940 and 2.7 percent in 1945, and the UE record was less impressive. Though the national union supported the NAACP, the Fair Employment Practices Commission (FEPC), and the campaign against the poll tax, it initiated no FEPC actions against discrimination by electrical companies, and only a handful of blacks served as convention delegates. Even then, Critchlow might be underestimating the record since the UE did elect a black to national union office in 1945. Moreover, Critchlow relied on a contrast between the apathy of the national union on racial issues and the activism of District 4 (New York/New Jersey) and District 8 (St. Louis) both of which worked with government agents against employer discrimination in their shops. Since, however, St. Louis district organizer William Senter was one of the few open Communists in the UE leadership, and both activist districts were led by Communists, it is reasonable to treat the evidence as supporting the interpretation of the Communist role as distinctively progressive on the issue of race.[76]

In their detailed study of the history of the Transport Workers Union (TWU) in New York and Philadelphia, August Meier and Elliott Rudwick suggest another qualification of communist activity on racial issues. They suggest that in spite of the union leaders' radical commitment to racial equality, their actions and policies were constrained by the "pervasive prejudice" of the predominantly white members. Only when the commitment of the union leaders was supplemented by outside pressure from black advancement organizations like the NAACP and the federal government was progress made in breaking down discriminatory practices of the employers and ensuring the interests of black members. The point is a good one, but it is not inconsistent with the argument that the Communist leadership deserved considerable credit for the remarkable gains in equality among white and black transport workers. In the union's first contract, for example, white workers' wages increased 10 percent, but the wages of the more poorly paid black porters increased 25 percent. Moreover, in 1941, after a month-long community boycott of the IRT bus lines in Harlem, Mike Quill signed an unprecedented agreement with the company and the leaders of the boycott providing for the waiving of seniority rights of ninety-one furloughed white workers, the hiring of 100 black drivers, and the alternate hiring of blacks and whites until blacks reached 17 percent of the work force.[77]

Conclusion

The main argument of this essay is that Communist influence on the labor movement took various forms at various times and that during the heyday of the Communist Party, its influence on CIO unions was substantial and beneficial. In the 1920s, Communist influence was largely agitational and educational and involved persuading workers to see the need for industrial unionism, the organization of the unorganized, and racial equality. In the Third Period, this influence was supplemented by another, providing an impulse for policies made by others. Here Communists played a major role in encouraging workers to protest unemployment, evictions, and police repression and to organize industrial unions and strikes. By these actions, Communists exercised a more important influence than in the 1920s by helping to force employers, established union leaders, and government officials to adopt policies favorable to workers. Among these policies were the cessation of wage cuts, the initiation of organizing drives among industrial workers, and the passage of the National Labor Relations Act. After 1934, Communists' influence advanced to another level, to the implementation of organizational and strike policies often decided by non-Communist unionists. With the establishment of many CIO unions which Communists controlled or in which they had a substantial voice, Communist influence assumed another form, the making of union policy. In such areas as political action, collective bargaining, internal democracy, racial equality, Communists exercised a distinctive influence that guided CIO unions under their influence toward greater political independence, more pro-labor contracts, and greater democracy and egalitarianism than would have been likely without their presence.

During World War II, Communist influence in the trade unions peaked. Communist-controlled unions contained about 25 percent of the CIO members, and unions where the Communists had substantial influence contained another 25 percent.[78] If the Communist influence was distinctive and significant, and if it was beneficial to unions and workers, why did it erode so quickly and apparently so completely?

No historian would deny that the cold war, and the postwar red scare, had much to do with this. The question that many historians have found most interesting is: to what extent were the Communists responsible for their own demise? Malcolm Sylvers and James Prickett have argued that the Popular Front, particularly the abolition of party shop units, weakened the party ideologically and organizationally.[79] Harvey Levenstein has argued that the party's Leninism and Popular Front alliances weakened the party by denying union leadership positions to Communists and their allies that they deserved and could have won.[80]

Nelson Lichtenstein has argued that the Communists' opposition to strikes during World War II undermined their position as shop floor militants.[81] Martin Halpern has, however, pointed out that there is no evidence of this for the UAW.[82] Elsewhere, I have argued that Earl Browder's insistence on labor-management cooperation unfavorable to the advancement of labor during World War II, and his attempt to convert the party into a political association, disoriented and disillusioned many rank-and-file Communists.[83] Maurice Isserman and Joseph Starobin have criticized what they consider to have been sectarian trade union policies pursued by

William Z. Foster after he replaced Browder as head of the party.[84] Without questioning the validity of these claims, I nevertheless submit that the opposition to and repression of Communists, which was spearheaded by the Chamber of Commerce, other employer groups, and the Republican Party, was due more to Communist achievements benefiting workers than to Communist limitations. In any case, opposition to Communism in the labor movement and outside it was so formidable because of the cold war that it was inconceivable that the party's influence could have survived in an organizational form under any leadership and following any policies (short of giving up its opposition to capitalism and support of socialism and the Soviet Union).

The Meiklejohn Civil Liberties Institute's two-volume *The Cold War Against Labor* is a recent reminder of the extensiveness of the repression.[85] A brief mention of the high points will suffice. Except for the brief period of the Nazi-Soviet pact (1939–1941), a strong consensus on domestic, foreign, and union policies existed between the CIO's left (the Communists and their allies) and the center (led by Lewis and then Murray) from the creation of the CIO through the War. By 1946 three events began to change labor's environment—the cold war, a management offensive against labor's wartime gains, and a red scare, which David Caute aptly called "The Great Fear."[86] Three signs of this new environment's effect on labor occurred that year. Walter Reuther defeated R. J. Thomas, who was backed by the Communists, for the presidency of the UAW. In Milwaukee, with the help of Reuther, a congressional investigation, and local newspapers, Allis-Chalmers turned a strike of UAW Local 248 into an hysterical anticommunist campaign. At the 1946 CIO convention, Phil Murray engineered the passage of the "resent and reject" resolution, condemning Communist interference in the unions. Major fissures soon opened. Reuther purged Communists from the UAW staff and worked to unseat local Communist officers. Murray fired Len DeCaux and Lee Pressman from the national CIO. Michael Quill of the Transport Workers Union and Joseph Curran of the National Maritime Union broke their Communist ties and purged their erstwhile supporters. In some unions, the Association of Catholic Trade Unionists served as shock troops for assaults against the left. The left and the center in the CIO were soon at odds over whether to comply with the non-Communist affidavits required by the Taft-Hartley Act, whether to support the Marshall Plan, whether to affiliate with the World Federation of Trade Unions, and whether to endorse Henry Wallace and the Progressive Party in the presidential election of 1948.

In 1949, to protest raids upon them by other CIO unions, the United Electrical Workers (UE) and the Farm Equipment Workers withdrew from the CIO. Between November 1949 and August 1950, the CIO formally expelled the UE, the Farm Workers and nine other unions for alleged Communist domination. The expulsions represented as many as one million workers, perhaps one third of the CIO's total membership. Subsequently, raids weakened the expelled unions and led some to disappear and others to merge with more viable unions. Twenty years later only four of the expelled unions still existed.[87]

Meanwhile, at the local level Communists experienced the brunt of a nationwide witch hunt led by the federal government and supplemented by many state governments and other sources as well. The Taft-Hartley Act requirement that all union officials sign non-Communist affidavits led, by 1956, to prison for twenty officers. The Communist Control Act of 1954 denied the services of the NLRB to any union that supported Communist "fronts" or whose leaders were identified with the CP. The Landrum-Griffin Act provided for a $10,000 fine and a year imprisonment for any union officer or member who failed to report their party membership.

By 1954 fifty-nine unions barred Communists from office, and forty barred Communists from being members. The NLRB and the courts upheld the practice of firing employees who pleaded the Fifth Amendment with regard to party membership.[88] By 1955 direct persecution and the great fear had purged nearly every trace of direct Communist influence in the trade unions. That year, as well, the labor movement began to experience a steady erosion of the percentage of workers represented by unions, an erosion that has continued uninterrupted to this very day. Whether or not one agrees with my thesis, that the Communists played a crucial role in the development of industrial unionism and the most progressive elements in the union movement, perhaps the persecution of the party and its elimination from an active role in the labor movement has had the greatest influence of all.

Notes

1. See Roger Keeran, *The Communist Party and the Auto Workers Unions* (Bloomington: Indiana University Press, 1980), p. 24.
2. See Harvey Klehr, *The Heyday of American Communism* (New York: Basic Books, 1984), pp. xi, 223–51, 415–16.
3. See August Meier and Elliott Rudwick, "Communist Unions and the Black Community: The Case of the Transport Workers Union, 1934–1944," *Labor History* (1982): 196–97.
4. See Malcolm Sylvers, "American Communists in the Popular Front Period: Reorganization or Disorganization?" *Journal of American Studies* 23 (1989): 392.
5. See R. Neal Tannahill, *The Communist Parties of Western Europe* (Westport, CT: Greenwood Press, 1978), p. 139.
6. See Len DeCaux, *Labor Radical* (Boston: Beacon Press, 1970), p. 245.
7. See Edward Levinson, *Labor on the March* (New York and London: Harper & Brothers, 1938), p. 282.
8. See Irving Bernstein, *Turbulent Years* (Boston: Houghton Mifflin, 1971), pp. 782–83.
9. See Eric Hobsbawm, *Revolutionaries* (New York: Pantheon Books, 1973), p. 3.
10. See Paul Buhle, *Marxism in the USA* (London: Verso, 1987), p. 131.
11. Foster quoted by Buhle, *Marxism in the USA*, p. 137.
12. See Philip S. Foner, *The T.U.E.L. to the End of the Gompers Era* (New York: International Publishers, 1991), pp. 133–34, 140, 152, 155, 335–36, and *passim*; see also Irving Howe and Lewis Coser, *The American Communist Party* (New York: Frederick A. Praeger, 1962), pp. 245–51.
13. See Theodore Draper, *American Communism and Soviet Russia* (New York: Viking Press, 1960), pp. 285–90.
14. See James Prickett, "The Forgotten Federation: New Perspectives on the Trade Union Unity League," unpublished ms., p. 1.
15. See William Z. Foster, *From Bryan to Stalin* (New York: International Publishers, 1937), pp. 216–81.
16. See Irving Bernstein, *The Lean Years* (Baltimore: Penguin Books, 1960), pp. 20–28; Theodore Draper, "Communists and Miners, 1928–1933," *Dissent* (Spring 1972): 371–92; and Vera Buch Weisbord, *A Radical Life* (Bloomington and London: Indiana University Press, 1977), pp. 298–372.
17. See Robin D.G. Kelly, *Hammer and Hoe* (Chapel Hill: University of North Carolina Press, 1990), pp. 39–56.
18. See Cletus Daniel, *Bitter Harvest* (Ithaca: Cornell University Press, 1981), pp. 105–221.

19. See Bruce Nelson, *Workers on the Waterfront* (Champaign: University of Illinois Press, 1988), pp. 79–98.
20. See Herbert Tank, *Communists on the Waterfront* (New York: New Century Publishers, 1946), pp. 63, 75.
21. See Joyce Peterson, *American Automobile Workers, 1900–1933* (Albany: State University of New York Press, 1987), pp. 126, 146.
22. See Roger Keeran, *The Communist Party and the Auto Workers Unions*, pp. 84–95.
23. See Michael Goldfield, "Worker Insurgency, Radical Organization, and New Deal Labor Legislation," Occasional Paper no. 8, Center for Labor-Management Policy Studies, Graduate School of City University of New York, 1990, p. 20.
24. See ibid.; Daniel J. Leab, "'United We Eat': The Creation and Organization of the Unemployed Councils in 1930," *Labor History* (Fall 1967); Roy Rosenzweig, "Organizing the Unemployed: The Early Years of the Great Depression, 1929–1933," *Radical America* (July-August 1976): 37–62.
25. See William Z. Foster, *History of the Communist Party* (New York: Greenwood Press, 1968), p. 299.
26. Goldfield, "Worker Insurgency," p. 28.
27. Ibid., p. 31.
28. Quoted in ibid., pp. 33–34.
29. See for example Howe and Coser, *The American Communist Party*, pp. 175–272.
30. Sylvers, "American Communists in the Popular Front Period," pp. 373–93.
31. Buhle, *Marxism in the USA*, pp. 151–52.
32. See Ronald Filippelli, "UE: The Formative Years, 1933–1937," *Labor History* (Summer 1976): 351–413.
33. Nelson, *Workers on the Waterfront*, pp. 108–55, 229.
34. See Joshua B. Freeman, "Catholics, Communists, and Republicans: Irish Workers and the Organization of the Transport Workers Union," in Michael Frisch and Daniel Walkowitz, eds., *Working-Class America* (Champaign: University of Illinois Press, 1983), pp. 257–83.
35. See Leon Fink and Brian Greenberg, *Upheaval in the Quiet Zone: A History of Hospital Workers' Union, Local 1199* (Champaign: University of Illinois Press, 1989).
36. See Jerry Lembcke and William Tattam, *One Union in Wood: A Political History of the International Woodworkers of America* (New York: International Publishers, 1984).
37. See Harvey Levenstein, *Communism, Anticommunism and the CIO* (Westport, CT: Greenwood Press, 1981), pp. 64–66.
38. Ibid., pp. 64–69.
39. See Victor Navasky, *Naming Names* (New York: Viking Press, 1990), p. 174.

40. See Levenstein, *Communism, Anticommunism and the CIO*, p. 70; Philip Foner, *The Fur and Leather Workers Union* (Newark: Nordan Press, 1950) pp. 343–58, 462–503; Lester Cole, *Hollywood Red* (Palo Alto, CA: Ramparts Press, 1981), pp. 12–128, 162–63.

41. See Bert Cochran, *Labor and Communism* (Princeton: Princeton University Press, 1977), pp. 57–58.

42. Keeran, *The Communist Party and the Auto Workers Unions*, pp. 96–145.

43. See Sidney Fine, *Sit-Down* (Ann Arbor: University of Michigan Press, 1970), p. 341.

44. See Wyndham Mortimer, *Organize!* (Boston: Beacon Press, 1972), pp. 103–04.

45. Keeran, *The Communist Party and the Auto Workers Unions*, pp. 148–85; see also Roger Keeran, "The International Workers Order and the Origins of the CIO," *Labor History* (Summer 1989): 385–408; and interview of Robert Travis by Neil Leighton, 13–15 December 1978, University of Michigan–Flint.

46. Keeran, *The Communist Party and the Auto Workers Unions*, pp. 148–85; see also Christopher Johnson, *Maurice Sugar* (Detroit: Wayne State University Press, 1988), p. 194.

47. Levenstein, *Communism, Anticommunism and the CIO*, pp. 49–51, 69.

48. See Staughton Lynd, "The Possibility of Radicalism in the Early 1930s: The Case of Steel," *Radical America* (November-December 1972): 37–64.

49. Foster, *History of the Communist Party*, p. 349.

50. See John Williamson, *Dangerous Scot* (New York: International Publishers, 1969), pp. 125–26.

51. Greene and Schmies quoted by Roger Keeran, "The International Workers Order," pp. 294–395.

52. Ibid., pp. 389–96.

53. See Irving Bernstein, *Turbulent Years*, pp. 467–73.

54. Cochran, *Labor and Communism*, pp. 100–1.

55. See Gerald Meyer, *Vito Marcantonio* (Albany: State University of New York Press, 1989), pp. 5–6, 25–26, 66.

56. See Jack Barbash, "Ideology and the Unions," *American Economic Review* (December 1943): 875.

57. Levenstein, *Communism, Anticommunism and the CIO*, p. 334.

58. See Martin Halpern, *UAW Politics in the Cold War Era* (Albany: State University Press of New York, 1988), p. 199.

59. See Earl Browder, "The Decline of the Left Wing of American Labor," unpublished paper, 1948, p. 25.

60. See Richard Boyer and Herbert Morais, *Labor's Untold Story* (New York: Cameron, 1955), p. 361.

61. See Walter Galenson, "Communists and Trade Union Democracy," *Industrial Relations* (October 1974): 242.

62. See Nelson Lichtenstein, *Labor's War at Home* (New York: Cambridge University Press, 1982); Martin Glaberman, *Wartime Strikes* (Detroit: Bewick, 1989); Joshua Freeman, "Delivering the Goods: Industrial Unionism During World War II," *Labor History* (Fall 1978): 570–93; Ed Jennings, "Wildcat! The Wartime Strike Wave in Auto," *Radical America* (July–August 1975): 77–113.

63. See Judith Stepan-Norris and Maurice Zeitlin, "'Red' Unions and 'Bourgeois' Contracts?" *American Journal of Sociology* (March 1991): 1161–167.

64. See James Prickett and Walter Galenson, "Communism and the Trade Unions: An Exchange," *Industrial Relations* (October 1974).

65. See Jerry Lembcke, *Capitalist Development and Class Capacities: Marxist Theory and Union Organization* (Westport, CT: Greenwood Press, 1988), pp. 133–34, 138, 153.

66. See Bruce Nelson, "Unions and the Popular Front: The West Coast Waterfront in the 1930s," *International Labor and Working-Class History* (Fall 1986): 60.

67. See James Prickett, "Communists and the Communist Issue in the American Labor Movement, 1920–1950," PhD diss., University of California, Los Angeles, 1975, pp. 422, 427.

68. See Wilson Record, *The Negro and the Communist Party* (Chapel Hill: University of North Carolina Press, 1951); Howe and Coser, *The American Communist Party*, pp. 415–16; and Harry Haywood, *Black Bolshevik* (Chicago: Liberator Press, 1978), pp. 499.

69. See Frank Marquart, *An Auto Worker's Journal* (University Park: Pennsylvania State University Press, 1975), p. 35.

70. Keeran, *The Communist Party and the Auto Workers Unions*, pp. 86–87.

71. See August Meier and Elliott Rudwick, *Black Detroit and the Rise of the UAW* (New York: Oxford University Press, 1979), pp. 42–44.

72. See Robin D.G. Kelley, "A New War in Dixie: Communists and the Unemployed in Birmingham, Alabama, 1930–1933," *Labor History* (Summer 1989): 384.

73. See Michael Honey, "The Popular Front in the American South: The View from Memphis," *International Labor and Working Class History* (Fall 1986): 51–52.

74. See Mark Naison, *Communists in Harlem During the Depression* (New York: Grove Press, 1984), pp. 178, 200; Meier and Rudwick, *Black Detroit*, pp. 28–33, 55–57.

75. Halpern, *UAW Politics*, pp. 126–27.

76. See Donald T. Critchlow, "Communist Unions and Racism," *Labor History* (Spring 1976): 230–44; Ronald Schatz, *The Electrical Workers* (Champaign: University of Illinois Press, 1983), p. 157; and Nelson, *Workers on the Waterfront*, p. 259.

77. See August Meier and Elliott Rudwick, "Communist Unions and the Black Community: The Case of the Transport Workers Union, 1934–1944," *Labor History* (1982): 165–97.
78. See David Milton, *The Politics of U.S. Labor* (New York and London: Monthly Review Press, 1982), p. 121.
79. Sylvers, "American Communists"; and Prickett, "The Forgotten Federation."
80. Levenstein, *Communism, Anticommunism, and the CIO*.
81. Lichtenstein, *Labor's War*.
82. Halpern, *UAW Politics*.
83. Keeran, *The Communist Party and the Auto Workers Union*.
84. See Maurice Isserman, *Which Side Were You On?* (Middletown, CT: Wesleyan University Press, 1982); and Joseph R. Starobin, *American Communism in Crisis, 1943–1957* (Cambridge: Harvard University Press, 1972).
85. See Ann Fagan Ginger and David Christiano, eds., *The Cold War Against Labor* (Berkeley: Meiklejohn Civil Liberties Institute, 1987).
86. See David Caute, *The Great Fear* (New York: Simon and Schuster, 1978).
87. See Frank Emspak, "The Break-up of the Congress of Industrial Organizations (CIO), 1945–1950," PhD. diss., University of Wisconsin, 1972; David Oshinsky, "Labor's Cold War: The CIO and the Communists," in Robert Griffith and Athan Theoharis, eds., *The Specter* (New York: Franklin Watts, 1974), pp. 116–51; and F.S. O'Brien, "The 'Communist-Dominated' Unions in the United States Since 1950," *Labor History* (Spring 1968): 184–209.
88. O'Brien, "'Communist-Dominated' Unions," pp. 188–91.

THE RED AND THE BLACK:
The Communist Party and African-Americans in Historical Perspective

Gerald Horne

Introduction

There is a saying among Los Angeles rock critics that most rock critics like Elvis Costello because most critics look like Elvis Costello. If one understands that point, one understands some of the problems of the historiography of the Communist Party. The isolation of its scholars, the fact that they are "lone rangers," that they are often not part of political collectives and often lack "real world" administrative or managerial experience—all of this colors the kind of political history they write. Yet, it is clear that whatever history of the CPUSA is written, it cannot avoid addressing the significance of party policy and activism to the African-American experience in the twentieth century.

One does not have to be of African descent to write African-American history or an activist to write the history of activists. Nevertheless, it does seem that the isolated scholar tends to valorize the maverick and/or the apostate when writing about left movements. The fact that this dovetails with the dominant rightist discourse no doubt helps to buoy the tendency.

It is a particularly mischievous one in the case of the historiography of the left. Scholarly isolation has, typically in this case, inhibited scholarly imagination in accounting for the articulation of left organizations within the fluid and diverse contexts in which they exist. The result has often been tendentious overemphases on specific events and, correspondingly, a tendency to narrow the evidentiary basis for evaluating the wider regional, national, and even international impacts of such organizations. This is evident in the mainstream historiography of the Communist Party, particularly in regard to the party's policies about race.[1]

"The Negro National Question"

African-Americans were, in a sense, predisposed to be receptive to the Communist Party, and were recruited by it. They were less anticommunist than other groups, and tended to view the party's emphasis on "white chauvinism" more favorably than others who saw it as exaggerated and as an error.[2] Nevertheless, one of the weaknesses of the CP's approach to race relations, and that of the entire progressive movement, has been a relative lack of attention to the question of geography and the nature of federalism.

Communists have been justifiably proud of the consistency with which they have advanced the notion of the "centrality" of the Negro national question. But this virtue presents its own difficulties in the tendency to overgeneralize. One must ask whether or not, and if so how, the party's way of defining the question has been responsive to the different economic, political, and cultural conditions that exist in the United States, in New Mexico, or the Dakotas, or Hawaii, or even California.[3] For example—and this is certainly arguable—the generality with which the party formulated its policy in regard to race may have been partly responsible for one of the party's most grievous blunders. When "Little Tokyo" in Los Angeles became "Bronzeville" and African-Americans began to replace Japanese-Americans, the party chose not to subject this variation on the general issue of race relations to a sensitive and forceful Marxist critique.[4]

In retrospect, it is reasonable to suggest that, along with the trade union question, the Negro national question was of central concern to the leadership of the CP. This is reflected to some extent in the career of Ben Davis, a Harvard-trained attorney and prominent black Communist between the 1930s and the 1960s. It was of central importance in his victorious campaign for election to the New York City Council in 1943, as it was during the party crisis of 1956. However, to understand the specific historical significance of the Negro national question, it is important to understand the more general aspects of the party's position on what Marxists called "the national question."

What drove the diverse and multifaceted system of alliances that the party expected would provide the basis of a broad anti-capitalist movement during the years leading up to the war, was a theory

Campaign poster highlighting demand for black national self-determination, 1932.
Courtesy of Tamiment Institute Library, New York University.

that simultaneously encompassed the notion of a "united front" and the "national question." In the context of the United States, this had to do with principles and policies in regard to the experience of the African-American community.

The "national question" was and remains, for many Marxists, one of the most complex questions in the social sciences. The position and experience of African-Americans in U.S. history substantiates the point. This was understood as much by the party's enemies as by its friends, as is indicated by Herbert Philbrick, a professional "stool pigeon," in his summary of his employers' views: "The importance of the race question to the Communist Party and its purposes is indicated by the fact that it has [devoted] more printed matter to the American Negro [than] any other segment of the American population."[5]

Unfortunately, in analyzing the complications of the party's position on race, many historians have resorted to simplistic invocations of the ubiquitous "hand of Moscow." For example, Bernard and Jewel Bellush tell us that "what was good for Mother Russia was good for American Communists.... At no time during the New Deal was the response of the CPUSA determined by factors indigenous to this nation...." In this regard, "the Communists contributed significantly to the demise of the left."[6]

This tends to be the consensus view still, despite evidence of what seems to be a new historiographical disposition to review the case. Eric Foner has noted the benefit of comparative study for understanding the post-emancipation South.[7] A fortiori, in an area where it is assumed that one nation has had so much influence on the policies of so many other nations—indeed virtually every nation—one would expect at least some North American scholars to have looked at Marxist-Leninist parties historically within a comparative framework. That they have not represents an intellectual failure of enormous magnitude, since it in effect constitutes an exemption of the historiography of the parties from even the minimal requirements for dealing with contextual factors in historical inquiry.

The issue is important since to see the CPUSA as merely a puppet is to see those to whom it appealed as passive and incapable of having chosen their politics rationally. In this case, the attractiveness of the party to African-Americans becomes extremely problematic.[8] What characterizes the new historians of Communism is their willingness to acknowledge the indigenous influences on party politics, and to demonstrate those influences by detailed accounts of the formulation and implementation of specific policies. In this essay, I will examine the way the party posed the "Negro national question," how it developed as an issue in the context of the African-American experience, and how the question presented itself in the context of an election that brought together the Red and the Black.

Admittedly, the U.S. party did see itself as the advanced detachment of the Communist International (CI, or Comintern) based in Moscow. But it does not follow that it was the International's puppet. This exaggeration was due in large part to a tendency only to credit the testimony of those who had left the party. On the other hand, it is useful to examine the viewpoint of Sam Darcy, one of the highest ranking party leaders until his departure in 1945. Darcy was posted by the U.S. party to Moscow and worked directly with both Stalin and Bukharin. He alleges that it is "completely wrong" to portray the CI as "monolithic" or "homogeneous." There was "constant inner struggle," often "with the most violent language used [by] contending factions." The CI "had no way of enforcing its decisions" but "moral influence." Thus, Darcy views Gerhart Eisler, CI representative in the United States, not only as the CI's voice in America but as a conciliator of the U.S. factions grouped variously around Jay Lovestone, Earl Browder and William Z. Foster. Darcy concludes: "From all I have said... about the international influence on the Communist Party I hope no one gets the idea that these class struggles were initiated by the Comintern or other outside forces.... They were born of conditions that exist in this country."[9]

At the Sixth Congress of the CI, in 1928, it was decided collectively that the party should reorient its policies toward blacks. The CI, like the CPUSA, operated on the principle of democratic centralism in which a democratic discussion is followed by a decision that all are expected to carry out. To that extent, the CPUSA must be understood as part of the CI. The "Black Belt" thesis that emerged from this meeting was that blacks in the Black Belt South constituted a nation with the right to self-determination. Due to the particular conditions under which the thesis could be converted to policy for the U.S., this simple idea was to cause more than a bit of grief for both the party and its chief black spokesperson, Benjamin J. Davis.

The United States delegation to the Sixth Congress had five African-Americans. But according to Philip Foner and James Allen, Harry Haywood "was the only American Black" to back the thesis; it was opposed by James Ford and Otto Hall. There was only one Soviet citizen on the subcommittee formulating the thesis. At the same time, the South African party's policies were also under discussion, and this inevitably influenced the U.S. debate. Yet, it is often forgotten that, by the end of the day, it was decided that the Black Belt thesis was to be for purposes of propaganda while the key theme of the struggle was to be equal rights. By most accounts, this complex resolution was the result of lengthy debate and was more influenced by the U.S. participants than by Stalin.[10] If one were to criticize the adoption of the "Black Belt" thesis, it would be more appropriate to say the hand of the world rather than that of Moscow was too intrusive.[11]

Benjamin Davis's comrade, James Ford, has been accused of refracting the Soviet view exclusively in his 1935 pamphlet, "The Negroes in a Soviet America." A United Soviet States of America would mean "complete independence of the Black Belt region"; blacks could choose "federation with or separation from" the U.S. The party would "urge and fight for federation" but "would respect" sovereignty. In the North, blacks could "remain in Harlem" or move. The latter would be encouraged as it would "hasten the destruction of all forms of separation." In the Black Belt Republic, blacks would play the "principal" but not an exclusive role: not the "dictatorship of the Negroes" but of the "workers," since the "Soviet Negro Republic" would not necessarily be all black. Though many whites might find all of this objectionable, there are still many African-Americans who find it a vision worth considering.[12]

To understand why the Black Belt thesis was adopted, it is more important to understand how established an idea it was, in many ways, in the context of the African-American experience in the United States, independent of Soviet influence. For example, Cyril Briggs of the African Blood Brotherhood had enunciated a Black Belt thesis at the beginning of the 1920s.[13] As early as 1918, blacks in Texas supported a plan to make part of it a forty-ninth state, for blacks—a view thought by some at the time to have been consistent with Woodrow Wilson's "Fourteen Points," which included self-determination. Memories of the struggle of Native Americans for their own land, e.g., in Oklahoma, and the successes of Marcus Garvey were also certainly part of the background of the debate. Those who gathered in Moscow in 1928 did not have to construct the Black Belt thesis from whole cloth.[14]

A number of writers have nevertheless claimed that the Black Belt thesis was out of touch with the African-American experience. However, the evidence suggests that this criticism is misleading. Abner Berry, who left the party in the 1950s after working in the South for some time, felt that the Black Belt thesis was received more favorably in the South than the North. Below the Mason-Dixon line, he writes, "memory is already there of how land had been taken from" blacks. Moreover, blacks in the South understood quite well the need for a "conspiratorial organization."

Like Darcy, Berry saw Eisler's role as CI representative in the U.S. as "not obtrusive" in regard to the Black Belt Thesis and related issues.[15] Davis agreed: "If one goes into the Black Belt today and asks a Negro farmer if he wants 'self-determination' he may not understand at once just what is meant. But if you explain, if you ask him if he wants the land, he will answer 'yes.'" Like Ford, Davis lauded the idea of a "Soviet America."[16]

Generally, the party was true to the original admonition to utilize the Black Belt thesis for propaganda and focus on the struggle for equal rights as a matter of praxis. The Foster-Ford presidential ticket of 1932 reflected this focus.[17] Their 1936 platform highlighted "full rights for Negroes," "complete equality," "death penalty for lynchers," and enforcement of the Civil War constitutional amendments. The Black Belt thesis was not even mentioned.[18]

In his 1938 party "Report on Negro Work," Robert Minor, the party's expert on the Negro question in the pre-World War II era, declared that "the main link to be seized is that link around employment discrimination or limitation in employment opportunities," and urged comrades to join black churches.[19] The 1938 "Election Platform Demands of the CP," like the platform of 1936, did not mention the Black Belt thesis.[20]

On balance, the Black Belt thesis was probably not an asset for the party, particularly during the postwar period when blacks moved en masse to the North and West. It was particularly unhelpful during Ben Davis's campaign for office. On the other hand, support for the thesis was understandable in the light of the relative success of the movement led and symbolized by Marcus Garvey.

Communists had direct experience with the Garvey movement. Claude Lightfoot, a long-time party leader in Illinois, was a member of the United Negro Improvement Association (UNIA) as a child: "I had an aunt who was a top leader; I had an uncle, a top leader and so forth and I used to go to the meetings and sing the songs and chant the slogans, etc., etc." What did he learn? "Black pride for one thing."[21] Party leader Israel Amter, who was not black, had a related experience: "In Cleveland, I also made contact with the Cleveland (UNIA).... There was something splendid about them.... The men and women who followed [Garvey] were wonderful. I felt privileged to be invited to their meetings.... They received me warmly.... Members of the UNIA came to speak at united front meetings organized by us on problems of those years, when the shadow of the big depression was descending upon all of us."[22] The Communists and the Garveyites clashed intellectually but were able to find unity in action.

Garvey was a complex and mercurial figure. Therefore, the party's response to him had to be flexible and sensitive. After the government initiated its investigation of his movement and began to issue indictments, Garvey's radicalism, formerly symbolized by his pro-Bolshevik comments, tended to ebb. He allied his movement with Tammany and even backed white Democrats against black Republicans.

There were other nationalist trends that the party viewed less benignly. During the "don't buy where you can't work" campaign in Harlem in the 1930s, the *Daily Worker* expressed these tensions in a vivid editorial: "We denounce the present methods of barring those sympathetic whites—workers, intellectuals, and professionals—who have manifested a desire to sincerely fight for the rights of the Negro people by picketing stores where whites are only employed at the present time. These [campaign] 'leaders' are taking advantage of the nationalist feelings of the much oppressed Negro people in order to gain security for themselves."[23]

Just as the First Amendment carries an inherent tension between the free exercise of religion clause and the clause prohibiting the government from supporting religion, the party's position on the Negro question was divided between a concept of self-determination which could have been taken to imply support for black separatism, and the idea of equal rights which could have been taken to imply support for integration. This tension is evident in most aspects of the party's relations with nationalists and nationalism.[24]

Ben Davis was particularly caustic in his analysis of certain nationalists. For example, he denounced Sufi Abdul Hamid, "Harlem's self-styled 'Black Hitler,'" and his comrades who stabbed an International Labor Defense leader as he was speaking in Harlem against low wages paid to black butchers. These black nationalists had been hired by Julius Malin, the owner of the market.[25] Similarly, one writer for the *New Masses* commented that "nationalist speakers who nightly attack" Harlem progressives "are said to be sponsored by Tammany."[26]

Davis himself remained a vigorous critic of black nationalism. When Garvey died in 1940, Davis wrote an article that attempted to show Garvey's "Back to Africa" theories as having "feet of clay":

> He organized perhaps the biggest movement of Negroes in the history of the country.... The Negro people were sound and progressive in their feelings for a government of their own and for independent existence as a nation.... [But this] fantastic dream of a trek to Africa [was] ridiculously impossible... He neither saw nor understood the class struggle, but instead saw as the solution the building of a parasitic Negro imperialism, [which amounted to] petty bourgeois nationalism.... Garvey's methodology was a sort of inverted segregation.... The real blow to Garveyism was given by the Communist Party....[27]

After charging Garvey with having supported Mussolini during the conflict with Ethiopia and accusing him of having broken strikes in Jamaica, Davis reiterated the Black Belt thesis. Yet, nowhere in the article did he perceive any connection between the party's view of self-determination and the early success of Garveyism.

Former party leader Dorothy Healey has observed about the CP, "... when we make mistakes, it's considered part of a terrible conspiracy; and when others do, it's just a momentary lapse of judgment."[28] This could be applied to perceptions of the Black Belt thesis. For despite its flaws, the party was probably unparalleled in fighting racism not just in society but within its own ranks as well. The 1930s are known already as the time when the party began to cast out members on the grounds of "white chauvinism."[29] However,

this was not satisfactory to some black members. At a 1932 meeting
in Harlem that featured Briggs and Haywood, among other nota-
bles, much dissatisfaction was expressed with the campaign
against white chauvinism.[30]

James Prickett's comments on red trade unionists should be
considered in that light: "As unionists, they were far superior to
their anticommunist counterparts, but they were poor Communists." Could this be applied more generally to the work of reds in
the black liberation movement? Were they poor Communists? It
could certainly have been argued that they were, insofar as they
maintained the Black Belt thesis even after the "facts on the
ground" had changed. Were they "far superior" to their "anticommunist counterparts?" Undoubtedly.[31]

Despite the tensions it produced, the attempt to walk the fine
line between class and race helps to explain the party's relative
success among African-Americans, especially given their lack of
political alternatives. Abner Berry believes that the political dislocation ignited by the Republican Party's attempt to oust blacks in
the early 1930s left the black community "thrashing around,"
looking for leadership. Berry argues that the party was able,
partially, to fill this vacuum. He concludes, however, that this was
a mixed blessing: it encouraged African-Americans to think of
themselves as "American" rather than to confront, more authentically, their alienation.[32]

Ben Davis: Theoretician and Activist

Davis was a staunch advocate of the Black Belt thesis over the
years, though there is no evidence indicating that he objected to
Browder's ditching of the thesis during the war. He was also the
major interpreter of black history within the party whose interpretations were fully consistent with the revolutionary tradition. At
times, his positions could be seen as reflections of "Browderism,"
for example, in a 1938 article in which Davis referred to Thomas
Jefferson as the "first Abolitionist," despite the fact that he "owned
slaves." Yet a more dominant theme was expressed in another
article published that same year, in which Davis outlined "the
revolutionary traditions of the Negro people," praising in that
regard Lincoln, Frederick Douglass and John Brown.[33]

Davis's awareness of the importance of history is evident in his essay on Wendell Phillips where he noted that Phillips "would have toured the country in support of the Southern Conference for Human Welfare...." When applying the lessons of Reconstruction, Davis pointed to "a new 'unholy alliance' between the reactionary Southern Democratic industrialists and landlords on the one hand and the Republican Tories in the North on the other." This historical awareness is evident in the terms in which Davis evaluated the party: "The Communist Party has performed an outstanding service to the country by re-discovering ... Negro achievements during the Reconstruction period, and by carrying them forward against the slanders of the Tories and the fascists."[34]

The persistence of lynching meant that invoking Reconstruction was not merely a theoretical position removed from practical reality. Davis spoke and wrote numerous times on this problem and its handmaiden, the poll-tax. Many times he brought to light concrete examples of lynching horrors and of people fighting back. On various occasions, he assailed Democrats and Republicans alike for their lethargy or refusal to oppose lynching and the poll-tax. He was particularly scornful of Senator Bilbo: "If someone put a burglar-proof [device] on Senator Bilbo's mouth, it would keep a little more poison out of the air we breathe." He referred to Governor Talmadge as a "pint-sized dictator" and a "menace to democracy." Roosevelt and Willkie he accused of being "tremendously interested in 'democracy' in far-away places ..." but not in the South. The Republican Party was a special target of his criticism. Davis called their filibuster against anti-lynch legislation, their aim of "talking the hind legs off of a donkey," a "brazen nullification of the Fifteenth Amendment." He accused "Senate Tories" of "the trick [of cutting] off the anti-lynching bill from the rest of the progressive measures to divide the forces in support of the bill." He used his considerable legal skill to unmask opponents of the anti-lynching bill. What this one-man campaign shows is that his support of the Black Belt thesis did not inhibit Davis in fighting for equal rights.[35]

As election day approached in 1943, the Davis campaign for election to the New York City Council had an air of victory about it. Crowds flocked to Davis's rallies. The climax of this campaign, and perhaps the apex of Communist influence in the U.S. to that point in the twentieth century, came in late October. Over seven thousand cheered Davis at two rallies. Subsequently, he recalled that "the Golden Gate was sold out ten days before the rally. On the day of the event, the fire department closed the hall two hours before the hour of performance when I, the guest of honor, appeared on the scene. It was all I could do to get in. Another 5,000 people had gathered outside the Golden Gate." A second hall had to be rented on the spot. The account published in the *Daily Worker* recalled that the hall was

> jammed to its 4,500-person capacity. By 3:15 the Renaissance, ... 121 W. 138th St., was crowded with an additional 2,300 and the fire department was turning away thousands of Negro and white citizens. When the Communist candidate walked down the aisle ... to the platform the entire audience leaped to its feet and rocked the hall with applause.

Among the speakers were Powell, Ella Reeve Bloor, Elizabeth Gurley Flynn, and James Ford. Hazel Scott performed, and Paul Robeson sang "The Purest Kind of Guy." Years later one participant recalled to Davis her little boy being carried to the platform and emptying "his piggy-bank into your hands to assure your election to the City Council."[36]

In addition to the size of the crowd, what was remarkable about the rally was the incredible number of African-American celebrities who saw fit to support the campaign of a member of the Communist Party, despite the danger of jeopardizing their careers. But Davis was so compelling a candidate, and the urgency so great that what would otherwise have been unusual became what was expected. The breadth of support for Davis from prominent people seemed to signal, in the popular phrase of the day, that a "new world is coming," though there had been notable cases of celebrity support for the party well before 1943. Pianist Teddy Wilson, who was chair of Davis's Artists Committee, played a key role in bringing Lena Horne, Duke Ellington, Count Basie, Mary Lou Williams, Coleman Hawkins, Billie Holiday, Jimmie Lunceford, Art Tatum, Ella Fitzgerald, Lucky Roberts, Josh White, Pearl Primus, and Fredi Washington to the rally to express publicly their support for Davis. Each member of the cast of *Oklahoma!* pledged $100 to his campaign. When Powell referred to Davis as "my logical successor," he was as much attempting to draw upon Davis's luster as he was trying to share his own. *The People's Voice* noted that the affair "brought out more top-flight stars than have ever honored any political candidate in the history of Harlem."[37]

This was so extraordinary that it merits further examination. The British musicologist, Ian Hall, has observed that many whites who relate to black music in Britain see it as a form of rebellion against the established order. Certainly the "established order" did not, in the 1930s and 1940s, embrace the kind of music made by those listed above; but the reds did, the later flap over "be-bop" notwithstanding. The role of writers close to the left, like Barney Josephson and John Hammond, in promoting this music is well-known. Yet what is even more striking is the fact that black artists and musicians, including Cab Calloway and Lionel Hampton (who subsequently became a Republican), continued to support Davis. In 1952, Charles "Yardbird" Parker was still performing in benefits; and in 1956, W.C. Handy referred to Davis as "my dear friend." As late as 1959 Ted Curson was still appearing at benefits for Davis just as Billie Holiday had been a regular at May Day celebrations during the 1940s.[38]

The capacity of the party to draw support from black writers and artists extended from the 1930s through much of the 1950s. While Davis was undoubtedly an exceptional figure and his campaign particularly attractive, support for him had the background of continual support for the party among many prominent African-Americans. Perhaps the best known celebrity in the party's orbit was Richard Wright, who had once been a member of Davis's party cell, and still supported him in 1943.

Davis admired Wright, though not uncritically. Margaret Walker refers to Davis as the "most important of the black reviewers" of *Native Son*. While Davis condemned the politically motivated closing of the Broadway version of *Native Son*, he was critical of the novel.[39] But he was by no means the most critical of the reviewers. Lloyd Brown recalled that he had been "much more critical," and Addison Gayle argues that Davis protected Wright from even harsher censure from party leaders like Ford. Indeed, while Davis's reaction to Wright's *Twelve Million Black Voices* was mixed, he called it "the first realistic, class-conscious narrative of the Negro people in the United States," though, "one could wish ... that the picture would have been a bit more balanced."[40]

But Wright's backing of Davis in the 1943 election was to be his swan song with the party for some time to come. Months later, he attacked the party publicly. Gayle describes an FBI tap that re-corded Davis's reluctance to respond to Wright: "I regard him as just another casualty of the movement of the people for freedom today.... To enter into a polemic with this guy is simply going to prolong that period during which they are going to try and exploit everything he can say about the Communists...."[41]

Davis ultimately did respond to Wright—sharply and publicly—for his "wholly unjustifiable attack upon the Communists—the very organization whose outlooks had helped him create his master-piece.... The Communist organization took no official position [on his work] but rather invited and stimulated broad, free discussion and comment upon it.... However, Wright sulked and chafed at all criticism; and rejected it all. Who was intolerant in this case?" Davis's rejoinder to Wright's statement that he left the party in 1940 ended with a question: "why did he wait until now" to an-nounce it? "Whether Wright wants to or not he is qualifying for very green open and prosperous pastures. Time will tell."[42]

Wright's association with C.L.R. James during this period might have influenced his decision to attack the party at that apparently late date.[43] In any event, when *Black Boy* was published, Davis denounced it unequivocally, but in literary rather than strictly political terms. Other critics have similarly found something of a decline in Wright's writing after his Communist period.

Nevertheless, Margaret Walker is probably correct when she says that "Wright seemed in 1956 to be revising both his feelings about black nationalism and his attitudes toward red internation-alism...."[44] Abner Berry, writing in the *Daily Worker* at that difficult moment of re-thinking by Communists, also departed somewhat from the negative view of Wright then held by some comrades.[45] This was a result, in part, of Wright's own public conduct during that period: he agreed to lead a committee in Paris to support freeing Henry Winston.[46]

Perhaps because of its own traditional support for the arts, and certainly because of the importance it came to attach to the arts in regard to the "national question," the Communist Party was able to sustain its attractiveness to the arts community, black and white. This may help to account for why the party's response to Wright did not prevent other writers from flocking to the party banner before, during, and after the 1943 election campaign.

Langston Hughes, the most prominent of them, was joined by, among others, Walter Lowenfels, Harold Cruse and José Yglesias.[47]

Davis was a naturally attractive figure among artists. His support from the artistic community was an extension of his own interest in the arts. He was an accomplished violinist and something of an art critic. He believed that "it is obvious that the Negro has had a profound and creative effect on the American dance, on literature, on drama and on nearly every other field of artistic endeavor." He consulted closely with the Negro Playwrights Company, which included George Murphy as well as Hughes and Locke. Paul Robeson, a close friend of Davis, had ties with the artistic community—for example with Lena Horne and José Ferrer. Support from that community was to prove important during the 1943 campaign. The prominent black actor of the 1940s, Rex Ingram, endorsed Davis, and Horne was repeatedly quoted as saying, "it is my duty as an American to endorse" him.[48]

The cultural base of Davis's campaign extended beyond the arts to sports. Joe Louis supported Davis avidly. Again, this had as much to do with Davis as it had with any tendency of the base to extend itself naturally beyond the arts. Davis, like Robeson, was a former athlete, and had been intimately involved in the effort to advance blacks in sports. The party acknowledged the value of these efforts.[49]

In fact, not enough has been written to this day about the importance of the party's activities in that regard. For example, the Communists, in 1943, presented thousands of signatures to Branch Rickey, general manager of the Brooklyn Dodgers, concerning the "need for adding star Negro players to the Dodgers." Later, Davis, Max Yergan, Pete Cacchione, Robeson, Robert Murphy of the *Afro-American*, and Ira Lewis of the *Pittsburgh Courier*, met with baseball moguls at New York's Hotel Roosevelt to discuss desegregation. This was bound to win support and votes in a sports-hungry black community.[50]

The ruling class never forgot the support the party, and Davis, received from celebrities in the arts. No doubt the red scare of the late 1940s and 1950s was inspired in part by the fear members of the ruling class had that the left would continue to grow, especially in the post-war context of strikes and the tremendous unsettling mobility of segments of the U.S. population. And it may well be that the backlash against left celebrities in the arts was prompted in part by the support the Davis campaign received from so many of them.

Merle Miller, an eminent producer in radio and television, was blacklisted due to his having backed Davis. So were Hazel Scott and Lena Horne. Professional stool pigeon Louis Budenz attempted to discredit José Ferrer by linking him to Davis, as the FBI sought similarly to discredit Sidney Poitier in the 1960s.[51] The *Daily Worker* summarized some of the consequences the red scare had for performers: "... such big agents as Moe Gale, Joe Glaser, the William Morris Agency and other managers had refused to okay the contracting of such stars as Erskine Hawkins, Louis Armstrong, Benny Goodman ... Count Basie and Billie Holiday ... [and] threatened the cancellation of contracts for recordings, television, dances and other engagements" unless they cut all ties with the left.[52]

But celebrity support alone could not have won the election; people had to have been mobilized and organized. The engine of the Davis campaign was the Communist Party, particularly the party section in Harlem. This was something of a change from 1934. Then, there were only two hundred blacks in the Harlem section. The *Party Organizer* complained that

> Harlem for a long time was one of the sorest points in the work of our party.... The weakest point in our work has been the inability of the Section Committee to enforce the most elementary discipline on its members. Petty personal questions have been on the order of business at the great majority of our section committee meetings.[53]

The Harlem party's fortunes improved with Davis's arrival. Davis noted this in 1936, and announced proudly that there were seven blacks on the central committee and 2,800 black reds overall, compared to the absence of blacks among the Socialist Party's leaders.[54] By 1938, the Harlem party reported a membership of 2,800.[55]

During the war, and especially in 1943, the membership of the Harlem party, and the numbers of Black communists generally, dramatically increased. This belies the notion that the Communists lagged on the civil rights front. If they had, such an expansion of the black membership would have been unlikely. The *Amsterdam News*, certainly no friend of the reds, touched on another underlying reason for this growth: "Many sincere non-Communist Americans find it impossible to reconcile our unabated national game of Red-baiting in the face of the incalculable aid the Red Army has been to the cause of democracy."[56]

The *Daily Worker* documented this trend in its report, in February 1943, that blacks were joining the party in "growing numbers"—forty-four out of ninety-four recruits in Michigan, fourteen of thirty-four in Maryland, eight of fifty-two in Wisconsin, eight of sixty-four in New England.[57] In the midst of this, Davis announced a recruiting competition between the Upper Harlem and Chicago Southside sections of the party. By April, with the eager assistance of three leading black women Communists, Audley Moore, Rose Gaulden, and Elizabeth Barker, 300 had been recruited in Harlem alone. That spring, 500 were recruited in Upper Harlem.[58]

The *Party Organizer* commented that "the winning of entire families ... inlaws and cousins, has been a feature of a new kind in our drive."[59] Doxey Wilkerson claimed that "nearly 5,000 Negroes joined the party [nationally] during the 1943 spring recruiting drive alone."[60] To Essie Robeson, Davis exclaimed that "the Harlem Section of the Communist Party is beginning to break records. We have doubled our membership [securing 400 new members in three months] since I've been here. We've just begun."[61]

Thus when Davis decided to throw his hat in the ring, he was acting in the context of a red resurgence. Si Gerson, a skilled Communist organizer who had worked with Cacchione, the party's other successful campaigner for City Council, and Liberal Republican Stanley Isaacs, points out that Davis "had observed the successful 1941 campaign closely and indeed had come to Brooklyn to make speeches for Pete and had patterned his own campaign after Pete's." What Davis noticed particularly was the value of energetic Communist cadre. One reason why the campaign literature of Davis and Cacchione was so effective was that it was prepared by two party clubs composed of "highly skilled advertising and public relations workers...."[62]

In Manhattan County alone there were 6,200 Communists at the time of the election and most if not all were active to some degree, working on Davis's behalf out of four offices in Harlem.[63] The *Daily Worker* constantly called on members to work on the campaign. By late October, there were "twenty-five sandwich-men—day and night ... five wagons, trucks with signs touring the city continuously ... [and] three sound trucks on [the] streets." There were "close to

1,000 canvassers" combing neighborhoods regularly in search of potential votes for Davis.

It was not unusual for Davis himself to address "thirty open-air meetings" in a single evening; he was in churches more often than pious sinners.[64] A certain lore built up around the campaign and the candidate. A writer for the *Party Organizer* recounted the story of a "first year high-school boy who came in day after day from his civics class to help us explain [proportional representation] to the voters and marched back triumphantly the day after the final count to prove to a skeptical civics teacher that Ben could be elected...."[65]

The Davis candidacy was truly a mass campaign. A striking feature of this Communist effort was the important role played by African-American women. Among the leaders was Audley Moore, now a nationalist leader in her nineties living in Harlem. Moore's father had been a deputy sheriff in Louisiana; his mother had been raped by a white man, his father. Moore's mother died when she was five. Afterward, Moore spent several years in a convent. She came to New York for the launching of the Black Star Line, was involved in Republican politics, and became a businesswoman. Scottsboro brought her to the Communist Party, but she says that she never left the Garvey movement even during her years of membership in the party, evidence that there was less sectarianism than is often thought to have been in the party. Moore was an extraordinarily talented recruiter for the party, topping the Harlem drive by recruiting thirty-seven members, twenty-seven of whom were women and all but one of whom were black. Davis himself managed to recruit sixteen members.

In addition to Moore, Dorothy Jenkins, Rose Gaulden, and Elizabeth Gurley Flynn were involved in Davis's campaign. Jenkins, born in Panama, was a hotel chambermaid who joined the party in 1940. Gaulden, a nurse at Harlem Hospital, was born in Thomasville, Georgia, and graduated in 1923 from Vorhees Institute in South Carolina.[66] Flynn was the top woman leader among the Communists. Thus, Davis's campaign organization crossed gender and nationality lines. As Israel Amter stated at the time, Davis "cannot be elected by the people of Harlem alone. This is the task of all Manhattan and particularly the white citizens of Manhattan."[67]

The *Daily Worker* considered the election of Davis to be a first priority, not just for the city and state but for the nation as a whole.

This determination was reflected most clearly on election day itself, as vote-stealing efforts were suppressed by a brigade of alert Communists.[68]

The Davis victory was a victory for the entire party and especially for state party leader Gil Green.[69] Yet, it would be one-sided to portray it as an unalloyed success. There were, most definitely, voices raised in objection to Davis and his party. For example, right after the election, the complaint of A. Philip Randolph and Walter White that the party was making serious inroads among blacks was deemed sufficiently important for the *New York Times* to print it, with a further suggestion by Randolph and White: "to counter this trend, [they] suggested that the other political parties assume a realistic approach to the Negro problem and make a sincere effort to combat existing prejudices."[70]

Oddly enough, it is through expressions of anticommunism by such figures as Randolph and White, and by the *Times*, that one glimpses the role played by the reds in hastening black liberation from Jim Crow. In fact, the black drift to the left was evidently seen as sufficiently threatening for representatives of the ruling class to make anti-racist concessions. Of greater interest to the party, however, was the fact signified by the *Daily Worker* headline immediately after the election: "Davis's Election Shows Negroes Reject Randolph's Red-Baiting."[71]

White and Randolph continued their attack on the Communists by focusing on the George Washington Carver School, which for some time had been accused of being a "Communist front." This was a reversal in part for Randolph, who had earlier defended school leader Gwen Bennett in the face of the same charge. Sensing that White and Randolph had larger fish to fry, Doxey Wilkerson pointed out that "it was not until after the election of Benjamin Davis to the City Council that the false issue of 'Communist control' was raised." But anticommunism was, in this case as in so many others, to have its way. The school was unable to survive such broadsides, and Harlem was the ultimate loser in the wake of this precursor of the red scare.[72]

Despite the success of the 1942 rally at Madison Square Garden, it appeared, by 1943, that Randolph's popularity and the popularity of his March on Washington Movement (MOWM) were waning. In this regard, Harvard Sitkoff has asked, "why ... did all the major civil rights spokesmen and Negro newspapers shun and denounce

Randolph's call for civil disobedience to protest Jim Crow schools and railroads?" Why did Randolph's convention in Chicago in 1943 "attract virtually no blacks other than a handful of Sleeping Car Porters?"[73] The *New York Age* questioned how Randolph and the MOWM could reconcile blasting local reds while praising reds in Moscow, and how they could praise integration yet bar whites and reds: "[they are] acting like the well-known ostrich which sticks its head in the sand to hide from its enemies.... What of the Negro Communists who are already in the organization but who, because they can do more effective work, prefer not to be known as Communists?"[74] The conservative *Amsterdam News* raised similar questions and added, "contradiction seems to be the keynote of MOWM." First they'll march, then they won't. First they exclude whites, "yet on the other hand the best programs sponsored by the group to date have been through interracial cooperation."[75]

It finally seemed as if Davis was winning his long-standing ideological battle with Randolph. However, despite the sharpness of his criticism of Randolph following the failure of the Chicago meeting, he agreed that "the Administration has not been sufficiently consistent in fighting Jim Crow."

At the same time, the line promoted by Davis and the party was gaining in popularity. That was evident in the success of their Negro Freedom Rally at Madison Square Garden in June 1943, a year after Randolph's own successful rally. Jim Crow and the Second Front were the themes, as 20,000 people gathered inside and 10,000 remained outside. Hughes, Robeson and Canada Lee, among others, supplied the art; Lester Granger, Tobias, Powell, and Davis supplied the words. The rally confirmed Davis's stature and enhanced his popularity. Its success undoubtedly contributed to his election months later.[76]

The election itself was a watershed, and the party was quick to recognize it as such. Davis received approximately 44,000 votes. Israel Amter summarized the distribution:

> ... 19,300 valid first choice ballots [that is, ballots properly marked and not spoiled] out of 34,000 to 35,000 first choice votes cast, were cast for Davis in greater Harlem. This represents between 55 and 60 percent of the first choice ballots by the Negroes in that area. 15,000 additional first choice votes in the white districts went to Davis.... In the final choice, 23,000 votes in the white districts outside of Harlem, out of a total of 44,000, were cast for Davis.

But Davis was not the only big winner. Cacchione had received the "largest first choice vote of any candidate in the city."[77] Party leader Gil Green put this in context in a November 15 speech delivered at the Manhattan Center to party workers:

> [In] the Councilmanic elections our party scored a great advance of far-reaching consequence. If correctly appraised and followed up it may well mark the turning point in the relationship of our party to the main forces in American political life—the beginning of full integration of our party in the camp of national unity.... While we have left the bush league, we are not yet in the major league.... [Our candidates] came out of their corners swinging both fists, landing upper-cuts to the jaw of their opponent instead of gentle slaps on the wrist.... They fought against every form of discrimination.

Green recalled the support Tobias had received even before Davis ran, and the thriftiness of Davis's campaign: "not ten dollars was spent on that day because our watchers gave of their time for a noble cause and not for a few paltry dollars."[78]

It was tragic for U.S. politics that Green was proven wrong. The election was indeed a turning point, but not in the direction he had hoped. Despite Davis's smashing re-election in 1945, 1943 was to be the high-water mark for the party in the U.S. The ruling class, frightened by the Communists' electoral success, could barely wait until the war ended before launching the red scare.

The red scare was a disaster for civil liberties and democracy. Yet there was a certain irony in the fact that while 1943 did not mark the "integration" of reds into the political life of the nation, it did mark the beginning of the "integration" of blacks. From the point of view of the ruling class, it was becoming clear that Jim Crow was not just hampering the war effort but was serving as one important basis of a growing domestic tendency aimed at the expropriation of the property of the economic royalists.[79]

What was remarkable about Davis's election was the fact that he won. But he barely defeated Samuel DiFalco, a Democratic incumbent, for the fourth seat from Manhattan. Parenthetically, the margin might have been greater since "the count in Manhattan was marked in its earlier stages by considerable confusion" and hints of fraud. The party moved swiftly to capitalize on the victory, adding 5,000 *Daily Worker* readers by February 1944, in New York alone.[80]

The response to the result in the black press was almost as ecstatic as that in the *Daily Worker*. Dominic Capeci wrote that the Davis "election proved to one black editor that whites would vote 'for qualified Negroes.'"[81] If whites would vote for a black with the added "handicap" of being red, then there was some reason to believe that racism was receding. The editors of the *Amsterdam News* concluded that "Davis's election confounded the professional politicians who had predicted that a Negro didn't have a chance to win this year. It was generally agreed ... that his supporters had waged one of the most effective campaigns ever carried on in a Negro's behalf locally." About Davis himself, they added: "he is thoroughly qualified ..., a close student of social problems, courageous, honest and highly educated ..., should be a real asset to the entire citizenry."

The black progressive, Eugene Gordon, drew a somewhat different but related conclusion from the victory: "the fact that Davis is a Communist is taken in two ways: either it is regarded as totally unimportant or is taken to be especially important in view of the Communists' known position on the Negro question." The *New York Age* concurred: "Negroes no longer look at a man's party label as the sole standard.... Voters in New York generally are becoming more liberal."[82]

Despite Walter White's cavil, others in the NAACP hailed the Davis victory. Theodore Spaulding, president of the Philadelphia chapter, called it "wonderful news." In Boston, the celebration brought together leaders from the CP and the NAACP. Roy Wilkins, writing in the *Amsterdam News*, was effusive:

> ... the town is in a dither.... What to do? What to do? A Negro in the council is bad enough but a Negro communist.... The *World-Telegram* has been throwing little fits with every editorial and the Hearst press is purple with apoplexy. And yet we have the *World-Telegram* wringing its hands because jolly Ben Davis shook hands with the Duke and rested next to Lena Horne.... More seriously, the *World Telegram* forgets the vicious racial and religious campaign carried on by the Republicans during the Lehman-Dewey race for governor. It is a great crime for the Communists to use racial appeals, but for the Republicans to do so only means a "hard fight" or a "bitter battle." Moreover the Communist appeals were not vicious or based on hatred, whereas the governorship battle was the slimiest waged here in many a decade.... If our system of government is so weak that two

Communists out of a Council of 17 members constitute a danger then we had better be looking to our foundations.

Wilkins wrote about Davis that

[He] is young and able. It is to be doubted whether there is a single council member of any higher calibre.... He is probably as good a politician as any man in the council.... [He] is affable and personable. He does not knock you down with a Communist argument if you should happen to mention that it is a fine day.[83]

The bourgeois press was predictably unhappy with the outcome of the election. The *World-Telegram* asserted that Davis won by "exploiting national, racial and religious feeling," in effect admitting that blacks were more willing to vote for a party that refused to compromise with Jim Crow, than for the GOP and the Democrats.[84] The *New York Herald Tribune* expressed much the same sentiment, while acknowledging the "emergence of the Communist Party as a strong factor," that the victory "had many of the political experts baffled," and that "almost everyone agreed that the Communists conducted the best organized, hardest hitting and, perhaps, the smartest campaign." What apparently confounded the experts was how Davis and Cacchione got 113,483 votes when there were presumably no more than 15,000 reds in the two boroughs combined. Even the existence of "more liberal tendencies at work these days," did not explain the results.[85]

One immediate consequence of the election was "a new drive," featured prominently in the pages of the *New York Times*, "to eliminate ... proportional representation." As part of an escalation of anticommunism, the drive was joined by, among other powerful figures in New York, Robert Moses, who privately contacted the president of the Bronx Chamber of Commerce, writing: "I can't take the lead [against proportional representation] because I am too busy, but I can help." One way in which he helped was to send the chamber president a pamphlet associating proportional representation with fascism.

Davis himself was elated by the victory. Election day had begun, he said, with the "worst downpour of the season...." But after the votes were counted and victory was assured, he acknowledged the epoch-making significance of the result. About Jim Crow, Davis commented that if the ruling class "should see that these inequalities are abolished, then no one would have to raise them" as issues.

At the same time, he denied that appeals to racialism could account for his triumph. The fact that 23,000 of his 44,000 votes were cast by whites showed that he was not "elected by Harlem alone or by the Communist Party alone." Indeed, Davis wrote fondly in his memoir about his support from Jewish people:

> The tremendous vote that I received from the Jewish working class community was one of the highlights of my election.... I was told by experienced election campaigners that my name had become as familiar to Jewish workers' as one of their own and that never before had a Negro candidate received such a high percentage of votes in a white neighborhood.... There were many Jewish candidates among the white aspirants for the Council posts but in certain Jewish districts I topped them all.... On each of the occasions that I spoke in the Jewish community at the other end of the Manhattan island, I received ovations and huge crowds that rivaled those in Harlem.... [86]

Davis's victory press conference at the Hotel Theresa in Harlem was jammed. Oddly, "there [were] as many newspapermen who want to tell [Davis] what they thought about his election as there were that wanted to ask him about it." His 1940 attack against the Congress's reluctance to enact anti-lynching legislation had made him a hero. Now he had reached an altogether different level. His reputation exceeded that of any Communist in U.S. history. When he entered one meeting in Harlem after his victory, "bedlam broke loose. The men, women and children laughed, screamed, wept, shouted, sang, hugged the winner and became breathlessly quiet to hear him talk." Then like a Pied Piper he went, entourage in tow, to Small's Paradise where he was greeted by "new rounds of applause, cheers...." Paul Robeson joined the crowd immediately after completing his performance in Othello.[87]

So a black Communist had won an election that neither a black nor a Communist were thought capable of winning. The anti-communists were stunned. It did seem for a moment that Gil Green's projection was accurate, that the election was the "turning point." But while there was little reason to doubt that it represented the beginning of the integration of blacks, a development aided in no small way by red activism, the reaction by the mainstream press provided at least a hint of the red scare to follow, a development that would almost destroy the party.

Party Wars, 1956–1959

On the other hand, while the party's subsequent decline was primarily due to the ferocity with which it was attacked by the state, it was accelerated by an internal ideological turn, known as "Browderism." This turn, whatever its causes, was mediated as well by unresolved and perhaps unresolvable organizational tensions within the party.

I have tried to show that the policies adopted in regard to, and the particular tensions around, the "Negro national question" reflected in complex ways the situation in the United States, as well as the debates that took place at the 1928 meeting of the Communist International. They cannot be understood as the result of unreflective acquiescence in an imperative structure of control exercised monolithically by Moscow. The history of the Davis victory by itself illustrates the point. It also illustrates the capacity of the party to respond to the particular conditions of life in the United States, suggesting that it might well, but for the repression that followed the war, have become an authentically national political force.

That the development of policies by the CP resolved tensions on the surface while leaving the differences they expressed submerged but still active, does not in any way distinguish the party from other political organizations. Action requires decision, and decision requires at least a momentary reconciliation of different points of view. But the suspension of differences does not eliminate them, and this inherent vulnerability is part of the development and changes that all political organizations experience.

That historians of the party have consistently denied its responsiveness to conditions and the fact that the Communist Party has in certain aspects of its political organization a great deal in common with other such organizations, has led those historians to treat the party as something *sui generis*, without internal life and without any local context. Because of that, their accounts have typically exaggerated the working relationship between the party and the Communist International, and seen the party as nothing more than the semblance of an organization, created by an outside force for its own purposes.

They have thereby tended to select as evidence for those accounts little more than the words of specific leaders, the testimony of

Woodcut by Oscar S. Frias in support of Benjamin J. Davis after his jailing under the Smith Act. Courtesy of Reference Center for Marxist Studies.

former members who left the party, and tendentiously selected documents; they have tended to take the Communists' commitment to social change on an international scale as evidence that the party operates essentially outside of life in the United States, rather than acknowledge the internationalist view of capitalism that it represents; they have, for the most part, neglected the various constituencies that have made up the party's base and provided support for it; they have, for the most part, slighted African-American history by either disregarding or minimizing the party's activities in regard to race relations and the role of black people in the history of the party; and they have ignored or denied the indigenous sources, in the 1930s and early 1940s, of the party's appeal to people in the United States.

The Davis campaign illustrates the political potential that had existed during the heyday of the Communist Party. It illustrates the role the party has played in the struggle against racism in the United States. But I believe that it also illustrates a more general point about political formations and constituencies, namely that differences within an organization that are suspended in the interest of acting responsively are likely to remain suspended so long as there is concrete political work to be done around issues of general interest.

However, when other events, such as war, overwhelm the capacity of a political organization to pursue a domestic agenda, or when the organization comes under an attack greater than its resources can bear, those differences are likely to emerge once again. Under those conditions, there is likely to be at least some disruption of the organization's integrity sufficient to lead to the sort of decline the Communists experienced as a result of the repressions of the postwar period.

The downside of the fight against this trend was the delay in retooling the Black Belt thesis. For Browder had proclaimed that blacks had chosen, and they had chosen for integration not self-determination. When he was dislodged in 1945, it was decided that all of his theses should go with him—including his thesis on integration. Hence, it was not until 1959 that the Black Belt thesis was jettisoned.

The Counter-Intelligence Program (COINTELPRO) of the FBI was a dominant factor in exacerbating and creating contradictions within the party in the post-1956 era. The FBI played on tensions created by the disclosures about Stalin, the Soviet intervention in Hungary, the Suez crisis, and, ironically, the burgeoning civil rights movement. Once again, at the epicenter of this political temblor was Ben Davis.

The anticommunist scholar Harvey Klehr has written, "Many people assume, erroneously, that with the collapse of the New Left in the early 1970s, American radicalism disappeared." He is right by a half. Though given post-mortems many times by various coroners—literary and otherwise—the U.S. left has been resilient. As Davis emerged from post-prison restrictions in 1956, a movement was emerging in Montgomery that highlighted the glaring blot on the U.S. escutcheon—racism. As many on the right saw it, this was a direct boon to the left internationally, headed by Moscow. And as Richard Gid Powers reminds us, the FBI began taking more serious notice of Dr. King "when it learned he had been introduced to Benjamin Davis." Hoover saw black organizations "as easy prey" for the reds and was "concerned with civil rights organizations almost exclusively in terms of their potential as targets for Communist infiltration." The party was still one of the few national organizations with a disciplined and sophisticated cadre of full-time black revolutionaries that included figures with many contacts and allies still within the emerging movement; William Patterson, Doxey Wilkerson, Henry Winston, James Ford, James Jackson, Ed Strong, Louis Burnham, Ted Bassett, Harry Haywood, Hosea Hudson, Augusta Strong, Bill Taylor, Abner Berry, Claude Lightfoot, and Geraldine Lightfoot were just a few of the black comrades surrounding Davis. The thought of them taking advantage of the moment to play a role in the movement, recruit and help to blare headlines abroad trumpeting Jim Crow, was of grave concern to the authorities.[88]

Controversies arising in the party in 1956 was like manna from heaven for the FBI. They seized the time by initiating COINTELPRO:

[There] is existing within the CP, a situation resulting from the developments at the Tenth (sic) Congress of the Soviet Union ... the Bureau is in a position to initiate on a broader scale than heretofore attempted, a counterintelligence program against the CP, not by harassment from the outside, which might only serve to bring the

various factions together, but by feeding and fostering from within
the internal fight currently raging ... informants ... will be briefed
and instructed to embark on a disruptive program within their own
clubs, sections, districts or even on a national level. Those informants
will raise objections and doubts as to the success of any proposed plan
of action by the CP leadership. They will seize every opportunity to
carry out the disruptive activity not only at meetings, conventions,
et cetera, but also during social and other contacts with CP members
and leaders.

This was one of the momentous memoranda emerging from the
period: COINTELPRO not only disrupted the party, it led to the
inflaming of black-Jewish tensions, it fed paranoia and helped to
frighten a generation away from open left ties. The talented journalist Louis Burnham expressed the wonder of the time: "... where
are so many of our friends: Balancing political angels and devils on
the heads of ideological needles. History has caught up with much
good theory and there has not been time to replace it. Meanwhile
we walk in a kind of limbo between the past and unknown future.
At least I do."[89]

With revelations about Soviet anti-Semitism and the Suez crisis,
Zionism reared its head in party ranks. Davis and other black
leaders were charged with anti-Semitism because they backed
Egypt and condemned Israeli aggression. Neither Davis nor other
party leaders reassessed their support for the creation of Israel.
This was doubly ironic for Davis since in the pre-1948 period, few
blacks—or Jews for that matter—were as active in Jewish affairs
as he.[90]

Since the party and Moscow were so fervent in backing a Jewish
state in Palestine, the entry of comrades to the party with Zionist
inclinations was facilitated. It was felt that Jews were dis-
proportionately sympathetic to the party. The events of 1956
worsened black-Jewish relations particularly. *Daily Worker* reporter A.B. Magil in May 1956 called on the party to raise the slogan
of "Arms for Israel." The Stalin-devaluation period and the
resultant glasnost allowed such ideas to be expressed. Then Ed
Strong, one of the more popular black leaders, denounced *Daily
Worker* editorials on the Suez Crisis which "departed seriously from
a Marxist-Leninist analysis"; it had been claimed that Egyptian
and Arab provocation led Israel to launch war.[91]

Then the *New York Times* entered the picture. It reported that the American Jewish Committee had done a study of the party that concluded:

> Most of the party's Negroes seem to be behind the Foster-Dennis-Davis pro-Soviet group.... The Negro members look upon racism and traditional colonialism as the prime evils to be fought and tend to relative indifference about Eastern Europe.

Jews in the party were split, with workers backing Foster on one side, and intellectuals and Yiddish-speaking activists on the other side. It was true that blacks were less susceptible to manipulation of the "iron curtain" issue as they had few relatives or brethren in Eastern Europe and were generally suspicious of initiatives that seemed to come from elites in any case.[92]

Davis took on Abner Berry, objecting to his "neutralist" stand on the Mideast; in passing he noted the "strong pro-Egyptian influence among the Negro masses expressed in part ... by the increasing growth of Moslem influence and organization in Negro communities.... I venture to say that Negroes are anything but neutral in this matter ... and they're right." He downplayed the idea that this harmed black-Jewish ties—but certain Zionists were out to prove him wrong; he came under attack. The *Times* charged that black Communists were "using the Jewish issue" and charging "Jewish bourgeois nationalism" in factional disputes. This got Davis going. He came back to the Berry piece and accused him of making an "apology for the pro-imperialist policies of the Ben-Gurion government" and condemned the "bourgeois nationalism among certain Jewish circles"; he added the obligatory, "Israel has a right to a secure existence as a state" but warned that "Israel is courting national suicide" because of its "brutal aggression" against Cairo. He railed against Zionist pressure on the *Los Angeles Herald Dispatch* and other black papers, though he disagreed with their calling Ben-Gurion "Hitler," terming it "harmful and unfortunate"; but the "chauvinist and far more prevalent slander is that of labelling Nasser as a 'dictator' and 'Hitler.'" The FBI was aware of these contradictions and sought to capitalize on them; intentionally or inadvertently they helped along the process of inflaming black-Jewish tensions instead of lessening them.[93]

Davis was on to something. The Suez crisis was an important

milestone in the revival of Islam among blacks; Nasser was seen as acting in the tradition of Bandung. African-Americans, as was their wont, reacted to the flood of negative publicity directed at Nasser by flocking to his banner. But that was not the only development in this general area. Montgomery signalled that the Black Belt thesis required retooling.

Yet, at the end of the day it could be fairly said that despite errors, misjudgments and the like, the Communist Party did play a signal role in disintegrating the stolid walls of Jim Crow. The question for today is what forces will be necessary to do away with racism altogether.

Notes

1. Staughton Lynd and Christopher Lasch allude to these points in Staughton Lynd, "Intellectuals, the University and the Movement," *Journal of American History* 76 (September 1989): 79–485; and Christopher Lasch, "Consensus: An Academic Question," *Journal of American History* 76 (September 1989): 457–59.
2. I discuss this question in my forthcoming book, *Black Liberation / Red Scare: Ben Davis and the Communist Party*.
3. I discussed this point in an interview with James Jackson on 6 April 1988 (in possession of author).
4. See Gerald Horne, "Black to the Future: Japan, Cold War, the 'Birth Dearth,' the Supreme Court, the Jewish Question, Rap Music and the Destiny of African-Americans," paper presented to the American Association for the Advancement of Science, New Orleans, 16 February 1990.
5. Herbert Philbrick and James D. Bales, *Communism and Race in America* (Searcy, Arkansas: Bales Bookstore, 1965), p. 15, Louis Budenz Papers.
6. Moscow must have had supermen in place in order to direct so many successful struggles in the 1930s in an era before electronic mail, fax machines, and express mail. On the issue of the *longa manus* of Moscow, see Bernard and Jewel Bellush, "A Radical Response to the Roosevelt Presidency: The Communist Party (1933–1945)," *Presidential Studies Quarterly* 10 (1980): 645–61; Jane Degras, ed., *The Communist International, 1919–1943, Documents* (London: Frank Cass, 1971); Maurice Thorez, *France Today and the People's Front* (New York: International, circa 1935), Communist Party Archives; Edward Mortimer, *The Rise of the French Communist Party* (London: Faber and Faber, 1984).
7. See Eric Foner, *Nothing But Freedom: Emancipation and Its Legacy* (Baton Rouge: Louisiana State University Press, 1983).

8. See Allison Blakely, *Russia and the Negro: Blacks in Russian History and Thought* (Washington, DC: Howard University Press, 1986), p. 160: "There is evidence that there was an especially intensive Soviet campaign in the 1920s to establish strong cultural ties between the Soviet Union and Negro America.... It was such efforts which convinced McKay, Robeson, Rudd and other Negro artists to visit the Soviet Union." Blacks were no doubt impressed with the militant line of the party which contrasted sharply with their recent experience with the Dixiecrat-influenced Democrats and the lily-white Republicans. See also Earl Browder, "For National Liberation of the Negroes! War Against White Chauvinism," *The Communist* 11 (April 1932): 295–309: "It is impossible for the Communist Party to lead the struggle for Negro liberation unless it begins by burning out (of) its own ranks every manifestation and trace of the influence of white chauvinism ... everything that touches upon the Negro question is for our Party a question of fundamental principle importance, a matter of life and death." But symptomatic of the apparent tension between self-determination and equal rights or integration is the fact that Browder carped at the idea of a "Negro Federation" within the party mirroring some of the language federations (pp. 297, 303).

9. Interview with Sam Darcy by Ron Filipelli, *Series I, Oral History of the American Left*, 23 March 1971, Box 3, Folder 32, Sam Darcy Papers.

10. Philip S. Foner and James Allen, eds., *American Communism and Black Americans: A Documentary History, 1919–1929* (Philadelphia: Temple University Press, 1987), pp. 180, 190; Harry Haywood, *Black Bolshevik* (Chicago: Liberator Press, 1972), pp. 218–280; Margaret Wilhemina Jackson, "Evolution of the Communist Party's Position on the American Negro Question," M.A. thesis, Howard University, 1938; Sam Darcy Manuscript, Box 3, Folder 34, Sam Darcy Papers; Hyman Kublin, *Asian Revolutionary: The Life of Sen Katayama* (Princeton: Princeton University Press, 1964), p. 319.

11. See Virginia Dominguez, *White by Definition: Social Classification in Creole Louisiana* (New Brunswick: Rutgers University Press, 1986); Patrick Washburn, *A Question of Sedition: The Federal Government's Investigation of the Black Press During World War II* (New York: Oxford University Press, 1986); Herbert Haines, *Black Radicals and the Civil Rights Mainstream, 1954–1970* (Knoxville: University of Tennessee Press, 1988); Mary L. Dudziak, "Desegregation as a Cold War Imperative," *Stanford Law Review* 41 (November 1988): 61–120; Juan Williams, *Eyes on the Prize: America's Civil Rights Years, 1954–1965* (New York: Penguin, 1988). See also *City Sun* (Brooklyn), 4–10 May 1988, recounting contemporary struggles regarding the notion of black self-determination. The recent effort in Boston to establish

"Mandela, Massachusetts," and efforts from the 1960s to ignite "black power," as well as the legacy of Malcolm X also reflect this trend.

12. See James Ford, "The Negroes in a Soviet America," William Patterson Papers. Also indicative of international influence: Ford cites the experience of Finland, which seceded from Soviet Russia, as an analogue. Many Communists were struck as well by the experience of the Jewish Autonomous Region in the USSR. See also Tom Johnson, pamphlet, "The Reds in Dixie: Who Are the Communists and What Do They Fight for in the South," Reel 15, Series 6, P293, circa 1935, Earl Browder Papers. This strongly anti-racist piece reflects party views of the era insofar as it stresses the class dimension of racism, i.e., how it splits the working class and drags down wage levels. Denied is the allegation that the party "demands" that blacks marry whites and vice versa, but it is noted that white males sleep with black women and "nor is it unknown for white women to sleep with Negro men. It's done under cover, that's all." The Black Belt thesis, he says, "does not mean we want to establish some sort of Jim Crow state." Ultimately, he says, the Black Belt should be "a federated part of the Soviet U.S."

13. The African Blood Brotherhood (ABB) had a membership of almost 5,000 in the 1919–1927 period. They had significant influence on Marcus Garvey's movement; the national anthem of the United Negro Improvement Association (UNIA) was written by the ABB; Bishop George A. McGuire, founder of the African Orthodox Church was an ABB man, along with UNIA Assistant President General Dr. J.D. Gordon, Cyril Crichlow (head of the UNIA mission to Liberia), two leading officers of the Black Star Line (the UNIA shipping company), and others. The main ship of the line was purchased by Cyril Briggs. In 1925 the ABB forces left the UNIA for the CP *en masse*. Their influence and perhaps the West Indian backgrounds of many of them is a more useful path of analyzing the evolution of the Black Belt thesis than the simplistic incantation of Moscow's hand.

14. See interview with W.A. Domingo, Box 21, Folder 3, Theodore Draper Papers. The interviews of Draper and his emissaries did not always go well. When Richard Moore, a prominent Harlem activist, was approached, he was reluctant to talk, though this was in 1958 and his close ties with the party had receded. The emissary refers to him as a "liar," perhaps because he did not echo the anticommunist line: see interview with Richard Moore, circa 1958, Box 21, Folder 3, Theodore Draper Papers.

15. See interview, Abner Berry, 2 December 1977, *Series I, Oral History of the American Left*.

16. See *Daily Worker*, 4 October 1936.

17. See *The Liberator*, 1 June 1932.

18. See *Daily Worker*, 30 October 1936.

19. See "Report on Negro Work," May 1938, Box 12, Robert Minor Papers.

20. See *Daily Worker*, 2 August 1938.

21. See interview, Claude Lightfoot, "Seeing Red," *Series IV, Oral History of the American Left*.

22. See Israel Amter, *Autobiographical Sketch,* Israel Amter Papers (Tamiment Institute, New York University), p. 93.

23. See *Daily Worker*, 19 October 1936.

24. See Edwin Lewinson, *Black Politics in New York City* (New York: Twayne, 1974), p. 60; *Negro Liberator*, 4 August 1934.

25. See *Daily Worker*, 19 October 1936.

26. See Frank O'Brien, "Harlem Shows the Way," *New Masses* 20 (18 August 1936): 17–18.

27. See *Daily Worker*, 14 June 1940.

28. See Dorothy Healey and Maurice Isserman, *Dorothy Healey Remembers: A Life in the American Communist Party* (New York: Oxford University Press, 1990), p. 330.

29. See *Daily Worker*, 4 May 1935.

30. See "Meeting with Negro Comrades, Harlem," 23 August 1932, Box 8, William Patterson Papers.

31. See James Robert Prickett, "Communists and the Communist Issue in the American Labor Movement, 1920–1950," Ph.D. diss., UCLA, 1975, p. 456.

32. Interview, Abner Berry, July 5, 1977, *Series I, Oral History of the American Left*. See also Steve Murdock, "California Communists— Their Years of Power," *Science and Society* 34, no. 4, pp. 478–87; William Edward Regensburger, "'Ground into Our Blood': The Origins of Working-Class Consciousness and Organization in Durably Unionized Southern Industries, 1930–1946," Ph.D. diss., University of California Los Angeles, 1987; George Lipsitz, "A Rainbow at Midnight: Strategies of Independence in the Post-War Working Class," Ph.D. diss., University of Wisconsin, 1979; Herbert Krugman, "The Interplay of Social and Psychological Factors in Political Deviance: An Inquiry into Some Factors Underlying the Motivation of Intellectuals Who Became Communists," B.A. thesis, Columbia University, 1952; Michele Fraser Ottanelli, "Origins of the Popular Front Policy in the United States, 1933–1935," unpublished paper, American Historical Association Graduate History Forum of Central New York State, SUNY-Cortland, 1983.

33. Davis called Douglass "one of the titanic figures of American history" though in the "latter part of his life he did not see clearly the relationship of class forces which were beginning to congeal into American imperialism." Again he linked past and present: "Just as Douglass's paper the *North Star* was assailed as being financed by 'British gold' so the Communist Party and the *Daily Worker* get attacked as financed by 'Moscow Gold.'" In reviewing a biography of Hiram Revels by Elizabeth Lawson, Davis cites words of the Reconstruction leader that

could be applied to himself: In "prejudice in this country" versus blacks "it matters not how colored people act; it matters not how well they behave themselves, how well they deport themselves, how intelligent they may be." Said Davis, "One can only say 'Amen' to that one." See *Daily Worker*, 5 June 1960.

34. See *Daily Worker*, 4 July 1938, 19 August 1937, 12 February 1938, 13 February 1938, 6 February 1939, 11 January 1938, 12 February 1939, 14 June 1939, 6 April 1941.

35. See *Daily Worker*, 27 June 1940. In *Daily Worker*, 23 January 1938, Davis hits the idea of "protecting Southern white womanhood" as a reason for opposing anti-lynch legislation as "phony blather." See also *Daily Worker*, 30 January 1938, 12 May 1937, 4 April 1937, 18 April 1937, 9 January 1938.

36. Flyer, 23 October 1943, Reel 2, Box 5, Peter Cacchione Papers; *Daily Worker*, 25 September 1943, 26 September 1943, 29 September 1943; Unexpurgated version of Ben Davis memoir, Ben Davis Papers.

37. Pamphlet, circa 1943, Ben Davis Vertical File, Schomburg; *Daily Worker*, 5 October 1943; *People's Voice*, 30 October 1943.

38. See interview, Ian Hall, WLIB-AM, New York City, 23 March 1988; interview, Phil Schaap, 5 June 1988. Schaap, the noted New York authority on jazz, places the Parker concert on September 26, 1952 at Rockland Palace. He points to Teddy Wilson as an influence on a number of musicians. Howard "Stretch" Johnson goes further and refers to Wilson as the "Marxist Mozart." He recalls Cy Oliver and Al Haig as also being sympathetic to the left and Dizzy Gillespie as being "quite revolutionary" in outlook. See also interview, Howard Johnson, 2 March 1988; W.C. Handy to Ben Davis, 1 February 1956, Ben Davis Papers; flyer, 2 January 1959, Ben Davis Papers; *Daily Worker*, 1 May 1941; *People's Voice*, 9 October 1943, 30 October 1943; *Daily Worker*, 22 November 1943, 7 December 1943, 28 October 1943; photos of Davis, Lena Horne and Cab Calloway, undated, Ben Davis Papers.

39. See *Daily Worker*, 1 March 1941, 9 December 1941. This review marks one of the few times Davis spoke of Blacks as a "nation."

40. See *Daily Worker*, 1 April 1941; Margaret Walker, *The Daemonic Genius of Richard Wright* (Washington, DC: Howard University Press, 1983), p. 155; interview, Lloyd Brown, 18 April 1988; Addison Gayle, *Richard Wright: Ordeal of a Native Son* (Garden City: Doubleday, 1980), p. 89.

41. Gayle, *Richard Wright*, pp. 162–63.

42. See *Daily Worker*, 6 August 1944; *New York Herald Tribune*, 28 Ju 1944; *New York Journal American*, 28 July 1944.

43. See C.L.R. James to Constance Webb, circa September 1944, Box 1, C.L.R. James Papers.

44. Walker, *The Daemonic Genius of Richard Wright*, p. 111.

45. See *Daily Worker*, 1 July 1956.
46. See *Daily Worker*, 1 April 1945.
47. See *Daily Worker*, 8 May 1943; Langston Hughes to "Dear Pat," 10 August 1964, Box 2, William Patterson Papers; "Sonnet for Ben Davis," by Walter Lowenfels, undated, Reel 23, Box 39, J-10, Civil Rights Congress Papers; Walter Lowenfels, *My Many Lives: The Autobiography of Walter Lowenfels*, vol. 2, *The Poetry of My Politics* (Homestead, Florida: Olivant Press, 1968); *Daily Worker*, 12 June 1949.
48. See *Daily Worker*, 15 September 1940. Davis was sensitive to the fact that at many of the massive Harlem rallies featuring these celebrities, African-Americans were not present in representative numbers.
49. See *Daily Worker*, 1 October 1943, 5 December 1943.
50. See Pete Cacchione to Branch Rickey, 7 June 1943, Box 4, Reel 2, Pete Cacchione Papers; *Daily Worker*, 5 December 1943.
51. See Merle Miller, *The Judges and the Judged* (Garden City: Doubleday, 1952), pp. 54–55; *Daily Worker*, 24 September 1950; Gail Lumet Buckley, *The Hornes: An American Family* (New York: Knopf, 1986), p. 208; Canada Lee to Ed Sullivan, 15 November 1949, Box 1, Canada Lee Papers; Louis Budenz, *The Cry Is Peace* (Chicago: Regnery, 1952), p. 23; Memorandum, 2 April 1964, 100-3-116, FBI.
52. See *Daily Worker*, 2 October 1949.
53. See Louis Sass, "On Some Problems of the Harlem Section," *Party Organizer* 7 (March 1934): 19–21.
54. At this point there were 16,000 Communists in the state, with 10,000 in the unions; see Israel Amter, "The Elections in New York," *The Communist* 15 (December 1936): 1141–53. In the *Daily Worker*, 9 June 1936, Davis stated, "Negro Communists capable of leading the 12,000,000 American Negroes will henceforth be the goal of the Communist Party in developing and training its Negro members." The *People's Voice* was an outgrowth of Harlem's All Peoples Party, "which in several election districts in lower Harlem last November ran second to the Democratic Party ..." and was backed avidly by Harlem reds; see *Daily Worker*, 2 June 1937.
55. See *Daily Worker*, 9 May 1938.
56. See *Amsterdam News*, 10 April 1943.
57. See *Daily Worker*, 19 February 1943.
58. See *Daily Worker*, 9 March 1943, 17 March 1943.
59. See Elizabeth Barker, "Building a Mass Party in Harlem," *Party Organizer* 1, no. 1 (1943): 9–12.
60. See Doxey Wilkerson, "The Negro in the War," *New Masses* 49 (14 December 1943): 18–19; *Daily Worker*, 6 September 1943.
61. See Ben Davis to Essie Robeson, 27 April 1943, Paul Robeson Papers.
62. See *Daily Worker*, 19 September 1943, 28 October 1943.

63. The 21st Assembly District office was at 702 St. Nicholas Avenue (at 145th Street). Other offices were at 428 Lenox Avenue, 321 West 125th Street, and 2163 8th Avenue.
64. See *Daily Worker*, 30 October 1943, 1 November 1943.
65. See Charles Lomax, "Harlem Plays a Winner," *Party Organizer* 1 (December 1943): 11–15. Patrick Washburn in *Question of Sedition* (Oxford University Press, 1984), p. 181, details red ties with the black press; the *Afro-American*, he suggests, had numerous "Communist connections." Carl Murphy "admitted that he still believed that so far as the solving of racial problems is concerned, the spirit of the Communists was greatly needed. They represent, he thought, the spirit of the abolitionists which seemed to abate after the seventies and was supplanted by an era of condescension. A militant approach to the race problem is needed, he believes, and the Communists are the only ones who have the courage to carry on this type of struggle." Ben Davis, Sr. campaigned enthusiastically for his son and his long-standing relationship with black leadership and the black press proved helpful; see *Daily Worker*, 8 October 1943.
66. Interview with Audley Moore, *Oral History of the American Left, Series I*.
67. See *Daily Worker*, 24 October 1943.
68. See *Daily Worker*, 27 October 1943.
69. Ben Davis to Elizabeth Gurley Flynn, 4 October 1943, Reel 4206, Elizabeth Gurley Flynn Papers.
70. See *New York Times*, 22 December 1943.
71. See *Daily Worker*, 29 November 1943. The FBI maintained a consistent interest in any NAACP friendliness to the party during this period, despite their not-infrequent clashes. Main File No. 62-78270, 100-136-34, FBI.
72. See *Daily Worker*, 30 December 1943, 30 November 1943.
73. See Harvard Sitkoff, "American Blacks in World War II: Rethinking the Militancy-Watershed Hypothesis," in James Titus, ed., *The Home Front and War in the Twentieth Century* (Washington, DC: GPO, 1982), p. 153.
74. See *New York Age*, 4 September 1943.
75. See *Amsterdam News*, 31 July 1943.
76. See *Daily Worker*, 31 January 1943, 18 July 1943, 14 September 1941; "Communists in the Struggle for Negro Rights," circa 1943, Communist Party Archives; *Daily Worker*, 23 May 1943, 8 June 1943. Despite Davis's souring relationship with labor leader Randolph, his overall ties with labor soared during this period.
77. See *Daily Worker*, 29 November 1943, 30 November 1943.
78. See Gil Green, "The New York City Elections," *The Communist* 22 (December 1943): 1103–10.
79. See *Daily Worker*, 10 November 1943, 12 November 1943.

80. See *New York Age*, 20 November 1943; *Amsterdam News*, 13 November 1943. John Ross, black Republican candidate, got 20,000 of his 23,390 votes "from the white folks downtown." This suggests that blacks were much more willing to vote red than whites were; see *Amsterdam News*, 20 November 1943. The Davis election "proves conclusively that white voters will vote for qualified Negroes for political offices...."; see *Daily Worker*, 12 December 1943.
81. See Dominic Capeci, *The Harlem Riot of 1943* (Philadelphia: Temple University Press, 1977), p. 161.
82. *Daily Worker*, 12 November 1943, 4 December 1943; *Amsterdam News*, 20 November 1943; *Daily Worker*, 23 November 1943; *New York Age*, 20 November 1943.
83. See *Amsterdam News*, 20 November 1943.
84. *New York World-Telegram*, 16 November 1943.
85. See *New York Herald Tribune*, 11 November 1943.
86. Davis memoir, p. 31/721, 15/705; *Daily Worker*, 31 December 1943; *New York Age*, 20 November 1943; *New York Times*, 14 November 1943; *New York Age*, 27 November 1943.
87. *Daily Worker*, 11 November 1943, 14 November 1943; Davis memoir, pp. 1/277. But with all his notoriety, in his memoir he recalls how he was still constantly mistaken for the other Ben Davis, the West Point military man.
88. See Harvey Klehr, *Far Left of Center: The American Radical Left Today* (New Brunswick: Transaction, 1988), p. xi; Richard Gid Powers, *Secrecy and Power: The Life of J. Edgar Hoover* (New York: Free Press, 1987), pp. 368, 324.
89. See Brian Glick, *War at Home: Covert Action Against U.S. Activists and What We Can Do About It* (Boston: South End Press, 1989), p. 74; and Ward Churchill and Jim Vander Wall, *COINTELPRO Papers* (Boston: South End Press, 1989).
90. See *Daily Worker*, 3 April 1938, 20 April 1938, 22 April 1938, 25 April 1938, 27 April 1938, 18 October 1943, 27 October 1943, 9 February 1944, 3 March 1944, 24 September 1944, 7 April 1945, 24 September 1945; *New Masses*, 23 October 1945; *Daily Worker*, 26 October 1945; flyer, circa 1945, Box 5, Robert Minor Papers; *People's Voice*, 22 January 1946; *Daily Worker*, 8 June 1946, 15 June 1946, 26 May 1947; press release, 26 May 1947, Box 2, Folder 1, Pete Cacchione Papers, and copy of preceding statement in *Daily Worker*, 9 March 1948; *Daily Worker*, 12 March 1948, 28 November 1948, 31 October 1948.
91. Arthur Liebman, "The Ties that Bind: The Jewish Support for the Left in the U.S.," *American Jewish Historical Quarterly* 66 (December 1976): 1–25; and *Daily Worker*, 30 May 1956, 31 May 1956, 23 July 1956, 31 October 1956, 1 November 1956, 2 November 1956, 22 November 1956.
92. See the *New York Times*, 27 January 1957. The press played more

than just a reporting role during this period; they were conscious actors. See James Aronson, *The Press and the Cold War* (1973: rev.ed., New York: Monthly Review Press, 1990).

93. See *Daily Worker*, 8 March 1957, 13 March 1957, 28 March 1957, 7 May 1957; *New York Times*, 18 March 1957, 28 March 1957; Sub-Committee of National Committee-CPUSA, "An Evaluation of the *Daily Worker*," *Political Affairs* 36 (September 1957): 26–33. On the Mideast the party organ "showed great sensitivity to the feelings of the Jewish people, though ... not the same awareness of the need to keep in mind the feelings and sentiments of the Negro people," J. Edgar Hoover to Gordon Gray, 23 July 1958, *FBI Series*, Box 2, FBI L-N (2), OSANSA, Staff Files, Dwight D. Eisenhower Papers.

"Lucky for him I believe in mass action."

One of a series of gag cartoons entitled "The Ruling Clawss," created by A. Redfield for the *New Masses* in the early 1930s. This "in-joke" (the class-conscious masseur resists the temptation to mangle a capitalist) assumes a broad familiarity with Communist politics. Courtesy of Reference Center for Marxist Studies.

THE CULTURAL WORLD
OF THE COMMUNIST PARTY:
An Historical Overview

Annette T. Rubinstein

Those of us who believe in the possibility and value of historical understanding have, I think, a serious responsibility for making the facts of our social experience available to the increasing number of open-minded young historians working to achieve an understanding of the most recent, and most deeply buried, period of North American radicalism. Much of this past can be, and has already been, rediscovered by the competent, diligent and imaginative exploration of printed material—official Communist Party directives, party periodicals, general newspaper reports, court proceedings, official or unofficial union publications, organizational minutes, the Congressional Record and contemporary fiction, poetry, or literary controversy. However there is much in the day-to-day activity on the left which such written records omit or which is so completely taken for granted that they give no idea of its relative importance.

Matters which absorbed most of the time, energy and interest of the average party member or "fellow traveller" are often barely mentioned in print. A constant flow of directives from headquarters reflect the leadership's concern with international affairs, but these were often received with a pious "Amen—file and forget" by hard-pressed local union or community leaders. Yet the printed material fills the archives and there is no written evidence to tell how often casual resolutions to implement national or state directives were unanimously passed and ignored while those who voted for them concentrated on more immediate concerns.

My own experience of some twenty years as a party activist, and another twelve or fifteen during which I worked closely with many party groups, was in many ways typical. My political work was almost never inside the party structure. Like most Communists in the 1930s and 1940s I was almost entirely absorbed by my work in

239

mass or united front organizations. Such organizations involved many times the 100,000 optimum estimate of actual card-carrying party membership, and most of us were deeply concerned with the development and objectives of those organizations to which we belonged.

Virtually all my time, except for the hours necessarily spent professionally, was occupied by such specific *ad hoc* projects as building a customers' committee to aid the Gimbel's strikers (the first victorious white collar strike), defending the Scottsboro Boys and the Trenton Six, chairing the West Side chapter of the American League Against War and Fascism, chairing the Fifth South club of American Labor Party, organizing mothers' committees for the Mayor's Committee for the Care of Young Children in Wartime to open low cost nursery schools, etc. Yet, except for sporadic accounts in the FBI files, there is little documentary evidence of all this and less of the work of other full time rank-and-file party members in similar organizations and unions. (There are newspaper reports of the innumerable rallies and public meetings at which I and other party speakers appeared, but even though each of us may have spoken at three, four, five or even six affairs a week, they occupied less time than the intense day-to-day activity demanded by un-financed organizational work—including the preparations for such meetings themselves.)

Written records give a similarly skewed picture of the cultural work on the left. It is, of course, possible to find copies of the major novels and anthologies written and/or edited by radicals in the thirties and forties. With sufficient diligence one can also exhume crumbling mimeographed copies of short-lived literary periodicals, created in hundreds of small amateur writers' workshops in the early thirties when the party organized and sponsored the national network of John Reed writers' clubs. But the tremendous import-ance of the left theater, in many ways the real cultural center of the radical movement during the Depression, is almost entirely irrecoverable, except through the personal memories of a rapidly disappearing generation.

Before addressing this phenomenon more specifically I want first to continue the discussion of the culture fostered by the Communist Party when it was a genuine force in U.S. life, using culture in its broader dictionary sense as "the sum total of ways of living built up by a group of human beings."

As Mark Naison has indicated earlier in this volume, and as other younger researchers have come to see, the early, largely cold war historians seriously misinterpreted our relation to the Soviet Union. It's perfectly true that the Soviet Union was a tremendously important factor in our lives, but it was most important in rather intangible ways. It was an inspiration, it created faith in the future, it legitimized optimism, it gave us a feeling of worldwide comradeship and a sense of participating directly in world history.

I don't mean that there weren't occasions when orders from the Soviet Union relayed by the central committee of the U.S. party came down very heavily. The most salient examples in my experience were the directives at the beginning of World War II (1939–1941) demanding approval of the Nazi-Soviet Pact and disapproval of the war as an imperialist war—simply a replay of the first world war. There were direct orders from headquarters that all Communist Party members work in their mass or united front organizations to get resolutions passed approving the pact, and disapproving any such infringement of neutrality as lend-lease to Britain. These orders were explicit, and they cost the party very heavily. In most united front organizations, as in the League of American Writers, there was a Pyrrhic victory. The party line would win by a narrow majority and all or most of the non-party members would leave so that there was no longer a united front organization in existence.

But in general, while directives coming down from headquarters to the CP members in a trade union, a consumers' group, a parent-teacher organization, or any other local body (often even a local CP club), may have amounted to a great deal of paper—that's all they amounted to. In many cases there was very little time or energy spent by local organizations, busy with their own problems and their own urgent agendas, in following directives through, unless they fitted in concretely with their own immediate concerns. (Of course these were formulated in terms of the party's general policy, but with wide variations depending on the members themselves and on local conditions.)

I speak of the party, but it is quite correct to say that the CPUSA was essentially a movement rather than a party, as others in this book have noted. I remember Congressman Vito Marcantonio saying over and over, "The American Labor Party is *not* a movement—it's a party, a political party. We can't take up this, that or any other good cause that is important somewhere in Greece or Australia. We must concentrate on what's happening here in New York, here in the USA." Marc was right. The American Labor Party, which re-elected him seven times, *was* a political party, but the CP was much more a movement than a party.

This was true not only in terms of size. It was true in terms of influence, in terms of the great number of large mass organizations established and led by its members, in terms of impressive demonstrations, huge popular delegations, petition campaigns and other forms of social pressure, including important sit-ins or strikes.

Here I want to note a sentiment common among most CP members and supporters; why was it possible in the depth of the Depression, without being hopelessly Pollyanna-ish, for us to maintain a sense of real optimism? I must take sharp issue with the not-infrequently heard claim that most, or an inordinate number, of party members got "burnt out." In all my more than sixty years of involvement with an immense variety of organizations I have found a much smaller percentage of members in the CP than in any other organization become "burnt out," and it seems clear to me that there were evident reasons for this ability to endure.

Perhaps the most important factor was that one always felt himself or herself to be a functioning part of something great and potentially powerful. Vivian Gornick uses a wonderful phrase in the introduction to her book, *The Romance of American Communism*. She says that when her parents and other needle trade workers, radical Russian-Jewish immigrants, sat down in their kitchens in the Bronx co-ops to discuss world affairs, "history sat down with them."

I believe this was the feeling most Communist Party members had; history sat down with us. We were a functioning part of history, a small part or a larger part depending on our specific contributions, but all parts of a tremendous and ultimately victorious movement. Of course the Soviet Union was, for us, a vital and legitimate part of that optimism; against all the odds it was incontrovertibly there.

One of us may have been working with the Unemployed Councils, another in the American Labor Party, another in the American

ANNETTE T. RUBINSTEIN 243

League for Peace and Democracy, another in the International
Workers Order, another in the early, radical Teachers Union or the
Civil Rights Congress, but we all felt part of a coherent whole.
Whatever we were doing, as members of the Communist Party we
were part of something larger. There was never the sense of
fragmentation, of isolation and futility, so prevalent and exhaust-
ing in so many dedicated radical groups today.

I've continued to be active politically in many different ways, not
only in the ten or fifteen years after I left the party in 1952, but also
long after I dropped any contact with it. In terms of time and energy
I have often been quite as active in such organizations as the
Charter Group against Racism in New York, the New York Center
for Marxist Education, and women's groups fighting for abortion
rights. But good and necessary as all these efforts are, I, in common
with many—perhaps most—of my co-workers feel that each is an
ad hoc committee, a sort of holding operation. It's an important
thing we're doing, but important only within its own narrow limits.
That is very different from the feeling we had when we believed
that what we were doing was a necessary small part of a tremendous concerted worldwide effort.

In our present fragmented world one is much more easily discouraged by defeat. Consider, for example, the total defeat that the
entire left felt at the time of the legalized murder of Sacco and
Vanzetti in Boston in the twenties. Compare that with the effect of
even so traumatic an experience as the fall of Madrid in the 1930s.
The repercussion, the expressions of anger and grief, are entirely
different. In the first we felt we had lost everything. We had lost
the war. In the second we'd lost a major battle—a very significant
battle, a very terrible loss, but nevertheless one battle and not the
war. Here are a few lines from Dos Passos' *USA* written shortly
after the execution of Sacco and Vanzetti. He wrote:

> All right, you have won. You will kill the brave men, our friends,
> tonight. There's nothing left to do. We are beaten. We the beaten
> crowd together in these dingy old school rooms on Salem Street,
> shuffle up and down the gritty creaking stairs, sit hunched with
> bowed heads on benches and hear the old words of the haters of
> oppression made new in sweat and agony tonight. ...

This is, I think, the most powerful passage in the entire *USA*
trilogy, but it expresses total irredeemable defeat.

In contrast, Edwin Rolfe, a veteran of the Abraham Lincoln Brigade who had been critically wounded in the defense of Madrid, wrote after the city fell to the fascists:

To Madrid, to Spain:

Who is not true to you is false to every man,
and he to whom your name means nothing never loved,
And if I die before I can return to you
or you in fullest freedom are restored to us,
my sons will love you as their father did.
Madrid, Madrid, Madrid.

The dreadful loss we all felt at the fall of Madrid is evident here but so too is Rolfe's feeling that this great struggle was part of something even greater, something which could not be defeated. That was truly how we, how Communists, felt through all the pain and desolation of the 1930s.

Speaking of the literature of the time, the critic Warren French called it "The exciting literature of a depressing age." Looking back I think that this was on the whole true. I have no space here to discuss the novels, poetry and critical battles of the period and regret it less given the contribution elsewhere in this book of Alan Wald, who has done and is doing such major work in the field.

There were a number of intellectual as well as emotional reasons for the feeling of buoyancy, of exhilaration, that radicals felt in the thirties and, with a difference, in the forties. One of these is summarized by an ode of, I believe, Horace's which begins, "Happy is he who knows the causes of things." This was one of my first reactions when I joined the party in the 1930s and began to read Marxism seriously. I had thought of myself as a socialist since childhood because my father had run for judge on the Socialist ticket during a Debs campaign and my mother had been one of five Hunter College graduates to organize an atheist socialist Sunday school in 1907. (A group of radical needle trade workers provided the loft, and the students and my mother planned the curriculum consisting largely of Shelley's poetry, Morgan's anthropology, Marx's *Manifesto* and Old Testament stories told as struggles for national liberation.) I gloried in this tradition, but lived in a wealthy suburb and my sheltered childhood provided a sort of unworldly utopian socialism with no practical application whatsoever. But, like many of my generation, when I graduated into the Depression in 1929 I wanted to understand why there were no jobs. We couldn't understand why stores were empty and breadlines long. Newspapers offered all sorts of idiotic explanations and remedies from (literally) sun spots to President Hoover's neighborly self-help.

In this situation the discovery of surplus value was a real event. It explained what was happening around us and to us. My family had been wealthy and a number of the men we knew committed suicide as their businesses were forced into bankruptcy. We had grown up in a very different world than the one we entered and those of us who turned to Marx—there were half a dozen editions of *Capital* published in the early thirties, including the popular Everyman and Modern Library series—had a sudden feeling of dazzling illumination.

We also felt we had to do something about it, and many of us began looking for allies. It was then that the party first really began to recruit U.S.-born, English-educated and, to some extent, privileged young people.

The mood of the time is well expressed in two very short verses, one written in 1931 just before the party impinged on our consciousness, and one in 1935 just after its membership had increased by at least 700 percent from some 7,000 largely foreign-born members in 1929. A collection of poetry called *Unrest* was published by the party in 1931. It included "The Paper Mill" by a mill worker, Joseph Callar, which began:

> The fires are banked and red changes to black.
> Steam is cold water. Silence is rust, and quiet spells hunger.
> Look at these men now standing before the iron gates mumbling,
> "Who could believe it? Who could believe?"

In the roaring twenties the idea that factories could close, that production and prosperity could decrease instead of increasing, that this could happen in the United States, was really something incredible.

A few years later Kenneth Fearing wrote in *Dynamo: A Journal of Revolutionary Poetry*:

> And all along the waterfront, there, where rats gnaw into the loading
> platforms, here, where the wind whips at the warehouse corners,
> look, there, here, everywhere huge across the walls and gates "Your

party lives," where there is no life, no breath, no sound, no touch, no warmth, no light but the lamp that shines on a trooper's drawn and ready bayonet. "Your party lives."

These two verses give a great deal of the spirit, the mood and the reason for the phenomenal growth of radical organization in the Depression.

As I have already said, there were a number of unsentimental reasons for the optimism radicals felt as their organization grew. The continuing activity itself was, psychologically at least, a cause of optimism. As William James discovered, we're often afraid just because we run, and while we may fight because of hope we often feel hopeful because we're fighting. Together with the exhilaration generated by this activity itself, there was also the fact of frequent, if not continual, small victories. We could actually unionize a shop, lead a group to sit in at the welfare office until they were given the benefits they were entitled to, force a restaurant to serve a black customer. These things were not going to change the course of history, but it was doubly worth mobilizing to get furniture put back into a house when you knew this would encourage the tenants' union to stop future evictions. There were enough of these successful actions in our own immediate consciousness, often as the result of our own personal participation, to make us know that victories were possible.

Another element in our radical culture, evidenced in 1930s fiction but not in official documents of the CP, was the curious pervasive democracy, emotional democracy, which characterized the party and the organizations it influenced, despite the undemocratic hierarchical structure up above. Within any local organization which met regularly, whether it was a Parent-Teacher Association chapter, or an American Labor Party club or a newly formed CIO local, there really was a feeling of genuine democracy. I'm not speaking of elections or resolutions but of a much more fundamental sense of equality.

What probably shocked me more than anything else about the young people of the New Left, whom in many ways I much admired, was to hear them say, time after time, about a necessary mailing or other such routine task: "I don't want to do that kind of shitwork." That was an attitude which would have been completely inconceivable to any of my comrades in the thirties and forties. Translating an Icelandic Edda, William Morris reports two chiefs, brothers, speaking to each other. One says, "There's the calf to be killed and the Viking to be fought. Which of us shall kill the calf and which shall fight the Viking?" That was exactly how we felt. If there were envelopes to be stuffed we stuffed envelopes. You might speak to a rally of several thousand at Manhattan Center one day, climb up on a soap box to attract a dozen passers-by another, and act as an usher in Madison Square Garden the next week. In the ALP we would ordinarily define the chairman as the one who set up the chairs. This was a simple fact since if you were chairing you had to be there early to open the place, and would naturally set things up while waiting.

There was also a serious sense of democratic responsibility. If you were not on the picket line you had promised to join, if you didn't appear for whatever action you had volunteered or been assigned to support, you felt you were deserting your comrades. Like acrobats on a trapeze, we were usually confident that whoever was supposed to be somewhere would be there. Our own sense of responsibility assured us of one another's.

Obviously one of the elements which made for this comradeship was the sense of being a beleaguered minority. Even at its largest the party never claimed more than eighty or a hundred thousand members so that we were always clearly outnumbered. Our opponents were strong and ruthless and many of us had good reason to be afraid. But there was also a sort of intoxication in the situation, certainly a strong emotional bond created by the shared danger. It was a feeling Henry V had expressed when he said, outnumbered a hundred to one at Agincourt, "We few, we happy few, we band of brothers."

While we all felt that each gain in living standards, civil liberties, racial equality, etc., was a step toward socialism, there was little discussion of socialism itself or even of the necessary transition. I don't think anyone I knew personally, except perhaps Mike Gold, really expected that he or she would ever live in a socialist United States, and even fewer expected to emigrate to the Soviet Union. But we were all sincere in believing that we were distinguished and empowered by belonging to the Communist Party; in fact, in most mass organizations and unions influenced by the party its members were the most dedicated and highly respected. The strong personal relations our radical culture fostered among its members were ethical rather than psychological. I don't remember ever discussing my state of mind or emotions or love affairs with any comrade. And yet it is true that all but one of my close friends today—that is, those of my own generation—are former members of the party I left some forty years ago. They all left too, at different times; some a little earlier, most a little later. But the bonds we forged in working together for an end we still, albeit less optimistically, believe in, hold. It has been said that true love doesn't mean looking steadfastly at one another; it means looking steadfastly in the same direction. That was essentially the meaning of our comradeship.

I have necessarily over-simplified, over-generalized and omitted more than I could include in this hasty survey of the cultural climate fostered by the Communist Party in the thirties and forties. For me this climate was best epitomized in the radical theater—not so much the plays as the actual theater experience of the so-called red decade, the thirties. It is to this topic that I now turn. Actually a small personal experience made me feel it was absolutely essential I do this.

Paul Buhle, an extremely able, very knowledgeable young cultural historian, conducted several oral interviews with me about the social and cultural life on the left in the thirties. At the end of the series he asked whether there were any important topics we hadn't touched on. I looked at him with utter amazement since he hadn't even mentioned the theater, and said I thought he had been saving that for a separate session. In equal amazement he asked whether there was really much to talk about there! Actually the theater was the center for a very large segment of radical social life. Ordinarily your plans would be to go to the theater with somebody and if you were having dinner you would go before or after the theater.

In the 1920s, with movies displacing road companies, the theater in the United States had come to mean a strip of fourteen blocks in the heart of Manhattan housing the glittering, technically sophisticated, extravagant Broadway productions available only to those in the upper income brackets. There were a few semi-professional acting companies organized by immigrant workers, notably the German-speaking Prolet-Buhne (Workers Stage) and the Yiddish speaking Arbeiter Teater Verband (Workers Theater League, known as ARTEF). There were also a number of less professional groups organized by various unions throughout the country such as the Chicago Blue Blouses, the Rebel Players of Los Angeles, and the Solidarity Players of Boston. These generally presented "agit-prop" plays, short sketches which required a minimum of scenery or costuming and could be mounted on the bare platform of a union hall or even at an outdoor street meeting.

In 1930 a number of other similar groups, including the Harlem Suitcase Theater which produced Langston Hughes' *Scottsboro Boys*, were founded. In 1931 the most professional of the English speaking groups, the New York Workers Laboratory Theater, encouraged by the growing interest among newly radicalized workers and the unemployed, launched a mimeographed magazine, *Workers Theater*. A hundred and thirty groups responded to its call for a national conference, including nineteen which had already established functioning companies. Hallie Flanagan, later appointed to head the Federal Works Progress Administration (WPA) Theater, reported in the major drama magazine, *Theater Arts*. She said, "... there are only two theaters in the country today that are clear as to their aim: one is the commercial theater which wants to make money; the other is the workers' theater which wants to make a new social order...."

Encouraged by the growth of a new working-class and left-leaning intellectual audience, two important groups of theater workers organized the Group Theater (1931–1940), and the Theater Union (1933–1937). Although both were forced to close by financial difficulties their critical success, and the enormous popular interest in theater which they evidenced and fostered, were factors in the establishment of the WPA Federal Theater.

The class nature of these theaters was clear, although a large part of the theater workers and much of the audience were, like Marx, Engels, Lenin, Brecht, and Zhou Enlai, self-enlisted under the proletarian banner. The Group Theater, with left-liberal leadership and, often, open debates between Communist Party members and other personnel, nevertheless produced plays like John Howard Lawson's *Success Story* and Clifford Odets's *Awake and Sing*. Its less expensive seats were always sold out but, except for an occasional hit, the front orchestra rows were rarely filled. The more explicitly revolutionary Theater Union, with a top price of

CP influence was felt in union drives among artists, writers, and actors. March against war, 1935. Courtesy of Robert F. Wagner Labor Archives, New York University. Charles Rivers Collection. Photo: Charles Rivers.

$1.50, subsisted largely on the revenue of theater parties through block ticket sales organized by and for such varied groups as Communist and Socialist Party clubs, the Jewelry Workers Union, the League of Woman Workers, IWO clubs, Nature Friends, the Flatbush Cultural Forum, etc. Buying the tickets that way contributed to a communal sense of going to the theater.

The contemporary impact of this short-lived but significant theater is captured in Harold Clurman's account of the first-night production of Clifford Odets' agit-prop *Waiting for Lefty*, presented as the winner of the New Theater League playwriting contest in January, 1935. In *The Fervent Years* Clurman says:

> The first scene of *Lefty* had not played two minutes when a shock of delighted recognition struck the audience like a tidal wave. Deep laughter, hot assent, a kind of joyous fervor seemed to sweep the audience toward the stage.... When the audience at the end of the play responded to the militant question from the stage ... with a spontaneous roar of "Strike! Strike!" it was something more than a tribute to the play's effectiveness.... It was the birth cry of the 30s.

The next year a large union, the International Ladies Garment Workers Union, produced *Pins and Needles*, the first of a number of very different, very radical, musical comedies. It announced its theme forthrightly when, in an early scene, a group of young women turn their backs on a group of lovesick swains ardently rhyming June and Moon. The girls reply:

> Sing us a song with social significance
> Or you can sing till you're blue—
> You must get hot with just what's what
> Or we won't love you.

"Picket Line Priscilla," one of the hit songs in the show, became well known all across the continent as it was used in innumerable small retail strike actions building the new Congress of Industrial Organizations (CIO) unions. Another similar musical, *Sing for Your Supper*, produced the next year by the Federal Theater, sang the joy of getting not a sweetheart, but a job. It was not so much a matter of preaching to the converted as strengthening one's faith; as the Catholic Church learned over the centuries, it is very important for the converted to be constantly refreshed in their adherence. This is what occurred in the theater. If you went to see a play like *Stevedore*, it would remind you that some white workers had broken ranks with their leadership and supported a black strike. It gave new life to the American Labor Party (ALP) slogan: "Black and white, unite and fight."

The Federal Theater (1935–1939), unprecedented in the United States, was by long odds the most innovative and influential dramatic project in our national history. Founded as one of the WPA Arts Projects to give jobs to unemployed theater workers in their own field—itself an extraordinarily imaginative New Deal proposal—the combination of a surprisingly progressive, exceedingly competent national director, Hallie Flanagan, and the growing popular interest in serious sociopolitical drama, soon made it the cultural center of the radical movement, a vital factor in a national cultural renaissance.

It presented searching mixed-media documentary plays, written by its own writers, like *One-Third of a Nation*, *Injunction Granted*, *Chalk Dust*, *Power*, *Triple-A Plowed Under*, *Spirochete*, *Ethiopia*. These, produced by a unit of the Federal Theater Project called "The Living Newspaper" under the leadership of a blacklisted former Newspaper Guild president, Morris Watson, were as radical in format as in viewpoint, and made theater history. The first play that they put on, *One-Third of a Nation*, was an enormous success. It had an incredibly creative stage set, and employed many artists in this. The major character was an old-line tenement house, which took up the whole stage, with a piece sheared away to reveal a number of apartments. The voice of the house was a triumph, a very hoarse old ogreish voice that played a large part in the presentation.

The Federal Theater also produced, but did not actually present Marc Blitzstein's censored *The Cradle Will Rock*, and did present Sinclair Lewis' *It Can't Happen Here*, as well as circuses, dance programs, vaudeville shows and children's plays. (One of these, *The Revolt of the Beavers*, by Oscar Saul and Lou Lantz, was cited as communist propaganda by the House Un-American Activities Committee, which also asked Hallie Flanagan whether Christopher Marlowe was another one of those Communist writers.) The Federal Theater made a rousing success with brilliant productions of classic plays by Shakespeare, Shaw, O'Neill and T.S. Eliot, which commercial producers had shied away from. When a play was successful, like Eliot's *Death in the Cathedral*, it would be taken over by the commercial theaters.

The Federal Theater had over two hundred production units in thirty-five states, including at least twelve black companies, and presented plays at an average admission price of fifty cents. These were seen by over an eighth of the people in the United States, most of whom had never seen live theater before. We kept getting reports from sections in the Midwest that audiences which had evidently been engrossed by a play didn't applaud but simply sat still after the final scene. When the manager came out to ask what they were waiting for they said, "to see it over." Their experience had been entirely with films which were then shown repeatedly, and people with time to kill often stayed for several showings in an afternoon if they liked the story. Many of the Federal Theater performances were presented outdoors or in old theaters left over from nineteenth century and pre-World War I road shows. It also produced shows in the Guild Co-ops and meeting halls, as well as churches or community centers connected with churches. People found out about these performances through notices on bulletin boards and announcements in the local paper. If it was a small town, a reporter was usually sent to cover the play. The Federal Theater guidelines said that not more than ten percent of the budget could be spent for non-theater jobs which limited advertisement.

Discussions were common after the play; they varied from city to city, with no uniformity to them at all. Some questions focused on subtle shadings of meaning; others, especially those of the Living Newspaper, were extremely naive and asked, for example, how a given sound effect was produced. There were also discussions before the play with actors or stage hands as they were setting up. In New York Elmer Rice was the director of the Federal Theater until he resigned because the Washington office of the WPA censored his dramatization of Italy's attack on Ethiopia, calling it "unkind to a friendly power." One of the landmark stagings was Sinclair Lewis' anti-Nazi *It Can't Happen Here*, depicting a fascist takeover of the United States, which I think made a better play than a novel. It opened simultaneously in twenty-two cities with twenty-two distinct and independent productions. Of course there was a great deal of struggle between Actors Equity and the *ad hoc* WPA theater workers' union. At first Actors Equity refused to recognize the WPA union—the stage hands never did—and part of what is now the accepted custom of actors moving their own furniture on and off the stage developed during that time.

The CP membership had quite a strong presence in most theater groups and when theater workers were protesting lay-offs, pink slips and the like, it was quite common to have a few auxiliary protesters on the line from the cultural clubs of the party, partly through natural friendships. I myself was on several picket lines related to support for the painters, because a friend of mine, Charles Humboldt, was an editor of their magazine *Art Front*.

Federal Veterans League Jeopardizes Project

"THE TRIPLE-A PLOWED UNDER" GOES TO PRESS

The Living Newspaper went to press with a resounding bang at the Biltmore with "Triple A Plowed Under." The thinking New Yorkers present were appreciative of a startling new and effective form of drama. Employing the methods of the newsreel combined with the stereoptician, a hard-biting, necessarily sketchy but honest review of the American farmers plight from 1917 to 1935 was presented in twenty-two fast moving scenes.

Opening with a scene in which farmers are being implored to raise more crops "to win the war" the story goes on to show the effects of post-war deflation on the farmer and the disparity in the price he received for his product and the price which the consumer was forced to pay. Passing hurriedly over the temporary "farmers holiday," the rolling scene reveal the steps which the landworkers took to protect themselves—the milk strikes, crop burnings and suppressed foreclosures.

Then with the Federal Government stepp'ng in the triple A farm program is inaugurated, only to be revealed as a dubious, self defeating device for aid'ng the oppressed. Tabloid evidence of its effects upon the farmer, the consumer and the speculator is presented, followed by a scene in which the Supreme Court's case against it is placed alongside arguments by Al Smith, Earl Browder and Thomas Jefferson. The story ends with a mass scene in

BULLETIN

As we went to press, word came that Major Ball, President of the Fascist inspired Federal Veterans League, was transfered to another project.

which farmers and workers join in a united front against the speculators.

Unfortunately, due to the activities of a handful of disruptive reactionaries the full significance of this new and graphic drama form was lost to some. Dramatic critics as a whole agreed however that a new, vital and telling form of drama had been born.

The idea of presenting living dramatization of current news events was conceived at a meeting of the re-employment Committee of the Newspaper Guild. To their credit it has been carried forward by Morris Watson and his capable staff of actors and reporters despite the subversive attempts of a few misguided "patriots" to hamper it.

The Living Newspaper with its staff of 243 which includes 46 reportes, re-write men and editors should be credited with a sensation beat in presenting this intensely intersesting drama for which should reflect credit on the entire project.

42,000 TO GO (?)

Hundreds of "Pink Slips." the U. S. Government starvation passports, are raining down on thousands of workers throughout the city as

Victor Ridder's plan to drop 42,00\. from W.P.A. projects get under way.

The first to go are "agitators," or those who had sufficient courage to exercise their constitutional privilege in insisting upon their inherent right to live. Despite all promises that dismissals would not be made discriminatory, Ridder is, nevertheless, firing first those who were known to be in the leadership of the various protective organizations on the project. However, thousands of workers who had absolutely nothing to do with any organization and submitted meekly to whatever the administration did, will feel the axe of "economy" very shortly. Ridder plans to dismiss 12,000 by the end of March.

The City Projects Council, the only union of white collared employees on the projects has already begun action to counteract Ridder's edict. Remembering that it was through picket lines and mass demonstrations that Ridder's previous order effecting the dismissal of 20,-000 workers was successfully combated last January, the CPC is now preparing a mass demonstration to be held March 28, at the Port Authority Building to force Ridder to see that the project workers, engaged on the most worthwhile, useful work, will not take these dismissals lying down.

Even arrest and Ridder's Fascist charge that the dismissed WPA workers who protest at his office (as on March 19) be charged with "is

(Continued on page 4)

The CP helped organize artists and technicians in the Federal Theatre Project. Note reference to Earl Browder's "appearance" in the production *Triple-A Plowed Under*. Courtesy of Tamiment Institute Library, New York University.

Actors or artists would call on their friends, and their friends tended to be in the CP. There were some occasions where Hallie Flanagan found herself opposing the theater group's demands, fairly explicitly CP demands, for more revolutionary content in the plays. As for a democratic spirit in the theater companies themselves, there was often the kind of discussion among actors, author and director that Brecht encouraged. This was especially true in the Living Newspaper, which itself emerged in this way, and in work on the classics that were often freshly reinterpreted, as in *Julius Caesar* set in contemporary Rome. There was also thoughtful planning at the national level, deciding which company did which play at what time.

The weekly audience of almost 400,000 made the Federal Theater a force to be reckoned with, and an increasingly conservative Congress finally succeeded in closing it in 1939, declaring it to be a "hotbed of communism." The report issued by the red-hunting Congressman Martin Dies declared that "A rather large number of employees ... are either members of the Communist Party or sympathizers...." For an excellent illustrated history of the Federal Theater see *Free, Adult, Uncensored: The Living History of the Federal Theater Project*, edited by John O'Connor and Lorraine Brown (Washington DC: New Republic Press, 1978).

In New York for a long time after, there were all kinds of small theater attempts either inspired by or tracing some of their members to the Federal Theater. The extremely lavish use of personnel had been a plus, not a minus. The WPA wanted to employ as many unemployed people as possible, and this assured that a director had the people he or she needed to do any kind of job. However, there wasn't really any continuum. The closest successors may have been some of the regional theaters and perhaps a number of union theater groups whose inspiration was the Federal Theater. In Harlem, where there were a great many clubs and cabarets, there was very little demand for written scripts until the Federal Theater. In this sense it may have been helpful in the development of black playwrights.

Some mention should be given to the party's general outlook with regard to the dynamic presence of progressive artists during the period. The CP cultural policy was an extremely confused one. There was the extreme proletarian attitude; Mike Gold, for example, wrote a scathing attack on Sean O'Casey's *Juno and the Peacock*, because it showed a drunken, lazy Irishman. This was not considered proper: it was seen as a stereotype that helped the enemy. But Mike Gold's criticism reflected his actual taste; what I thought was worse was people like V. J. Jerome, who in their own homes would have abstract modern art, but in their writing would argue very strongly for the simplest kind of realism.

On the whole I don't think the CP took the cultural front seriously enough to develop a coherent perspective, but in general the membership was very enthusiastic about the theater. There wasn't the kind of theoretical debate that one had in the Soviet Union; there was not the material for it. After all, almost everybody in the art world in the CPUSA was unemployed and wanted, if possible, to get a job. So the CP influence if anything was through the weight of membership in the theater groups and did not stem from any formal directives.

The party's concentration on the situation of the unemployed, and on the Negro people *as a people*, provided the closest thing to a cultural focus; on the whole, there was no embrace of anything like Zhdanov's debased and fraudulent "socialist realism." The class-oriented John Reed Clubs were dissolved when the shift was made to the united front line in 1937, and, while perfectly correct politically, this line was generally devastating to serious development in the arts. For a serious writer to say less than he or she knows in order to broaden his audience destroys any creative depth in the arts. An anti-Nazi film that was widely accepted was considered perfectly appropriate, even if it did not provide any deeper analysis than the *New York Times*. By becoming concerned with casting such a wide net much of the critical thrust of the work was compromised.

One can't underestimate the political importance of the united front, but writers can't undercut themselves by saying less than they understand. Three of us presented this problem to the board of the party's Jefferson School, and were amazed by their indifference and antagonism.

The very nature of drama, which can never fully come to life on the printed page, has made necessary much more discussion of practical organization and audience than would be relevant in a consideration of fiction or poetry. Now we must also attempt some exploration of a theoretical question. Why should the Depression decade of the thirties in the United States have been the only time since Elizabethan England when an English-speaking stage found itself the center of a national culture? What, if anything, did the two periods have in common with the nature of drama that helped to create such an effect?

Sixteenth-century London was, of course, the self-conscious center of a society in transition. A new bourgeois society had matured within the womb of the feudal world, age-old verities had been called in question, men and women were seeking answers to new questions. The very shape of the earth, changed for the eyes of scientists two centuries earlier by men like Copernicus and Galileo, were now changed for the eyes of the less learned by men like Amerigo Vespucci and Christopher Columbus.

Not only were explorers bringing home stories of strange races and customs in remote islands; Christendom itself was no longer one. Luther, Calvin, and Henry VIII had led the way to unthinkable divisions in the very heart of European civilization when, for that civilization, religion was all-pervasive. It had for centuries been assumed that Catholic was also catholic—that is, universal. Every political and economic controversy from struggles for national independence to the regulation of "usury" or interest rates was argued in religious terminology after centuries when such arguments were inconceivable.

Of course no society is ever really static. But sometimes things change so slowly that no movement is discernible within a lifetime, while at other periods institutions and traditions seem to disappear and reform with bewildering rapidity. If one had asked the average twelfth century Englishman, "What will the world be like twenty years from now?" the answer would almost certainly have been "what do you mean? Just like it's always been." But the ordinary sixteenth century Elizabethan, the Londoner who had seen his city quadruple in his own lifetime, was sure that, for good or ill, the future would be very different from the past.

Similarly, before World War I, few North Americans expected anything but a continual expansion of established ways while, as Tennyson had complacently expressed the Victorian faith, "Freedom slowly broadens out/ From precedent to precedent." Even in the feverish twenties, while the United States celebrated the new hedonism of free love and free spending it never questioned free trade or the permanent beneficent growth of free enterprise. But whatever average people of the thirties hoped or feared from the future they knew there was no turning back to the world of their childhood. And many, if not the average person, then thought the Russian experiment might, for good or ill, offer a hint about the future.

Unlike the 1920s, when the essential choices seemed to be individual ones and the conflicts largely generational, when politics seemed irrelevant to daily life, every hotly contested government decision in the thirties was fateful. Struggles on the floor of Congress about money to be appropriated for home relief or WPA jobs, about a moratorium in foreclosing family farms, about the legality of strikes and picket lines affected one's daily life. Nor did people stand by watching, concerned but helpless spectators, while these issues were decided. It had become apparent that groups of men and women acting together could bring effective pressure to bear on local officials, on Congressmen, even on the President himself. Few groups could win all their demands but many could win some. It was this sense of the possibility, as well as the need, for collective struggle that informed what Warren French called "the exciting literature of a depressing age."

So drama which, to be dramatic, must involve struggle, had naturally an important part to play in that literature. Every play centers about some conflict. It may be, for example, simply the personal conflict between two men in love with the same girl; it may be the conflict between a woman and her society should she wish to marry a man of another class or race; it may be the conflict between two societies, like the war Homer tells us the Greeks and Trojans fought over Helen's elopement or the war twentieth century Germany, France, and England fought over colonies; it may be the conflict within a man if the woman he loves is a forbidden sister or daughter. Several types of conflict may be interwoven as in Shakespeare's *Hamlet, Prince of Denmark*, where the prince's attempt to revenge his father is complicated by his struggle with his own reluctance to kill the usurper. But whether it's a love story or a political or religious one, without opposition and action, however trivial, there is no drama.

And powerful drama requires a conflict that is vitally significant for its time, although the actual plot material may seem trivial. So in *Othello, the Moor of Venice*, what might have been simply a pathetic story of mistaken jealousy becomes tragically significant when we see how subtly Iago uses the unconscious sense of difference and sexual inferiority implanted in the Moor by a racist society. It is that, and not the conventional handkerchief plot, through which Shakespeare shows why Othello cannot understand or trust "our women"; it is that which makes the man believe it is impossible for a Venetian lady really to love a "thick lipped blackamoor."

The Hungarian Marxist critic György Lukács says in his remarkable book, *The Historical Novel*, that whereas a great novel must seem to present to the reader "a totality of objects," an entire world, a great drama seems to present only "a totality of forces"—that is, the major conflicts of its time, embodied in its protagonists. The actual plot material need not be of epic proportions. A very minor instance, such as a taxi drivers' strike or the unprecedented victory made possible by a newly united black and white group of dock workers, may represent vital contemporary forces and signal a momentous shift in power. But the example chosen, whether symbolic or realistic, must be rooted in the significant conflicts of its own time, though the action may take place in another place and some past or future time. Thus great drama is, of all literary forms, the one most aptly used to express an age of visible struggle and rapid change.

Another, perhaps equally important reason contributed to the popularity of the theater in the 1930s, a popularity not achieved in the United States before or since. That is the necessarily collective nature of theater, the social nature not only of its creation but also of its reception.

A play is and must be a shared experience, appealing to a common emotional denominator in its audience. They may respond on different levels with varying degrees of intensity but there must be some basic element in its message which moves them all, and moves them almost instantaneously. A reader can proceed at his or her own pace, can pause to relish a sense of personal familiarity with the characters in a novel, may choose to dwell on minor figures or descriptive touches or verbal felicities in the text. Spectators have no such options. If they are to enjoy the play they have to accept the tempo and emphases with which it is presented.

Furthermore the response of one audience member will be heightened by the participation of others who are moved by the same regret or angered by the same inhumanity or amused by the same absurdity or delighted at the same triumph. Every actor and every experienced playgoer knows how much individual emotions are deepened by the resonance of a group response. This mutual strengthening of concern and hope was something sought, consciously or unconsciously, by millions shocked and terrified as the American dream fell shattered about them in the thirties. Emerging from the debris, often "the hands of the unlucky found one another." There was emotional reassurance as well as practical help in newly formed community organizations, unemployed councils, unions and mass meetings. Many also found such support in the socially concerned theater.

THE NEW YORK WORKERS SCHOOL, 1923–1944:
Communist Education in American Society

Marvin E. Gettleman

Before 1919, when virtually every Socialist Party split into two wings (the left usually becoming the Communist Party), socialists in the United States and elsewhere had long assigned to schools a central role in developing and propagating their political vision. U.S. communists inherited this emphasis on propagandistic education, and soon after the U.S. Communist Party appeared, schools to teach Marxism and the party line sprung up. This essay describes the New York Workers School, which opened in 1923, became the model for similar schools elsewhere (including anticommunist schools), and merged in 1944 into another Communist Party educational enterprise, the Jefferson School of Social Science.[1]

The New York Workers School accepted its first students in October 1923. Located initially on University Place near Union Square, it moved to Communist Party headquarters at 28 East Fourteenth Street and later still to 35 East Twelfth Street, all on Manhattan's Lower East Side. These various sites were grimly utilitarian. An FBI informer reported the Twelfth Street building to have been so "dingy, makeshift and old ... that it recalls the evils of a fire trap that should have been condemned."

> The walls ... are filthy, their paint and crumbling edges covered for the most part with ... Red posters done in several languages.... [C]lassrooms on the fourth floor ... [were] divided by aged folding partitions constructed of glass.... More propaganda is found tacked and pasted to the walls; pictures of Stalin and other well-known Soviet characters; [cartoons] that have been splashed out of the ink pot in bold, bright colors ...; notices of coming Communistic festivities and demonstrations, and chalk and pencil effigies of [President Herbert] Hoover, [Mayor] Jim Walker, Grover Whalen, Mussolini,

261

the Pope, the eternal boss and a hundred other public figures that have drawn the hatred of these poor radicals.[2]

What this hostile observer did not, and possibly could not, detect beneath the school's undoubtedly grubby exterior was its animating conception: that of a militantly oppositional education right in the midst of capitalist America.

This vision received expression in the Workers School's ambitiously stated aims: to advance "true proletarian education," and to train workers "for effective leadership in the American Labor Movement."[3] By "true proletarian education" school spokesmen meant the effort "to make permanent the class knowledge of the working class," the "knowledge of revolutionary theory and tactics, and labor history, which is essential for militant activity in the struggle against capitalism."[4] Co-director Ben Davidson (writing under his *nom de guerre*, D. Benjamin) elaborated in 1927 on the Workers School's class-based, cooperative educational purposes and how they differed from those of "the capitalist schools."

> [Whether these capitalist schools be] ... of a private or public nature ..., [e]ducation [there] is a means of self-advancement—prestige, contact, training are all advantageous in a capitalist world.... In the [Workers School, however] ... the students are workers devoted to the working class movement who take courses in order to prepare themselves for better service to their unions and to the labor movement as a whole. They work hard all day ...; they smuggle in a few hours at the Workers School during the week so as to be better equipped for the working class struggle.... It is easy to see that [this] ... movement is not a leisure class movement. The students do not attend [the Workers School] with the aim of surpassing others in knowledge for the purpose of forging ahead of fellow students. The class is rather a cooperative enterprise, each learning as much as possible from the other[s], everyone contributing with an objective common to all—a better and stronger organization of the U.S. working class.[5]

Not only did Communist militants of the 1920s deem their Workers School a more authentic instrument for proletarian education than the schools of the capitalist society, but they also considered it the historic successor to such Socialist institutions as the Rand School of Social Science. This sense of succession was expressed by Sender Garlin, a young teacher at the Workers School who had earlier studied at the Rand School. But he and others who went over to communism believed that the Rand School had politically deteriorated: It had become a "tomb." Lectures on Marxism, Garlin charged, now drew people who arrived in chauffeured limousines, its curriculum included presumably objectionable courses in "interpretative dancing, psycho-analysis and the Ring of the Niebelung."[6] While this may have been an underestimation of the revolutionary potential of studying Freud, Wagner, and even modern dance (most of which would eventually make their way into the curricula of later Communist Party schools),[7] it did express the conviction that the old Socialist educational efforts were being eclipsed by the rising red star of the Workers School. Despite elements of polemical exaggeration in both the denigration of other left educational enterprises and in the contrasting characterization of the excellences of Communist Party schools, surviving evidence (including the oral testimony of former students and staff) suggests that educational practice at the New York Workers School was essentially what it set out to be—a systematic effort to mobilize learning to support the workers' side in the class struggle. On one level, of course, this meant that the curriculum was dictated by the party line of the moment. But educational historians have come to understand that actual pedagogy can never be reduced to the formal curriculum. Schools, like other collective movements, take on a dynamic of their own, and at the Workers School the pedagogical spirit stressed a close connection between learning and action: the fusing of theory and practice, in the spirit of Marx's celebrated "Eleventh Thesis on Feuerbach." From such an activist perspective, the undeniably fading Rand School and its parent Socialist Party (SP) had looked pretty feeble. There was by the mid-1920s little ongoing Socialist Party practice that could be invigorated by connection with parallel educational work.[8]

Thus, the Communist Workers School, in its pursuit of an education that would hasten the overthrow of capitalism (a goal muted in SP circles by the mid-1920s), devoted itself mainly to the necessary preliminary activity—earnest work in that area which, if any did, embodied the spirit of revolution: the labor movement. It is in this linkage between trade unionism and education that the U.S. Communists made their most significant contribution, one that is all but forgotten nowadays.[9] To grasp (but not necessarily to endorse) this vision of an engaged, activist education, it is best to look at Communist efforts against the background of other concepts of U.S. education.

Two aspects of twentieth century educational theory are particularly relevant for this comparative perspective. The first is the widespread, almost universal, view that authentic education is entirely different from education-for-action, or even advocacy of action. The second is the "Progressive Education" outlook of John Dewey and his followers. By the early 1930s, as Robert Westbrook shows in his recent *John Dewey and American Democracy*, Deweyites were locked in a many-levelled struggle with Communists, who believed that whatever might have once been the spark of radicalism in Deweyite progressivism had been drained away by an unwillingness to confront class issues in education, and by Dewey's own increasingly strident anticommunism.[10] The other view, less attacked by Communists but surely more widespread and more antithetical to the Communist vision than was Deweyite progressivism, was the view that action and advocacy are opposed to true education. In conventional circles, by the early 1920s at least, this notion had come to have the authority of "the way things are, or should be," but it was itself a historical phenomenon of relatively recent appearance. The best account is Mary O. Furner's brilliant but insufficiently known 1975 book, *Advocacy and Objectivity*, an analysis of the Faustian bargain struck in the 1890s that shaped all later official conceptions of U.S. education. Furner shows that, in a series of celebrated academic freedom cases, the professors under attack surrendered their original position that classroom advocacy of egalitarian social change is a legitimate educational goal, and adopted the ivory tower pose of detached, scholarly objectivity.[11] That retreat became the academic way of life in the U.S., with the significant proviso that support of positions consistent with the official state apparatus, or the interests of institutional donors, were deemed the only legitimate departures from the selective ban on advocacy.[12]

By contrast, Communist educational practice and (until the party grasped at straws in its final defense against the McCarthyist onslaught of the 1950s)[13] its openly announced conceptual rationale explicitly rejected this ivory tower model. A brochure of 1943 stated that:

It is the aim of the Workers School to *avoid* the academic approach. Its teaching is permeated with the live issues of the day, with the practical activity of the American people, with history in the making. The success of the Workers School lies in the fact that its students actively participate in its discussions and find in it a constant guide for the problems they face, as well as a source of inspiration to carry on the good fight for a free and democratic America. (Emphasis added.)[14]

It is true that the political concepts which animated communist educational work included the dubious belief that these goals for the United States—"freedom," "democracy," and especially social-ism—would be defined in terms of the ambiguous model of Bolshevik Russia. But in this author's view, it would be an error to hold that the support of what would become Stalinism in the Soviet Union vitiated each and every activity by dedicated Communists on U.S. shores, as conventional interpretations would have it. In any case, the question cannot be settled by a priori judgments, but rather it must be assessed on the basis of empirical investigation of actual party work, including its educational endeavors. (And it is precisely that task that has been shirked and even explicitly denigrated by conventional scholars.)[15]

Party educational efforts arose doctrinally from what was believed to be the Marxist idea that at bottom all significant human activity, including intellectual activity, expressed the prevailing social class divisions. But the practical orientation of the New York Workers School was also a response to what the students wanted and expected. In conformity with its name, the Workers School attracted a largely proletarian student body. Hundreds, and by the 1930s, thousands, of mainly foreign-born adult student workers came to the school at its various sites in downtown Manhattan, or to its annexes in Harlem, Brooklyn, and New Jersey. They were mostly drawn from the shops and factories where trade union organizing efforts were underway—the shoe, jewelry, light electrical and food preparation industries, retail and building and needle trades were most heavily represented. Some were already Communist Party members or sympathizers when they enrolled at the Workers School. Others could—and did—join on the basis of what went on in and out of classes at the school.[16]

And what did go on? The *Announcement of Classes*, issued at the beginning of each term, provides a starting point. In the very first term, the fall of 1923, there were a dozen courses. Marxism, of course, was featured, but there were others too: American applied economics (taught by Solon DeLeon, son of the celebrated socialist, Daniel); contemporary Europe; the history of the Three Internationals (taught by Communist editor Ludwig Lore). Party theorist Alexander Bittelman offered an analysis of tactics of the Third International. There was also a course on "Biologic and Social Evolution," and several on elementary and advanced English, "speech improvement" (i.e., getting rid of foreign accents), and platform speaking.[17]

Four years later the array of courses had tripled, and several luminaries had joined the school's advisory council, including labor historian David Saposs, Communist militant Elizabeth Gurley Flynn, and writers Floyd Dell and John Dos Passos. Courses now included "Citizenship and Naturalization," labor journalism (taught by veteran writer Harvey O'Connor), and a related course on "workers correspondence"—how to put out shop papers, leaflets, and the like (taught by Sender Garlin and Whittaker Chambers),[18] "Problems of the Needle Trades" (taught by another Lovestoneite-to-be, Benjamin Gitlow, and "open only to active, left wing needle trade workers"), "History of the American Working Class" (taught by pioneering social historian Arthur C. Calhoun), imperialism (taught by Scott Nearing, not yet expelled from the Communist Party), and a "Proletarian Writers Workshop" conducted by Mike Gold, the admission to which was based upon submission of two specimens of writing.[19] In 1926–1927, when the Workers School had enrolled over 1,000 students, Director Bertram D. Wolfe offered what seemed to have been something like an advanced seminar on "The American Mind," covering such themes as Puritanism, Transcendentalism, Fundamentalism, Mormonism, Pragmatism, etc. Increasingly, top party leaders would teach courses or give special lectures on such topics as the Chinese Revolution (Earl Browder) and trade union issues (William Z. Foster).[20]

An important, perhaps the most important, aspect of Communist educational work, in this and later periods, was its egalitarian and anti-racist thrust. (This is also true of party work generally, as Mark Naison and more recently Robin Kelley have convincingly demonstrated, and as Gerald Horne also points out in his contribution to this volume.)[21] At the Workers School, and later at the Jefferson School of Social Science, a dedicated group of white and black Communist educators, such as the writer Elizabeth Lawson, the Columbia-educated historian Herbert Aptheker, and the former Howard University faculty member Doxey A. Wilkerson, developed courses and teaching aids for a fresh, positive history of resistance to oppression by what were then called Negro Americans.[22]

By 1927, the "core course" at the Workers School, "Fundamentals of Communism," was being taught in six sections, including a day class for workers on the night shift. Several years later as many as fifty sections would be offered throughout the city. The course was sometimes a prerequisite for advanced courses, such as A.B. Magil's 1936 course on "Fascist Trends and Tendencies in the United States."[23] The content of "Fundamentals of Communism" varied somewhat as the CPUSA went through its sectarian Third Period phase, which by the mid-1930s gave way to the United Front conception of legitimate collaboration with "progressive" non-communists. These positions were developed at each stage through study of such Marxist classics as Lenin's *State and Revolution* and *What Is to Be Done?*, which were made available in one penny and five cent Workers School editions. Party educators contemptuously dismissed existing textbooks as being "full of poisonous capitalist and anti-labor propaganda,"[24] so in addition to its reprints, the Workers School also issued its own textbooks for the "Fundamentals" course. One of them, *Why Communism?* by Moissaye Olgin, the Russian-born Communist author, translator, and editor of the Yiddish daily *Freiheit*,[25] written in a vivid, colloquial style, captures much of the tone of political education in Workers School classes.

Why Communism? was specifically addressed to militant workers who were deemed on the verge of joining the party but needed a basic grounding in Communist principles and strategies. An evident subtext was also its demonstration to party members of how Communist beliefs ought to be presented to promising recruits. The 1935 revision opened with a bitter evocation of working class life in Depression America: the firing of a worker, after which the employer "goes to his country estate or abroad to have a good time." If the worker tries to remain at the plant or shop "to produce" for his benefit and others, the police or militia would soon arrive to club, shoot and arrest people "for the sole crime of wanting to continue working at the machines and with the materials you and the like of you have produced." Having set the stage in ordinary life for discussion of class, exploitation and the futility of looking to the capitalist-controlled government for relief, the pamphlet presents "the cure": that "all land and buildings, all manufacturing, mines, railroads ... [become] the common property of all those who work." This goal cannot be reached by "the poisonous theory" of "gradual transformation" espoused by the Socialists, nor will Roosevelt's "tinkering" be of any avail. Supporting the capitalist political parties, as so-called labor leaders do, is no better. "The exploiters won't give up their loot." "We Communists say that there is one way to abolish the capitalist state, and that is to smash it by force." Then, as was done in Russia, create a state that is "the instrument of the workers' and poor farmers' power."[26]

Education had an essential role to play in this process, according to Olgin's pamphlet. The Communists, he argued, "are the only social scientists in the world today." They are also "dreamers," but their dreams are "forecasts of realities to come" when "[h]ighly cultured men and women [workers], bred in a spirit of collective life" will make up the coming ruling class. The Communist Party, and its constituent organizations are "in fact... training schools" for this new class, assisting it in choosing the correct tactics, including forming a united front against capitalism, convincing white workers that their struggle must include alliance with the "super-exploited" Negro people. So instructed the American workers will become "masters of nature and their own society...."[27]

Thus, as courses in "Fundamentals" (as well as the numerous and varied "elective" offerings) indicate, the Workers School was in doctrine a distinctly Communist enterprise. This was also apparent in the advocacy/action component of classroom teaching, the pedagogical expression of a party formally committed to the unity of theory and practice. The classroom was not considered a self-contained unit, sealed from the surrounding world. On the contrary, great effort was made to forge and maintain links to the outside world of labor and struggle. In such an educational environment, the idea of value-free scholarly neutrality got short shrift. Communist educators dismissed such notions on the grounds that so-called

WINTER TERM, 1937

Room	Course	Instructor	Room	Course	Instructor
MondayT7-8:30 P. M.			**Monday—8:40-10:10 P. M.**		
308	Principles of Communism 1	Gabriel Kent	207	Principles of Communism 5	Chas. Elstein
207	Principles of Communism 2	Chas. Elstein	203	Principles of Communism 6	Barbara Rand
307	Principles of Communism 3	Martha Murray	206	Principles of Communism 7	Julius Low
203	Principles of Communism 4	Barbara Rand	308	Political Economy Ic	Gabriel Kent
305	Political Economy Ia	Edw. Smith	205	Political Economy Id	Abraham Markoff
202	Political Economy Ib	Julius Low	202	Political Economy II	Morris Colman
309	Political Economy II	James Field	309	Advanced Political Economy	James Field
208	Introduction to Dialectical		202	Marxism-Leninism I	Beatrice Blosser
	Materialism	Harry Martel	208	Marxism-Leninism II	Harry Martel
205	History of the Communist Party		307	Social and Political Forces in	
	of the Soviet Union	Abraham Markoff		American History	Martha Murray
206	Negro America and the Struggle		204	History of the Communist Inter-	
	Against Reaction	Theo. Bassett		national	Alberto Moreau
204	Marxism and Colonial Question	Alberto Moreau	303	Elementary Russian	Zachary Gisenkin
306	Labor Journalism	Morris Colman	304	Intermediate English C	J. Edwards
304	Elementary English	Ben Shaw	305	Advanced English	Roy Norton
303	Intermediate English B	Jules Carter			
Tuesday—7-8:30 P. M.			**Tuesday—8:40-10:10 P. M.**		
309	Principles of Communism 8	Carl Brodsky	309	Principles of Communism II	Harry Mann
305	Principles of Communism 9	Arthur Carey	307	Political Economy Ig	Chas. Elstein
306	Principles of Communism 10	Frieda Ludwig			
308	Political Economy Ic	Gabriel Kent			
307	Political Economy If	Chas. Elstein			
Wednesday—7-8:30 P. M.			**Wednesday—8:40-10:10 P. M.**		
207	Principles of Communism 12	Timothy Holmes	308	Principles of Communism 16	Art Stein
205	Principles of Communism 13	Isidor Begun	306	Principles of Communism 17	Steve Kingston
305	Principles of Communism 14	Gilbert Douglass	202	Principles of Communism 18	Neil Brant
307	Principles of Communism 15	Carl Wilson	204	Political Economy Ij	Meyer Weise
208	Political Economy Ih	Geo. Lewis	203	Political Economy Ik	Harry Mann
306	Political Economy Ii	Steve Kingston	208	Political Economy II	Geo. Lewis
202	Political Economy II	Neil Brant	304	Marxism-Leninism I	Gilbert Douglass
309	Advanced Political Economy	James Field	307	Marxism-Leninism I	Carl Wilson
204	Marxism-Leninism I	Meyer Weise	205	Fundamental Study of Marxian	
308	Marxism-Leninism II	Art Stein		Classics	Milton Howard
206	History of American Labor		309	Public Speaking	Joseph Arch
	Movement	Charlotte Todes	207	Theories of Literary Criticism	Angel Flores
203	Social and Political Forces in		303	Intermediate Russian	Zachary Gisenkin
	American History	Fred Day	305	Advanced English	Roy Norton
304	Elementary English	Ben Shaw			
303	Intermediate English A	Jo. Austin			
Thursday—7-8:30 P. M.			**Thursday—8:40-10:10 P. M.**		
308	Principles of Communism 19	Gabriel Kent	306	Principles of Communism 23	Philip Cabot
306	Principles of Communism 20	Philip Cabot	307	Principles of Communism 24	Beatrice Blosser
207	Principles of Communism 21	Chas. Elstein	202	Principles of Communism 25	William Hart
305	Principles of Communism 22	Fred Nelson	203	Political Economy In	Eliz. Lawson
203	Political Economy IL	Eliz. Lawson	206	Political Economy Io	F. H. Meyer
202	Political Economy Im	William Hart	308	Political Economy Ip	Gabriel Kent
304	Political Economy II	William Roberts	309	Advanced Political Economy	Alfred Goldstein
309	Advanced Political Economy	Alfred Goldstein	305	Social and Political Forces in	
307	Marxism-Leninism I	Beatrice Blosser		American History	Fred Nelson
205	Fascist Trends and Tendencies in		207	History of Class Struggle in Epoch	
	the U. S.	A. B. Magil		of Industrial Captalism	Chas. Elstein
204	Current Trade Union Problems	Alan Ross	204	Trade Union Theory and Practice	Alan Ross
208	Shop Paper and Leaflet		208	Shop Paper Leaflet Preparation	P. Culver-M. Pass
	Preparation	P. Culver-M. Pass	205	Organization Principles	Rina Epstein
303	Intermediate English B	Jules Carter	303	Elementary Russian	Zachary Gisenkin
			304	Intermediate English C	J. Edwards
Friday—7-8:30 P. M.			**Friday—8:40-10:10 P. M.**		
207	Principles of Communism 26	Chas. Elstein	304	Principles of Communism 28	A. H. Hartfield
305	Principles of Communism 27	Geo. Lewis	207	Principles of Communism 29	Chas. Elstein
307	Political Economy Ip	Eliz. Lawson	306	Political Economy Ir	Bill Reich
306	Political Economy Iq	Leonard Mins	307	Political Economy Is	Eliz. Lawson
309	Marxism-Leninism I	Alfred Goldstein	309	Political Economy II	Alfred Goldstein
208	Historical Materialism	I. Stamler	308	Science and Dialectical	
304	Trade Unionism: Theory and			Materialism	James Leonard
	Practice	A. H. Hartfield	205	Health and Hygiene	M. A. B.
205	Critical Periods in American Trade		303	Intermediate Russian	Zachary Gisenkin
	Union History	Louis F. Budenz			
202	Social Trends in Contemporary				
	Literature	Angel Flores			
308	History and Method of Science	James Leonard			
203	A Marxian Survey of Psychology	R. Gley			
206	Research Methods	L. R. A. Staff			
204	Modern Economic Theories	E. C. Blake			
303	Intermediate English A	Jo. Austin			

A course list for the New York Workers School. Reproduced from *Isms*, 2nd ed. (Indianapolis: American Legion, 1937).

objectivity tacitly supports passive acceptance of, rather than militant opposition to, the evils of the day.[28]

At its most ceremonial level, the conception of education linked to political action brought students, teachers and staff of the Workers School (and later party schools) to march under Communist banners at the annual May Day parades. Less ceremonially, and more closely related to classroom subject matter, were such extensions to the outside world as, for example, the natural spillover of classes on black history that led to organized demonstrations against lynching; support of the Scottsboro defense effort; aid in getting evicted New Yorkers back into their homes; and letter writing campaigns on behalf of such legislative proposals as bills to repeal poll taxes.

Study of trade union tactics led to support of actual ongoing strikes, including supplying experienced speakers from the Workers School staff and student body to assist local strike committees, and providing "organizers for unorganized workers." The succeeding *Announcements of Courses* proudly stated that students and staff members "participated in such campaigns as the fight for Sacco and Vanzetti, the Hands Off China campaign, Passaic relief, etc."[29] Courses on international relations included what could be called "field trips" to protests against such Fascist atrocities as the Italian invasion of Ethiopia, or Japanese incursions into China. During the Nazi-Soviet Pact era, with somewhat diminished fervor, Communist educators and students rallied against what the party, taking its cue from Moscow, labelled as "imperialist war."[30] The student *Weekly* at the Workers School amplified the message of engaged education, preaching the necessity of "going out into the field and put[ting] into practice what you have learned." Under the heading "Demonstrate With Your School," the *Weekly* urged students and staff where and when to register their opposition to the Scottsboro frameup, or their support of Gastonia (North Carolina) workers.[31]

There were moments in the institutional life of the Workers School when political obligations might be relaxed: at volleyball games (one in the spring of 1931 pitted the Workers School team against "Prolecult Bronx") and summer swimming outings to "give us comradely atmosphere and relaxation." Literary discussions about such writers as D.H. Lawrence, Aldous Huxley, and Hugh Walpole also took place at the school.[32]

Administration of the Workers School in this same spirit of engaged, non-academic, activist-oriented inquiry was at first entrusted to co-directors Wolfe and Davidson. But after the ouster from the Communist Party of the Lovestoneites in 1929,[33] the task was taken over by Abraham Markoff, a politically orthodox New York pharmacist, who served as head of the Workers School until his death in the late 1930s. In a 1936 essay on "Tasks and Problems of the Workers Schools" that explicitly invoked the directives of the Seventh Congress of the Communist International, Markoff stressed the need to reach out to non-communist trade union schools and other "nonpartisan" educational institutions in the spirit of the united front policy. He had in mind "joint conferences for the discussion of teaching methods," exchange of texts, lecturers, and common efforts to fight reactionary legislation threatening "academic freedom in schools generally," and "interference with workers' education particularly." Nothing seems to have come of this, especially since Markoff insisted that the Communist schools themselves must remain true to Marxism-Leninism, and it would be hard to conceive of such teaching materials as Olgin's *Why Communism?*, which vilified liberals, Socialists and non-Communist labor leaders, appealing to schools run by these very people. In 1938 the position of Workers School director devolved on former top party leader William Weinstone.[34]

Although Communist Party financial records, if they exist, are not available to scholars, it seems that the New York Workers School was largely self-supporting, rather than running on party subsidies or "Moscow Gold." Student tuition kept the school going, including paying modest salaries for some of the teachers and administrative staff. In 1923, $3.50 paid for a standard twelve-session one-night-a-week course at the Workers School. In 1927 the cost rose to $4.00, and twice-weekly English courses were six dollars. Reduced rates were made available to trade unions, working-class fraternal organizations or foreign language associations. For a payment of $25.00 such groups could send a student to take four courses each term.[35]

Although anticommunist scholars consider the Workers School and its successors as nothing but indoctrination agencies to instill party dogmas into the uninstructed faithful,[36] the actual situation seems to have been that these schools also had to offer something more than dry recitations of the party line, especially for the unaffiliated left-leaning students who came voluntarily (and might leave anytime) and whose recruitment as Communist militants could possibly be brought about or accelerated by attending party-run classes.[37]

Thus, much pressure fell on teachers, most of whom were self-educated part-time volunteers, selected "not only on the basis of their ability and experience but also on the basis of their close contact with the struggles of the workers and familiarity with their lives and needs."[38] There was a core staff of about ten regulars who handled the "Fundamentals of Communism" and other key courses. These teachers earned $12.00 a week for the heavy teaching load of ten to fifteen two-hour weekly classes.[39] The task they faced was not so much to transmit the correct party line (usually only trusted party cadres would be on staff, especially for the more sensitive classes) but to maintain attendance by lively teaching. An instructor whose enrollment dwindled to three or four by the second or third week was sure to be taken aside by a fellow teacher or staff member, counselled on how better to hold his or her students' attention, and told generally to shape up.

Politically and financially the school could not afford to retain teachers who drove students away, especially those promising proletarians who had little patience for high-flying intellectual posturing. Variations on "What good is Aristotle for the workers?" were frequently heard in classes. On the other hand, actual workers harbored fewer of what their teachers called "bourgeois illusions." Especially as Depression conditions arrived and worsened, these Workers School students were often eager to grasp explanations of the exploitation and misery that they experienced daily, especially since the doctrines taught promised eventual liberation into what they hoped would be a future socialist or even "Soviet" United States.[40]

In 1944 the Workers School was absorbed into what was part of the last major effort of the U.S. Communist Party at adult education in the U.S. mainstream—the Jefferson School of Social Science. Although there were major differences between these two educational enterprises, as well as between both and the transitional School for Democracy (1941 to 1944),[41] the similarities seem far more significant. First of all, neither the Communist Party nor its educational institutions, despite their encouragement of a variety of political advocacy causes and actions, were instrumentalities of anything approaching direct revolutionary effort. Anticommunist ideologues entertained lurid fantasies of party cadres stepping right out from a classroom discussion of one of Lenin's pamphlets and violently assaulting the U.S. Government.[42] But, despite the rhetoric of direct action, and student-staff willingness to apply communist doctrines on the streets, on picket lines, or in union struggles, there is no evidence that would suggest that the Workers School, or any other party educational enterprise, was some U.S. equivalent of the Smolny Institute, the academy from which the Russian Bolsheviks made their successful armed seizure of state power in 1917.

What then were these party schools, dedicated as they were to an eventual socialist revolution in the United States, if not bases for actual revolutionary action? The slogan emblazoned on the bulletins announcing classes, and even on receipts for tuition payment, and expressed in such texts as *Why Communism?*, was "Education for the Class Struggle." The hypothesis offered here is that these schools approximated an indirect but necessary path to revolutionary transformation, one that had been charted by the Italian Marxist Antonio Gramsci (1891–1937) who more clearly than perhaps anyone else in the world Communist movement perceived that the Leninist model of armed seizure of power in a period of severe governmental breakdown would not work in advanced industrial countries. Although much of Gramsci's relevant writing on these issues was done while he was confined to fascist prisons, and was elliptically phrased as a series of running commentaries on bourgeois and fascist educational policies, it is possible to derive from the *Prison Notebooks* the theoretical basis for a Marxian theory of hegemony which encompasses a particular conception of educational practice. This is not the place to discuss such a theory, but merely to indicate its basic premise, which is that long before the eventual decisive assumption of political power, Communist parties, for an indefinite period, must be engaged in a protracted struggle over cultural hegemony to prepare the proletariat for its destined role as the ruling class under socialism.[43]

Gramsci's work, unknown in U.S. Marxist circles before the late 1940s, would take another decade or more to be assimilated. It is the main point of this paper that even before the U.S. discovery of Gramsci's ideas,[44] the U.S. Communist Party was following them anyway—especially in its educational work—because essentially there was no alternative. In addition to helping explain Communist educational work, this Gramscian hypothesis may help clarify several other features of the Communist experience in such advanced industrial countries as the United States. It suggests how Communist militants in these areas could and did conduct such open day-to-day activities as running a school (or participating—but rarely as open Communists—in trade union efforts) without any sense that they had thereby abandoned long-term insurrectionary goals; the short-term reformist actions were precisely the kinds of contests for cultural hegemony deemed necessary as preludes to the decisive revolutionary struggles to come in the Gramscian, not the Leninist sense. Of course, in Communist circles, the Leninist doctrine of the primacy of armed struggle could not be formally repudiated. It lingered on as a rhetorical device, used mainly in the sometimes fierce intra-party wrangling that characterized CPUSA history.[45]

The importance of the Communists' educational program to contest bourgeois cultural hegemony is revealed in several ways. One is the copying of much of these Workers Schools' curricula by the anticommunist Roman Catholic labor schools established from the mid-1930s onward.[46] Another such indirect and inadvertent indication of the significance of the Communist Party's educational work is the U.S. government's own repressive strategy, that (in the words of the 1941 Smith Act) was mainly directed against the party's "teaching and advocacy."[47] Recognizing implicitly what few anticommunists would acknowledge (that the CPUSA was no revolutionary threat), the U.S. government's anticommunist directors, as Ellen Schrecker points out elsewhere in this volume,[48] mounted a campaign of a scope and power that dwarfed any defensive reaction by the party and its ancillary organizations, most of which were destroyed in the 1950s. I suggest in this paper that the overkill of McCarthyist repression was a tacit recognition of the considerable success of the U.S. Communists' Gramscian efforts to create through their schools and other party activities a genuine cultural alternative to the official "bourgeois" value system. That may have been threat enough.

Notes

Earlier versions of this essay were presented at a symposium on "The Marxian Tradition and the Study of Higher Education" held at the American Educational Research Association's annual meeting, April 6, 1988, as well as at the City University of New York conference on Seventy Years of American Communism, November 9, 1989. I gratefully acknowledge assistance from several sources: the staffs of the Reference Center for Marxist Studies at U.S. Communist Party headquarters in New York City; the Tamiment Library at New York University; the State Historical Society of Wisconsin; and the New York Public Library. Comradely advice, information and criticism came from David Goldway, Ben Harris, Emily Jones, Henry Levin, Randy Martin, Mark Naison, Annette T. Rubinstein, Sheila Slaughter, Alan Wald, and of course, Ellen W. Schrecker. This essay is dedicated to the memory of David Goldway (1907–1990).

1. For brief accounts of both the New York Workers School and the Jefferson School of Social Science, see my entries in Mary Jo Buhle, Paul Buhle, and Dan Georgakas, eds., *Encyclopedia of the American Left* (New York: Garland, 1990; paperback edition, University of Illinois Press, 1992), pp. 853–55, 389–90. It should be mentioned that the Communist educational work carried out in such open party schools as the New York Workers School was only one of several types of educational/propaganda work carried out by U.S. Communists. Another was teaching by Communist teachers in regular primary and secondary schools and colleges. There were also regular educational programs carried out in most party clubs and units. Special cadre schools for training party functionaries and leaders from the rank and file would be held from time to time. For a vivid account of one such cadre school, see Junius Scales and Richard Nickson, *Cause at Heart: A Former Communist Remembers* (Athens, GA: University of Georgia Press, 1987), chap. 7.

2. Anonymous report on the New York Workers School (n.d., but in late or mid-1920s), Workers School folder, Hoover Institution Library, Palo Alto, CA. (I am grateful to Professor Ben Harris of the University of Wisconsin for sending me a photocopy of this report.)

3. Untitled Workers School brochure (New York, 1923), in New York Public Library (Annex).

4. Ibid.; statement on inside back cover of *The Heritage of Jefferson* (New York: Workers School Pamphlet, May 1943).

5. D. Benjamin [*pseud.*], "Capitalist Schools and Workers Schools," *The* [Workers School] *Student-Worker* 1, no. 1 (February 1927): 10.

6. S.A. Garlin, "The Rand School: A Memory," ibid., pp. 6–7.

7. On the curricula of later party schools, see the previously-mentioned Jefferson School entry, *Encyclopedia of the American Left*, p. 389; Gettleman, "'Education for Victory and Action': The California Labor School in the Popular Front Era," paper presented at the History of Education Society's 1990 annual meeting. A full account will appear in Gettleman, *"Training for the Class Struggle": American Communism and Education, 1923–1957* (Philadelphia: Temple University Press, forthcoming, 1993).

8. On the decline of the Socialist Party, see David Shannon, *The Socialist Party of America: A History* (New York: The Macmillan Company, 1955), chaps. 7–9. On the Rand School, see the two relevant dissertations: Frederic Cornell's "History of the Rand School ...," Columbia University Teachers College, 1976, and Rachel C. Schwartz, "Rand School ...," State University of New York at Buffalo, 1984 (both available from University Microfilms).

9. Several studies of U.S. workers education have recently appeared. The best is Richard J. Altenbaugh, *Education for Struggle: American Labor Colleges of the 1920s and 1930s* (Philadelphia: Temple University Press, 1990). Another survey is Steven H. London, Elvira R. Tarr, and Joseph F. Wilson, eds., *The Re-education of the American Working Class* (Westport CT: Greenwood Press, 1990). Neither book so much as mentions Communist labor schools.

10. For left disenchantment with Deweyite "progressive education," see Barry Rubin, "Marxism and Education: Radical Thought and Educational Theory in the 1930s," *Science and Society* 36 (Summer 1972): 171–201. For a penetrating recent discussion of Dewey's anticommunism, a hostility fully reciprocated by the Communists (in part due to his association with the international committee to evaluate Stalin's charges against Trotsky), see Robert B. Westbrook, *John Dewey and American Democracy* (Ithaca: Cornell University Press, 1991), chaps. 12, 13. (One serious flaw in Westbrook's otherwise judicious book is his misunderstanding of Dewey's relation with the Teachers Union [see pp. 478–79]. For a corrective, see Marjorie Murphy, *Blackboard Unions: The AFT and the NEA, 1900–1980* [Ithaca: Cornell University Press, 1990].)

11. Mary O. Furner, *Advocacy and Objectivity: A Crisis in the Professionalization of American Social Science, 1865–1905* (Lexington: University Press of Kentucky, 1975), *passim*, esp. Chap. 9.

12. The literature on objectivity in social science is enormous. Among the main sources are Loren Baritz, *Servants of Power: Social Science in American Industry* (Middletown, CT: Wesleyan University Press, 1960); E.H. Carr, *What Is History?* (New York: Alfred A. Knopf, 1963); Gunnar Myrdal, *Objectivity in Social Research* (New York: Pantheon Books, 1969); Sheila Slaughter and Edward Silva, *Serving Power: The*

Making of the Academic Social Science Expert (Westport, CT: Greenwood Press, 1984).

13. For the legal rhetoric developed in connection with the Jefferson School's self-defense against the Justice Department's Subversive Activities Control Board prosecution, see Harry Sacher, "In Defense of the Right to Learn" (1954), Jefferson School of Social Sciences Papers, Tamiment Library, New York University; Howard Selsam, letter to the *New York Times*, 6 January 1954.

14. Workers School, *Heritage of Jefferson* (cited above, note 4).

15. Some mention must be made, however brief, of certain methodological issues in the historiography of U.S. Communism, and especially of what was obviously intended to be the standard work on Communist education, the volume in the Ford Foundation series, "Communism in American Life," attributed to Robert W. Iversen; see Clinton Rossiter, ed., *Communists and the Schools* (New York: Harcourt, Brace, 1959). This volume offers the conventional cold war view (in both its methodological and substantive form): that everything important about the CPUSA can be encompassed from an international top-down perspective, since the party and the schools it operated were completely dominated by the party leadership which was in turn the ever-compliant tool of the Communist International in Moscow. A corollary drawn was that the expulsion of Communist teachers from the regular schools where they taught, as well as the closing of party schools, was a justifiable and legitimate enterprise. Authored by an ex-Communist who earlier taught at the Workers School in Chicago and at the Jefferson School in New York City, another volume in the same Ford Foundation series has (for this project on Communist education) the promising title *The Moulding of Communists: The Training of the Communist Cadre* (New York: Harcourt, Brace & Co., 1961). While it does mention party schools (pp. 161–62), it also invokes a mood of anticommunism so extreme that it cannot locate its subject in historical time and space, and instead invokes an ageless model of eschatology that renders it useless. Meyers's 1956 testimony against the Jefferson School in the Subversive Activities Control Board (SACB) trials (microfilm edition of National Archives SACB hearings, reel 29) is far more useful. A more recent expression of the conventional wisdom is John E. Haynes' editorial *obiter dictum* in the preface to his comprehensive *Communism and Anti-communism in the United States: An Annotated Guide to Historical Writings* (New York: Garland, 1987), where he invokes the extra-historical principle that since U.S. Communists supported Stalin, little that they did in the United States can be viewed in any sort of positive light. Party educational work was not carried out by top Communist leaders, but originated in the middle and lower ranks of party adherents—many of whom left

the Communist Party in or around 1956. People like Theodore Draper (who produced some of the best historical scholarship on the early history of the CPUSA) now denigrate any study of the CP that allows for a significant sphere of rank-and-file initiative. Although Draper himself carried out extensive interviews (see the Draper Collection, Emory University Library, Atlanta, GA), some of his epigones deny the value of oral history data. See, for example, Harvey Klehr, whose *Heyday of American Communism: The Depression Decade* (New York: Basic Books, 1984) emulates Draper's conclusions and methodology faithfully, except for his refusal (p. xii) to utilize such data. The polemical literature (up to about 1987) surrounding the Draper/Klehr denigration of "bottom-up" studies of U.S. Communism is all listed in Haynes' bibliographic survey, including the many accusatory ideological pronunciamentos masquerading as methodology. Cutting through much of the confusion is Allan Brikley's recent bibliographical essay (in *The New York Review of Books*, 28 June 1990) that invokes the wholesome substantive criterion that good empirical work vindicates the methodology that produced it.

16. Interviews with David Goldway, 4 February 1988; Annette T. Rubinstein, 13 March 1989; Sender Garlin (telephone), 12 February 1988; Doxey Wilkerson, 18 July 1990.

17. Workers School brochure (1923), cited above, note 3.

18. Workers School, *Announcement of Courses, 1926–7* ([New York, 1926?]), p. 10, New York Public Library (Annex). In his *Witness* (New York: Random House, 1952), pp. 197, 217, Whittaker Chambers claimed that Garlin recruited him into the CPUSA, a claim which Garlin (telephone interview, 12 February 1988) denies.

19. Workers School, *Announcement of Courses, 1926–7, passim.*

20. Workers School, *Announcement of Courses, 1927–8*, p. 7.

21. For CPUSA antiracism, see Mark Naison, *Communists in Harlem During the Depression* (Urbana: University of Illinois Press, 1983); Robin D.G. Kelley, *Hammer and Hoe: Alabama Communists During the Great Depression* (Chapel Hill: University of North Carolina Press, 1990), and Gerald Horne's essay in this volume, "The Red and the Black: The Communist Party and African-Americans in Historical Perspective."

22. See Elizabeth Lawson (Chair, History Department, New York Workers School), "Study Outline: History of the American Negro People, 1619–1918" (New York, 1939).

23. Workers School, *Announcement of Courses*, Fall Term, 1936, p. 15.

24. Workers School, *Announcement of Courses, 1930–31*, p. 5.

25. For Olgin (whose life and career deserves careful study), see Harvey Klehr's entry in Bernard K. Johnpoll and Harvey Klehr, eds., *Biographical Dictionary of the American Left* (Westport, CT: Greenwood Press, 1986), pp. 297–98.

26. M.J. Olgin, *Why Communism? Plain Talks on Vital Problems* (rev. ed., New York: Workers Library, 1935), *passim*. The first edition of this work appeared in 1933.

27. Ibid.

28. For just one of many denigrations of "objectivity" by Communist educators in this period, see Howard Selsam, "Where the People Go to School," *Daily Worker*, 2 October 1947, p. 11. Admittedly this essay derived from a slightly later period, but it reflects dominant Communist views on the subject.

29. Workers School, *Announcement of Courses, 1929–30*, p. 3.

30. Ibid.

31. *Workers School Weekly* 4 (4 May; 20 April 1931), in Sam Darcy Papers, Tamiment Library, New York University.

32. Ibid.

33. On the expulsion of the Lovestoneites, see Theodore Draper, *American Communism and Soviet Russia* (New York: Viking/Compass Books, 1960), chap. 30.

34. See A. Markoff, "Tasks and Problems of the Workers Schools," *Party Organizer* 9 (April 1936): 43–46; *Daily Worker*, 30–31 August 1938 (Markoff obituary). On Weinstone, see Klehr, "Weinstone," *Biographical Dictionary*, p. 411.

35. Workers School, *Announcements of Classes, 1923–36, passim*.

36. Iversen, *Communists and the Schools*, p. 80.

37. Interviews, cited above, note 16.

38. Workers School, *Announcement of Courses, 1930–1*, p. 5.

39. Interviews, cited above, note 16.

40. Ibid.

41. For The School for Democracy, set up to provide teaching positions for New York City academics fired from the municipal colleges in the Rapp-Coudert purges of 1940–1941, see my entry in *Encyclopedia of the American Left*, p. 644; Alvah Bessie, "School for Democracy," *New Masses* 40 (27 January 1942): 12–13.

42. For just one example of the anticommunist fantasies of the early cold war period (which includes much material on Communist schools), see *Red Fascism: Boring from Within by the Subversive Forces of Communism*, compiled by Jack B. Tenney (Los Angeles: Federal Printing Co., 1947), *passim*.

43. Among the vast Gramsci literature, Gwynn Williams, "Gramsci's Concept of *egemonia*," *Journal of the History of Ideas* 21 (October/December 1960), John Cammett, *Antonio Gramsci and the Origins of Italian Communism* (Stanford, CA: Stanford University Press, 1967), and Eugene D. Genovese's 1967 review article, reprinted in *In Red and Black: Marxian Explorations in Southern and Afro-American History* (New York: Pantheon, 1971), chap. 19, have been most useful to me.

Gramsci's own writings are available in the multi-volumed *Opere* (Turin: Einaudi, 1947—) and (on the topic of this essay) Gramsci's *La formazione dell'uomo: Scritti di pedagogia* (Rome, 1967). For materials in English, see Quintin Hoare and Geoffrey Nowell Smith, eds., *Selections from the Prison Notebooks of Antonio Gramsci* (New York: International Publishers, 1971), pp. 5–43 and *passim*. Any further study of Gramsci must now begin with John Cammett's massive *Bibliografia Gramsciana, 1922–1988* (Rome: Fondazione Istituto Gramsci, 1991).

44. Apparently the first mention of Gramsci in the United States was an excerpt from his *Prison Letters* which appeared in *Science and Society* 10 (Summer 1946): 283–92 under the title "Benedetto Croce and His Concept of Liberty."

45. The CPUSA has done little to clarify its own history. Books like *Highlights of a Fighting History: 60 Years of the Communist Party, USA* (New York: International Publishers, 1979) are—or aim at being—uncritical works of institutional hagiography. There apparently has been in the United States little self-critical work comparable to the Italian Communist Party's efforts described in Franco Andreucci and Malcolm Sylvers, "The Italian Communists Write their History," *Science and Society* 40 (1976): 28–56.

46. For the Roman Catholic schools modelled on the Workers School, see Steve Rosswurm, "The Catholic Church and the Left-Led Unions: Labor Priests, Labor Schools and the ACTU," in Rosswurm, ed., *The CIO's Left-Led Unions* (New Brunswick, NJ: Rutgers University Press, 1992), pp. 119–37.

47. See especially the Circuit Court papers in *Dennis v. U.S.*, 341 US 495 (1951), available on reel 27 of the microfilm edition of the *Collection of Trials Relating to ... the Communist Party, etc., 1919–53*, in New York Public Library.

48. See Ellen W. Schrecker's essay in this volume: "McCarthyism and the Decline of American Communism, 1945–1960" and Schrecker, "McCarthyism and the Labor Movement: The Role of the State," in Rosswurm, ed., *The CIO's Left-Led Unions*, pp. 139–57.

CULTURE AND COMMITMENT:
U.S. Communist Writers Reconsidered

Alan Wald

Introduction: Class War Against the Literary Canon

After Walter Lowenfels, the Lost Generation poet turned Communist journalist, was arrested in 1953 by federal agents for violating the Smith Act, he protested that the charges against him were inadequate: "A large part of my adult life has been spent trying to overthrow not only the government but the universe."[1] In the strategy session before his trial, Lowenfels, sequestered with the eight other defendants, was asked to give his opinion: "Comrades, I have made many mistakes during my years in the Party. Some were left sectarian; others were right opportunist. During this trial of ours, I want to be sure all my errors are straight down the middle." The decision was unanimous that perhaps the best contribution Walter might make to the defense would be to keep to writing his poetry.

During the trial itself, Walter was astonished at the verbiage of the stool-pigeons and informers, who transformed Marxist thought and terminology into a "long-drawn-out gobbledegook of 'proletariat,' 'cadres,' etc." He predicted to his Communist co-defendants: "This jury is going to find us guilty of having endured boredom and convict us of talking nonsense." And so it did.

When higher courts later overturned his conviction, Walter was disappointed that the grounds were "for lack of evidence." Did the learned judges not know Emerson's dictum that one must "Beware of poets; they leave nothing unchanged; they overturn everything"?

These excerpts from letters of Walter Lowenfels, published in Robert Gover's *The Portable Walter* (1968), ought to remind one how partisan and irresponsible it is to reduce the hundreds of poets, fiction writers and critics drawn to the U.S. Communist movement throughout its seventy-year history to tools, dupes, acolytes, or other mere instruments of "the party line." As these quotations suggest, imaginative writers, whether Communists or vegetarians, are primarily engaged in recreating human experience through language and situating themselves in relation to traditions among contemporaries and earlier generations of writers. Whatever their political delusions and human flaws, left-wing artists possess other distinctive characteristics that make them unique and complex.

Indeed, the very fact that so many of the most extraordinary U.S. writers felt, for longer or shorter amounts of time, that the ideals of Communism and the organized Communist movement held out the best hope for humanity, ought to be understood as an augmentation, complication and enrichment of their literary lives. The choice of Marxist commitment, no matter how ill-founded in inaccurate information about the Soviet Union, ought not to be perverted into a means of dismissing their cultural contributions.

The additional fact that so many of the Communist writers who once appeared in the *Daily Worker, New Masses, Dynamo, Rebel Poet, Anvil, International Literature, Directions, Harlem Quarterly, Jewish Life, California Quarterly, Contemporary Reader, Mainstream* and other publications are entirely absent from extant literary histories, anthologies, and the lists of publishing houses, should by no means be taken as a sign of the "inferiority" of their writings. Increasing evidence shows that the authentic history of twentieth century United States literary practice has yet to be written, especially in regard to the left.[2]

The 1990s, the first decade when the implosion of Stalinist societies in Eastern Europe may finally strike the overdue death blow to cold war mythologies of "Communist monolithism," is probably an appropriate occasion to start reversing the disgraceful and unfair treatment accorded the study of the varying impact of U.S. Communism on writers. In terms of scholarly advances, there has not been a more propitious moment in the past twenty-five years. A quarter of a century ago, coming out of the McCarthyite witch-hunt era, several new books appeared analyzing the impact of Communism that were widely discussed.

The authors of those new books, Walter Rideout, who published *The Radical Novel in the United States, 1900–1954* in 1956, and Daniel Aaron, who published *Writers On the Left: Episodes in American Literary Communism* in 1961, did not write as militant partisans of a revolutionary new social order; rather, they depicted Communist writers as people of good will naively deceived by utopian illusions. Although dated by the scholars' failure to predict the spectacular rebirth of literary Marxism in the West and in the third world in the 1960s and after, such an approach was a vast improvement over the earlier view that communists of any kind were lemming-like agents of an international conspiracy.[3]

Even though Aaron and Rideout conducted their research in the 1950s, their work was an indication of the breakdown and invalidation of McCarthyite versions of the literary left. Rideout argued for a modest although genuine contribution on the part of the radical novel to United States literary history, and Aaron expressly honored the writers and their good intentions. Thus, while the Communist novelist Philip Bonosky wrote a harsh critique of Rideout for the party's theoretical journal *Political Affairs*,[4] the editor of the party-sponsored literary review *Mainstream*, Charles Humboldt, praised the same book as a "singularly fair study."[5] A few years later, Bonosky was more generous with Aaron's work, and Philip Stevenson, a Communist novelist, playwright and screenwriter who played a major part in sustaining the journal *California Quarterly*, hailed *Writers on the Left* as "heroic."[6] The concluding sentences to Aaron's book even appear as the epigraph to the International Publishers 1969 anthology of the *New Masses* edited by Joseph North.[7]

Nevertheless, subsequent books and dissertations on communist writers that have appeared in the last decades have been accorded far less attention than Aaron and Rideout by scholars as well as left-wing cultural workers. Three decades after publication, their two books remain the *loci classicus* for scholarship on the communist literary left, although there are signs that the situation is changing in the early 1990s with the appearance of new research by Cary Nelson, Paula Rabinowitz, Constance Coiner, and several others.[8] To some extent this apparent lack of continuing impact may be due to exceptional quality and success of the first two books, which are unusually rich and accurate, giving the appearance of having exhausted the subject far more than actually was the case. The fault may also lie with some of the subsequent scholars, who, with some exceptions, tended to recycle old material about a dozen or so top male, mostly white, figures, neglecting the hundreds who made up the infrastructure of a politico-cultural movement unparalleled in U.S. history, with the one possible exception of the Black Arts movement in the 1960s.[9]

Still, it is surprising that, even though we have been living through more than two decades of sustained assaults against the dominant literary canon in the universities—assaults that have resulted in real though inadequate changes in the literary representation of women and people of color—the situation in regard to the study of Communist writers has stagnated until just recently. Although some radical novels reissued in paperback in the 1960s and 1970s are no longer in print, new ones are becoming available for the first time.[10] Moreover, a few of the literary histories that are being updated in so many areas are now for the first time presenting fresh material about the literary left.[11]

Thus it appears that, in the wake of all the "culture wars" of recent decades, a new war is beginning to be waged, a second front has been opened, against the literary canon, and it is one that needs to be in part a "class" war. This is because, even though Communist-influenced fiction-writers and poets did pioneer issues of importance to women and people of color in their writings, if not always in their critical theorizations, it was specifically the promotion of class culture, and culture viewed through the prism of class, that was understood as the hallmark of the Communist effort.

Conversely, as in so many other areas of politico-cultural repression in the United States, the silencing and distortion of the Communist literary tradition has turned out really to be a means of silencing the larger radical and working-class tradition in literature. As has been well-documented by now, the ideology of "anticommunism" in the United States has little to do with genuine opposition to the brutal and authoritarian policies of the Stalin and post-Stalin regimes.[12] It is more often a means of discrediting the entire effort of the left by tainting all radicals with the crimes of the Soviet ruling group, real or fabricated—although today we must recognize that most of those crimes were real.

One result of this kind of anticommunist ideology in literary studies is the disempowerment of the population of ordinary people who are denied a genuine history of their own cultural activities through access to authors who wrote about strikes, rebellions, mass movements, the work experience, famous political trials, the tribulations of political commitment, as well as about love, sex, the family, nature, and war from a class-conscious, internationalist, socialist-feminist, and antiracist point of view. Instead, the population is often exclusively presented with literary role models that inculcate notions of culture that distort visions of possibilities for social transformation.

If many institutions today teach the outstanding African-American novelists Toni Morrison and Alice Walker alongside Saul Bellow and Henry James, it is not simply because the professors on their own discovered "literary merit" outside the traditional canon. It is partly because students took over campus buildings; African-Americans rebelled in the streets; and the colonies of the West rose up arms in hand. Something analogous may have to happen before the red tradition also gets a foot in the door of academia.

At present, so far as any writers from the Communist tradition go, Walter Lowenfels, the Marxist poet with whose reminiscences I began these remarks, is one of the lucky ones. In the decades prior to his death, he was able to get a number of books into print, and he became something of an entrepreneur in the promotion of counter-literary anthologies that might be characterized as "prematurely anti-canon." These include *Poets of Today* (1964), *Where Is Vietnam?* (1967), *In a Time of Revolution: Poems from Our Third World* (1969), *The Writing on the Wall* (1969), and *For Neruda, For Chile* (1975).

But in my estimate there are several hundred U.S. Communist-influenced novelists and poets of real merit who have received *no* critical attention, and whose names never appear in literary histories except sometimes in those long lists of endorsers of various Writers Congresses and other Communist causes catalogued for us in Eugene Lyons's conspiracy fantasy, *The Red Decade* (1940). The most comprehensive source I have been able to locate on their activities is, in fact, not the multivolume *Dictionary of Literary Biography* but the national and local files of the FBI.

In the remainder of this essay I will suggest several new angles of approach for recognizing this important legacy. The underlying premise is that one must abandon the view that a writer drawn to the Communist movement necessarily demonstrates certain stylistic or thematic qualities demanded by the political character of Stalinism as a movement. The meaning of the Communist experience is less a matter of literary form or content than of commitment to racial equality, antifascism, anticapitalism, national independence of colonies, and similar values, even though all of these attitudes were variously qualified by the erroneous belief that the Soviet Union was a living example of socialism that must be preserved and defended. A new generation of scholars must put less emphasis on the claim that Communism "created" a literary/cultural movement, although there were certainly efforts in that direction, and more on the view that Communist institutions, ideology, and committed cadres "gave voice" in variously effective ways (some beneficial and prophetic; other deleterious and retrograde) to a large number of diverse writers radicalized by the inequities of capitalism.

Part 1: Communist Writers in Perspective

The new perspectives suggested in this essay are based on substantially fresh empirical research that includes not only the examination of previously unexplored archives, oral histories, and unanalyzed literary texts, but also interviews with participants who have not been sought out previously or who have not spoken up earlier. This includes officers of the John Reed Clubs, League of American writers and the National Council for the Arts, Sciences and Professions (ASP); editors of *Dynamo*, the *New Masses*, *Mainstream*, *California Quarterly*, *Jewish Life* and many similar pro-Communist publications; numerous left-wing novelists, critics and poets; and surviving reds in Hollywood. This research has convinced me of the importance of reconsidering the centrality of the Communist experience in United States cultural history.

There are many reasons why it is crucial to recognize that "Communism," by which I mean official Communist Party "communism," and not the other more heterodox varieties of Marxism to which I myself am more partial, is at the center of what one might call cultural "commitment" from the 1920s until the New Left of the 1960s. One is that the Communist cultural movement was the largest and most coherent expression of twentieth century rebellion by workers, women, people of color, and committed intellectuals prior to the 1960s. It touched the lives of millions—not only the

New Masses covers from the mid-1930s illustrate the scope of CP concerns in the academic and literary spheres. Reproduced from *Isms*, 2nd ed. (Indianapolis: American Legion, 1937).

perhaps one million who passed directly through membership, but the many millions influenced by Communist ideas in literary publications, trade unions, civil rights and peace organizations, and elsewhere.

But to defend Communism as central to the legacy of the committed is also to present ourselves with a host of problems, the most important of which is the wholly mistaken view of the Soviet Union as an authentic socialist society that was doing the best it could under Stalin to abolish inequality, achieve a genuine democracy, and protect the interests of the poor and oppressed throughout the world. For those who really want to learn the lessons of the past, this flaw in the otherwise insightful and humane vision of the pro-Communist writers cannot be ignored or even minimized.

Indeed, "flaw" is hardly a sufficiently strong adjective. Stalin and his policies were virtually deified in the official declarations of the United States Party up until 1956, as any reading of *The Communist* and *Political Affairs* will demonstrate.[13] Afterward, it was mainly pronouncements from abroad—the 1956 Khrushchev revelations—that precipitated a partial reevaluation. Ideologically, then, in terms of formal adherence to policy, the CPUSA was dogmatically Stalinist. But this characterization of official program has turned out to have less importance for the local practice of Communist cultural workers and even the individual consciousness of pro-party writers than I, as one trained in textual analysis and theoretical critique, had previously imagined.

The "tragic" side of the Communist literary movement is that, from the perspective of the movement's creative potential, a tremendous amount of energy by devoted and intelligent people was canalized into promoting literary practice in order to bolster a political orientation based on such a mistaken premise. On the other hand, the counterpart to trivializing this real "flaw" is very often to try to *reduce* the whole complex experience *to* the flaw; that is, to sneer at those who failed to see Stalinism for the system of bureaucratic tyranny that it was. This reduction violates the historical record because, so far as I can tell, for the most part, the people involved and their dreams were superb, and many of their writings explore fresh terrain with insight and power unmatched by more familiar texts.

As the poet and critic Stanley Burnshaw wrote in a letter years after he had abandoned Communism: "I'm bitterly anti-Soviet, but I still believe I behaved as I'd want to behave during my Thirties period, for we were all moved by what Michael Gold described as the passionate view of the future's powerful beauty."[14] Novelist Guy Endore, in his UCLA Oral History interview, held a similar view: "The truth about the Communist Party was that it was a dedicated group of people who wanted to improve the world.... [The members were] for the most part very decent people who gave of their time and of their money and contributed everything they could to this movement, which was not going to benefit them in any way."[15]

For a less familiar approach than personal testimony, one might turn to the vividly dramatized view of that shared dream for "a better world" appearing in Ben Barzman's 1960 Marxist science fiction classic, *Echo X*. Here the familiar twin-planets motif is used to contrast our own post-holocaust and cold war world with one in which the "premature anti-fascists" had won out in the 1930s, saving the Spanish Republic and preventing World War II.

Part 2: Obfuscation of the Left Cultural Tradition

In my view, two major constraints have limited scholarship on U.S. Communist writers up to the present moment. The first is the experience of the McCarthyite witch-hunt that forced a generation of writers to conceal, dissemble, and even to actually forget what they had gone through. The second has been the limitations of liberal thought as manifest in politics and literary criticism.

In regard to the former situation, even as late as the 1980s, writers significantly influenced by Communism omit that fact when submitting their own autobiographical statements for publication. In regard to the latter, the critics who created the "field" of U.S. literary radicalism were, as were many who followed them, still prisoners of literary categories that occluded from vision vast amounts of literary practice. This is usually writing by women, people of color, radicals, people from the non-elite classes, people who wrote in what were stigmatized as more popular forms, and also people from many regions, especially outside big northern and West Coast urban centers. The field was designed in such a way that what these others wrote didn't fit; much of this creative practice wasn't even "seen."

The prevailing approach was not to pursue in an open-ended manner the question, what kinds of writing did people sympathetic to Communism produce? Instead, many scholars perhaps precipitously created special categories—helped by the fact that certain Communist critics themselves wanted to create special categories—of proletarian novels and revolutionary poetry for the early 1930s, and radical novels and social poetry for the popular front.[16] This was an advance that, in the absence of further inquiry, eventually became transformed into a barrier.

Moreover, scholars almost always declared that this Communist literary phenomenon for all practical purposes came to a halt at the time of the Nazi-Soviet Pact when several key academic party members, such as Granville Hicks and Robert Gorham Davis, resigned, and a few fellow-traveling critics, such as Malcolm Cowley, disassociated themselves. However, whatever moral blow the Nazi-Soviet Pact was to the Communist movement at that time and retrospectively, the majority of left writers remained willing to work closely with the Communists. For example, the League of American Writers membership lists indicate that seven-eighths of these weathered the year-and-a-half-long crisis.[17] That is one of the reasons why a new study of literary Communism should not be limited to a 1930s act of nostalgia, but should go all the way up to the early 1970s and the experience of *American Dialogue*.

The research I have undertaken to date confirms the work of those younger historians of U.S. Communism—such as Paul Buhle, Mark Naison, Robin Kelley, and Maurice Isserman—who see the party as a war of a good many voices, but with the political and (I now add) literary orientations from Moscow (which tended to be narrowly functionalist in demanding political conformity) ultimately hegemonic.[18] While I have my own Marxist political opinions, I agree with the argument that in interpreting the reality of U.S. Communism, there has been much too much emphasis on what was said in central committee directives or (in regard to writers) by a few select party critics. What actually happens in a trade union or in the pages of a novel is usually far more dependent on matters such as the personalities and abilities of those who are the human agents, and the context in which those agents are active.

It is true that one can document that Michael Gold offered many
simplistic and half-baked judgments in his "Change the World"
column, as his own comrades sometimes protested. One can show
that John Howard Lawson and V.J. Jerome liked to review manu-
scripts by party members prior to publication and that they would
not hesitate to insist that material that might be interpreted as
"defeatist" or that might possibly militate against class unity be
altered or held back from print. But one can also show that Gold
upheld some important values in difficult times, and that the
majority of Communist writers either ignored or bypassed the
informal supervision of party institutions such as Lawson's "Writers Clinic" in Hollywood. Moreover, almost every Communist critic
progressively evolved in one way or another to embrace the argument of Leon Trotsky's *Literature and Revolution* (1922): that a
Marxist political party should encourage literary practice, especially by workers, but not try to lead a partisan literary movement
with a "line" in the way one tries to lead trade union and other
struggles.

An important weakness of much scholarship on the Communist
literary Left is that non-membership among sympathetic writers
is sometimes taken as a sign of superior talent, morality and
intellect to those who joined. This means that considerable effort
has been devoted to attempts (often futile) to determine who did or
didn't have the equivalent of a "card." If a writer turns out to have
had one, then a scholar who is sympathetic to the writer (for
example, to Meridel LeSueur, Edwin Rolfe, or Thomas McGrath)
must prove that the writer was really a "maverick" or earned the
ire of some higher-up Stalinist "official." If no "card" can be produced, then the critic's task of humanizing the writer becomes
easier.

This approach fails to take into account many subtleties, such
as the evidence that artistic autonomy often survived official membership and that some writers in the broader Communist "movement" beyond the party might have had opportunist reasons for
staying at arm's length. In fact, the typical pattern seems to be that
numerous writers considered themselves devoted Communists in
one way or another, but, due to their desire to spend all their spare
moments writing, rather than going to meetings, they simply could
not find the time or a good reason to join up. Stanley Burnshaw

wrote that "I was never a party member. [But] The matter is not of importance. What counts is the attitude, the public position."[19] Thus the non-member Burnshaw considered himself a Communist by his own account up until the 1952 Doctors' Plot, which is at least twenty years. The situation is much the same in regard to many others who retrospectively claimed that they were not actually party "members"—Kenneth Fearing, Ralph Ellison, Josephine Herbst, Nelson Algren, Jack Conroy, James T. Farrell, Irwin Shaw, and so forth.

Due to McCarthyism, which virtually forced writers to find some way to claim that they had never been party members, or, if they had been, to say that the party had abused them, the public statements of writers themselves are often unreliable. In his auto-biography, *The House on Jefferson Street* (1971), Horace Gregory first introduces his association with Communism in the following manner: "At this time (circa 1929–1931) I was moving closer to the Communist orbit...."[20] But back in February 1935, in the pages of a *New Masses* debate with Meridel LeSueur, he wrote: "Ever since I left college (that is, 1923), my political interests have centered in the work of the Communist Party. Ever since 1924 my poetry has contained social implications that can be resolved only by the success of the Communist Party in America."[21]

Another problem with the "membership fixation" is that it doesn't respond to the reality of political repression. Writers, like union activists, might be fired or blacklisted if they could be pegged as a party member. So it became possible and often desirable to be a member in practice with no material evidence. That is, one didn't have a card, one didn't pay dues in the regular manner, and one's name didn't appear on a list of members. Moreover, one's presence at a branch, unit, club or fraction meeting of the party was proof of nothing definite because it was known that sometimes non-members were present at such times (as a recruitment technique, or to facilitate collaboration on some project) and people didn't go around the room identifying themselves as "in" or "out." The entire Holly-wood branch of the party was organized in this manner. Similarly, the diverse African-American writers drawn to the left in New York, Chicago, and at Howard University in Washington, D.C., cannot be put into clear-cut boxes by virtue of membership or not; they constituted a kind of continuum of relationships to Communist ideology and organizations with all sorts of complex interactions. Terms such as "unorganized Communists" or "non-Party Bolsheviks," used on occasion by the activists of the left themselves, are never used by the scholars, who are fixated on "card-carrying members" who are most often seen as dour "hacks," and "fellow-travelers" who are depicted as "dupes," cynics, or "innocent" liberals.

Unfortunately, such problems as the inability to explain how one might be significantly influenced by Communist thought, but not in a formal sense a member, have caused large-scale confusion among academics and thus produced a cliché-ridden simplification in cultural history of this major phenomenon. The major biographer of Sherwood Anderson, apparently uncertain about how to explain that Anderson said he was a Communist but didn't join, ended up with the following formulation: "Whether or not [Theodore] Dreiser or Anderson joined the Party, which neither ever did, whether or not they went to the Soviet Union, which Dreiser did and Anderson did not ... as Anderson knew full well, the Party wasn't terribly interested in the likes of them."[22] This statement suggests that, even though Anderson claimed to be a Communist, he was farther away from this source of all evil than was Dreiser, who dirtied his hands by visiting the USSR but at least refused to commit the unpardonable sin of signing a card. However, this familiar trope of anti-communism does violence to the facts, for Dreiser *did* join the party; his letter of application is a public party document that reads:

> These historic years have deepened my conviction that widespread membership in the Communist movements will greatly strengthen the American people, together with the anti-fascist forces throughout the world, in completely stamping out fascism and achieving new heights of world democracy, economic progress and free culture. Belief in the greatness and dignity of man has been the guiding principle of my life and work. The logic of my life and work leads me therefore to apply for membership in the Communist Party.[23]

A different type of confusion exists about the politics of Mari Sandoz, a prolific author of Western U.S. literature such as *Old Jules* (1935), *Slogum House* (1937), and *Cheyenne Autumn* (1953). Her biographer writes only the following of her views:

Mari was not a pessimist; she was, more than she realized, an idealist. She believed that although there were ills, people, once aware of them, could cure them, but she did not approve of some of the cures offered. Many writers, discouraged by the government's failure to solve the country's problems, became communists, but the extreme left never attracted Mari. She read the proletarian novels of the 1920s and '30s (some of her ideas in *Capital City* may have come from them), but she believed as strongly as her father in democracy.[24]

Nevertheless, Sandoz's name appears as a member of the Communist-initiated-and-led League of American Writers in the mid-1930s. In and of itself, that might not be significant, but in 1982 *Colorado Heritage* published a memoir of Sandoz by a close literary friend, Caroline Bancroft. This sketchy memoir starts by attributing symbolic significance to Sandoz's red hair: "its color represented her firebrand political bias." The memoir then recounts Sandoz's sympathy for the Foundation for Soviet-American Friendship during World War II. Finally Bancroft recalls that: "... by 1950 I had become completely disillusioned with the Soviets and was definitely anti-Communist.... [But] She had grown to admire the Communist system more and more and was berating me sharply for my shift.... (I do not know if Mari was ever a card-carrying member of the Communist party, but there were a number of years when I was suspicious.)"[25]

The primary research on Sandoz's politics was apparently never thoroughly done, and it may be impossible to determine the full truth at this late date; but it is evident that Sandoz cannot be boxed into pristine alternative categories of "card-carrying member" or "democrat." However, it would be unfair to attribute such misrepresentations as these references to Dreiser and Sandoz to poor or sloppy scholarship on an individual basis; it is a generalized phenomenon that many literary scholars have trouble talking accurately and with subtlety about the relation to Communism of a whole generation, including both major and minor figures.

Part 3: Agenda for Research

Where to begin in terms of rectifying this situation? Here are some of the areas that require fuller research and theorization.

1. *Jewish-Americans*: What is taught today in Judaic studies programs and English literature departments as the "Jewish-American literary tradition" is still a tiny portion of a huge body of literature, a surprising amount of which was pioneered by Communist-influenced writers. Some of the early studies of Jewish-American literature such as Judd Teller's *Strangers and Natives* (1968) and Bernard Sherman's *The Invention of the Jew* (1969) offer a few pages on Communists Isidor Schneider and Mike Gold. Moreover, Henry Roth has received substantial scholarship, although none of it deals substantively with the fact that Roth spent twenty years as a party member and another fifteen years as a self-proclaimed independent "Titoist."[26] However, ever since Irving Malin's *Jews and Americans* (1965), almost all the attention has gone to Saul Bellow, Bernard Malamud, and Philip Roth. The most recent book, Mark Shechner's *After the Revolution* (1987), is being hailed by some as the greatest work ever on Jewish-American literature, even though Jewish Communist writers are never mentioned. In the past few years Louis Harap has published a three-volume work about Jewish-American writers that is enormously helpful, but, since he casts his net so wide, a great deal more depth and detail needs to be filled in by successors.[27]

What is ignored is that, especially in the 1930s, although before and after as well, there existed major groups of Jewish-American Communist poets and novelists who wrote in English (not to mention those who wrote in Yiddish) and very often on Jewish subjects. At least three Jewish pro-Communist women poets won the Yale Younger Poets Award and had their works published by Yale University Press: Muriel Rukeyser, Joy Davidman (also author of the Jewish proletarian novel *Anya* in 1940), and Eve Merriam (an extraordinarily prolific writer in many genres). Norman Rosten, the Jewish-American leftist author of what might be regarded as the major epic poem of the 1930s, *The Fourth Decade* (1943), also won that prize.

A beginning list of Jewish-American fiction and poetry writers on the left should also include Martin Abzug, Nelson Algren (born

Nelson Abraham), Benjamin Appel, Nathan Asch, Ben Barzman, Alexander Bergman, Alvah Bessie, Beatrice Bisno, William Blake (born Blech), Michael Blankfort, Maxwell Bodenheim (born Bodenheimer), Stanley Burnshaw, Laura Caspary, Lester Cohen, Edward Dahlberg, Guy Endore (born Samuel Goldstein), Howard Fast, Kenneth Fearing, Joseph Freeman, Ben Field (born Moe Bragin), Sol Funaroff, Robert Gessner, Michael Gold, Albert Halper, Alfred Hayes, Maurice Hindus, V. J. Jerome (born Jerome Isaac Romaine), Gordon Kahn, Aaron Kramer, Melvin Levy, Walter Lowenfels, A. B. Magil, Albert Maltz, Martha Millet, Arthur Miller (author of an antiracist novel and collection of short fiction), Tillie Olsen (born Tillie Lerner), George Oppen, Sam Ornitz, Abraham Polonsky, Naomi Replansky, Edwin Rolfe (born Sol Fishman), Sam Ross (born Sam Rosen), John Sanford (born Julian Shapiro), Edwin Seaver, Isidor Schneider, Budd Schulberg, Edith Segal, George Sklar, Tess Slesinger, Herman Spector, Joseph Vogel, Len Zinberg (better known as "Ed Lacy"), Leanne Zugsmith, and Louis Zukofsky.

These names hardly exhaust the field. Jewish-American Communist writers had their own publication, *Jewish Life*, later called *Jewish Currents* as it became increasingly independent, which started in November 1946 and contains fascinating material excluded from the version of Jewish-American literature propagated by the universities. One revealing document is a polemic against anti-Semitism in the United States by John Howard Lawson.[28] Lawson, whose family name was Levy, is a figure rarely treated as Jewish in any of the canonical studies of the cultural left, although he wrote on specifically Jewish themes as in *Success Story* (1932). In fact, six of the "Hollywood Ten" were Jewish, and, long before synagogues burst forth in vigorous debate about Philip Roth's *Portnoy's Complaint* (1969), they were thrown into turmoil by *Bride of the Sabbath* (1952), written by Samuel Ornitz while serving his prison sentence.

2. *African-Americans*: A second area that deserves serious and fresh attention is the profound interconnection between Communism and African-American cultural theory and practice. There is no doubt that the Communist effort to defend the black nation thesis in the early 1930s rebounded against powerful themes of African-American cultural autonomy, pride and resistance evident

in much radical Black writing. Much is known about the Communist associations of Paul Robeson, W.E.B. Du Bois, Langston Hughes, Countee Cullen, and Richard Wright, all highly influential figures; but less about Lorraine Hansberry, Margaret Walker, Alice Childress, Shirley Graham, Margaret Burroughs, Arna Bontemps, Ralph Ellison, Sterling Brown, Robert Hayden, John O. Killens, Julian Mayfield, Lance Jeffers, William Attaway, Willard Motley, Chester Himes, Douglas Turner, Lonnie Elder III, and many others.

3. *The Premature Socialist-Feminists*: A third area of importance that is just beginning to receive discussion is that of women writers attracted to Communism. I have already mentioned Sandoz, but Meridel LeSueur and Tillie Olsen are the figures who have received the most attention, while Anna Louise Strong and Agnes Smedley, both of whom wrote novels, have just recently been the subject of full-length books.[29] Josephine Herbst is featured not only in a fine 1984 biography by Elinor Langer, *Josephine Herbst: The Story She Could Never Tell*, but in a half-dozen doctoral dissertations.

Yet little has been written in regard to the U.S. cultural left about the complex case of Christina Stead. She was an Australian by birth, but spent the 1930s and 1940s active in the Communist cultural Left in New York and Hollywood. Well-known leftists Ruth McKenney, Grace Lumpkin, and Dorothy Myra Page wrote novels, but both have lapsed into obscurity. So has Leanne Zugsmith, who claimed not to be a party member but was a Communist ideologically. Laura Caspary has been pegged as a prolific "romantic mystery writer"; but her numerous novels dramatize many concerns and perspectives reflective of her years as a member and then a friend of the Communist Party.

Sanora Babb, Beatrice Bisno, Bessie Breuer, Catherine Brody, Henrietta Buckmaster, Fielding Burke (a pseudonym for Olive Tilford Dargon), Olga Cabral, Joy Davidman, Martha Dodd, Martha Gellhorn, Josephine Johnson, Jean Karsavina, Margaret Larkin, Gerda Lerner, Irene Paull, Ruth Suckow, Caroline Slade, Evelyn Scott, Janet Stevenson, Genevieve Taggard, Frances Winwar, and Helen Yglesias are all intriguing left-wing women fiction writers and poets who have for the most part been "disappeared."

4. *Writers in Popular Genres*: To my knowledge, despite the

highly apt tools available to Marxists, we have not even made a rudimentary beginning of an examination of the major contributions of leftist writers to the historical novel (for example, William Blake and Howard Fast) and to the radical farm novel (for example, Ruth Suckow and Paul Corey) in the United States. In addition, the topics of Communist producers of mass culture, detective fiction, horror fiction, pulp fiction, children's fiction, and science fiction have received no attention beyond the famous instances of Dashiell Hammett's party membership and the Hollywood Ten case. Yet this is the primary site of cultural production by the left after the Depression.

Howard Fast, a best-selling historical novelist from the 1930s to the present, published much detective fiction (often as "E.V. Cunningham") and a fair amount of science fiction. A prolific Communist journalist, Mike Quin, is well-known on the left for his classic *The Big Strike*, about the 1934 longshore strike, but under the name Robert Finnegan was developing a reputation as a pulp novelist for books such as *The Lying Ladies* (1946), *The Bandaged Nude* (1948), and *Many a Monster* (1949) when he died prematurely in 1947.

Robert Carse, a leftist known mainly for sea stories, turned to pulp fiction in *Drums of Empire* (1959), set during the Haitian slave revolt with Toussaint L'Ouverture among the characters. Although the dust jacket reads, "The fire of revolution made them enemies ... the flame of desire made them lovers," the plot concerns a white man won over to fight on the side of the Black rebels. Margaret Larkin (married to Albert Maltz) wrote a nonfiction mystery thriller, *Seven Shares in a Gold Mine* (1959). Guy Endore not only wrote mystery thrillers such as *Methinks the Lady* (1945) and *Detour at Midnight* (1959), but also the most famous werewolf novel in the English language—*The Werewolf of Paris* (1933), which has been compared to Stoker's *Dracula* and Shelley's *Frankenstein*.

Kenneth Fearing wrote numerous successful detective novels. Edwin Rolfe wrote at least one. So did Abraham Polonsky. William Lindsay Gresham wrote *Nightmare Alley* (1946) and *Limbo Tower* (1949). The core of the group of major science fiction writers known as the "Futurians," such as Frederik Pohl, also held membership in the Flatbush chapter of the Young Communist League.

5. *Writers Treating "Race" and Cultural Difference*: A fifth area never discussed is the contemporary ways in which many Commu-

nist writers, in contrast to some critics and theoreticians, depicted issues of cultural difference. For example, the Communist movement was an important avenue of expression for the forgotten Chinese-American writer H.T. Tsiang and the great Filipino writer Carlos Bulosan. In the Depression era, Japanese-American Communists in Los Angeles organized the Japanese Proletarian Art League. The group published a monthly magazine called *Proletarian Art*, which lasted from December 1928 until January 1932, when the Los Angeles Red Squad raided a party meeting, arresting forty-five Japanese-Americans and deporting most of the writers.

The contemporary issue of representing "cultural difference" is among the most recurring concerns in Communist cultural activities. For example, there are representations of Native American Indians in left-wing novels by Robert Gessner (*Broken Arrow*, 1933), Robert Cantwell (*The Land of Plenty*, 1934), and Howard Fast (*The Last Frontier*, 1944), and the significant use of Native American Indian cultures in the radical Modernist poetry of Norman MacLeod and Thomas McGrath. Franklin Folsom, who was for five years the full-time executive secretary of the League of American Writers, wrote *Red Power on the Rio Grande: The Native American Revolution of 1680* (1973); Alfonso Oritz wrote for the book-jacket, "For the first time, I feel that someone is writing about my [Pueblo] people...."

Daniel James, a descendant of Jesse James who was a Communist political activist and screenwriter in the 1940s, gained a national reputation before his death when he published under the pseudonym "Danny Santiago" the novel *Famous All Over Town* (1983) depicting the world through the eyes of a fourteen-year-old Chicano. There are also dramatizations of Mexican-American miners struggles in Philip Stevenson's unfinished series of novels called "The Seed," published under the name Lars Lawrence: *Morning, Noon and Night* (1954), *Out of the Dust* (1956), *Old Father Antic* (1961), and *The Hoax* (1961). Gordan Kahn's posthumously published *A Long Way From Home* (1989), written in the early 1950s, depicts a Chicano draft resister during the Korean war.

There are representations by Jewish-Americans of African-Americans as major characters in novels by Len Zinberg (*Walk Hard—Talk Loud*, 1940), John Sanford (*The People from Heaven*, 1943), Benjamin Appel (*The Dark Stain*, 1943), Howard Fast (*Free-*

dom Road, 1944), David Alman (*The Well of Compassion*, 1948), Earl Conrad (*Gulf Stream North*, 1954), and the poetry of Aaron Kramer (*Denmark Vesey*, 1952), as well as the work of many others. There are also black dialect poems by Sol Funaroff. One scholar of African-American fiction called Scott Nearing's 1931 Communist novel, *Free Born*, "the first revolutionary novel of Negro life."[30] There is a representation of the Jew as midwife to radicalism in Alexander Saxton's *The Grand Crossing* (1943).

Surely a provocative case is that of Jewish-American Communist Guy Endore's 1934 *Babouk*, just republished by Monthly Review Press. After *The Werewolf of Paris*, Endore obtained a publisher's contract to write a romance in the period of the slave trade. Arriving in Haiti to do primary research, he became entranced by the tales of African resistance. Soon he found himself, in his own words, "becoming Black."[31] The result was a startlingly original novel about the anti-slavery resistance of captive African-Americans that gives voice to a colonial subject in a manner far outdistancing most works of its day.

Conclusion: Recovering the Radical Tradition

As another decade passes, with the 1980s becoming the 1990s, the urgency only grows, not diminishes, to come to terms with the Communist foundation of the left movement in this country. Even as the problematic of the cold war disintegrates, nothing fundamental has changed in regard to the need to profoundly transform and restructure U.S. capitalism. Moreover, there still remains no more attractive, meaningful, and creative life for a young person in this society today than to devote himself or herself to "being all that he or she can be" by remaking the United States through organizing the unorganized, battling to extirpate the filth of racism and anti-Semitism, democratizing wealth, fighting for the extension of the rights of women and gay people, defending the environment, and, most of all, spreading the internationalist ideas of self-determination in the Middle East, Africa, Latin America and Asia. Without doubt, the recent experiences of social change in every part of the globe during the 1970s and 1980s have made every aspect of this effort infinitely more complex. But on moral and practical grounds, there can hardly be a more meaningful life than that of what used to be called a "red."

However, in order to build upon the red tradition effectively, to truly overcome the grave errors and yet still draw sustenance from the real glories, one must know the past. Here the left must be reminded of the lesson taught to us so well by the feminist historians and historians of people of color: If one does not represent oneself, whether in regard to red writers or red trade unionists or red political parties or red student activists, others will do the representation for one. Moreover, despite some substantial achievements, for the past twenty-five years the "others" have been doing a seriously inadequate job. Just as Marx argued that the overthrow of capitalism and the construction of socialism must be carried out and administered by the producers themselves—not any self-proclaimed surrogates making decisions for others "for their own good"—so the telling of the story of the literary left remains the long overdue and the urgent task of left cultural workers themselves.

Notes

1. These and all the following quotations from Lowenfels appear in Robert Gover, ed., *The Portable Walter* (New York: International, 1968), pp. 34–39.
2. It would take many pages to list the materials that have arisen in the "canon debate" of the past twenty years. However, to gain some insight into the new approaches to United States literature and an awareness of some of the writers who are in the process of rehabilitation, one might examine Emory Elliot et al., *Columbia Literary History of the United States* (New York: Columbia University Press, 1988), and Paul Lauter et al., *The Heath Anthology of American Literature,* 2 vols. (Lexington, MA: D.C. Heath and Co, 1990).
3. This image was partly created by Eugene Lyons, whose view is explicitly stated in his opening chapter of *The Red Decade* called "In Defense of Red-Baiting": "During the Red Decade we are confronted, in the main, with a horde of part-time pseudo-rebels who have neither courage nor convictions, but only a muddy emotionalism and a mental fog which made them an easy prey for the arbiters of a political racket" (New York: Bobbs-Merrill, 1941, p. 16). The tropes of vulgar red-bait-

ing were reinforced by the title and some of the writings in *The God That Failed* (1950) and Whittaker Chambers's *Witness* (1952).

4. Philip Bonosky, "The 'Thirties' in American Culture," *Political Affairs* 38, no. 5 (May 1959): 27–40.

5. Charles Humboldt, "Fiction on the Left," *Mainstream* 10, no. 3 (March 1957): 48.

6. Philip Bonosky, "On *Writers on the Left*," *Political Affairs* (September 1962): 41–47; and unpublished review of *Writers on the Left*, Philip Stevenson papers, Wisconsin State Historical Society.

7. By mistake, Professor Aaron's words are attributed to the working-class novelist Jack Conroy.

8. Cary Nelson, *Repression and Recovery: Modern American Poetry and the Politics of Cultural Memory, 1910–1945* (Madison: University of Wisconsin Press, 1989); Paula Rabinowitz, *Labor and Desire: Women's Revolutionary Fiction in Depression America* (Chapel Hill, NC: University of North Carolina Press, 1991); Constance Coiner, "Literature of Resistance: The Intersection of Feminism and the Communist Left in Meridel LeSueur and Tillie Olsen," in Lennard J. Davis and M. Bella Mirabella, eds., *Left Politics and the Literary Profession* (New York: Columbia University Press, 1990).

9. The main departure in focus was James B. Gilbert's *Writers and Partisans: A History of Literary Radicalism in America* (New York: John Wiley and Sons, 1968), integrating the history of *Partisan Review* into the larger story of the cultural left. Richard Pells presented a striking synthesis in *Radical Visions and American Dreams* (1973), but his literary material consists of brief discussions of relatively familiar figures. References to female creative writers in Pells's study come to one out of 424 pages; the book contains no mention at all of the major women writers such as Herbst, Lumpkin, Page, McKenney, or Slesinger. Pells provides no consideration of writers of color other than a few pages on Richard Wright and some brief references to Langston Hughes. Marcus Klein's *Foreigners: The Making of American Literature, 1900–1940* (1981) treats many more women writers in passing and takes a fresh look at a number of neglected literary anthologies. Yet Klein's work is nearly as limited as Pells's in regard to writers of color, treating in detail only the well-known figures of Mike Gold, Nathaniel West, and Richard Wright.

Among the many impressive unpublished dissertations on the literary left, there is a common pattern of focusing chapters on the same group of texts most familiar within the category of radical writing. This might be justified if there were conclusive evidence that this relative handful were the richest works of the hundreds that qualify for the genres discussed; but I don't see evidence that such judgments

ALAN WALD 303

are being made through rigorous first-hand comparisons with a broad sample. For example, Cheryl Davis's "A Rhetorical Study of Selected Proletarian Novels of the 1930s" (University of Utah, 1976) discusses mainly the widely known novels by Conroy, Cantwell, Gold, and Roth; Calvin Harris's "Twentieth Century American Political Fiction: An Analysis of Proletarian Fiction" (University of Oregon, 1979), treats the most famous novels by Dos Passos, Steinbeck, Conroy, Lumpkin, Herbst, and Cantwell; K.L. Ledbetter's "The Idea of a Proletarian Novel in America, 1927–1939" (University of Illinois, 1963) focuses on Gold, Roth and Fuchs; and Joel Wingard's "Toward a Workers' America: The Theory and Practice of the American Proletarian Novel" (Louisiana State University, 1979) treats the most frequently cited novels of Gold, Conroy, Cantwell, and Farrell. Of course, the discussions of the writers in these works have many virtues and are not repetitive in other ways. But it is surprising how few of them refer to earlier scholarly studies other than Aaron and Rideout. Some useful observations on the treatment of radical women writers in anthologies is presented in Paula Rabinowitz's "Women and U.S. Literary Radicalism," in Charlotte Nekola and Paula Rabinowitz, eds., *Writing Red* (New York: Feminist Press, 1987), pp. 1–16.

10. As I write, it is no longer possible to obtain for classroom use the paperback reprints once available of James T. Farrell's *Studs Lonigan* trilogy; Josephine Herbst's *Pity Is Not Enough* and *The Executioner Waits*; and Grace Lumpkin's *The Wedding* (although a hardback is available and inexpensive). However, there are new paperback editions with useful introductions of William Attaway's *Blood on the Forge* (New York: Monthly Review Press, 1987), Fielding Burke's *Call Home the Heart* (New York: Feminist Press, 1983), Jesus Colon's *A Puerto Rican in New York* (New York: International, 1982), Alice Childress's *Like One of the Family* (Boston: Beacon, 1986), Guy Endore's *Babouk* (New York: Monthly Review Press, 1991), Josephine Herbst's *Rope of Gold* (New York: Feminist Press, 1984), Myra Page's *Daughter of the Hills* (New York: Feminist Press, 1986), Tess Slesinger's *The Unpossessed* (New York: Feminist Press, 1984), and Joseph Vogel's *Man's Courage* (New York: Syracuse University Press, 1989).

Moreover, West End Press has reprinted many writings by Don West in *In a Land of Plenty* (1982), and collected numerous writings by Meridel LeSueur in *I Hear Men Talking* (1984), *Harvest Song* (1990), and *The Girl* (1982). At the present time, Omnigraphics, Inc., is in the process of issuing hardback reprints of Nathan Asch's *Pay Day*, Louis Adamic's *Grandsons*, Daniel Fuchs's *Homage to Blenholt*, Albert Halper's *Union Square*, and Clara Weatherwax's *Marching! Marching!*

In addition, Volume 2 of the new *Heath Anthology of American Literature* has short excerpts from Michael Gold, Albert Maltz, Lillian Hellman, Clifford Odets, Meridel LeSueur, and several writers of color who were variously drawn to Communism.

11. An example of the current crossroads in scholarship on the literary left can be seen in a comparison of several chapters of *The Columbia Literary History of the United States* (New York: Columbia University Press, 1988). In a section called "Literary Scenes and Literary Movements, 1910–45," Daniel Aaron devotes the last dozen pages to presenting the left cultural movement as he saw it in *Writers on the Left*. Complementing this, Elaine Showalter considers a number of left-wing women writers in a segment called "Women Writers Between the Wars," and Cary Nelson discusses quite a few neglected radical poets in "The Diversity of American Poetry."

12. See the landmark volume edited by Ralph Miliband, John Saville and Marcel Liebman, eds., *Socialist Register 1984: The Uses of Anti-Communism* (London: Merlin, 1984), especially "Reflections on Anti-Communism" by Miliband and Liebman, pp. 1–22.

13. At the time of Stalin's death, party leaders tried to outdo each other in presenting the most disgusting accolades to this bloody tyrant. He was characterized by William Z. Foster, Elizabeth Gurley Flynn, and Pettis Perry as "the best loved man on earth, enshrined in the hearts of people everywhere, to whose well-being his life was selflessly devoted." See "On the Loss of Stalin," *Political Affairs* 32, no. 3 (April 1953): 4.

14. Undated letter to Elinor Langer, Stanley Burnshaw papers, National Humanities Center.

15. Oral History of Guy Endore, UCLA Library.

16. Granville Hicks was among the more aggressive Communist critics in promoting categories. Among the most creative were those of "Complex and Collective Novels" in his series on "Revolution and the Novel" that ran in seven issues of the *New Masses* in April and May 1934. The series is reprinted in Jack Alan Robbins, ed., *Granville Hicks in the New Masses* (Port Washington, NY: Kennikat Press, 1974), pp. 19–66. The most influential scholarly theorist of categories of the radical novel is Walter Rideout who in *The Radical Novel* argued that most works written by leftists "can be fitted fairly easily on the basis of content or subject matter into four main groups: 1) those centered around a strike; 2) those concerned with the development of an individual's class-consciousness and his conversion to communism; 3) those dealing with the 'bottom dogs,' the lowest layer of society; and 4) those describing the decay of the middle class" (p. 171).

17. The papers of the League are at the University of California at Berkeley library.

18. See Paul Buhle, *Marxism in the United States* (London: Verso, 1989); Maurice Isserman, *Which Side Were You On? The Communist Party in World War II* (Middletown, CT: Wesleyan University Press, 1982); Robin Kelley, *Hammer and Hoe* (Chapel Hill, NC: University of North Carolina Press, 1989); and Mark Naison, *Communists and Harlem During the Depression* (Chicago: University of Illinois Press, 1983).
19. Undated letter to Elinor Langer, Stanley Burnshaw Papers, National Humanities Center.
20. Horace Gregory, *The House on Jefferson Street* (New York: Holt, Rinehart and Winston, 1971), p. 182.
21. Horace Gregory, "One Writer's Position," *New Masses*, 12 February 1935, pp. 21–22.
22. Kim Townsend, *Sherwood Anderson* (Boston: Houghton Mifflin, 1987), p. 272.
23. The letter appears in Philip Bart et al., eds., *Highlights of a Fighting History: 60 Years of the Communist Party USA* (New York: International Publishers, 1979), p. 486. The letter is dated July 1945.
24. Helen Winter Stauffer, *Mari Sandoz: Story Catcher of the Plains* (Lincoln: University of Nebraska Press, 1982), pp. 127–28.
25. Caroline Bancroft, "Two Women Writers," *Colorado Heritage* 1 (1982): 103, 108.
26. Wald interview with Henry Roth, New Mexico, 1989.
27. See Greenwood Press's *Creative Awakening* (1987), *In the Mainstream* (1987), and *Dramatic Encounters* (1987).
28. John Howard Lawson, "The Politics of Anti-Semitism," *Jewish Life*, September 1950: 10–13.
29. Tracy B. Strong and Helene Keysar, *Right in Her Soul: The Life of Anna Louise Strong* (New York: Random House, 1983) and Janice R. MacKinnon and Stephen R. MacKinnon, *Agnes Smedley: The Life and Times of an American Radical* (Berkeley: University of California Press, 1988).
30. Hugh M. Gloster, *Negro Voices in American Fiction* (Chapel Hill, NC: University of North Carolina Press, 1948), p. 197.
31. Undated letter, Guy Endore papers, UCLA.

INTERVIEW WITH GIL GREEN

Anders Stephanson

Anders Stephanson: You joined the party in 1924 as an eighteen-year-old Jewish working-class kid from Chicago and instantly lost your job as a result of it.

Gil Green: Yes, I lost my job at an oil refinery because they learned I was trying to organize a union and was a Communist. Later, towards the end of the twenties, I moved to New York and became an official of the Young Communist League. As such, I also attended a number of meetings of the Young Communist International in Moscow.

AS: And in 1935 and 1936 you even became a member of the Comintern executive.

GG: That story is interesting. In 1934 a gathering which called itself the American Youth Congress took place in New York City. It was organized to serve a rather conservative end, but was transformed into a progressive national movement. We considered it an important development, and the Young Communist League was represented on its leading committee.

This took place in August 1934. Around November I received a cable from Moscow asking me to attend a special meeting of the Young Communist International. I had no idea what it was all about. But when I got there I learned that it had been called to discuss the "deviation" of the American and French youth organizations. A resolution had been prepared condemning us and demanding a change in our policies. We were accused of participating in a mixed-class movement which could only result in dulling working-class consciousness. Raymond Guyot, the head of the French league, had also been called to Moscow for the same "deviation." I had never met Guyot before, but we got along beautifully, for we both stood our ground and would not accept the criticism. We accused them of failing to understand, even at this late date, the reason for the terrible defeat of the Communist, Socialist, and democratic forces in Germany by the victory of Hitlerian fascism. Had they been united that would not have happened.

After three weeks of endless debate, we were warned by Shemadonov, the representative of the Russian league and the secretary of the Young Communist International, that Guyot and I had to agree with and accept their resolution condemning us within a few days or be condemned by a final meeting of their committee with a recommendation to our leagues that we be removed from office. But Guyot and I refused to budge from our position. But before that final meeting took place, Shemadonov, as we later learned, brought their proposed action against us to the attention of the Comintern secretariat. It would not go along. Thus, when that final meeting took place, to our immense surprise, Shemadonov rose and told the committee "we wish to withdraw our resolution, comrades Guyot and Green are right; we were wrong." With that the meeting was adjourned.

The background of this changed position by the Comintern secretariat had to do with the depth of discussion and reevaluation taking place upon the release of Georgi Dimitrov from Nazi Germany, and his arrival in the Soviet Union. Having lived in Germany for some years he knew the situation there quite well and the terrible mistakes made by the German CP in failing to work for all-inclusive anti-fascist unity, even seeing the Social Democrats as the main "enemy." He charged that a fascist takeover could have been prevented had unity of all the anti-fascist forces been established. So when Shemadonov came to the secretariat with his resolution condemning the French and American youth leagues for following a policy of left and progressive unity, it of course turned the resolution down. That's how the resolution against us was dropped. It was only after that fundamental shift in policy that the Seventh World Congress of the Comintern could be called. It took place the following summer.

AS: This is in 1935, consequently, a moment of success for you.

GG: Guyot and I became examples of the united front policy that was favored for the youth leagues. Thus when they elected the new Comintern executive committee they included Guyot and me on it as exemplifying the new policies advocated for the youth movement. Actually, however, I was never called to a single meeting.

AS: Because the Seventh Congress was really the end of the

THE NEW "STAR OF BETHLEHEM"   *by Phil Bard*

Daily Worker cartoon, Christmas 1935.

Comintern, more or less. The 1943 dissolution, often referred to as
Stalin's grand concession to the West, was really codification of an
already existing state of affairs. We are now, then, in the 1940s. So
where did you spend the war? Did you go into the armed services?

GG: No, I had a wife and two young children. I was not drafted.
I volunteered, but they insisted that I get the signature of my wife.
My wife had more sense than I. She refused to sign it. So I did not
serve in the armed forces.

AS: You continued to work for the Communist Party, or did you
become a laborer?

GG: I became the head of the party in New York.

AS: So when the "Duclos Article" sprang upon you in the spring of 1945, you were an important functionary.

GG: Yes. Just about the end of the war, we suddenly learned of this article. It had appeared in a French Communist magazine.

AS: Before discussing this controversy, you might say something about your relations with Browder and Foster.

GG: Browder and Foster were the two main party leaders. Both left their mark on the party. Browder and I had never been close. He was not the kind of a person that you really got close to, but you respected him. Foster had his eyes set in one direction, how to organize the working class into industrial unions. He made an immense contribution on that score. Foster was a very interesting personality and a man you could talk to without being made to feel that he was the "great, great leader." I disagreed with him a number of times, but I also respected him highly. Browder, on the other hand, had a deeper feeling for the country itself.

AS: He was from Kansas, after all.

GG: Yes, he was from Kansas. And he knew this country as different from others, with a history all its own. Nor did he make the sectarian mistake of thinking everything bourgeois was bad. He understood the psychology of the country better and attempted to incorporate it into his politics. The interesting thing about both of them is that they complemented each other. They were constantly at odds, but they checked each other from going to extremes.

Take for example the case of John L. Lewis when he finally decided to establish the Committee for Industrial Organization in 1934 or 1935, in order to organize the unorganized. Lewis let the party know that he wanted some young Communists on his staff, because we alone at that time had experience in organizing the unorganized workers. A number of left-led unions had been formed. The party leadership discussed Lewis's request, and Foster warned about cooperating with him: "You can't trust that son-of-a-bitch." Browder took a somewhat different point of view: "At this time, for whatever reasons, Lewis wants to organize. This is a period in which workers can be organized. We don't have the means or the ability to do it by ourselves. If this period passes, and we don't know how long it may last, the present opportune moment will pass without our knowing when another one will arise. The question, therefore, is, not John L. Lewis, but what can we do to take advantage of the present favorable climate. We should give Lewis some of our young people, but with their eyes open; comrades who understand what this guy's record has been, and we'll have the means to check on what changes he may undergo." So that's the kind of relationship they had.

AS: But in 1945 Browder went out as a result of Duclos's attack on his coalition line.

GG: I was terribly shocked by the article. But in my naiveté and innocence, I was shocked because I was supposed to have been involved in what was a betrayal of Marxism. This was undoubtedly coming from Moscow, and had greater significance than an article by some leader of the French party who suddenly attacks the line of the American party without even letting us know his views beforehand. According to the Italians, later on, there is evidence that it was not aimed so much at Browder and the party here as at the Italian and French parties. The fear was that, with their underground fighting against the Nazis, they would emerge with tremendous prestige and be able to take an independent course. And while the blow was struck against us here, it wasn't necessarily concerned with us alone.

AS: Browder, at any rate, was finished.

GG: Browder did go overboard on some questions. He did believe after a while that he had some contacts that brought whatever ideas he had directly to Roosevelt. And he began to believe that *he* was partially running the policy in Washington, thinking he had much greater influence than he did. And he didn't realize what was going to happen after the war; he thought everything was going to be hunky-dory, all major conflicts would be resolved. However, he played a tremendous role in helping to Americanize the party, by enabling us to see American reality, while Foster saw the labor movement and made a great contribution there, but often had a much narrower approach in the political arena.

AS: In the early cold war period, then, the party becomes the target of intense repression, initiated with the indictment of the twelve party leaders in 1949, of whom you were one.

GG: Foster was let off because of his heart ailment.

AS: You were also one of the three that, when your appeal to the

Supreme Court failed in 1951, were sent underground, jumping bail on orders from the party. The rest of the leadership took their prison sentences.

GG: Not knowing what was going to happen and with the press saying that our conviction was going to be followed by a whole series of other raids against Communists everywhere, the executive committee decided that a number of people should stay out and not turn themselves in.

AS: So you spent more than four years underground, moving from place to place, chiefly together with Henry Winston.

GG: Yes. There were a number of us, but it ended up with only Winston and me still functioning, not being picked up by the police.

AS: You finally surrendered in early 1956, after Gene Dennis and the rest of the leadership had finished their sentences. And you then spent five years in prison?

GG: I had a five-year sentence, but three years were added for my jumping bail. So I had eight years. I spent close to six years in Leavenworth Penitentiary in Kansas.

AS: So you were out of the circulation of the party mainstream between 1951 and 1961. As a fugitive you couldn't openly participate except in certain very special occasions.

GG: ...and by communications.

AS: And going into prison you were out of party affairs for the duration of the fifties, during the McCarthyist repression, during the time of the Soviet invasion of Hungary in 1956 and the secret Khrushchev speech at the Twentieth Soviet Communist Party Congress, all of which were exceedingly trying events and caused internal turmoil. How did you, from the distance, react to these events?

GG: Let me confess that at times I was glad I was in prison. That seemed to be a lesser punishment [laughter]. My wife would visit me, and then I had a brother, a younger brother in Chicago, seven years my junior, a wonderful person and also a party member, who had a right to visit me once a month. They would inform me about what was happening. I definitely opposed the intervention in Hungary, just as I did later in Czechoslovakia. That to me was a violation of principle. No party has a right, no country has a right to intervene in another. Yes, there was upheaval in Hungary, but you couldn't put that upheaval down by an army from the outside. It had to be resolved by the people themselves. Khrushchev's revelations of the Stalin period were terribly shocking.

AS: They came as a total surprise to you?

GG: Well, yes and no. I had been disturbed over many years about so many top people disappearing or charged with treason, the trials they had. I knew something must be wrong when people who played such roles in the revolution itself suddenly were accused of treason. If it was true it indicated that something was basically wrong, and if it was not true, it was a frame-up. Then it was even worse. So my wife and brother, during the hour I got every month, told me in capsule form what the essence of the document was. But I was saved from what happened in the leadership itself. And I was grateful—I don't want to be quoted on this—that I was not outside [laughter].

AS: And what happened in the leadership in the mid-to-late 1950s, with the emergence and rapid departure of Gene Dennis as a leader?

GG: Dennis was easy to get along with if you were not a competitor of his, and I certainly was not. But he was uptight all the time, very high-strung. When there was a large national board meeting in New York, I would come in the night before from Chicago and go to his home for dinner with him and his wife. And he would pace the floor for two hours before he could relax enough to eat. Uptight all the time. Frightened of speaking in public. Certainly not the kind of person who could be a figure. So, obviously Foster was the person behind the scene, but when I came out of prison Foster was dead, Dennis was dead.

AS: And Gus Hall was the new leader.

GG: Yes, Gus Hall, with whom I had spent about a year in Leavenworth.

AS: How would you describe Gus Hall? An old-style Finnish communist?

GG: A man taken up with his own importance.

AS: Did you experience him that way in the prison as well?

GG: Well, no. We were friendly, but we were never friends; there's a distinction there. In prison he never became warm to anybody.

People in prison are human beings, even in a penitentiary, so I made quite a few friends. In fact, there was a man in prison for bank robbery with whom for a time I lost contact, but just a while ago he finally found out where I was and sent me air fare. He now lives in Arizona. He insisted I must come and visit him and his wife. And I'm going. I do want to see him very much.

When I got out of prison, I was told not to leave Chicago as I was on early release for good behavior and still subject to finishing my sentence "on the street." I remained there with my wife, Lillian, who was suffering from cancer. After she died the party asked me to move to New York in 1964, and I became the leader of the New York State party. Bob Thompson had had a sudden heart attack. He was the head, so I was asked to come in to take his place.

AS: You had been out of commission for more or less a decade. You had been underground, you had been in prison, but you had escaped the whole upheaval that happened as a result of 1956—on the one hand the people who disagreed with the Hungarian developments, on the other hand the people who had difficulties accepting the revelations about Stalin. We have the advent of John F. Kennedy in the White House. There's an immense intensification of the cold war at the same time over Cuba, over Berlin, and then the relaxation after 1963. The party at that stage is really in bad straits, because of the repression, because of the cold war climate, and also presumably because of the relative prosperity of the 1950s. How would you describe the situation of the party in 1961 when you get out and you see what was going on?

GG: The party at its high point in the 1930s had had a hundred thousand members. And the Young Communist League had twenty thousand, and in those years we counted by actual dues payments. Now, the party had lost most of its members, it was only a shadow of its former self—no question. At one time the party had some four thousand auto workers in its ranks. Some two thousand in Detroit. You know how many auto workers we have in Detroit today? One. A single member in the auto industry. Of course, there were also people in that period who were frightened away—people in jail, etc.—but mainly it was the sectarianism of the party. To give you an example, the party leadership did not support the decades-long rank-and-file upheaval in the Teamsters union. Why? Because they learned, whether true or false, that it had begun somewhere in California with two members who were Trotskyists [laughter].

Let me give you another example. In 1961 the party organized, through its contacts, a trade union conference of militants. And it was surprisingly successful, it was a mass gathering—some 700 militant workers from key areas of the economy. Out of it came the TUAD, the Trade Unions for Action and Democracy, to oppose bureaucracy and stultification in the unions. *Political Affairs*, the party monthly magazine, even carried a leading article by Gus Hall entitled "The Turning Point in Labor." But TUAD fell on its face. Why? Because you can't have a united front with yourself. It was a rank-and-file movement, expressing the beginnings of an upsurge. But the party viewed it as *its* movement. It is easy then to choose the leadership. You have a majority but a *mechanical* majority. Then you begin to use the mechanical majority to run the thing and do not permit it to take on its own character. And so you kill it. So that's the narrowness, the idea that you build everything by controlling it. Thus TUAD is out of existence and there's never been an accounting to the party as to why that happened.

So when I got out of prison it was evident that the party had shrunk terribly. Many very fine people with mass connections were leaving because of the sectarianism of the party, the attempt to make people follow one path, one approach. I argued against this: "You can't have a united front with yourself. A united front means you've got to have a united front with others who in one way or another may disagree with you but are united with you on what your objectives are in this particular movement."

AS: What were the immediate causes of this sectarianism?

GG: The party was fighting for its life. Therefore, it turned inward in many ways. People who had mass connections, who were doing mass work, were expected to be good Communists in a narrow sense, to hold the fort. So a lot of very good people left because of this sectarianism. The approach was false because it was as if *we* were the movement, instead of recognizing the changes outside. They misread the new upheaval amongst young people as "petty bourgeois" because it happened mainly in colleges.

AS: Were there contradictions in the leadership over the emergence of the New Left? On the one hand we have this new, shall we say, oppositional, "petty bourgeois" movement emerging in the universities. On the other we have a number of third world revolutions: there is Cuba in 1959; there is Algeria continuously in the late fifties; there is the intensification of the Vietnamese revolution.

Something is obviously going on here. So instead of taking this into account the party, in your view, sticks its head in the sand, saying "We're in bad straits, we've lost a lot; if we just hold on, 'turn inward,' we can probably weather the storm, we can actually survive, and eventually the right line will actually gain currency, and we will come out on top. Things will get better in the future as a result of these various developments in the third world and because of the continuing improvements of the Soviet Union in the cold war." Reasoning something along these lines. What's peculiar about this sectarianism, however, is that after all, the orthodox mainstream line of the Communist Party and the Moscow line itself is one of *class coalition*. There is no return in the Khrushchev or Brezhnev-Kosygin era to the policy of "class against class," the policy of the 1928–1934 period. On the contrary, it is an anti-monopolist coalition policy. Why, then, doesn't the party open up, why doesn't it try and connect up with various "popular" movements, anything that looks like an anti-monopolist movement or people's front?

GG: Because any movement had to be directly controlled by the party.

AS: So that's why the New Left is suspect. Not only is it petty bourgeois, but it cannot be controlled.

GG: Yes. And because they didn't follow what we considered to be the correct line.

AS: And what was the correct line?

GG: [Laughter] It seems to me at that point the correct line *should* have been to try to turn this upheaval amongst young people into a permanent kind of a movement while letting its dynamics work itself out with our participation. Without any attempt to tell it what it must do.

AS: Did you actually have contacts outside the party with the New Left? Did the members who disagreed with Gus Hall's decision or the official line, have connections with the anti-war movement, with the New Left?

GG: I did. I attended most SDS conventions. Not as a delegate, but as a spectator; I saw something new arising, something important. And a hell of a lot of them were sons and daughters of former party members. It was an interesting phenomenon to see the new generation, whose parents I knew, come forward. The fact is that today there are many working-class youth who go to college. I went to high school for only two years, but my oldest son is a professor, the head of a science lab and a Ph.D.!

AS: So you had fairly extensive contacts, personal contacts with the SDS. What about the rest of the party? Were you the only one who did this sort of thing?

GG: No, I wasn't the only one. The younger people in the party—I think at that point it was the Du Bois Clubs—definitely had close contacts. But the stress of the leadership was to break that contact. This was a "petty bourgeois" movement. And the term petty bourgeois is a derogatory term.

AS: One area of traditional strength in the party has been its work among African-Americans. What happened there in the 1960s? Among the cultural radicals of the 1960s, we have the civil rights movement, in some ways *the* leading oppositional movement. This was an independent movement.

GG: We definitely supported Martin Luther King. And in his group there were people who were very close to the party.

AS: But yet it was not controlled by the party.

GG: No, not at all. Absolutely not.

AS: But nevertheless you supported him, even though he must have been, classically speaking, petty bourgeois as well. So why support that and not the college students?

GG: There's a positive and a negative side to that. The positive side is that the party did have a very, very strong position on the race question. It was the first of the socialist movements in this country that did, to its credit. And that's why today the party has more black leaders than any other formation I know of that's mixed. So that we favored an upsurge of black people, definitely. Take the Southern Negro Youth Congress, which was really a forerunner of the King movement. It was a tremendous movement. At every southern college that had any blacks, they had an organization. From that they all came into the King movement. The party couldn't control it, and they didn't attempt it.

AS: How did the party react to the Black Panther Party and the most militant forms of black liberation?

GG: We didn't support the Black Panthers. We were hostile to them, saw them as anarchists, engaging in individual violence. This and that and the other thing: they would drive people away, they would counter the ability to build a powerful black movement, and create unnecessary divisions with the whites and so on.

AS: The same thing vis-à-vis the Muslims, the nationalist Black Muslim movements?

GG: We stayed away from them too. We didn't attack it, we stayed away. We considered it a sect.

AS: But the party, in so far as it had strengths anywhere, did so in the black community.

GG: In the 1940s, the Harlem city councilman was Benjamin Davis, Jr., a black party member. The party had a few thousand members, at least a few thousand, in Harlem.

AS: Let's go back to the impact of the third world revolutions. At the same time as the Soviet Union and the United States become friendlier, or at least more predictable in their relationship, we have the emergence of a very radical critique from Beijing, from Maoism, a critique which takes as its primary target precisely this new "hegemonic superpower relationship," as they would call it, deemed then to be detrimental to the emergence of revolutionary movements everywhere. How did the party take all of this, the rapprochement between Moscow and Washington and the Maoist critique?

GG: Actually we felt that the Soviet Union had to be recognized as a world power and that this new balance of forces could prevent U.S. imperialism from doing everything and anything it wanted.

AS: Was there any support at all for the Maoists? Was there any kind of mute support for it?

GG: There were some, but not much, but then the party didn't accept the fact that the Chinese revolutionary leaders were Marxists.

AS: What about expanding third world movements? Surely, these were looked upon as a great boon to the party?

GG: Actually, not always. In regard to Cuba, which I know more intimately, for a period of time the relations between Havana and Moscow were rather cool. And so the relations of the American party to Cuba were cool. The party leadership didn't believe that it was possible to have a socialist revolution which was not lead by the Communist Party. And therefore Castro was an imposter. Nor did they agree with the whole tactic of guerilla warfare. Castro was just an adventurer.

Of course, now they're trying to wave the Cuban flag. Why? Because they use it against the Russians. The Russians have "betrayed" Cuba, and so now they're all for Cuba. How deep that feeling is, [laughter] is more than questionable. And the same holds with regard to, say, China or anywhere else: it all depended upon what the relations with the Soviet Union were.

AS: Let's talk about what happens to the party in 1968, which is a devastating year from a whole series of angles. You have upheavals everywhere not controlled by the party, or the parties. There is May 1968 and ten million workers on strike in France; there are revolutions, there is the Tet offensive in Vietnam, there are the domestic assassinations and revolts. There are upheavals that the party must analyze, or that the party is forced to account for within the context of its own analysis. But what really is difficult to deal with for most communist parties is the invasion of Czechoslovakia, since in contrast to 1956, Moscow is dealing here with a leader, Dubcek, who is a reform Communist, a person actually attaching himself to socialist ideals in the Prague Spring of 1968. Can you tell me how the party took this and how you yourself came to act? You didn't leave the party, but you left all your official positions.

GG: Yes. I have not been a functionary since then, for twenty-four years. I was *not* alone; there were many who were opposed to the intervention. But only a few spoke up. On a matter of this kind I wanted to go to the public. I gave an interview to the *New York Times*, in which I declared my opposition to the Soviet intervention in Czechoslovakia. I could have told them no, but in this case I grabbed the chance, because it was a matter of principle, not a tactical question. And that's what upset the party: it was "treason."

AS: By 1968 you didn't go along with it and by mutual agreement you ceased being a functionary. But you stayed in the party.

GG: Yes, I didn't leave the party, but I had to find a job. I got one at the World Trade Center then being built. I was sixty-two years old, but I went to work as a laborer. Jim Haughton of the Fightback organization in Harlem helped me get in.

AS: You were not in fact expelled.

GG: No, because, after all, I've been in this party long enough.

AS: But they expelled Bittelman, I think, in the early 1960s because of what he said about monopoly capital, which is a far less important issue than the intervention. (When I interviewed him in 1976, nevertheless, he was still diligently reading the *People's World*).

GG: The times were different. After all, this business of using armed force in Czechoslovakia did have an effect on the ranks. But Bittelman went around the country lecturing a point of view that didn't correspond to orthodoxy.

AS: How did the upheavals and the new oppositional movements, such as feminism and ecology, new questions that were not linked to the traditional centrality of the working class, affect the party? Was there a theoretical re-assessment?

GG: No. There was lip service to the ecology movement, as a problem, but nothing by way of helping to build a movement. On the women's question, the party was very backward. There was and is a women's commission, but here we are, after all, in a country with the most impressive women's movement in the world. And we're only at the beginning of things. But the leadership refuses to believe that anything new comes out of anywhere but themselves.

AS: In the thirty years since you got out of prison, have there been any fundamental theoretical debates, Marxist debates, fundamental debates about basic Marxist concepts? A lot of things have happened in Marxist theory in that period of time.

GG: Debate in the party? No, except for the last few years, where the differences were so sharp that prohibiting debate over them was impossible.

AS: How would you describe the organizational structure of the party and how it has changed or not changed, as the case may be, over the last thirty-five years? It's always been a rigidly hierarchical, "democratic centralist" form of organization. Has that changed at all in the last thirty years?

GG: It has changed but not because there was a conscious policy of change at the top. Because life itself dictated change. The concept of democratic centralism meant that the stress was on centralism, that leadership had total control. But now things are changing. New York has the largest organization. It had a convention recently and elected new leadership, overwhelmingly opposed to Gus Hall. But Gus controls all the money, and I'm amazed at how easy it is to bribe some people. I know it takes place.

AS: How so?

GG: Mike Zagarell was the editor of the *People's World* and wanted to leave. He was sick of the whole thing, the dictation from above. So he went to Gus Hall and said, "I'm out." But Gus didn't want Carl Bloice, the associate editor, to take over. So he asked Zagarell to stay on. Zagarell refused. So Gus told him to see his secretary and she hands him an envelope. He opens the envelope; there's two thousand dollars in it. He tosses it back and says, "I don't take bribes." The objective of getting him to stay a little bit longer was to keep Carl Bloice from becoming the editor, because he could not be dictated to. Gus Hall, by the way, has had problems with Afro-Americans. That this is a true story can be seen by this incident: at a meeting of the national committee, Zagarell told the national committee exactly what had happened and nobody dared to challenge it; not Gus Hall, nor any of his henchpeople—so sort of obviously it's true.

AS: It's become a kind of petty fiefdom. How was the party financed? How did the actual finances work after the 1950s?

GG: The party has been very clever in organizing money, not people. Take a few years ago: they advised a scheme called "advanced wills," that is, they went to older people and said, "Look, we know you have some money. And you may need it; you should hold on to it. But let us hold it for you. We'll put in your name in a bank account. If you want the interest on the money, you get it. But when you die, if you have not used that money, and you don't indicate that your children should get it, it goes to us." The party has from six to eight million dollars in that advanced wills fund.

AS: There have been revelations that the Communist Party in Britain received a very substantial subsidy from Moscow, and similarly so in the American case.

GG: I read that the party here got two million dollars. Whether that's true or not I do not know. If it is true only Gus Hall and maybe one other person that he trusts in matters of this kind would know. At the recent national convention there was a demand for a financial accounting. It was denied. No financial account is ever made. Before, the argument was, "Well, the repression in the country ..." and this and that. Now, that's all bullshit. Gus Hall does what he wants. Envelopes go all over.

AS: So this suggests corruption. But is there now a real opposition to this, a very strong opposition?

GG: Yes. As a matter of fact, the party is split, with some of the most important and largest districts leaving it. This is the case with northern California, the second largest district, and with New York State, the largest one. There are a number of others that have left to form Committees of Correspondence as a transition form to something new.

AS: So Gus will have a nice retirement on the six to eight million dollars, what?

GG: But he won't retire, he'll stay until he dies. However, this has nothing to do with what you're here for....

AS: Yes it does, in a way. It does have a very clear symptomatic meaning to me in terms of what has happened to the party since the fifties. One can understand how an isolated and repressed party movement which is very sectarian is hanging on to a distant yet present party affiliation with the Soviet Union. But how would you explain that in the last three or four decades the party has stayed so close to Moscow when other parties, such as the Italian and even the French for a short period of time, went their own way or at least distanced themselves?

GG: Well, how do you account for the fact that just recently, after the attempted coup in the Soviet Union, Gus Hall said in an interview with the *New York Times* that he doesn't consider it a socialist country anymore, and then goes on to advise workers to go to North Korea for their vacation; that's where you have an example of what socialism can be [*derisive laughter*]. The only communist country with a monarchy! A communist place where the son is crown prince! So how do you account for that?

AS: It is a way of surviving with some sort of identity intact, I suppose.

GG: On the question of subsidies, I can understand aid to parties in poor third world countries but not to parties in countries such as this.

AS: But there is something aside from petty corrupt instances. There is the control over a personal fiefdom that needs to be organized from the top down, and here, presumably, it's functional to have an identity with Moscow because of the precarious situation in which this organization finds itself. The party's *raison d'être* comes from that connection in a way that was never the case in Italy, for example. Nevertheless, the support has to come from somewhere: individuals who are in agreement with this kind of policy. And when you talk about Kim Il Sung as the leading star of the straight and narrow road, then you're really reaching the level of absurdity. But it isn't wholly absurd from the inside. Why is that?

GG: People often believe what they want to believe. And people who have given years to something have to defend themselves in the sense of "I've done the right thing." And therefore anything that touches their own beliefs is an attack upon them personally. That's the attitude of a whole section of old people towards Gus Hall: not that they know him personally, but he identifies with how they feel.

AS: This must be related as well to the events in the Soviet Union and Eastern Europe, which must have put an intolerable strain on the party after 1985. How has that "world-historical" process affected it?

GG: From the outset Gus was against Gorbachev, because Gus is against democratization. He was hostile from beginning to end: he took a "principled stand" [laughter], although he wouldn't openly say it. Of course now he claims that he was right. When that view comes up I usually say, "Look, comrades, I know how to fry an egg, but I'll be damned if I know how to unfry it. And that's the problem they've got there." How to get out of the situation. Now, of course, a lot of blunders remain.

I have also come to a conclusion, again, that in Gus's case it relates to money. He came back a few months ago from Moscow and said that there's no longer any spirit of internationalism there. And what were his examples?: Three. First, that they no longer intend to take bundles of the *Daily World* and pay for them—which means that they don't want the Soviet people to see a western communist paper that takes issue on important questions. In other words, he didn't say: "If they can't pay for it we'll send them a bundle free." No, he was talking about the fact that a good chunk of money was coming in via the paper, and the party was charging them the subscription rate. Second, he reveals that they no longer want to finance the American-Soviet Friendship Council. This shocked me: Since when do we expect *them* to finance an American organization? And the third example is that International Publishers is in difficulties because the Russians no longer buy large quantities of its books. So you could see the mentality of the man when he gives those three examples to prove that they're no longer internationalists. Only when that story about the two million dollars broke did I say, well, maybe there's something more to it.

AS: But there is the attachment to the old Brezhnevite position within the CPUSA. How did the party manage during these last years? There must have been an immense strain.

GG: It's been a terrible shock, to have the world movement collapse like that. It's a shock to *me*. But Gus believes that it was because Gorbachev did something, not that there was something wrong there....

AS: It seems to me, though, that it must have been extremely difficult for a person such as Gus Hall to navigate in these years between the emergence of a new line and his attachment to the old line, while at the same time maintaining a strong identity with the Soviet party. When the Soviet party officially is going in the direction that he loathes—perestroika and, moreover, glasnost, openness—he must have been extremely uncomfortable. At the end he could insist that he had been right all along: once the Berlin wall comes down and, moreover, the party falls to pieces in the Soviet Union, he could argue that. But *during* the time when it happened the Moscow-orthodox mind had to be, precisely, Moscow-orthodox, and being orthodox in that sense means being for perestroika and glasnost. Hence a conflict.

GG: But remember that there was a double game going on. Actually the Soviet party was against Gorbachev and against democratization. To Gus the Soviet party was still the Soviet party, and it's Gorbachev and the others that have broken with it. When Gus went to the Soviet Union last year, he met with people who had been part of the coup. In fact, the first thing he did regarding the coup was to support it. Then, when it failed he changed his mind, publicly. And those who know him closely believe that he had been given some inkling that something like that was going to happen.

AS: Yes, but during the time when it begins to happen—say 1985 to 1988—perestroika and glasnost is the official papal line.

GG: Yes, but Gus had his own ties.

AS: Outside the leading cadres.

GG: No, inside. He had inside information from his own connections, that they weren't going to stand for this too long, that something was going to happen.

AS: What about the party membership? How would you characterize the reaction over these years of the party membership?

GG: There was a growing opposition in the party, which also related to what was happening internationally. Of course some people are cast in iron and that's it. Their point of view was settled a quarter of a century ago and that's still it. They can't even talk with their own children. And it's my generation. As for the young generation, unfortunately, the party doesn't have many.

AS: What about Angela Davis?

GG: Remember that she was on trial, and a very serious case too, and that Charlene Mitchell, a party leader, was sent to organize a defense for her, and that it became not only a national defense but an international defense. Angela won her case, and she felt a duty to those who defended her so successfully and so militantly. But though she became a member of the national committee, she very rarely spoke up.

AS: Looking back at sixty-one years of political engagement in the Communist Party, how do you now ponder that experience at a personal level?

GG: I've thought it over. I've given it all these years. What if I had to do it over again? And I say I don't know where else I could have gone and got that feeling of participation, and actual participation in so many struggles. There's one attribute the party does have, different from the Socialist Party: it is a party of activists. The party was involved, its membership was involved. That's it. I really remain in the party for only one reason. People say: "We know you have an independent view on many things. Why do you stay in the party?" And I say, "Look, I don't believe that I as an individual can get anywhere without organization. If any of you here can tell me there's a better organization I'll join that." So that's my reason. I don't see anything else that I would join. But now things are changing rapidly. The party is split down the middle, and an entirely new formation is being considered and worked for.

In my own area of the city there's a Chelsea for Peace movement, which has every religious institution in the area as a part of it, except for the Jewish synagogue: the best people in the area. Our people put it together but they don't try to run it. There's also a sister-city project here with a town in Nicaragua. It finances a full-time person in Nicaragua, in that town, assisting in a water project. Then there's a housing movement, a tenants' movement here.

AS: So you would do the same thing over again. I can see this for I have the same sort of feeling about what I did in the 1960s and the 1970s, I don't have any regrets about it, even though one did absurd things at times. I don't have any regrets about it because, all things considered, the alternatives were mostly worse. Yet there are of course specific things that I deeply regret. How do you feel about that sort of thing? For instance, would you not have broken on the question of Stalin's repression?

GG: Of course, my God, I'm ashamed to think of that even now. I'm not talking about that, I'm talking about other aspects of the party.

March 1992

CONTRIBUTORS

Rosalyn Fraad Baxandall is a feminist activist and professor of American studies at State University of New York at Old Westbury. She is the author of *Words on Fire: The Biography and Writings of Elizabeth Gurley Flynn* (Newark, NJ: Rutgers University Press, 1985), co-editor of *American Working Women: The History of Women in Work, 1607–1976* (New York: Random House, 1976), and co-author (with Elizabeth Ewen) of *Picture Windows: Race and Gender in Suburbia, 1945–1990* (New York: Basic Books, forthcoming).

Michael E. Brown is chair of the Department of Anthropology and Sociology at Northeastern University. He is the co-author of *Collective Behavior* (Goodyear, 1973) and the author of *The Production of Society: A Marxian Foundation for Social Theory* (Totowa, NJ: Rowman, 1986). He is an editor of *Socialism and Democracy* and *Social Text* and has published a number of articles on the historiography of Communism.

John Gerassi is professor of political science at Queens College and the Graduate Center of the City University of New York. He is the author of ten books on development and revolution in the third world, as well as of *The Premature Antifascists: North American Volunteers in the Spanish Civil War* (New York: Praeger, 1986) and *Jean-Paul Sartre: Hated Conscience of His Century, Volume I, Protestant or Protestor* (Chicago: University of Chicago Press, 1989). Volume II, entitled *Rebel or Revolutionary*, is scheduled for publication in 1994.

Marvin E. Gettleman is professor of history at Polytechnic University in Brooklyn. He is co-author of *Vietnam and America* (New York: Grove Press, 1985) In addition to his work on Communist education, he is co-editor of *The Middle East Reader* (New York: Hill & Wang, 1992) and is a member of the editorial board of *Science and Society*.

Gil Green is the author of *Cold War Fugitive: A Personal Story of the McCarthy Era* (New York: International Publishers, 1984) and *What's Happening in Labor?* (New York: International Publishers, 1976). He is currently working on a history of the Communist Party.

Gerald Horne is professor and chair of the Black Studies Department at the University of California-Santa Barbara and was a candidate for the U.S. Senate in California in 1992. He is the author of *Communist Front? The Civil Rights Congress, 1946–56* (London: Associated University Presses, 1988) and two forthcoming books: *Black Liberation / Red Scare: Ben Davis and the Communist Party* and *Fire This Time: The Watts Uprising and the Meaning of the 1960s*.

Roger Keeran is professor of history and chair of the Master of Arts Program in Labor and Policy Studies, Empire State College (SUNY) in New York City. He is the author of *The Communist Party and the Auto Workers Unions* (Bloomington: Indiana University Press, 1980). He is currently doing research on the International Workers Order.

Stephen Leberstein is the executive director of the City College Center for Worker Education, where he teaches history. His research interests included working-class culture, labor, and politics; he has also written on French syndicalism.

Randy Martin is associate professor of sociology at Pratt Institute and author of *Performance as Political Act* (Westport, CT: Greenwood Press, 1989) and a forthcoming study of theater in Cuba and Nicaragua. He works with the journals *Socialism and Democracy* and *Social Text*.

Mark Naison is professor of African-American studies and history at Fordham University. He is the author of *Communists in Harlem During the Depression* (Champaign: University of Illinois Press, 1983).

Frank Rosengarten is professor emeritus of Italian and comparative literature at Queens College and the Graduate School of the City University. With Michael E. Brown, he founded the Research Group on Socialism and Democracy in 1984. The author of three books and various essays on Italian political and cultural history, he is currently editing an integral English-language translation of Antonio Gramsci's *Letters from Prison*, scheduled for publication in the latter part of 1993.

Annette T. Rubinstein, Ph.D., is the author of two major critical histories, *The Great Tradition in English Literature* and *American Literature: Root and Flower*. She has also written a number of political pamphlets, including *The Strange Case of the Harlem Six, The Black Panther Party*, and *Attica*, and edited *Schools Against Children* and *I Vote My Conscience: Debates, Speeches, and Writings of Vito Marcantonio*. Formerly a high school principal and New York State chair of the American Labor Party, she is now on the editorial board of *Jewish Currents* and of the independent Marxist quarterly *Science & Society*, and is a teacher at the New York Marxist School.

Ellen Schrecker is associate professor of history at Yeshiva University. She is the author of *No Ivory Tower: McCarthyism and the Universities*, and is presently working on a general study of anticommunist political repression during the 1940s and 1950s.

George Snedeker teaches sociology at the State University of New York at Old Westbury. He has published articles on Social Theory in *Science and Society, Nature, Society and Thought*, and *Rethinking Marxism*. He is currently working on a book entitled *Between Criticism and Social Theory*.

Anders Stephanson is assistant professor of history at Columbia University. He is the author of *Kennan and the Art of Foreign Policy* (Cambridge, MA: Harvard University Press, 1989) and is a member of the editorial committee of *Social Text*.

Alan Wald is Professor of English literature and American culture at the University of Michigan and cultural editor of *Against the Current*. His books on the U.S. cultural left are *James T. Farrell: The Revolutionary Socialist Years* (New York: New York University Press, 1978), *The Revolutionary Imagination* (Chapel Hill: University of North Carolina Press, 1983), *The New York Intellectuals* (Chapel Hill: University of North Carolina Press, 1987), and *The Responsibility of Intellectuals: Selected Essays on Marxist Traditions in Cultural Commitment* (Atlantic Highlands, NJ: Humanities Press International, 1992). He is presently completing a non-canonical history of Marxist writers, *Exiles From a Future Time: The Left in U.S. Literature Reconsidered*.